The Life of
Lidian Jackson Emerson

Lidian Jackson Emerson

The Life of Lidian Jackson Emerson

by *Ellen Tucker Emerson*

EDITED BY
DELORES BIRD CARPENTER

Michigan State University Press
East Lansing
1992

Introduction and Notes
© 1992 Delores Bird Carpenter
Ellen Tucker Emerson's *The Life of Lidian Jackson Emerson*
© Ralph Waldo Emerson Memorial Association

Partial funding for this edition was provided by the Ralph Waldo Emerson
Memorial Association

Revised Edition
Michigan State University Press 1992
Originally published by Twayne Publishers 1980

All Michigan State University Press Books are produced on paper which
meets the requirements of American National Standard of Information
Sciences — Permanence of paper for printed materials ANSI Z39.48-1984.

Michigan State University Press
East Lansing, Michigan 48823-5202

Printed in the United States of America

00 99 98 97 96 95 94 93 92 91 1 2 3 4 5 6 7 8 9 10

Library of Congress Cataloging in Publication Data

Emerson, Ellen Tucker.
    The life of Lidian Jackson Emerson / by Ellen Tucker Emerson ; edited
by Delores Bird Carpenter.
        p.   cm.
    Originally published: Boston : Twayne Publishers, 1980.
    Includes index.
    ISBN 0-87013-303-9
    1. Emerson, Lidian Jackson, 1802–1892.   2. Emerson, Ralph Waldo,
1803–1882—Biography—Marriage.   3. Authors, American—19th century
—Biography.   4. Authors' wives—United States—Biography.
I. Carpenter, Delores Bird.   II. Title.
PS1632.E48   1992
814'.3—dc20
    [B]   91-29778
                                                                   CIP

Cover design: Michael M. Smith

Front cover photo: Lydian Jackson Emerson with son Edward Waldo/by
permission of the Concord Free Public Library

Back cover photo: Ellen Tucker Emerson/by permission of the Concord
Free Public Library

To the Memory of
M. Estelle Cooper Hawkins (1881–1904)
and her daughter, my mother,
Hazel L. Hawkins Bird (1903–1989)
who did for me
"love's austere and lonely offices"

Contents

Acknowledgments

I am grateful to the Ralph Waldo Emerson Memorial Association for a grant to assist in reissuing *The Life of Lidian Jackson Emerson*. I thank Margaret E. Bancroft, president of the association, for her interest in the project, for her prompt and faithful correspondence, and for her help with photographs.

I am grateful to Rodney Dennis, Curator of Manuscripts at the Houghton Library, Harvard University, and to Marte Shaw in the Reading Room, who befriended and assisted me in many ways during my work on the first edition. I continue to be obligated to those at the Houghton Library, for I found it necessary to return to examine Ellen Tucker Emerson's letters in typescript which I used in the introduction. With the 1980 edition of this text, I used a combination of Ellen's letters at the Houghton and some in typescript from Edith Emerson Webster Gregg, some of which were either not at the Houghton or not exactly the same as those at the Houghton. I intended to use for this edition Ellen's letters as published by Edith Emerson Webster Gregg, since Mrs. Gregg published them where possible from the originals. I found either that I had used letters that are not in the two published volumes or that Mrs. Gregg had omitted material in letters that I had included or that there are differences which cannot be accounted for as the originals are not available to the public. Therefore, I have followed where possible the letters in typescript at the Houghton Library.

I am grateful to Ernest Carleton Nickerson who did many things for this reprint from picking up electroprints at the Houghton Library to reading articles and books for relevant material. I also thank Robert D. Richardson, Jr. and Robert Sattelmeyer with whom I briefly discussed new material in the introduction on the Lidian-Henry relationship. I am grateful to Keith William Bull for his help in reviewing galleys. Marcia Moss of the Concord Free Public Library helped with the new photograph of "Graciosa." I thank Fred C. Bohm, Julie L. Loehr and Kristine M. Blakeslee of the Michigan State University Press, for their roles in the reprinting of the *Life*.

I continue to remember with gratitude those who criticized the dissertation draft of this text: Professors Paul Boyer, Everett Emerson, Sidney Kaplan, and James Matlack. I am grateful to Gay Wilson Allen of New

York University, who directed my attention to the *Life*. I thank Joel Myerson who edited Twayne's American Literary Manuscripts Series of which this was a part. For the first edition, a number of Concordians and members of the Emerson family corresponded faithfully with me: Amelia Forbes Emerson, Edith Emerson Webster Gregg, Mary Fenn, Isabel Gerty, and Mrs. John Dempsey. I still recall with pleasure Mr. and Mrs. David Emerson, thanking them for their warm reception and for his prompt attention to my many requests. Their daughter, Ellen Emerson Kohler, sent me photographs of "Diamond" for the first edition. Beyond Concord, a host of librarians and historians responded to many inquires. Among these I am especially indebted to Grace M. Greenwood of Plymouth and Doris Fautaux, who was reference librarian at Cape Cod Community College. I remain grateful to the many friends who served as proofreaders for the first printing and for the hospitality of Claude and Kim Winters of Natick who made it possible for me to work at the Houghton Library for extended periods.

Introduction

Part I

It would be an understatement to say that Lidian Emerson has not loomed large in biographies of her husband. O. W. Firkins, in his 1915 biography of Emerson, wrote concerning Mrs. Emerson: "The tread of this lady through the unfrequented paths of Emerson's domestic life is so noiseless that only a rare footfall here and there reaches the ear of the questioning biographer." With the exception of the chapter on Lidian in Ralph Rusk's biography, which draws on Ellen's manuscript, Firkin's comment is verified by book after book in the long Emerson bibliography.[1] With two books on Emerson's romantic and tragically brief first marriage, a biography of Lidian Emerson, especially this authoritative one, is very useful. She was Emerson's wife of forty-six years, mother of his four children, and hostess to Bush, their Concord home, during a period of great literary and historical interest. To the feminist she will come forth as a very capable woman, caught by the "cult of true womanhood" in the nineteenth century.[2] Lidian, herself, was unhappy with her lot as a woman. She longed to speak out, to become a writer. "I don't do it for a few good reasons, chief of which is that I am nobody & editors would not publish anything I wrote. Another, that I don't know well enough how to write English not to make myself ridiculous—and if I published in my language how would Papa like that? I have done enough in that line already" (28 April 1873). Readers of her letters, of her "Transcendental Bible," and of the testimony offered by her family and friends to her verbal powers can only regret that the climate for women was not such to encourage Lidian to express herself.

Although there is little about Lidian in published sources, material abounds in Ellen's seventeen volumes of letters and in Lidian's letters, as well as in Ellen's life of her mother, all in the Houghton Library at Harvard. Ellen's letters, in sharing domestic trifles with her sister Edith and her brother Edward, display Lidian's wit, her great ability as a conversationalist, her devotion to animals, her Christianity, her health problems, and her contribution in forces that formulated the man, Emerson. For the scholar of Emerson, we often receive glimpses of Emerson's responses to these aspects of his wife's personality.

Emerson, himself, especially appreciated her wit, an outlet, perhaps for her frustration over the nineteenth-century expectation of submission. The very full revelation of this wit, greatly admired by her daughter, is one of the contributions of Ellen's manuscript. Her wit is also suggested in Lidian's largely ignored letters as well as Ellen's. A mild example is in a letter from Plymouth in 1866 when Lidian tells of being stung by a wasp. Since she had nursed Emerson through a similar sting, she told him that in expressing his overflowing sympathy he might limit himself to two pages. A more powerful dose of her wit is in 1873 when, writing from Milton, she describes the new wallpaper for the study which was much the same color as the old, with sprigs of lily of the valley: "I observed to Edith that I should exhort her Papa to let the pattern of his paper be a constant teacher of Humility. . . . Tell him it is not in the power of 'Sulphur' homeopathic to cure 'Pride ugly Pride'—but a good hymn is always a good medicine. Please burn this most presumptuous document—lest it should confound the antiquary of 1973" (7 January 1873). Edith had suggested that they frame two lines for the study from Taylor's hymn,

> Come my love and do not spurn
> From a little flower to learn.

Another example of Lidian's wit occurs in this letter to Ellen:

As for your and your Father's being "ambitious" that depends upon what "ambition" means. Does it [mean] love of excellence—or of fame or of power! I imagine ambition is good or evil according to its aim. As obstinacy—or resolution—are the result of having a strong will. Where there is sense & kindness and principle—the one; where these qualities are lacking—the other. I think our Ellen is ambitious to be good and useful and beneficial to all the world. Papa is certainly ambitious to excel as a writer—and to enlighten his fellow creatures—*according to his light!* tell him from Mamma. (25 April 1873)

Lidian was the family actress or comedienne, as Ellen seems to have occasionally recognized. The point is illustrated by what Ellen called a very ordinary home tale:

Last night, having sworn John to carry them early in the morning to be mended, I moved two disabled chairs out of Mother's room into her entry. When I went to bed she came to see me, and came without her spectacles, so she went back for them. I heard her safely descend and ascend the three steps and then arose a scream. I knew too well what had happened, poor Mamma! if there is any snare in the way she is so sure to be caught! I arose and hollered to know the extent of the injury, she replied by moans and mingled exclamations of "It is exactly what I *knew* would happen." and "I had no idea of such a trap!" and Papa below is heard to spring from his chair and tramp hastily to the door to ask what it is. Mother cries out anew with a second spasm of distress and frightens Father. "What? What?" he calls. "Oh dreadful!" exclaims Mother with that extremity of suffering peculiar to her, then remembering other people's standards "It is no matter; that is, I have not hurt myself at all." Then recurring to the cause she cries out "A horrid pitfall!" and Father rushes up stairs and bears away the chairs. This morning at breakfast Father and I laughed to recall the scene and Father pitied the "various calamities that mark her course from day to day. She loves a good delivering scream" he ended. It is so innocent, so pathetic, and so funny. I don't think any family before has ever contained so curious, and interesting a character as she is. I contemplate her all the time with increasing pleasure, and find her innocence unfathomable. I wonder if she could have got into a family more unlike her than the Emersons who are hardly born innocent, and cannot stay so. (30 January 1872)

Lidian's verbal ability was well known in her circle. Ellen quoted her brother Edward as observing that

"Conversations seem to be Mother's natural field. I regularly hear when there has been one either that 'It was a failure because Mrs. E. wasn't there,' or 'Oh yes they talked a good deal about cats and rats and sealing-wax and whether pigs had wings, but at last Mrs. Emerson spoke, and then all the fools were silent.'" I always hear the same thing. People tell me they were "thankful for every word my Mother said the other night," and they do rejoice when she speaks. Father exults greatly, he often is present and hears her, and says "I like to see her security and I know that whatever stranger is present will soon recognize the weight of what she says. She is equal to anything they may bring up." Mother is really a great belle, she has more invitations than she can accept. (12 September 1878)

Lidian's verbal skills are displayed several times in the manuscript, especially in her "Transcendental Bible" and in one of the highest points of the biography, the historically rich description of the visit to the Shaker community where Lidian is exposed as a brilliant, determined negotiator who could later speak extemporaneously to a large group of both sexes and could make a lasting impression on at least some of the young female Shakers. The letters are full of praise of her art.

Her contemporaries did not doubt Lidian's contribution to the forces that made Emerson the man he was. Ellen quoted Franklin B. Sanborn:

He said the worship of Father was nothing new, Father had been surrounded by it from his youth. Mrs. C. [Chamberlaine] was incredulous, and said, "Why do you believe people appreciated him years ago and felt about him as they do now,—as I do, for instance." "Yes, people of superior minds recognized him from the beginning. Mrs. Emerson did. . . ." Later in the evening Mrs. Chamberlaine said, "Mr. Emerson doesn't quote. He thinks out all his thoughts himself,—doesn't borrow them." "Yet you often hear the thoughts of others in what he says," said Mr. Sanborn. "Yes," said Lizzy, "don't you think sometimes he says things he learned from Mrs. Emerson?" "Often!" said Mr. Sanborn decidedly. When Lizzy said this I remembered Mrs. Nathan Brooks's remark, "Mr. Emerson wouldn't be the man he is if it weren't for Mrs. Emerson. People have no idea how much he owes to his wife." (1 June 1895)

Lidian, herself, reveals in a letter from 1863 the closeness and dependence of Emerson on her: "Father has come to my room several times a day lately to talk over his Dartmouth Oration—with which I was well pleased. I have sat with him most of the evenings in his study and—on two of them he read the Dialog[u]es of Socrates with his disciples."

Ellen's biography reveals how deeply Lidian Emerson was influenced by the nineteenth-century movement for the more humane treatment of animals. She became an associate member of the Massachusetts Society for the Prevention of Cruelty to Animals in the year of its founding, 1867, and served as its vice-president for Concord in 1872. In December 1871, she attended the Dumb Animal's Fair in Boston and in 1875 gave Ellen a hundred copies of *Our Dumb Animals* to distribute on the church pews. About the same time, Lidian went to downtown Concord to enter a protest against the bleeding of calves, a popular issue, armed with a copy of the Society's laws and instructions on how to proceed. (Calves were bled alive until they were too weak to stand; the benefit was apparently the changing of the color of the meat.)

The letters contain many anecdotes of Lidian's intensely sympathetic attitude toward God's creatures. When Emerson and Ellen returned from the garden chore of killing rose bugs, Ellen caught one in her hand and laid him on a magazine on the table.

No sooner did Father see him than, as I had hoped, he swiftly reached out his right hand of extermination but swifter Mercy in the shape of Mother caught sight of him at the same moment, and snatched him, magazine and all, away just as that fell finger and thumb were within an inch of him, and bore him to the open window. I deeply enjoyed the play, the more so as each parent seemed wholly unconscious of the intent or presence of the other, each simply and abstractedly followed their natural bent. (28 June 1880)

As is clear from the *Life*, Lidian's favorite animals were cats. When "Twenty" had three kittens in 1877, Lidian sent a note to Ellen that she could not come down to dinner, for the cat cried so piteously in the closet that it would be cruel to abuse kitty's confidence in her affection. Ellen called her mother to the bay window to admire a March snowstorm when Lidian exclaimed, " 'Now here is trouble indeed! The cats will get under the piazza and won't be able to get out, and they will suffer!' It seemed to me most characteristic, the far-fetched difficulty relating to the dumb animal is as spontaneous in her thought as it is foreign to everybody else's" (12 March 1888).

If she had an unusual sensitivity to cruelty to animals, she had also a deep concern for human beings, especially slaves. Lidian had refused to permit Edward to go to the war unless it were for universal freedom. She said that the South shall beat the North for all she would let Eddy do to hinder them and then the Emersons would seek country in China or Haiti. Lidian wrote about a newspaper story of a black soldier who said that he had always hated the American flag, feeling that it was the flag of the enemy, but that now that it was beginning to stand for Liberty he would fight under it and be willing to die for it. Lidian's responses resemble those of Henry David Thoreau in his essays on John Brown and "Slavery in Massachusetts": "That is just what I have always felt; that the Stars and Stripes were on the Flag of a nation at war against the dearest and most sacred rights of Humanity; a nation to which I was sad to belong. I could not love but must hate such a Country. Now I begin to feel that I may love the Country and its Flag—it will before long be the sign of Freedom for all. 'Union' is *comparatively* dust in the balance" (1863).

We have only few glimpses from both published and unpublished sources of Lidian's religious and philosophical views. Her reception of Jesus as the Christ differs from Emerson's position and from the generally conceived Unitarian stand. In 1863, Lidian wrote her son Edward, "I trust you and Annie may be 'married in Christ.' " Emerson recognized the difference. He wrote to Carlyle, "My wife Lidian is an incarnation of christianity,—I call her Asia—& keeps my philosophy from Antinomianism."[3] Lidian was well-read in the philosophies of the day and was certainly aware of the Unitarian controversy over the "latest form of infidelity." She attempted to think for herself on these issues and left herself latitude for a change in her position. All of these points are illustrated by a letter to Edward:

That it seems to me two of our modern Infidel Philosophies—(with Infidel *tendencies*, is the *best* I can say of them) nullify each other—Certain Rationalists (or whatever they are called), believing that the universe is a machine set a-going ages since, and then left to itself to grind on at its own stupid will,— and who shrink from nothing so much as the idea of a Providence—or a "Father in Heaven"—say, that nature is reckless of the Individual but careful to preserve the Type.—The Darwinians whose Philosophy seems to me—to use an old expression—"The latest form of Infidelity—" say on the contrary that there *are* no fixed types—but that one type is perpetually shading—blending, into another, so that all creatures beast bird and fish, came from one germ or monad—making *itself* first one thing and then another, till it became Monkey and then Man! The monad was an ovum, but whether of fish or flesh is not known. Whether this made itself, or Nature made it not imagining what she had set a-going—I don't know. I think I truly state the Darwin doctrine but am not sure. I hope it is not quite so foolish. Wise men receive it, among whom Mr Agassiz is not. I have read his refutation of it. (18 January 1864)

Though the religious and philosophical insights may be scanty, we learn a great deal about Lidian's health problems. The *Life* is full of vaguely described illnesses and accounts of periodic depressions that seemed chronically to plague her. These complaints are perhaps related to hypochondria and an obsessive preoccupation with minor fluctuations of health. (Two of the more obvious examples of the obsessive element in her personality are her intense anxiety over the real or imagined sufferings of animals and her habit of getting up in the night to remove a large book that had been left on top of a smaller one.) The fact that Ellen could frequently divert her attention from her physical condition with food or reading further suggests a psychosomatic source.

What were the reasons for these psychosomatic illnesses, depressions, and complaints? First, her early, austere habits and childhood illnesses may have contributed to delicate health in her mature years. As a teenager she sat long hours in the cold at night, slept only four hours, and believed that the food that she did not eat did her more good than the food she ate. Ellen's ability to restore Lidian with food could also suggest that a major contributor to her poor physical condition was her failure to eat properly. Second, it is clear from the *Life* that Lidian was happy in Plymouth and did not wish to leave her birthplace. It is significant that she had unusual energy on each cherished visit there following her marriage. She seems to have brooded over the loss of her true home and her absence from her lifelong friends. A third factor is the role she played as mother and homemaker—the definitive expectation of the nineteenth-century woman. Before marriage, she confessed an unsuitableness for domestic responsibilities, and although Emerson appears to have had little reason to complain of the results, household duties and the management of servants did from time to time prove onerous. This frustration might have contributed to her depression and vague aches and pains.

The realization that she and her husband did not share identical religious views deeply grieved and perhaps depressed her. Very likely the issue of submissiveness, a fourth consideration, was the rub. This was the era when a book of advice to brides could warn: "Oh, young and lovely bride, watch well the first moments when your will conflicts with his to whom God and society have given the control."[4] Lidian followed the advice exactly during labor for her first born (see page 69) but defiantly refused to submit only hours before the birth of Ellen. She possessed an often terse wit, a love of controversy, and a keen intellect that was up to debate with such a man as Concord's revered Judge Hoar; she must have often felt restrained. In a day that condemned Margaret Fuller and Harriet Martineau and in a town where women's suffrage made only slight showing, Lidian's sickness and depression had obvious sources.

Lidian Emerson's tendency toward hypochondria may also be related to her interest in the ill. According to Barbara Welter, woman's privilege in Mrs. Emerson's day was nursing the sick. Female delicacy was set aside when it came to knowledge of medical terminology and sick-room practice. Lidian's letters describe detailed treatment of her children's ailments and illnesses when she was away from them, complete with medicine and elaborate instructions. She treated her husband for his balding. She gained her medical knowledge, at least in part, by studying her uncle's medical books.

Lidian's illnesses surely are related to the fact that in her day normal female functions and phases such as menstruation, menopause, and hormone changes were often ignored, shrouded in mystery, and surrounded by superstitions. Emerson sincerely believed that Lidian might die during her first pregnancy and could not understand why the woman, alone, must suffer. The doctor's response was that he never lost a case and that the woman was compensated with the pleasures of lactation. Modern understanding of the hormonal changes in pregnancy and menopause would alone explain away some of the ups and downs of her health.

It is also a very real possibility that grief over the death of her first-born child, Waldo, caused some of her periods of depression and anguish. She wrote in a letter to her husband on 17 February 1843 the following: "She [Ellen] is a year in advance of Waldo in reading. Torn is my heart as I write that cherished name. The wound of separation is as fresh as it was a year ago—at least it seems so to me. I am bruised in heart—and cannot be healed by Time. Only a new spiritual experience can bring balm to that wound. 'Time heals not the heart-stricken.' 'They think that I forget'—but I never forget. Flowers grow over the grave— Yet it is a grave no less. I know there is healing but it has not yet come to me. I trust it will—though probably not in this life." The very fact that she interpreted Emerson's dying words to be in reference to Waldo suggests to me how constant he was in her mind.

In a letter of September 1871, Ellen summarizes Lidian's report on her ailments and a diagnosis:

So Mother began with her Father's disease and death, her own youthful thin-ness, scarlet fever, rush of blood to the head, dyspepsia. Here he [a Dr. Clarke] began to ask questions and Mother answered most beautifully, the tones and phrases I had heard all my life, sounded so descriptive of her daily state I thought he must get a glimpse at her troubles. "I shall have to ask you ques-tions about half an hour longer," he said at last "but not for sixteen days." "I haven't told you all yet," said Mother, "my heart, (or it may be my lungs,) gives me an odd sensation here." "It is very likely to be your heart," he said, "but I shall postpone that. There are several organs I haven't interrogated yet. I am going to give you phosphates of soda and lime to mix with your food, and see how they affect you, and after that I can judge better of your estate, and I mean then to apply some tests to the nervous system." (21 September 1871)

In November, when Ellen tricked her mother into a return visit to Dr. Clarke, he came to what I suspect was a sound evaluation of the case as far as it went:

"Drugs of course can not do so much for her as hygienic life. Disease owing to non-hygienic life for many years. You must persuade her to regularity in eating, sleep and exercise. Also she has I think an introverted habit. Very bad. Watching an organ puts it out of order, habitually watching can bring chronic disease, watching for effect of drug perverts effect. If she is watching and expecting to be better she may not be better. If she can really be kept from expecting it, I think she has some chance of being better in 6 months." (17 November 1871)

Despite her illnesses, Lidian Emerson remained active in her later years. In November 1878, she walked up town for her shopping on six consecutive days and on the seventh she walked there to see Edward. In March 1881, Ellen wrote that Lidian went out two or three nights a week as usual and had gotten up twice to go with her to Boston on the ten o'clock train for shopping. At Ellen's forty-second birthday ball, when Lidian was seventy-nine, Lidian danced most of the dances. In 1883 she visited the state's prison. In July 1885, Lidian was going twice a day to every session of the Concord School of Philosophy and thrived upon it as she did morning and evening in 1887. Even as late as March 1892, the year of her death, she was active as her club met at Bush and discussed the Indian question.

By permission of the Houghton Library, Harvard University

Ellen Tucker Emerson

Part II

Ellen Tucker Emerson (1839–1909), the second child of Ralph Waldo Emerson, figures but dimly in the vast biographical literature on her famous father. Ralph L. Rusk, in *The Life of Ralph Waldo Emerson*, develops an image of her in Emerson's mature years as his traveling companion and general assistant, his memory, his judgment, and the general manager of his literary compositions. Ellen serves as Emerson's social historian, especially as Rusk traces with minute detail Ellen and her father's trip to Europe following the 1872 fire at Bush.

Her contemporaries, however, saw not only the filial reverence but also commented on aspects of her personality and character that reveal a warmth and glow not found in Rusk's biography. Annie Fields, wife of the Boston publisher, James T. Fields, recalls her as being full of good works.[5] Mrs. Daniel Chester French's tribute to Ellen begins by declaring there was never anybody like Miss Ellen: "An admirer once said that when she gazed upon the face of Emerson she always felt that that face had seen God. The same might have been said of Miss Ellen. She certainly saw God. Some people claim that she never saw anything else—a difficult situation in this over-practical world. She went through life shedding glory by way of her smile; small wonder that she took no account of changing style, of foods, of passing states of mind. How could anyone be practical who lived in the realm of the Beatitudes?"[6]

The many obituaries of her bear this same tone, of course, in proper obituary spirit. On 15 January 1909, the *Boston Herald*, recording that Concord's saint had died, observed: "She came to be in the course of time a link between the old and the new, an incarnation of the past for the benefit of moderns. Beautiful and dignified, modest yet resolute, sympathetic yet searching in judgment, unique in attire, distinguished in speech, an apostle of simplicity, purity and good will, she was a personality once seen never to be forgotten." The *Springfield Republican* more modestly suggests that she was social in disposition, simple and sincere in manner, and never failing in kindness and cordial fellowship. A. W. Jackson, in a eulogy printed in the 28 January 1909 *Christian Register*, wrote: "What biographies we shall have when simple worth is esteemed biographical, when they are written not less to show high character than conspicuous deeds! That such a life as Miss Emerson's will be an enviable theme." Jackson feels that in her the Emersonian philosophy of life became flesh. Yet he is insistent that

while in constant contact with those to whom Emerson's words were hardly less than sacred scripture she lived almost as independently of him as if she had never known his love or heard the voices of his fame. She saw with joy the blossoms along his pathway, yet kept to a pathway of her own. She loved the church, loved traditions as her father could not do. In her religious attitude she was distinctly, some would say extremely, conservative. Even over passages of her father's writings it was possible to get into smiling debate with her, in which she would criticize him as frankly as she would Addison or Montaigne. In these particulars she illustrated the Emersonian respect for the integrities of the individual mind, and witnessed an ingenuousness of spirit from which not even daughterly reverence and daughterly pride could divert her.

There are two sources left to us which intimately reveal Ellen's person, her character, and her soul: *I Remember the Emersons* by Mary Miller Engel,[7] whose grandmother was Lidian's Aunt Cotton, and Ellen's letters in the possession of Mrs. Edith Emerson Webster Gregg, Edith's granddaughter. A seventeen-volume typescript of these letters, undoubtedly the best source for Ellen's life and personality, is at the Houghton Library, dating from January 1850, when Ellen was eleven years old, to 2 November 1908, within a few months of her death.

Ellen's letters are a significant contribution to that now lost epistolary art. Her brother Edward in 1892, realizing her talent, suggested:

That the art be not lost after being carried to such a high pitch by you, why don't you let Isaiah & Jeroboam slide, give 'em a rest for a year, & teach your S. S. & other clients the art of letter-sketching, courses in instantaneous domestic pictures, verisimilitudinous memory-tales, interesting arguments of chapters that time serves not to chronicle? Why! the School of Philosophy was but a passing deliration and would be remembered 20 years but you (I speak now in the utmost seriousness) could 'furbish new the name of' Concord by doing this. . . . [H]ere is a real mission perfectly practicable and if you could take hold of it for an avocation, would be the best you could ever have. (26 January 1892)

Edward knew the value of her letters as early as 1873, when we find Lidian writing to Ellen: "Edward says your letters ought to be published and if, a hundred years hence, they are found in a garret, the fortunate finder will rejoice as one that findeth great sport; and strait way let them enlighten the world and make his fortune" (15 February).

Ellen Tucker Emerson was born on 24 February 1839. We know little of her earliest years apart from what we learn in her biography of her mother, but a good deal of information is available for the years beginning when she was fourteen. In June 1853, Ellen was enrolled in a school for girls at Lenox, Massachusetts, which was managed during the school's existence from 1828 to 1864 by Mrs. Charles Sedgwick, wife of the Clerk of the Courts. Mrs. Sedgwick was an authority on children's books, and her sister-in-law was the novelist Catherine Sedgwick. The school employed modern ideas such as field trips to such places as Bash-bish Falls and Salisbury Lakes in Connecticut. In the beginning Ellen boarded at a Mrs. Farley's. She found the lodgings, the school, and everything else very pleasant. All the girls were very kind to her, but Ellen soon found that she did not like those who evaded the rules. The girls were in class from eight to one and sewed from four till five while Mrs. Sedgwick read aloud.

As a child Ellen was obedient, zealous to do right, conscience-stricken when in the wrong, and eager to seek and obey parental advice. She wrote to her mother that she and one or two other girls had such appetites that they were ashamed to satisfy themselves at dinner time. So one night when the girls were alone she carried away from the table a piece of bread and butter, and several others followed her example. It soon became a habit to eat a second supper. She realized that it was underhanded and that her mother had taught her never to do anything of which she would be ashamed, and she realized that should Mrs. Sedgwick find her eating the illegal food she would feel shame. When her mother wrote the expected admonition, Ellen thanked her a thousand times.

On Christmas Day 1853, when the girls' mottoes were read, Ellen felt perfectly horrid as the room looked at her when hers was read.

> My fitful jaded muse
> Assumes a modest timid look
> That no courageous flight will brook
> When I invoke her aid
> That something meet be said
> To the fair lassie with the arched head
> And threatens to refuse
> Because she kindred has with one
> Who is higher Muse's son.
>
> But though of poet born
> And loving nature with a poet's eye
> Which that in Heaven and earth can spy
> That's hid to vulgar gaze
> Life's common duties she essays

And treads most faithful found, its common ways.
Not with a look forlorn
But cheerful with a heart at rest
Where all sweet virtues make their nest.

Ellen complained to her mother from Lenox in 1854 that she could not gain that habit of "intense study" which Miss Jane Whiting, an earlier teacher, had recommended. Ellen believed that she learned more from her than in any other two years of her life. In the same year she describes herself as a very dignified young woman who had on the second day of December received a book dedicated to her, Louisa May Alcott's *Flower Fables.*

In the spring of 1855, she briefly attended Franklin Sanborn's school in Concord, where she made numerous mistakes in Latin and where she felt that in algebra she was the only stupid one in the class.

That September she enrolled in the Agassiz school in Cambridge. In this family-run school, the Harvard botanist Louis Agassiz lectured once a day; his wife Elizabeth Cary Agassiz taught English; his son Alex was in charge of mathematics and Latin; and his daughter Ida handled French and German. Ellen commuted in the beginning. She and her contemporary "Aunt Birdy" Cheney rose at 5:45 and arrived at the depot at 7:00, where they took a train to Porter's, Cambridge, at 7:45, and then walked about a mile to the Agassiz House, but by November she was boarding at Mrs. G. S. Hillard's at 62 Pinckney Street and taking the omnibus to school. The only trouble with the school, in Ellen's view, was that she had to go riding and to dancing schools—a dancing school which boys also attended!

In September 1857, she wrote her Cousin Haven that she did not plan to go to school for a year. In November her only instruction was reading Livy aloud to Lidian and Ruskin's *Elements of Drawing* to herself and listening to Dr. Solger's lectures on Ethnology.

In 1859 Ellen again attended Franklin Sanborn's school. Sanborn tells of first seeing her in her childhood. She was descending a stairway and reminded him of "some angel in Allston's 'Jacob's Dream.' "[8] Ellen found Sanborn's school delightful: "Here at this school we have a head, that is a great thing, one master of all, under whose eye we sit, and this master is a wise, and joyful and handsome man who holds the hearts of all the school. The teaching here is much better and more thorough, and broader too, in most things than it is at Mr Agassiz's. Then the boys and girls go together here which I think is essential to a good school. They do not play together. I don't think that could be done in this generation, but it will be in the next, but the girls have at least the recreation of seeing the boys play, and it is a great one" (22 January 1859).

When she was not at school, she was occupied in house-affairs or in having company. After the very sad breakingup of the school in the summer came the disappointment of losing a long-dreamed-for vacation in Waterford, Maine, because of her father's sprained ankle, but Ellen soon found herself happy with the prospects of managing the home while Edith and her mother were away. With Edith and Lidian at Naushon, near Cape Cod, and with the cook and chambermaid dismissed, twenty-year-old Ellen, with help only from the seamstress, worked from five in the morning until nightfall, losing all sense of time. She enjoyed the experiment and felt that her attempt at cooking and housekeeping had been successful.

In February 1860, Captain John Brown's daughters began to attend school in Concord and stayed with the Emersons. These girls in odd clothes, brought up in the primitive spinning, weaving, sheep-tending, and butter-making times, proved of great interest to both Ellen and her mother.

The Civil War obsessed Ellen as perhaps few things did in her life. She thought news of every new recruit who joined a great thing and regretted that no one nearer than a second cousin had gone. Her only grief was that in her view the country could not make up its mind what it was fighting for. She followed closely news of the Massachusetts Fifth Regiment, fearful when there were rumors they had thrown their colors away and joyful when, having lost members of four Concord families, they returned for the town's reception. She was proud of Captain Prescott, whom she believed to be the only one in the army to share the fate and quarters of his men. In July 1862, she and Edith, visiting Mrs. Clarke in Newport, requested linen to make lint for bandages for the eighteen hundred wounded. When 1865 came, she wrote her cousin Haven:

And one thing rather surprised me—that I am really sorry to part with the War, and feel as if I never could have such a living interest in anything again as I have had in it. That hereafter "my country" will sound as quiet and commonplace as it used to, and "the government" absolutely uninteresting, instead of making me a little excited as it has whenever it has been named these last years. It is a great blessing ever to have known these fires, and it is hard to think they must go out. Mother often says adversity is really the best happiness, and that I never could bear to hear, it seemed an ungrateful way of treating prosperity. But when I think now of War and Peace I begin to be afraid that I agree with Mother. (5 May 1865)

In writing to Mrs. Herman Grimm after the war, Ellen says: "I think they were the best years of life, and that the strength of feeling and the love of country and the power of work that war brings and keeps alive, impossible in peace, were so enjoyed by everyone, that people who did not lose their friends in the war look back on those years with great affection" (2 March 1868).

During the war Ellen changed her schedule when her mother complained that she never saw her daughter. She gave up housekeeping and two or three regular engagements and spent much of the day with Lidian reading over her old papers and letters to see what should be burned. Following the war in 1866, apparently for the first time Ellen had a real understanding of her mission to her mother that was so to dominate her life, as the Civil War had. She discovered from her Aunt Susan a method of treating Lidian in periods of difficulty that was to be frequently successful. One day Lidian was upset as Ellen had kept her waiting all day or forgot her till by night her condition was frightening. Ellen set off for Aunt Susan's, who impressed on her mind her mother's danger, telling her the only way to save her was to surprise her every two hours with some small thing that she could eat. "I came home repentant, and found everything upside down, the family crying for supper, Mother very faint, the kitchen gloomy at the late hour, John [Clahan] gone home without seeing him. And yet that dreadful day came at last to an end, though new tragedies filled the evening, and Saturday was a day just like the rest, everything prosperous, and not a trace of the horrors of Friday" (16 July 1866).

She persisted in her dedication to her mother, for on 10 August 1866, she explains in a letter to Edward: "Your poor mamma is in a very sad condition, so utterly weak and broken down, and I see that no pains must be spared and nothing must be allowed to prevent me from doing for her every minute that she wants me. A year's devotion and absolute giving up of every other occupation would be cheap to give if she could be restored, and I seem to feel much more clearly than I ever did that it is necessary that she should have all she wants of care and reading, so whenever I feel as if I had a minute and could write to you children I run into her room first and ask if she would like to be read to. Of course she always says yes, and she shall have what she wants now. She never has before, and now I mean to comfort her if I can." Ellen's extreme efforts to protect her mother from any mental anxiety continued until Lidian's death.

Ellen's role as a sister and aunt was always a central priority for her, next only to being a daughter to her mother. She was not quite at the pinnacle of pride when Edward was admitted to the Hasty Pudding

Club: "You must wait till the day when I see my sister walk out with Will [Forbes, whom Edith married] in Concord streets, followed by her admiring family. That day I shall strut my grandest. Picture it" (6 May 1865). And she did! The majority of her extant letters are to Edith and they reveal deep affection and much love. Ellen never failed on the appropriate day of the year to remind Edith that her wedding day was the happiest day of Ellen's life. In 1881 she says it was the "crowning festivity of my life"; two years later, she calls it the brightest day of her life but admits that seems ungrateful as she has known many dazzling days of glory. And on Edith's twenty-fifth wedding anniversary Ellen wrote the following poem:

To
Will and Edith
On Their Silver Wedding Day

Let me, beloved, recall that Day
When that befell which was to me
And more to you the shining way
From joy to greater joys to be.

I see you on its blessed eve
Laugh the glad laugh of full content
As all of good man can conceive
Seemed in your cup by Heaven blent.

I see the Wedding Day's fair morn
To fairest noon still fairer grow
And friendly hands the house adorn
With genial autumn's brightest show.

The Bridegroom, watched with love and pride
By both the happy kindreds, stands
Our hearts' dear Rose a blessed bride
Beside him, dressed by holy hands.

Never before nor since have I
Seen in the Marriage Service shine
Such solemn power, such beauty high
Of human love and Grace Divine.

And with you through its opening gate
We saw a golden future smile
Of hopes on sure foundations set,
Good faith, good sense, hearts without guile,

And will to serve your fellow men
And keep God's laws in great and small.
And youth and health and love were then
Your portion—richest mercies all.

All that we hoped we now confess
With grateful hearts has been your share
And more, much more. For fancy's bliss
Can *not* with actual gifts compare.
                                    (29 September 1890)

It became the custom for Ellen to visit and help her married sister Edith in Milton, which she called Paradise, at the birth of each child. Ellen examined each new arrival with critical eye, praising or plainly condemning the shape of the head, the shape of the mouth, the closeness of the ears to the head, the size of the feet, and the complexion. The letters are full of recordings of the first words in baby dialect and of the actions of each child. As the children grew older, she chronicled their every advance; she wrote them and always remembered with joy their dates of birth.

From 26 June 1866 to 18 October 1868, Ellen made frequent, short trips. She went to Monadnock camping, to Milton, to Nahant, to Boston, back to Milton for Christmas at Mrs. Forbes, to Newport, to Beverly, to Naushon, to Boston to hear Dickens, to Milton, to New York, to Newport again, to New York for Haven Emerson (her first cousin) and Susy Tompkins's wedding, to Boston with Lidian, to their favorite camping spot again at Monadnock, to Princeton, to Middlebury and Rutland, Vermont, to Princeton, to Beverly, to Mt. Mansfield, Vermont, and to Boston. Such trips continued with frequency throughout Ellen's life. On the April 1868 trip to New York, Ellen not only heard Henry Ward Beecher but also saw General Grant, who had on an army hat but was dressed in old, shabby clothes, nothing in the least military about him. In August 1868, she met her father at Fitchburg and accompanied him to Middlebury for an oration and then to Rutland for the night. She grieved about separation from her mother: "Was ever anyone in such a dilemma between their parents? But Mother was strong on Father's side and insisted on my coming" (11 August 1868). And on the thirteenth she wrote to her "dear forsaken Mamma. . . . I keep thinking of you as a poor unsheltered lamb in the wilderness, and feel quite distracted lest you should be homesick, or should find your new quarters uncomfortable. For Father calmly says it is impossible to restore me to you before Saturday night."

The year 1868 was a precarious time to leave Concord. Someone had to stay home to protect the silver cream pitcher because of an outbreak of burglary in town. Five times in a fortnight houses were entered. Once, while her parents were in Milton, Ellen and May Alcott guarded Bush armed with a pistol, and May was disappointed when no one came.

Ellen's trips thus far had always been short in miles and brief in duration, but a Saturday morning in October 1868, "a bolt fell from a clear sky, and tore me up by the roots. My family told me to pack my trunks, settle my affairs, make my will and go to Fayal [in the Azores] on Wednesday, 28th to stay till June. . . . I must lose Thanksgiving but come the more to console poor Papa and Mamma who are torn up by the roots even more than I, and wonder at their own resolution in sending me away." She was apparently sent away for her health, but there is no indication of what is actually wrong. More than a year earlier she said she was gaining vigor. She said the fact that she could run up the stairs to within two steps of the top before feeling any difficulty showed a great improvement since she had had to crawl upstairs hitherto. The letters following her return from Fayal show that she went to bed just after eight in the evening, feeling it was her one hold on health. In 1878, she tells Edith of an illness of Lidian and confides that if it is as bad and is going to have as much effect on her as Ellen's own illness of 1867 which lasted seven years, she felt she may well tremble.

She sailed on the *Fredonia* on 30 October. It was nine days before she came on deck, and she was very weak. The only letter at the Houghton Library from Fayal is written to Ellen's "adopted" daughter, Edith Davidson, a young lady whose natural family conditions apparently warranted Ellen's care.

Ellen's best letters, full of loving religious instruction, are written to Edith Davidson, who died in 1877 in Mentone in the Azores where she was sent for her health. We gain much insight into the religious and moral values of Ellen by considering those letters. From these letters and from other letters on Unitarianism to be considered later, we know that Ellen was a Christian believer. In 1870, she scolds Edith for her behavior in philosophy class and reminds her that by her fruits she will be known: "I want you to know our Lord personally, and feel engaged to follow his example. . . . [W]hen you have him (Jesus) you are safe in any company. There is so much to be said on this subject! It seems to include everything" (24 May 1870). In 1873, she feels very sorry that to the boys of the present generation there seems to be no such thing as Christianity, "the only sufficing answer and motive seems as far removed from them and as inaccessible as it ever was to heathen people of old. They seem to be where Tacitus and all good, earnest,

seeking and sad men of culture were before the Christian centuries"
(13 August 1873).

Ellen writes Edith from Paris explaining that she talks to her in her
mind constantly, that she hears and reads sermons with her, and that
she always prays for her to live in Christ and to have grace to take her
cross bravely. These letters to Edith are especially important as they show
us the guiding principles in Ellen's own life.

From the time of her return from Fayal till her next major trip in
1872, Ellen was fully engaged in community and church affairs. During
this time she continued her frequent trips to Boston, to Milton, and to
Naushon. She also traveled to Springfield, to Worcester, twice to New
York, to Williamsburg, twice to Providence, twice to Amherst, to Barre,
to Greenwich, to Princeton, to Monadnock, to Cohasset, and twice to
Beverly. The trip to Egypt in 1872 with her father was prompted by the
fire that badly damaged the Emerson house and the loving generosity
of Emerson's friends. The fire, which occurred in Ellen's absence, was
surely the most dramatic event for her since Fayal but ironically and
in true Emersonian spirit, it could not be said to be traumatic. "Why
didn't the fire hurt? In a great measure because our house is to me
associated with dirt, waste, bottomless abysses of expense to no profit,
deceit, ill-temper and shirking" (30 July 1872).

In August, Ellen and her father went to Portland, Waterford, and Nor-
way, Maine, for a rest and change of air. For five or six years Emerson's
memory had been failing and for the last three years he was unable to
remember what he was asked to do even when reminded of the details
of the asking. In conversation about facts he could not remember words
or names of things, but he still had no difficulty in conversation with
people who were interested on his own ground. In Waterford, he began
to comment on the future of his manuscripts. He dreaded that Moncure
D. Conway or Sanborn might get hold of them; rather he commented
that Frederic Henry Hedge and James Elliot Cabot might be trusted with
them.

In October, Emerson and his daughter Ellen began an extended trip
abroad; they met Edward in Chester, but Ellen was lame from a sprained
ankle. Rusk records this trip, with Egypt as its ultimate destination, in
full detail.

Ellen confessed to Edith that when she went to galleries with people who knew about pictures she was discouraged to realize that she
never liked the good pictures and those she did like were considered
bad. Ruskin was the man who most interested her. His sadness went to
her heart; she valued him immensely for his sincerity. Emerson thought

him to be willfully gloomy. When they returned to the very elaborately planned town reception, Ellen noticed the schools marshaled under their own teachers, even the outer districts of schools three and four miles off; she believed, according to her letters, that this turnout was for her, apparently because of her membership on the school committee. For whatever reason, Fayal was a much greater experience for Ellen than this tour with her father.

Ellen made one other trip to Europe with Edward and his family. She was in Venice in May 1893, finding the temptation to buy in Paris nothing to that created by the shop windows in Venice. In Oxford and Cambridge she called the beautiful Oxford colleges "Rag-bag exteriors!" much to Edward's horror. She boarded in a house in Lincolnshire near Hull on one pound a week, which included an evening fire. She stayed two weeks in Salisbury. In the winter of 1893–1894 she was in Antibes, France, with Edward and the others. She encouraged her friends and her fellow members in Concord's Frolic Club to join her in Europe.

Ellen was unquestionably a daughter of the nineteenth century rather than a procreator of the twentieth century. Lidian consistently held more avant-garde ideas than her daughter. The most obvious point of departure is on the question of woman's role in society. The Emersons, with very independent minds, frequently had diverse opinions among themselves, but these opinions were respected, tolerated, and indeed sometimes enjoyed by one of an exactly opposite view. If one feels that the only intolerable thing is a difference of opinion, then that person is bound to interpret vigorous exchanges in the Emerson circle as discord. Ellen's letters determine once and for all that that simply is not the case.

One example of Ellen's stand on woman's role came on 30 October 1871, when a lady came trying to enlist Ellen's sympathy and labor for the Woman's Suffrage Fair. She pitied her and tried to look mild as she expressed hostile sentiments. Ellen said that her mother was an ardent advocate of the cause and a feeble opponent of Fairs whereupon the lady left Mrs. Emerson a circular and heaped coals of fire on Ellen's head by hoping that some day she would be able to further her charitable labors in some direction she was interested in. When she confessed the interview to her mother, Lidian wondered that Ellen could stand unabashed and express such selfish, blind, and cruel views.

In November, Ellen spoke against Woman's Suffrage at the Freedmen's Aid Society meeting at Bush. At tea with the family that same evening, she reported in a letter: "Mother mounts her most bolting and snorting warhorse and leaves us all nowhere in less than no time. Edith on a pony of the same breed charges valiantly on her presuming sister and tells her the least those inferior and selfish minds that cannot see the benefit and the privilege of voting can do is to hold their idle tongues. Father won't speak one word till particularly requested he gives his views and as a reward has directly the fury of all his household levelled at him" (17 November 1871). A Woman's Suffrage Convention was held in 1887. Since Ellen thought attendance would improve Lidian's downcast spirits, she got Dr. Titcomb to encourage her, and the two of them, plus Lidian's favorite green rocker, went. In September 1886, she sent Edith a letter from the Woman Suffragists and told her to "read it and judge of my state of mind. It resembled Edward's when asked to contribute towards giving the Putnams a large dog,—but my case was worse, for he could refuse, and I was morally certain Mother would consent to the meeting with its triple offence, Woman Suffrage, a Fair, and a Reverend lady. To my surprise and relief she at once said she was not well enough, and with joyous speed I have communicated this reply to the authorities."

Ellen also struggled with the idea of women speaking in public or doing public work (and Lidian obviously did not). Ellen in 1872 reported that a Mrs. Foss gave a dramatic reading that Lidian went with zeal to hear because Mrs. Foss was a woman. She said very little about her distasteful performance for the same reason. Yet Ellen enjoyed the sight of Effie Lowell speaking but felt she must explain that it was not against her principles as it was not a woman speaking in public but rather a member of a board of charities doing a member's duty at a meeting of boards of charities so that she felt free to admire the beauty of Effie's performance.

Ellen was extremely active in both community and church affairs, but she could not make herself step into territory that she felt to be strange for a woman. Her classic struggle took place during a sermon when the minister found that the darkness prevented him from reading his sermon and his struggle was so great that perspiration poured down his face although the temperature was sixty degrees. A lamp was badly needed. Ellen knew where the lamp was and how to fill it. A man went down for it but did not know how to fill it. While the preacher read "let no one say that this or that is not the province of woman and you, my sister, don't fear to carry on the work that is in your heart because you are a woman," Ellen would not move because she was a woman.

If Ellen was not in the forefront of the struggle on the behalf of womankind, her contributions to both church and community were nevertheless impressive and represent real leadership within the confines of her sense of what was acceptable. She was the first woman to serve on the Concord school committee, and, after her election in 1870, the delight in her being the first woman was talked over by all her callers with the hope that other women would also serve. When she attended her first school committee meeting in August 1870, Mr. Lang told her that Mr. Hurd had polished up the room on her election, since things ought to look fit for a lady, and she was grieved that not once had she appeared to see the improvement. One of Ellen's duties was to be annual examiner in the schools.

This is the week of annual examinations of the schools, and every morning I start off right after breakfast and every noon after dinner, two examinations a day. So many pleasures! Each child dressed in its prettiest, each schoolroom just scoured. The sight alone does one good. Half the children are really pretty. In most schools I know nearly everyone and understand their beauty. They sing, they recite so perfectly, they speak their pieces, often beautiful ones, they perform their gymnastics. . . . Three primary-school teachers are my own dear lambs, this is their first examination. On Sunday and the Sunday before I had all their fear and flutter. The first hymn last Sunday was something about "though anxious care may hang upon our way, we will not let it enter here; all shall be Thine at least today." One of them said when I came down into Sunday-school, "Oh Miss Ellen did you notice the first hymn? We did: we thought it was meant for the school-teachers."

Then our minister Mr Reynolds is Superintendent of Schools and Chairman of School-committee, and no one ever was better fitted for that office than he, it is beautiful to see how skilfully he manages to conduct everything, so that there is no possibility of fraud, and so the parents may see there is none, and at the same time smooths the way and often adroitly saves a child from failing. More surprising still is his clear memory of each child's history and capacity, and of the state of things last year in each school. Father says he is a Ulysses. (23 February 1871)

When examining the Intermediate School, she was treated with amusing deference, as she was asked to examine the class.

After reading I must hear them spell. An opportunity! Arise, O class, spell grief, receive, believe, stationary (ery), disappoint, separate, agreeable, skilful. They accepted the challenge, they spelt with zeal, and very well, Ellen had to use all her wits to collect words fast enough, she bethought her of Edward's letters and gave out *necessary*. They stumbled. But no one could complain that it wasn't a well-taught class. Scarcely one mistake in all the ei and ie words. . . . Miss Bull next set them to arithmetic and had them demonstrate their work and give the rule, with wonderful exactness. It showed scholarship and discipline but as I was questioning in my mind whether it was worthwhile to spend so much labour in committing to memory and so much time in reciting on this work which the children of my generation understood perfectly without it, Miss Bull said, "What do you think of this? Is it a good plan?" as if she had doubts too. I couldn't answer. I didn't know enough. (8 December 1871)

Ellen grew to love the meetings of the committee: "I went to a school committee meeting. Oh the delights that fill my days! No one knows how much I enjoy hearing with my own ears the talks in that room" (1 April 1872).

We can be fairly certain that Ellen was conservative in her views on education, for she admits as much in telling of a dinner she once had when both Bret Harte and Bronson Alcott were present. Ellen listened with interest to Alcott for perhaps ten minutes, but afterward her "narrow and conservative mind" was so riled by what seemed to her fanciful ideas that she could not bear them very well (3 November 1871). She regretted in 1883, in reflection on separating the rich from the poor, that the Forbeses had kept their children out of public schools.

In 1875, Ellen's brother, Edward, who had been graduated the year before from Harvard and was assistant to Dr. Bartlett, took Ellen's place on the school committee. In 1877 she grieved that she was no longer on the school committee: "Our School examinations are going on this week, I mourn that they no longer belong to me. I mean to go to two of them, however, and don't I wish I could sit with the committee and hear what they say to each other! Few relations are more delightful than the relations of a committee among themselves, they are so intimate, and full of the delight of the common work. Yet they fall to pieces in a moment when you leave the committee. You are at once an outsider and no matter what the disposition of your old associates may be they no longer have a right to open their minds freely to you as of old" (28 February 1877).

She served on another educational committee beginning in February 1895. In September a series of lectures began under the auspices of the American Society for the Extension of University Teaching. They enjoyed an audience of over fifty at two lectures.

Her interest in community affairs began as early as 1857 when she depicted the Cattleshow day as the famous day of the year in Concord where the Emersons displayed their pears and sage grapes. In 1867, she complained that her sociable did not prosper that year, as there were few there, little money, and no parents present. In the same year she attended a singing school in which she sang alto. There are several public occasions recorded where she sang alto. This singing would at least weaken Engel's statement that she only mouthed the words.[9] For example, she sang alto in a chorus on Decoration Day in 1883.

In November 1871, the Freedmen's Aid Society met at Bush. In

January 1872, Ellen attended the first meeting of the Sociable Committee. Mrs. Hoar was president of a 1872 Chicago Sewing Society which Ellen attended. They were sewing for twenty of sixty babies who were expected and who were unprovided for. Ellen attended once or twice a week and was reminded of the Soldier's Aid Society. She attended cooking school from time to time, visiting in 1887 Mrs. Hemenway's Cooking School. In 1885, she attended for the first time the Charitable Society. In the same year, she visited with Edward and Abby Hosmer the Idiot School in South Boston. The horrors of seeing the children eat was unexpected to her and shocked even more Edward, who told the attendants that they fed the helpless too fast. She mentions the Frolic Club from 1883 through 1887. One day she attended the club with Cary Hoar at Alice Wheildon's house where they observed a play that was written by Alice. In 1886, she declined an invitation from Edith rather than miss the Frolic Club's annual play as that year Miss Ball and Harriet Buttrick were to make their debuts. In January 1887, the Frolic Club held a twelfth-night celebration at Alice Wheildon's, and on another occasion they played beanbags at Cary Hoar's. Through the years she gave parties for the school children. In 1874, she held a carnival of youth. She had Ralph, Violet, and Ethel Davidson with the children she taught, Cora and Lucy Bowditch and Una Hawthorne, for a week or more. She immediately afterward began to plan a carnival of the mind or of wisdom to include more of her father's friends than her own.

Ellen was very active in church work. She joined the First Parish Church on 4 March 1867 and became a part of a Monday Bible Class. Ellen must have early taken a class of Sunday Scholars, since in January 1867, before joining the church after giving her name for membership, she was at a Teachers' Meeting where Edward, Mrs. Hoar, Judge Hoar, Dr. Bartlett, Mr. and Mrs. Simon Brown, and Mr. John Brown (of Concord) were present. She was deeply committed to her Sunday Scholars and found great joy in them.

On Friday night another Parish Party, a season of delight. I have been reading Job with my class the past two months, and by dint of faithful labour we have acquired a respectable degree of familiarity with it, and become correspondingly attached to it, a result agreeable to me, and a delight and real surprise to my girls, who, naturally enough, were nothing less than disgusted with it at the first taste. Coming to Arcturus, Orion, and the Pleiades, I found the children had never seen Orion. I had the planisphere and Celestial chart down in Sunday School, and the interest and ardour with which they hunted out the constellations thereon, was a refreshment to my aged mind. As I was coming home early from the Parish Party, I saw the stars peculiarly brilliant, Arcturus flashing and changing from red to green over the hill, and Orion glorious in the south. A bright idea struck me, I went back and asked Edward to call out my class and show them the stars. When he came home he was in high feather, he and they had enjoyed it so much. They gave 3 cheers for Orion, he said. (13 March 1871)

Later in the same year she asked her Sunday School babes to be true evangelical peacocks whereupon they consented to give up Christmas and send presents to Chicago's destitute children. In the winter of 1877 her Sunday Class was better than ever: "As the girls grow older they naturally talk more, and a new idea possesses them, the desire to hear what the whole class thinks. It is no longer a talk between me and one pupil at once, I choosing who shall answer and drawing the answers out. It is a furious burst of question and answer all round and my new office is that of chairman in an excited meeting, deciding who shall speak and keeping the others still" (28 February 1877). She had Judge Hoar's daughter, Clara, for a Sunday Scholar for at least ten years, and she was still teaching as late as 1900.

Another organization about which she frequently writes is Bible Society. In 1883, she had fifty at Bush for Bible Society, the largest meeting she ever had; they met there again in 1890. As late as 1899, she talks of the annual meeting of the Bible Society as a buzz of affection, enthusiasm, and sociability.

Ellen attended many church-related conferences and conventions. In 1874, she attended a conference at Arlington. In August of that year she was proposed as a delegate from her church to the National Convention in September, which she attended. In September 1878, she was a delegate to the National Unitarian Conference at Saratoga. She attended a Unitarian meeting at the Weirs, New Hampshire, in July 1879. In 1882, she was once again in Saratoga for a conference when they collected $158 for New Orleans, reparations for the Civil War. That same fall, she went to a Framingham Convention. She attended Conference board meetings in Boston, and in 1883 she reflected on the Saratoga conference and compared the religious status of the 1882 conference with that of 1878: "Saratoga was delightful in a social way and very interesting, but as in 1878 I came away in 1882 with a sense that there was nothing religious in the Conference. We do not seem to me to be a religious people; we have good sense, good moral principles, cheerful views, are a highly civilized set, and like to be friendly and generous. That is all. Those to whom I complained four years ago said, 'but you didn't go to morning-meeting. If you had you would have seen the religion and felt it through the day.' So this time I went to every morning-meeting, but my impression was only confirmed"

(2 April 1883). Other lay persons were clearly of Ellen's persuasion. They were unhappy with radical elements of their church but did not feel at home in any other church. Mary Blake complained to Ellen about Emerson's lifelong friend, the Reverend William Furness, that he was a radical and that she went to church only to cry. Believing that she could never go again, she tried the Episcopal church, but not feeling at home there, she longed for a Christian Unitarian church as did all her friends.

It is usually assumed that the religious convictions of a child follow those of the parents, but Ellen differed from her father. From what little has been written, one would suspect that Ellen's source for Christian belief is Lidian, but while mother and daughter were probably very close in their Christian views, it is not probable that they were dictated to the younger.

The major religious issue for Ellen remained the discrepancy between the minister and his congregation over Christianity. At a Sunday School Convention in January 1878, where the Emersons had fourteen to spend the night—eight of them ministers—and twenty-two for dinner the next day, she observed that the ministers that particular year believed that Christ was a man, a real man, not God manifest in the flesh. He is the sun but not the son, and he is the head of the church. When the Reverend Grindall Reynolds left Concord to become the secretary of the Unitarian Association, Ellen at first had little hope in finding a "Christian" Unitarian minister:

I find that my expectations are not high it does not seem as if there were any young ministers in the denomination who were Christians, and how can I like to receive a minister of the modern kind who is distinctly persuaded that Christ was a man, only a man, and that, as two ministers have said to me, he was valuable to the human race, "exactly as Washington was, as a moral example." For a long time I had great hopes of the Unitarians, the tide had turned I felt, and they were becoming more Christian; but since I have learned *how* they have become more Christian I am only pained by their preaching. At least they have learned to study the Gospels and to own in Christ their best example and teacher, and to confess it plainly, and that is something to be thankful for, and for a long time while I regarded this as a stage I enjoyed it; but now the older men, almost without exception have settled into the same place, and I seem to see that even if it is only a stage it is one that is likely to last these many years. Of course the first thing that occurs is, if the Unitarians don't please me why stay with them? Because I belong to them. I cannot find another home, in every other church the whole atmosphere and all the methods are strange and seem less healthy and right. I must stay where I belong and hope that the new light the Unitarians need, and that not I alone but most of the people I hear talk feel the need of, will shine in my day. The worst of the situation is that the ministers seem content, and believe that they have what the people want. But the laity are hungry and find the food the ministers offer does not satisfy,—I call this the one ground, the strongest ground for hope. Where many are so eager there will be something for them. (28 July 1881)

When the second-year divinity student, Benjamin Bulkeley, only about eighteen came and stayed with them, Ellen instantly admired him as all the others did. Among her early observations were that his feet were smaller than her own, that he was the eighth great-grandson of Peter Bulkeley (Concord's first minister) though he did not pronounce or spell his name right, and that he was a natural minister with no rhetoric. She was happy to find a precedent for choosing a young man who was yet to be ordained. Her grandfather had been chosen minister in February 1765, but was not ordained until 1 January 1766, when he was nearly twenty-three. In 1882, both Mr. and Mrs. Emerson were attending Bulkeley's services zealously. Ellen found him to be a Christian humanitarian who knew what the usual Unitarian mind had never dreamed of so that their children would not likely grow up heathen under his teaching.

Ellen held interesting views of the prospects of Christianity for the twentieth century:

One man preached here two years ago—perhaps I told you—who said "Religious interest still centres in the person of Jesus. Fifty years ago we Unitarians began to think we might advance beyond him, might leave him out, but as we stripped away the divine honours which had till then clothed him, the man Jesus drew our eyes and we do not yet feel that we know him.". . . the people who will live in the next century are a new race. Judging by the few I see I should say a pagan race for their parents have carefully defended them from hearing a word about religion so I make my little prophecy that Christianity will be rediscovered and be as new as it was to Rome, and that all the good and wise benevolent work that is started all over the world will make itself felt more and more and the new Christianity suddenly prosper and vivify it, and good will make mighty strides at last. (February 1897)

Other than church and community involvement, Ellen, in her later years, had two other interests, both rather advanced from older concepts of woman's domain. One was her intense interest in finances and investments, quite in contrast to Lidian's view of economy. She obviously knew little about money in 1879, for she tells that a Mr. Horton, an authority on money, and William Forbes, at that time President of the

Bell Telephone Company, talked on high themes to her which constantly soared beyond the reach of her female mind. Just ten years later, in a series of business letters to someone named Sally, she is very comfortable on the issue of investment of money. These letters to Sally, dealing exclusively with her investment of Sally's funds, continue until June 1908, when she returned her money with regret explaining that she could no longer remember well enough to be responsible. Brokers said they had learned by experience that when Ellen bought stock, it was safe for them to recommend it to others. Her letters to Sally frequently reveal the workings of her mind on the subject.

The other endeavor is her work with James Elliot Cabot on Emerson's literary remains. Cabot helped Emerson as early as 1877, and the next year when a Mr. Rice came from the publishing fraternity, Emerson admitted that the work was Cabot's and Ellen's compilation. Ellen wanted her father to take credit: "And I sat peacefully and listened but within I was stamping wildly about tearing my hair and uttering ever new shrieks of surprise and dismay. Still it was all true, and truth does no real harm" (30 January 1878). In 1880, Cabot came about twice a month. In 1883, Ellen worked with both Cabot and Edward on the essay, "Education," a lecture that gave the family many laughs in 1878. Emerson was to read it at Edward's house and later at the Lyceum. He could not remember the subject of the lecture, asking what it was every minute. He also thought it rather high-soaring for a Concord audience and laughed saying, "'A funny occasion it will be—a lecturer who had no idea what he's lecturing about, and an audience who don't know what he *can* mean!'" He delivered the lecture successfully (6 February 1878). After Emerson's death, Cabot gave the family in 1885 the initial eighty pages of his manuscript of the life of Emerson. The family was delighted with it. Later, the family gathered to read the first draft as they received it from him, reading as much as one hundred and fifty pages a visit.

In 1868 when Ellen's Aunt Susan and Aunt Lucy were ill, she said that her aunts were her sole business. In her later years her father's Haskins cousins were her dominant care and concern. They were double first cousins of Emerson, his mother's brother's children, and also his father's sister's. They were three widowed sisters, about the same age and always dressed in black. Their brother, the Reverend Samuel Haskins, rector of St. Mark's Episcopal Church in Brooklyn, kept Charlotte, Sarah Ansley, and Hannah Parsons until his death. A letter describing their welfare shows Ellen's responsibility: "They are perfectly well all the time, but it is lose, lose, lose. It seems impossible for Cousin Sarah to find her way round the house half the time. . . . Every day is Sunday and Miss Myers keeps her bonnet locked up to prevent her putting it on to go to church three times a day. . . . Then there are frequent interviews with Grandpa Ripley to tell of, and every white object or loaf of bread is welcomed with joy as a dear little baby" (4 April 1905).

Ellen could be very philosophical about her own aging process in a letter to Miss Dabney, with whom she developed a long friendship in Fayal: "You praise my fifty years dear Miss Clara [Dabney], and I can truly say that I seem to myself to have been quite singled out with favour. I am very much interested in growing old, and spectacles, gray hair and decrease of energy all amuse me like playthings, but there are parts of it that have a sad effect rather. It keeps coming to me in one way or another that instead of getting ready to live as, hitherto, I thought I was doing, I *have been* living, all I ever shall, and now all that made it possible is gone, the planning mind, memory, confidence, power of performance, and the rest of my years are to be decline. . . . I promise and forget, and in every arrangement drop two or three stitches. I was always in my best days accused of dropping *one*" (2 April 1888). Almost a decade later she admits the one thing about aging that she does not like at all: "I am grieved, often shocked, to see my contemporaries and worse still my juniors grow old. There is something so pathetic about that that first I wonder why I never minded it in the least with my elders, and second I see that I must for consolation resort to a great confidence that the succeeding life is going to be really better. Otherwise I should hate to see them fade and weaken as they do" (24 February 1892).

In July 1898, she had trouble with her knee swelling; she was on crutches for six months from a fall in the tub. In September, Edward sent her to Cousin Mary Dewey's boarding house at 96 Chestnut Street to get well where she stayed until the end of October. She had a private nurse in March 1900 for what she calls a slight illness but was irate over the twenty-one dollars a week for a service that anyone devoted to the sick-room could do as well. She went in the spring of 1908 to Hot Springs, Virginia, for treatment of her knee, and Dr. Pole assured her that when she was home she could ride her bicycle again. Her housekeeping ended on 10 September 1908, when she went to Edward and Margaret's in Milton. Miss Richardson (see note 398) found a new home, and Miss Leavitt (see note 382), Miss Grace A. Hurd, and Miss Legate (see note 372) stayed on at Bush. Her last letter in the Houghton Library is to Haven and Susan, telling them that she is sick in bed at her niece, Edith's; and that her future is yet to be constructed. She died on 14 January 1909. The coffin was put in the study of Bush in front of the bookcases as Lidian's had been. The church bells tolled her death; the funeral was in the Unitarian Church. The services were conducted by the

Reverend Leon B. MacDonald, the pastor, and the Reverend Benjamin R. Bulkeley of Beverly. Both ministers had lived for a short time with the Emersons. In front of and on both sides of the altar were masses of flowers, and on Ellen's pew door was a cluster of white pinks and mignonette. Among the pallbearers were nephews: William F. Emerson of Concord, Ralph E. Forbes, Gerrit Forbes, Waldo Forbes, Alexander Forbes and Edward Forbes of Milton, Haven Emerson of New York, and Kenneth Webster of Cambridge. The service included a Scripture reading by both ministers, a selection from Emerson's writings: "In the hours of clear vision how slight a thing it is to die! Let us hope infinitely. Nothing is so young and untaught as time." There was a prayer by the pastor and the benediction pronounced by Bulkeley. A quartet sang "I Heard a Voice From Heaven" and "Lord, Now Lettest Thou Thy Servant Depart in Peace," and the congregation sang one of Ellen's favorites, "While Thee I Seek Protecting Power." This hymn, written by Helen M. Williams in 1790, bespeaks Ellen's life:

> While Thee I seek, protecting Power.
> Be my vain wishes stilled;
> And may this consecrated hour
> With better hopes be filled.
>
> Thy love the power of thought bestowed,
> To Thee my thoughts would soar:
> Thy mercy o'er my life has flowed,
> That mercy I adore.
>
> In each event of life, how clear
> Thy ruling hand I see;
> Each blessing to my soul more dear,
> Because conferred by Thee.
>
> In every joy that crown my days,
> In every pain I bear,
> My heart shall find delight in praise,
> Or seek relief in prayer.
>
> When gladness wings my favored hour,
> Thy love my thoughts shall fill;
> Resigned when storms of sorrow lower,
> My soul shall meet Thy will.
>
> My lifted eye, without a tear,
> The gathering storms shall see;

My steadfast heart shall know no fear
That heart will rest on Thee.

The organist was Miss Edith May Lang of Boston. The ushers were Edward J. Bartlett, Charles W. Prescott, Woodward Hudson, Allen French, George S. Keyes, Thomas Hollis, Samuel Hoar, Henry Smith, Jr., Frederick W. Eaton, and Reginald F. Jones, all of Concord, Henry S. Forbes, Theodore S. Watson, and James S. Russell of Milton. The flags were at half-mast until after the funeral. Her remains were cremated at Mt. Auburn and buried in Sleepy Hollow.

Ellen's views on death remained consistent through the years. When she was twenty-one, she could not give her correspondent any idea of how sweet it was to see the deceased in the coffin. She liked to hear of things that made it seem probable that in the hereafter one would go right on, keeping the same consciousness and seeing old friends.

In telling Miss Dabney of the death of her niece, Ellen Randolph Forbes, and her nephew, Charles Emerson, Ellen reveals, "And alas! I see more and more that I am not made like other people, that to have people die doesn't affect me except as any beautiful and affecting event does. I am not grieved, I wish I were, I am only deeply interested" (30 April 1881). Of the death of her own mother she was thankful that the days of losing, losing, losing were over and felt that some day she might feel the loss out of this world sadly, but death seemed to her only beautiful: "The house does not seem to me so different as people think it must. Life looks as full and as interesting as it did before. I see that I am not made exactly like other people and death does not grieve me no matter how near it comes" (7 December 1892). If we make allowance for a measure of hyperbole in Ellen's and Emerson's correspondingly similar convictions on death, theirs is a healthy view, though, perhaps, not the normal one. In face of the inevitable do wailing and gnashing of teeth make sense?

Helen A. Legate wrote a letter to Edith on 24 February 1920: "I have been thinking a great deal about Miss Ellen yesterday and today, her birthday. . . . I never think of her as old for as long as she lived she had all the attributes of youth. I often think with wonder of the miracle that brought her with her fine exalted character into my life. The inspiration and stimulation she has been to me I can never estimate. I feel that I am far short of what I would like to be, but I know that her example and influence has helped me to come nearer to my ideals. I have told you all this before, but I like to tell you again, on her birthday. Your mother once said 'Ellen is a Christian Philosopher,' and it seemed such a fine description of Miss Ellen." The expression which always seemed to occur to Lidian in thinking of Ellen was "She walks in light."[10]

Part III

Ellen Emerson possessed the ingredients of a good biographer and overcame quite well what could have been her greatest weakness, a lack of objectivity. Her greatest asset was her knowledge of her subject. Ellen makes an obvious attempt to depict her mother clearly; for example, she frequently emphasized characteristics with the occasional touch that tells secrets, showing her devotion to the truth.

Ellen is best as a biographer when she not only presents the fact of an incident but also supplies jewels of conversation delivered in exciting settings. One such high point is the visit to the Shaker village. Her letters are richer in this gift than the biography. One incident, about the shy cat in the garden (see page 167), is supplied in a note with quotations from a letter written at the time of the incident, years earlier, for the reader not only to test Ellen's accuracy in recollection but also to see her skill in setting up a little drama. In this case the letter is clearly superior writing.

In a good biography, the storehouse of material must be treated with authentic precision. From what one can judge by means of Ellen's letters, the facts in her text are accurate, but, unfortunately, the sense of time is very fuzzy. The covers of the writing tablets that Ellen used give the span of years covered; they divide the manuscript into four periods. They do little, however, to satisfy one's need for dates. The dates supplied throughout the introduction, together with the chronology, should give the reader a sense of time in the text. Dates also appear in the text and notes. Ellen's transitional devices are occasionally rough, especially in the beginning, which is only a string of anecdotes. Since Ellen could not know personally the period prior to her birth nor remember well the first few years following her birth, information came to her from her mother's reminiscences. Apparently Lidian was given to telling anecdotes and to recalling earlier days, especially Plymouth days.

While one may criticize Ellen's lack of historical development or sense of historical context, the *Life* is rich in material for the student of middle-class domestic and religious life, especially nineteenth-century practices in the home, in education of children, in religious training of children, and in discipline. (Ellen's letters are also rich in such material.) Discipline in the Emerson household, for example, was consistent with the acceptable and recommended discipline of the day. The *Life* also provides a look at education and religious training in the Plymouth of Lidian's girlhood. Ellen suggests what kinds of entertainment were open to the nineteenth-century family, the occupational possibilities, and the opportunities for community or public services. In addition, the *Life* offers a glimpse into the structure of the household, the parents and children, the wider kin connections, the number of servants, and the relationship between the servants and mistress. For the historian and the psychologist there are accounts of medical care and of attitudes toward death. Ellen's *Life* offers much information on married life, love, and family.

Probably unwittingly, Ellen provides an introduction to her subject in a manner which became the vogue in her century. According to Joseph Kett, biographers and autobiographers in the seventeenth and eighteenth centuries either ignored the childhood of their subjects or treated the childhood simply as indications of later developments, focusing only on remarkable instances such as close scrapes with death; after 1800 biographers were more likely to recount unexceptional events of childhood.[12] Ellen does not attempt to show organic growth from infancy through childhood and into adolescence; rather, she seems to be intent on remembering all the early stories she can. But however formulaic and chronicle-like the early section of the work, if Ellen had chosen to begin with the courtship of her mother and father, the *Life* would have lost much of its richness.

Some readers may regret that the biography describes only briefly the courtship of Emerson and Lidian. Indeed, the only glimpse of their courtship we have occurs in a letter from Ellen to her sister recalling stories she had heard from her father's cousin Sarah, who, as a nineteen-year-old girl, had happened to ride from Concord to Boston with Emerson as he was en route to Plymouth for his wedding:

You remember that the chaise came up to the Manse on the Sunday P.M. with new bright yellow reins, and Cousin Sarah said Father's first care was to stop at the stable to have them changed for green ones "lest people should think he had been weaving them of goldenrod." She does not remember much about the ride, except that she asked Father about Swedenborg and his replies settled it in her mind that it would be a waste of time to read his writings. "But you don't mean that he didn't talk about Mother?" I said. "Oh no! he talked of her very beautifully, but the only words I remember are, 'The'—I can't remember the word but it means the people who didn't know as much as they ought to—'baptized her Lydia, but her name is Lidian.' " He took her to Grandfather Haskin's, but went himself to a hotel, and continued to ride to Plymouth the next day. I asked her if he looked handsome to her then. "Oh yes always! that is, he was lovely-looking just as he remained, just as you knew him. Charles was the handsomest. It was always a time of rejoicing at the old house when any of them appeared." (24 August 1885)

The reader will sense other losses in the biography as well. Biographers and students of Henry David Thoreau, for example, prompted in part by Thoreau's letters to Lidian, have made speculations of varying degrees of plausibility about their relationship. This biography sheds little new light on Emerson's now-famous Concord neighbor. Ellen and her siblings, indeed, the entire Emerson family, held Thoreau in esteem. There is less of Thoreau than one might wish because Ellen made a conscious effort to focus on her mother, so she resisted the temptation to relate something (see page 172) that was not part of her mother's story.

In February 1878, long after Thoreau's death, when a company of friends were suggesting names for Edward's new baby, Ellen thought of Henry Thoreau and thought that Ellery Channing did, too, but she "prudently" (as she wrote in a letter) held her tongue. One can only speculate on why "prudently." Perhaps it had something to do with the eccentric character of Thoreau and Concord's view of him.

I am sure that the same qualities in Lidian that attracted Jones Very attracted Thoreau. According to Edwin Gittleman, Emerson alluded to the almost scandalous personal interest Very was taking in Lidian and her spiritual welfare.[11] Lidian was a brilliant conversationalist and, no doubt, a very good listener. The letters of Ellen, if not the *Life*, show her to be a belle. One day, while traveling by train, the new church organist Mr. Gilman took such pleasure in her company that Emerson jokingly said he guessed he would have to get his pistol out.

Ellen contends that the Emersons met Thoreau in 1837 through Lidian's elder sister Lucy Jackson Brown, who was boarding at the Thoreau's (see pages 67–68). It is certain that Thoreau moved into the Emerson's home 26 April 1841, staying two years and moved in again in October 1847 when Emerson sailed for England.

Lidian's letters support the commonly held view that Thoreau was a handyman in the Emerson household. He planted trees; he duly killed the curculios on the plum trees; he skillfully dug snow paths, and he helped Lidian decide on the economy of purchasing a new pump.

Her letters enhance the view that we never seem to tire of—that of Henry David Thoreau with children, so effectively described in Edward Emerson's account of his remembrances of Thoreau. Lidian records a go-to-bed frolic between Eddy and Henry in which Eddy informed her that Thoreau first swallowed a book, then pulled it out of Eddy's nose, and then put it into Thoreau's "pantalettes." "I tell Henry I shall send you word he is in his second childhood, a wearer of pantalettes. He says it is so, according to the younger Edda; the poetic, not the prose Edda" (17 May 1848). Edward loved for Thoreau to put him in a chair and carry him high about the room. In a dictated letter to her father,

Edith said, "Mr Thoreau jumps us every night," to which Eddy added, "Mother, and tell him Mr Thoreau jumped a chair over me tonight!" (29 November 1847). Thoreau has long been known as a master of huckle berrying. He was equally valued as a master of ceremonies at a popcorn parching.

Susan [Bridge Jackson, Lidian's sister-in-law] and her children [Alice and Eliza-beth] are here—and after breakfast the little girls all, petitioned to have some pop-corn parched—so I brought the warming pan into the dining-room and the corn was quickly shelled into it and held over the fire by Henry who was master of ceremonies—and enjoyed the frolic as well as any child of us all. . . . I shall send you some of it and you must eat it in memory of those who were at its parching. Henry says that warming pans need not be banished under the new dispensation—as they will cook the grain more to the mind of the new fashioned epicures than any other utensil. (1 February 1843)

Thoreau that evening prompted Lidian to write: "I am wishing you here dear Husband. It is 'after dinner'—and your peerless Edith is look-ing most beautifully as she dances with Henry or lays her innocent head on his music box that she may drink yet deeper of its sweetness. Now am I interrupted by an exclamation from all present—the cherub face appears above the screen for Uncle Henry takes care that Edie shall take as high flights in Papa's absence as ever—she rides on his shoul-der or is held high up in the air—I think he adds to her happiness, and she no less to his" (1 February 1843). Lidian genuinely appreciated Thoreau's abilities and sensibilities. What mother is not biased toward one who shows sincere love for and natural skill with her children? Lid-ian saw more: "Richard Fuller [Margaret Fuller's brother] sent him a music box as a N. Year's gift and it was delightful to see Henrys child like joy. I never saw any one made so happy by a new possession. He said nothing could have been so acceptable. After we had heard its per-formance he said he must hasten to exhibit it to his sisters & mother. My heart really warmed with sympathy, and admiration at his whole de-meanour on the occasion—and I like human nature better than I did" (15 January 1843).

Recognizing Thoreau's skills as a thinker and a lecturer, Lidian did much "behind the scenes" to promote him, a respectable method of in-fluence for women in her day. Lidian was familiar with the work of Mary Abigail Dodge as she read her controversial *A Battle of the Books* hot off the press in 1870. Miss Dodge was against woman's suffrage because it would only double the suffrage without real benefit; therefore, she in-sisted women would do better to exert indirect political influence. While Lidian supported suffrage, she had for years recognized and utilized this avenue open to discerning, socially and politically oriented females. In the cause on behalf of the Cherokee Indians, Lidian wrote her sister in Plymouth:

Doing good you know is all out of fashion but there happens just now to occur a case so urgent that one must lay aside for awhile all new-fangled notions—and attempt in the good old way to do a little good—by speaking our word, and doing what deeds we may in behalf of the poor Cherokee nation.... Every town and every individual that does not at least raise a *voice* in condemnation of such an outrage on humanity—must share the disgrace and the blame of its perpetration. So I pray you do your share in calling the attention of some of the friends of goodness to this evil that Plymouth may speedily follow Concord in cleansing its hands of it wholly. Speak to Mary Russell—Jane Goodwin—& Mrs [George Ware] Briggs that they may mention it to the gentlemen most likely to care that something be done. But do not let this letter be spoken of—it may seem an impertinence.... Ask Mary and Jane G. directly from me—to speak to the gentlemen if they think it worth while—and speak yourself to G.[eorge] P.[artridge] B.[radford] if you should see him—which you can any day that you sit at the *window* .... I repeat that I hope you will not let my name be spoken if you can help it. Tell M. & J. not to speak of this letter. (23 April 1838)

Can we doubt for a moment now the force behind Emerson's very singular action of writing President Van Buren on the behalf of the Cherokee nation?

In similar fashion in several letters she implores Emerson to do all he can to help her brother, Dr. Charles T. Jackson, in his battle to prove his claim for the discovery of the anesthetic use of ether. In one letter she cites Thoreau's verification of the rightness of the cause: "Charles has at last succeeded in getting his Defence written & printed, and all whom I hear speak of it say it is complete to the overthrow of M[orton]'s claim. Even Henry who has been perverse, & mystified me much, by his view of the matter, now says that 'the claim of Dr J now stands as clear as if Morton had never tried to wrest it from him'" (4 June 1848). It was only natural then when Thoreau was cheated by his publisher that Lidian would use this method of influence in an appeal to her husband: "Did I tell you that Bradbury & Soden have refused to pay Henry more than two thirds of the money they promised for his 'Walk to W,' and that they postpone the payment even of that? Will it not do for you to call on your return through Boston and demand it for him?..." (17 February 1843).

As the evidence multiplies, we can safely assume that Lidian played no small role in developing Emerson's appreciation of Thoreau. After

Thoreau's lecture on Sir Walter Raleigh, Lidian urges Emerson's support for him: "Henrys Lecture pleased me much—and I have reason to believe others liked it. Henry tells me he is so happy as to have received Mr [John S.] *Keyes's* suffrage and the Concord paper has spoken well of it. I think you would have been a well pleased listener. I should like to hear it two or three times more. Henry ought to be known as a man who can give a Lecture. You must advertise him to the extent of your power. A few Lyceum fees would satisfy his moderate wants—to say nothing of the improvement and happiness it would give both him & his fellow creatures if he could utter what is 'most within him'—and be heard" (12 February 1843). Lidian more than once coaxed Emerson to stay on top of his correspondence with their young friend, "I think you have made Henry wait a reasonable—or *un*reasonable time for an answer to his letter" (12 February 1843).

Thoreau was indisputably a handyman for Lidian. He was undeniably endeared to her motherly heart through his brotherly-fatherly attention to her children. It has been demonstrated that he was a protégé whom she could promote. Canby claimed, "Thoreau was what the common man would call in love with Emerson's wife." Moreover, he placed a statement from a letter to Lidian from Thoreau as a caption under her picture: "You must know that you represent to me woman." There *are* all the ingredients for romance: a husband hung up on his first wife (wives of widowers do have a tendency to have been saints), a husband who was away for long periods of time, the presence of a young man who did chores for her, who charmed and adored her children, who was mentally stimulating, who flattered her, and who wrote her a letter that the editors note: "To almost anyone who will read the text with an open mind, this is a love letter."[13] In the past faced with such circumstantial evidence and offended by its soap opera aura, I would elevate my nose ever so slightly and say, "Considering each person individually, there is absolutely nothing in the character of either Henry or Lidian that would suggest the possibility of a physically intimate relationship." And there isn't! But we are suspicious that under the guise of love that things can "seem" right and that lovers are most noted for acting out of character. I do not believe that they were romantically involved, but when I say that, I am not addressing how they felt about each other. Neither am I suggesting that their Spartan characters, their fear of scandal or fear of pregnancy, their age difference, or a houseful of children and servants, or the presence of Emerson's mother or possibly homoeroticism in Thoreau, or the argument that Thoreau's female friends were mostly "safe, older women," or their mutual respect for Ralph Waldo Emerson, or Lidian's love for Emerson be accepted as proof of my position. The

proof I offer is this. The energy in the relationship suggests an unconsummated one. It's the kind of energy we find in Keats's "Ode on a
Grecian Urn" as he describes the beauty of the young musician posed
with lips so close to the fair maiden yet never to kiss with the electricity
being exactly in the fact that frozen there in time in an art form that
forever will that moment exist. "Heard melodies are sweet, but those
unheard / Are sweeter."

We have the expression, "The honeymoon is over," which doesn't
mean the couple is divorcing. It means that the excitement and ecstasy
of the new and unfamiliar have been replaced with that which is comfortable and steadfast. That energy of an unconsummated relationship
is always apparent to me when I address Henry and Lidian as members of the opposite sex. Perhaps, consciously or subconsciously sensing
their "chemistry" was what prompted Emerson to help establish Henry
in Emerson's brother's home in New York from which Thoreau wrote
his well-known letters to Lidian.

Friendship between members of the opposite sex had been risked
before. Consider Emerson's friendship with Margaret Fuller or Elizabeth
Hoar or Thoreau's friendship with Lidian's sister Lucy who boarded
with the Thoreaus. There's romantic energy in the bunch of violets and
the accompanying poem that Thoreau schoolboyishly tossed through the
window to Lucy and in Thoreau's intense interest in conversing with
Lidian's sister-in-law, a pleasure so intense that Thoreau wouldn't take
an hour to write Emerson a letter. Are we to conclude based on letters
we have read, letters that may shed more light on the conventions of the
day than on the relationships themselves, that Emerson and Thoreau had
affairs with these women?

If Lidian and Thoreau didn't have a physical relationship, where did
they channel all the dynamic energy that prompted Canby to risk such a
commotion? It's really rather obvious—in Conversations, in intellectual
companionship—a popular entertainment of the day. They were both
really very good at it. Remember Edward's observation that "Conversations seem to be Mother's natural field. . . ." I believe that Lidian and
Henry were *mind-bonded* which resulted in their being soul mates of the
highest order. Henry was but one of a circle of Lidian's intellectual companions as Ellen Emerson records in her biography of her mother: "But
to return to the company of which I was speaking, Mother really valued,
and had some intimacy with, Miss Fuller and Miss Sturgis, and Mr Newcomb even more; and Mr Alcott, Uncle George [Partridge Bradford] and
Mr Thoreau were to her near personal friends. The other gentlemen she
liked very well but they cared especially for Father" (see page 83). By the
same token as already noted, Lidian was only one of Thoreau's mature,

female companions of the mind. One such friend [Lidian's sister-in-law] is revealed for the first time in the letters. "Henry will not write. He too having nothing to say—I believe it is partly because he will not deny himself an hour of Susan Jackson's society to spend it in writing—Susan has been here since Sunday—" (17 February 1843).

We can only speculate on the subjects of Lidian's and Thoreau's intellectual pursuits. In a letter to Lidian, Henry alludes to the great questions of Fate, Freewill and Foreknowledge absolute, which used to be discussed in Concord. He shares views on a poet he has been reading and offers to copy a few such sentences as he would read to her if present. No doubt, they battled theological questions. Lidian seems to disagree with every one on religion except her daughter Ellen and possibly Emerson's mother. Lidian believed that Jesus was the son of God—a belief necessary not only for redemption but also for happiness in marriage. On Henry's deathbed when a friend of the family asked, "'how he stood affected toward Christ,' he replied that 'a snow-storm was more to him than Christ.'"[14] In 1843 Lidian wrote Emerson that she had discussed Thoreau's heresies with him. Letters indicate that the utopian schemes, especially Fruitlands, would certainly have been considered. Both Lidian's and Thoreau's commitments to anti-slavery efforts and the similarities between her anti-slavery thoughts and governmental attitudes and material in Thoreau's essays make safe the assumption that they must have often shared these views. One fourth of July Lidian, considering the country wholly lost to any sense of righteousness and seeing the flags go up in celebration of the day, asked Emerson's permission to cover the gates with a pall. When he smiled and consented, she took a quantity of black cambric and made a great show of it on the front gate and gateposts (see page 125).

There is one other area in which they were unquestionably bonded. That is in grief, in their handling the losses of Thoreau's brother, John, and the Emersons' little Waldo—the two deaths occurring only two weeks apart. Lidian, about half a year before Waldo died, could philosophize on the death of her little niece:

My visit to Boston was a happy one—can you believe it? When I heard of the death of that dear little Susan [Frances Jackson] I felt a grief and regret that I thought would be long in departing. But after I had joined my tears with the parents' tears, and looked at the little fair dead form—I began to feel as if a beautiful and deeply joyful event had occurred;—not losing sight of the earthly loss and disappointment, I saw the blessedness of the child's fate. I realized glorious spiritual things.—If she had been visibly carried by angels to her true home and the bosom of her Father, it would not have created in me a stronger faith than the *inward persuasion* given me that all was more than well. I saw the ineffable tenderness of Providence in all they told me of the circumstances of the bereavement—and the parents too, saw and rejoiced in it. (14 July 1841)

Only days before Waldo's death she wrote her sister of John Thoreau's death, of the nobleness of one knowing how to die, on the beauty of one knowing how to grieve:

Monday John was given over by the physicians—and to-day he died—retaining his senses and some power of speech to the last. He said from the first he knew he should die—but was perfectly quiet and trustful—saying that God had always been good to him and he could trust Him now. His words and behavior throughout were what Mr. Emerson calls manly—even *great.* Henry has been here this evening and seen Mr Emerson but no one else. He says John took leave of all the family on Monday with perfect calmness and more than resignation. It is a beautiful fate that has been granted him and I think he was worthy of it. At first it seemed not beautiful but terrible. Since I have heard particulars and recollected all the good I have heard of him I feel as if a pure spirit had been translated. Henry has just been here—(it is now Wednesday noon) I love him for the feeling he showed and the effort he made to be cheerful. He did not give way in the least but his whole demeanour was that of one struggling with sickness of heart." (11 January 1842)

When five-year-old Waldo died from scarlet fever, Lidian sent an extract to Emerson from a letter Thoreau wrote Lucy Jackson. His words are similar to Lidian's earlier observations on the death of Susan Jackson:

As for Waldo, he died as the mist rises from the brook which the sun will soon dart his rays through. Do not the flowers die every autumn? He had not even taken root here. I was not startled to hear that he was dead, it seemed the most natural event that could happen. His fine organization demanded it, and Nature gently yielded its request. It would have been strange if he had lived. Neither will Nature manifest any sorrow at his death, but soon the note of the lark will be heard down in the meadow, and fresh dandelions will spring from the old stock where he plucked them last summer. (10 March 1842)

We know Thoreau soon went into a depression, even developing "sympathy" symptoms of the lockjaw that killed his brother. We know from Lidian's letters that he complained of sick headaches, cold and weak eyes, and spasmodic affection. And Lidian—she developed a history of hypochondriacal illnesses as already noted. She shared, at least with Emerson, her deep grief, which was in vivid contrast to her previous ability to set death on a lofty and rhetorical, religious plane, quite removed from the frailty of deeply hidden human emotions.

It is clear that Lidian, on the deaths of Susan Jackson and John Thoreau, and Henry, on little Waldo's death, could feel that a divine Providence looks over all, deeming best that Earth is really not the finest dwelling place for sensitive souls and that it was beautiful to witness one's translation to more ethereal ground. The effect of John's death on Thoreau has been amply recorded. For Lidian, a whole year after little Waldo died, where was the "beautiful and deeply joyful event" of death? Where was the "ineffable tenderness of Providence"? Where was the *inward persuasion* "that all was more than well"? Perhaps the reader is critical of the ineptitude of Henry and Lidian to rise above their losses to their higher ideals. For me, "I like human nature better than I did" (15 January 1843).

Part IV

The manuscript "The Life of Lidian Jackson Emerson" by her daughter Ellen Tucker Emerson in the Houghton Library contains about 115,000 words. It begins with anecdotes of her mother's early life as told to her daughter. In the course of her writing, Ellen discusses life in the Emerson household and in the Concord community until 1892, the time of her mother's death.

This manuscript, which has been at Harvard since April 1969, has apparently received little use. Ralph L. Rusk used it in his chapter on "Lidian" in *The Life of Ralph Waldo Emerson*. The manuscript provides a lively picture of an attractive, individualistic woman; it gives us a valuable insight into nineteenth-century American life as well as a close look at Emerson's milieu. It contains material written by Mrs. Emerson herself, including a few satirical pages entitled "The Transcendental Bible."

The biography that Ellen Emerson prepared was the result of much research, for Ellen Emerson truly can be said to have devoted her life to her mother. There is evidence in Ellen's letters that she and Lidian read Lidian's early correspondence, burning much of it, but, no doubt, adding to Ellen's biographical heap. She sought information about her mother's early years. One letter, for example, indicates that on 29 August 1895, Ellen Emerson made a visit to Nina Lowell, daughter of Francis Cabot Lowell, Jr., the sole object of which was to write of Lidian. But finding that she lacked necessary information, she inquired of a Miss Cornish, who was born in Plymouth and who lived there until she was sixteen, and who shared with Ellen her knowledge of the town. She also felt a need to go to Plymouth to consult a cousin, Mary Watson, and visited her there in July 1896.

She "published" her biography by reading portions aloud to friends and relatives. We learn from her letters that Aunt Susan, Susy [Haven], Cousin Charlotte, and others listened for two hours to the stories of Lidian, and that in October 1897, her Concord friends, Mrs. Sanborn, Miss Leavitt, and Lizzy Bartlett came for a reading. There is evidence in the manuscript that it was read aloud; from time to time a portion is marked *not* to be read aloud.

I speculate that the manuscript is both the first and final draft; that is, the first draft was heavily revised on the manuscript itself. The manuscript is numbered three times. Through numbered page 384 a number appears in the upper right-hand corner, but there are also pages numbered A, B, C, D. The middle bottom of the page sometimes carries a number that generally corresponds to the one in the upper right-hand corner. In the bottom left-hand corner of most pages is a number in pencil, circled through 496. Since some clean sheets are numbered thus, I suspect that Ellen numbered her writing pads prior to writing. The loose pages, measuring five by eight inches, are contained in fifty-nine folders; occasionally, the cover of a Cupid writing pad is included.

The indentation for a new paragraph is not always clear in the manuscript. Only occasionally is a paragraph indented. Most of the time, I suspect a new paragraph is intended, since a line of writing stops somewhere before the right-hand margin and the next line begins at the left-hand margin. Here I silently begin a new paragraph. Many times, a new paragraph is signified in the manuscript by the sign for a new paragraph; here, too, I silently begin a new paragraph. Otherwise, the manuscript is transcribed as it appears.

The author rarely puts periods after "Mr.," "Mrs.," or "Dr." I have let these remain as in the manuscript without further comment. I supply a period inside brackets at the end of a sentence if the next sentence begins with a capital letter. If a declarative sentence lacking a period is followed by a sentence beginning with a small letter, either a semi-colon in brackets or a period in brackets is added. If a period is added, the small letter is silently capitalized. If there is a period but the first letter following the period is a small letter, I capitalize it and put it in brackets. I silently add quotation marks or parentheses that are missing from intended pairs. Punctuation of items in a series, since the author habitually set them off, is silently inserted where omitted in manuscript. Apostrophes have been silently inserted in possessives and contractions. Many needed commas are missing, for example, after introductory dependent clauses and around parenthetical expressions. I leave the manuscript as it is without comma additions unless the meaning absolutely requires it; then, the added comma is in brackets. The author habitually puts punctuation inside the quotation marks; however, occasionally the punctuation is under or outside the quotation marks. I silently place the punctuation inside the quotation marks.

The author rarely misspells a word. Spelling has been normalized, but old spelling of words remains as in the manuscript without comment. The author uses both the word and the ampersand for *and*. I follow the manuscript.

I silently omit cancellations, slips of the pen, false starts at words, careless repetitions of a single word, and the author's occasional carets under insertions which are assimilated into the text.

Comments and additions by Edith and Edward appear from time to time. As interesting to the reader as they are, they break into the flow of the biography and, therefore, have been set in notes. The most disturbing chronological break is the discussion following the account of Lidian's death, following manuscript pages 378 through 384. They are numbered to suggest that they were written last and not simply misplaced by someone. They appear here in a note.

The biography is graced from time to time with delicately sketched illustrations. A copy of each manuscript page with an illustration appears near the printed page on which it would occur. The copies of sketches made in ink are excellent, but the penciled ones, which are sometimes faded in the original, vary in quality.

Notes

1. Firkins, *Ralph Waldo Emerson* (Boston: Houghton Mifflin, 1915) p. 50; Ralph L. Rusk, *The Life of Ralph Waldo Emerson* (New York: Scribners, 1949).

2. According to Barbara Welter, in "The Cult of True Womanhood: 1820–1860," the four cardinal virtues were piety, purity, submissiveness, and domesticity. The role of woman was daughter, sister, and—most important—wife and mother. Religion was vital to a woman, and women were warned not to let their literary or intellectual pursuits take them away from God. Death was to be preferred to the loss of purity or innocence. To tamper with the expectation of submission was to tamper with the very order of the universe. Since true woman's place was unquestionably her own fireside, a most prized virtue was her understanding and faithful performance of household duties (*American Quarterly*, 18 [Summer 1966]: 151–174).

3. 10 May 1838, *The Correspondence of Emerson and Carlyle*, ed. Joseph Slater (New York: Columbia University Press, 1964), p. 184.

4. Welter, "The Cult of True Womanhood: 1820–1860," pp. 151–174.

5. *Memories of a Hostess: A Chronicle of Eminent Friendship*, ed. M. A. DeWolfe Howe (Boston: Atlantic Monthly Press, 1922), p. 94.

6. *Memories of a Sculptor's Wife* (Boston: Houghton Mifflin, 1928), p. 95.

7. (Los Angeles: Times-Mirror, 1941).

8. *Christian Register*, 28 January 1909.

9. Mary Miller Engel claims that Ellen could not sing and only mouthed the words (*I Remember the Emersons*, p. 14). Ellen's involvement in singing school would tend to discredit Engel's statement.

10. Lidian's letter of November 1871. One of the few occasions when students of American literature have been exposed to Ellen Emerson is a letter which she wrote on behalf of her

father to Mrs. Samuel Clemens, which appears in Albert B. Paine, *A Biography: The Personal and Literary Life of Samuel Langhorne Clemens* (New York: Harpers, 1912), 2: 608–609.

11. *Jones Very: The Effective Years, 1833–1840* (New York: Columbia University Press, 1967), p. 355. The visit alluded to is in June 1839. Very visited also during October 1838.

12. Joseph Kett, "Adolescence and Youth in Nineteenth-Century America," *The Family in History*, ed. Theodore K. Rabb and Robert Rothberg (New York: Harper & Row, 1971), pp. 95–110.

13. Walter Harding and Carl Bode, eds., *The Correspondence of Henry David Thoreau* (Washington Square: New York University Press, 1958), p. 121.

14. Walter Harding, *The Days of Henry Thoreau: A Biography* (New York: Dover Publications, Inc., 1962), p. 464.

Chronology

The following is a partial chronology from Lidian's life, based on dates given in Ellen's biography and from Ellen's letters.

1802 Born 20 September in Plymouth, fifth child of Charles and Lucy (Cotton) Jackson.

1812 For one year Lidian and Sister Lucy at boarding school kept by Mrs. Saunders and Miss Beach on the English plan at Dorchester.

1818 Her father died on 4 August.
Her mother died on 15 October.
In December 1818 or January 1819, Lucy and Lidian were at Mrs. McKeige's school in Jamaica Plain. They returned in 1819 to board with aunts and uncles.

1820 Lidian's sister, Lucy, married to Charles Brown on 18 September.
Celebration of the 200th anniversary of the landing of the Pilgrims in Plymouth on 22 December.
After 1820 Lidian boarded for twelve years with Rossiter and Priscilla (Jackson) Cotton.

1821 Scarlet fever attack marks the beginning of Lidian's ill health.

1825 Lidian went to Woods Hole and spent three weeks with Aunt Parker, where she read Scott's *Betrothed* and felt she had entered into a new state with preparation for the future.
During this year, she became a Christian.
Started a Sunday School Class.

1828 Her brother, Charles, went to Paris to study medicine.

1833? Heard Ralph Waldo Emerson preach at the Twelfth Congregational Church in Chambers Street.

1834 Her brother, Charles, married Susan Bridge on 27 February.
Ralph Waldo Emerson to Plymouth (two sermons and a lecture).

1835 Lidian received the letter containing Emerson's proposal for marriage on 27 January.
Discourse on 200th Anniversary Celebration of the settling of Concord on 12 September.
Lidian and Emerson married on 14 September in Winslow House in Plymouth.
She sees Bush, their Concord home, for the first time on 15 September.

1836 Charles C. Emerson, Emerson's brother, died on 9 May.
8 September, first meeting of the Transcendental Club.
In October, her first child, Waldo, was born.

1837? To Plymouth with little Waldo.

1837 Financial crash.

1839 In February, her second child, Ellen, was born.
Jones Very, Margaret Fuller, and Bronson Alcott came to Concord.

1840–
1845 The "Transcendental Times," when she wrote her "Transcendental Bible."

1840 In the winter, she attended Margaret Fuller's Boston Conversations.
Joined the Anti-Slavery Society.

1841 Lidian sensed that she had lost nearness to God.
Met the Swedenborgian lady Sarah Searle of Brookline and started reading Sweden-borg.
Took Ellen to Plymouth.
Because of illness, went with Elizabeth Hoar to Staten Island to spend some weeks with William and Susan Emerson.
John Thoreau took little Waldo for his daguerreotype.
In November, her third child, Edith, was born.

1842 Waldo died on 27 January.

1844 In July, her fourth child, Edward, was born.

1845? George Bradford spent the winter with them and took a school in Concord.

1845 Miss Sophia Foord of Dedham was governess to the Emerson and Alcott children; in late 1846 and early 1847, she lived with the Emersons.

1846 Jackson-Morton controversy over the discovery of the medical use for ether.

1847 Emerson sailed for England in October, and Thoreau came to live with them.
Lidian was ill, jaundiced.

1848 Emerson returned from Europe in the summer.

1850 Emerson's first journey west (St. Louis and Chicago).
Margaret Fuller Ossoli died in July.

1852 Louis Kossuth visited Concord.

1853 or

1854 4 July, Lidian hung cambric over the front gate and gate posts in protest of slavery.

1853? Visited Aunt Susan in Plymouth in the house where she was born.

1853 In November, Emerson's mother, Ruth, died.

1854 Took Edith and Edward to Plymouth to board for two or three weeks.

1857 Began acquaintance with the family of John Forbes and visited them on Naushon.
Emerson went in 1857, and all of them visited in 1858.

Late

1850s Visit to the Shakers in Harvard to remove Mary Hamlin.

1858? Emerson and Lidian visited Mrs. Bancroft in Newport.
Visited Mary Howland Russell in Seconnet.
Emerson and Lidian visited Sarah Clarke.

1859? In April, Walden Woods burned.
Edward had typhoid fever.

From

1860 William Emerson's family spent the summers in Concord.

1860s Attended lectures in Boston with Emerson.

1861 In April, the Civil War.

1862 In May, Thoreau died.
Attended funeral for Mary Howland Russell in Plymouth.
Aunt Susan Emerson stayed all summer at the Emersons' home.
Edith Davidson came to live with the Emersons, becoming Ellen's daughter and stayed for three years.

1865 Wedding of Edith Emerson and William H. Forbes.

1866 In the summer, Lidian had a long illness.
In October, she took a Sunday School class of girls.

1868 William and Susan Emerson and Lucy Jackson Brown died.

1871? Went to Naushon to see Edith's new home.

1871 Edward engaged to Annie Keyes.
Edward had smallpox while Emerson was on trip to California.
In March, Lidian had erysipelas.

1872   The fire at Bush in July. The Emersons went to the Manse.
       Emerson and Ellen make trip to Egypt in October.
       Lidian goes to Naushon.
1873   On 28 May, Ellen and Emerson return from France and England. Lidian stayed with
       Edith in their absence.
1874   Edward married Annie Keyes on 19 September.
1875   18 January, Lidian distributed 100 copies of *Our Dumb Animals* and protested against
       the bleeding of calves.
       Centennial Commemoration of Concord Fight on 20 April.
1878   Lidian at Milton for New Year's.
       Elizabeth Hoar died on 7 April.
1879–
1888   Summer sessions of the Concord School of Philosophy. Attended by Lidian the first
       time on 26 July 1883.
1881   Lidian dancing at Ellen's birthday party ball in Town Hall for Ellen's forty-second
       birthday.
1882   Emerson died on 27 April.
1883   Lidian visited the State Prison on 6 August.
1884   Week in Plymouth in May.
       One month at Edith's for Christmas and New Year's.
1885   In July, two times a day to the School of Philosophy.
       12 September, 250th anniversary of founding of Concord.
       To Plymouth on 14 September, to celebrate her fiftieth wedding anniversary.
1887   In July, two times a day to school of Philosophy.
       To Naushon in the summer.
1889   Last trip to Boston.
1892   Lidian died on 13 November.

The Life of Lidian Jackson Emerson
by *Ellen Tucker Emerson*

"Not afraid of the face of clay"

Aunt Lucy[1] once told me that when she and mother were late in being dressed for church (their Mother was not going) their Father said he would not wait for them they might follow him. So they did and when they got there church had begun, the doors were shut and no one was to be seen. So she was frightened and said she would go right home, but Mother was determined to stay. "How old were you?" I asked her. "I was seven and your mother was three. We had on our new winter-coats-&-capes, mine was dark green and your Mother's was scarlet. So she stood on tip-toe and rattled the latch till the sexton came to see what was the matter, and she marched in but I ran home. When they came home Father was delighted. He said 'this child isn't afraid of the face of clay. She made them let her in and walked up the aisle to the pew all alone.' "

When she was three years old some near relative died. Everyone must wear mourning and as there was not time to make all that was wanted for the funeral Mother was sent to a neighbour to borrow the mourning-bonnet of her little girl. The neighbour said "Let's try it on first. Why! you have a *bushel* of hair, dear, haven't you?" This Mother told me when I was asking how she looked. I gathered that she was got up something in this way. [See Sketch] Her hair never was cut in her life. As soon as it had any length it was done up in a twist with a comb. It never was braided or curled. This remark of the neighbour leads her to suppose it was thick. It was dark brown. Her garments from her earliest memory were a chemise, a petticoat, (sometimes two) and a short-sleeved low-necked long dress. Nothing else but her shoes & stockings. She on one occasion mentioned an apron—that at the school-room fire one day her apron caught fire and she laughed and shook it to call attention of the other children without a thought of danger, but the school-mistress rushed at her without stopping to raise herself from the sitting posture, [See Sketch] gathered the apron in her hands and clapped out the fire not without burning herself, I believe. When Mother told us this story she usually added that on one occasion Uncle Charles,[2] a very little boy laid a small train of gunpowder from the school-room fire to the school-ma'am's chair. He asked to go to the fire, started the train which worked beautifully, and had the ineffable joy of seeing the school-ma'am leap from her seat crying "Lud'a'massy! I should think I was aboard a man-of-war!"

3

When she was three years old
~~In that three year~~ her Grandmother
Lyme, near relative died
~~Stockton died.~~ Everyone must wear mourning
and as there was not time to make all
                    for the funeral:
that was wanted Mother was sent to a
neighbour to borrow the mourning-bonnet
of her little girl. The neighbour said
"Let's try it on first. Why! you have a
bushel of hair, dear, haven't you?"
This Mother told me when I was asking
how she looked. I gathered that she
was got up something in this way
Her hair never was cut in her life. As
soon as it had any length it was done
up in a twist with a comb. It never was
braided or curled. This remark of the

neighbour leads her to suppose it was [4]
thick. It was dark brown. Her garments from
her earliest memory were a chemise, a petticoat,
(sometimes two) and a short-sleeved low-necked
longdress. Nothing else but her shoes & stockings.
She on one occasion mentioned an apron —
that at the school-room fire one day her
apron caught fire and she laughed and
shook it to call the attention of the
other children without a thought of
danger, but the school-mistress rushed at
her without stopping to raise   herself
from the sitting posture, gathers
the apron in her hands and clapped out
the fire not without burning herself, I believe.
                Insert A opposite.
        I desire here to pin onto this
paper a pattern of a little calico
dress that her Mother made for her
it had a cape of the same, with
a narrow ruffle round it. It is

I desire here to pin onto this paper a pattern of a little calico dress that her Mother made for her[;] it had a cape of the same, with a narrow ruffle round it.[3] It is glazed, and when it was put on her, cape and all, she went out and sat down on the front door-step to enjoy its shining newness. A boy opposite looked at her and laughed. She was abashed and hurt. She got up and went right into the house. Her youngest brother, the last child, was born when she was nearly five, in August, 1807. He lived to be two years old, was handsome, with dark eyes and hair and was named John Cotton. His Father used to exclaim "When this child grows up, he'll be the greatest Jackson that ever wore a head!" They were all devoted to him, of course, as the youngest. He went into his Mother's room one day and, finding the lower door of a cupboard there open, proceeded to examine the interior. There was a small firkin there; it contained potash. He got the lid off and thought it was brown sugar. Of course he helped himself. He presently rushed to his Mother with loud screams, and the whole household was terrified when they saw what had happened[.] Mother remembered it all, and how her Mother had him in her lap washing his mouth out with vinegar. It turned out that he hadn't swallowed any, only taken the skin off his mouth, so he wasn't seriously injured. In 1885 when we visited the house the sight of the cupboard reminded Mother of this. "The dear little creature thought it was sugar," she said.

One day Mother was left at home with little John in her care. She wanted to go through Spooner's Alley to see I forget what friend and was half afraid she ought not to. Certainly she must not leave the baby, and probably she ought not to take him. But she went, leading him along and when she was well in she found a horse was coming to meet them. It looked to her as if there was no room for him to pass, and oh! little John! She flatted him up with his back hard against the wall, placed herself in front of him and made herself as flat as possible. The great horse, a white one, came walking by, hurt no one, trod on no toes, and left them safe to pursue their journey. This was an experience she always remembered and in 1885 she took me through Spooner's Alley and showed me the very place. He was two in August and he lived till the following January[4] only more and more charming from day to day. One afternoon Uncle Charles who was a little fellow of four and a half brought a little bit of a pumpkin into the room and played with it with him. I think I remember they quarreled over it and Mother took it from them and tossed it about the room. "And it amused him!" she said, "dear little angel! how he laughed! And at last it hit the looking glass and broke it. That was the last time I played with him. He had the croup in the night. In two days he was dead." The family always believed they had lost the finest of their children. Mother mourned him all her life. She bought the engraving of Master Lambton[5] when she was a young lady because it looked like the little John Cotton, and it hung in her room as a portrait of him. After his death her Father one day brought to her a magazine and asked her to read him a poem in it. I have forgotten alas! the name of the magazine, and I fear there is no copy of the poem, so I will write here such lines as I recall. Mother used often to recite it to me:

"Hark, hark! I hear the sound of angels' wings"

Then followed the description of a Mother watching her little boy in his last moments.

"The angel-guards conduct the child
In peace along the spangled sky.
The infant talked, the angels smiled—
'The moon—I thought it not so high.
When often of a summer night
I prattled on my Mother's knee
I thought the stars and this fair light—
A fancy strange!—was made by me.' "

Here Mother used to stop and say "Your Father admires *that*." Then she went on

"But since my Mother taught me how
The great Creator made them all
I in his glorious presence bow
And lowly at his feet would fall[.]"

There is more of it which I do not succeed in bringing back, no more narrative but pious talk of the child,—of the same nature as this last. Little John was so brought back by the beginning of the poem that Mother could hardly read and before she had read many lines she gave up and cried. Her Mother came in and looked at her and then at her Father, questioning. "The subject affects her" he said.

This a pattern of one of John Cotton's little dresses.[6] Aunt Lucy found among her possessions six or seven scraps of calico left from those earliest days and brought them over to show to Mother. It may have been about 1855[.] I shall add them as I come to the history of the date at which they were worn. Mother's ecstasy of tenderness over each little piece was most interesting to behold. "Oh! *that* was John Cotton's!"

she exclaimed[.] "Little darling! little darling! Oh can't you see him *in* it?" The red calico you have just seen was in the collection[.]

Aunt Lucy and Mother seem always to have gone to school together though of such different ages. They went to one on the same side of North Street as their Father's house. [I]t was kept by someone named Weston[.][7] The school-ma'am sat with a very long stick beside her with which she could reach and strike any naughty child. One part of the room which had a bench in it was called Bantam, Mother didn't know why. It seemed to have no peculiar quality or attribute; to visit it was considered neither punishment nor reward; but a child would often ask, "Please ma'am, may I go over to Bantam?" and was usually allowed to do so. All the girls sewed most of the time. The mistress basted their seams & hems, till they were old enough to do it themselves, inspected all their work and had bad sewing picked out. Each had her "stent." They all recited their catechism. Once a sudden memory of it (say in 1888) came to Mother when she was telling me of school and in a high voice like the teacher's she asked "What is the chief end of Man?" And then rattled off in the stentorian tones of the school "The chief end of man is to glorify God and to enjoy him forever." It was really glorious to hear this sound from the past. I often reminded Mother of it and asked her to do it again, but she couldn't remember anything about it nor that she had once done it, though when I told her what she had said she said "Certainly, we used to have that every day." She learned her alphabet from the New England Primer. She, and all Plymouth, called a doll a dawl, and when she said after her mistress

"in Adam's fall, we sinned all"

she wondered what sort of dawl was a sinny dawl. She and the other children made what they called baby-houses on steep grass banks, but I think they should have been called china-closets[;] they watched for scraps of broken dishes and ranged them in rows, with great delight. They looked so like dishes on shelves! And if they by chance found a piece of real china, especially if it was distinguished looking from having a flower on it, or gilding why it was an event. She sometimes was asked by the other girls to play at their houses and stay to tea and one day a little friend did invite her without asking her Mother and was ashamed either to confess it to her or to tell her Mother that she had asked Lydia. Accordingly she flagged as tea-time approached in her attention to her poor little guest, and finally when called to the table went and sat down with the family. Mother remained sitting on the window-seat, full of mortification, not knowing what to do. At last the lady of the house said "Won't you stay and have supper with us, Liddy?" "Oh I was so mortified! You may be sure I never went anywhere again without asking 'Did your Mother tell you to ask me?' You must be careful never to go anywhere till you have had a message from the lady of the house." This Mother told me when I was a little girl. Once she and Aunt Lucy went home one afternoon with their Mother's girl. Her family were very poor and I suppose not tidy. The children were of opinion that the place was repulsive and uncomfortable, but one of the family was sewing and had a handsome pair of bright new scissors. I forgot whether it was Lucy or Lydia, but one of them was overwhelmed with compassion that those beautiful scissors should have so miserable a dwelling-place, so she took them and carried them home thinking how thankful they would be for the change. The scissors were discovered and returned and the child had a lesson on stealing, but it was simply to deliver the scissors from their hard lot that the thing was done.

Among their teachers was a Miss Mary Russell,[8] really a cousin, but Mother never dared to remember that so exalted a person could be related to her. Miss Russell made a very gentle and interesting teacher and Mother loved her. Once they met in the street and Miss Russell bowed to her. Mother could hardly credit it that such an honour had been paid her. Once she made a call on Grandmother Jackson and condescended to talk a little to Mother who was overwhelmed with gratitude & joy.

She used to recur to this when young girls and little children showed their elders that they considered any attention from them rather an intrusion to be endured than a politeness, and say "Times have changed!"

While they were still young—I think Mother was eight—there was an examination or exhibition of their school, the parents were invited. Both she & Aunt Lucy spoke pieces and so beautifully as to wake the audience to enthusiasm, and gratify their parents, especially their Father. Mother burst forth with "Lucy said hers very well, but Lydia said hers charmingly," just as she heard someone say it at the time.

Aunt Lucy began to learn painting, and it was decided that Mother also should have lessons. I don't think they carried it far. But at this time a cartload of sand had been[9] thrown in the road near their Father's house and Mother seized the opportunity to make mud pies. While she was wholly occupied with them her Aunt Lydia came along and remarked "Pretty business for a young lady who is taking lessons in painting! How do you think your hands look?" "Oh! there's plenty of water in the akyduct." (Plymouth pronounciation in those days.) Mother answered, going on with her work[.] Her Aunt Lydia passed on in silence, but she was pleased with the answer and reported it to the family. Mother by and by began to hear it quoted and found she was considered to have made a bright speech.

A French dancing-master came to Plymouth and had a class. Aunt Lucy & Mother belonged. The hour was seven in the morning. He was a very good teacher and required the young ladies to stand in the stocks[10] for an hour or more every day. He used to say "I can tell as soon as the ladies begin to dance how much they have stood in the stocks." Mother was faithful, never omitted her hour and learned her lessons standing in them, not only that winter but always, and she thought she owed to that habit and to the good teaching of her master her beautiful walk. How beautiful it was! Of course she never saw it and couldn't know its charm, but she heard it praised, of course, all her life long. In those days dancing meant very great skill and agility, the boys were taught to spring into the air and "change their feet" three times before they came down. There was a variety of pretty and intricate balances to learn, and every change in the cotillon had its "steps[.]" Mother made it a rule to practise her dancing-steps daily, as good exercise, and did it for some twenty years after the dancing-school was over. When the exhibition-day of the class came the Master required that the young ladies should all wear black slippers spangled. Mother enjoyed the class very much. But her Calvinist Aunts talked to her very seriously against it and told her to remember she was dancing over hell-fire. I don't know which Aunts these could have been.

In the church in those days they used Watts's[11] hymns and Mother pored over the hymn book in church-time very much. The awful pictures of God's wrath and the Judgment-Day interested and impressed her and she could recite them by the half page as long as she could remember anything. She said terror was bred in her bones, terror at least of death and future punishment, and though her mind didn't believe it, and in health she could see how wrong and groundless it was, the moment she was sick or tired she became a prey to it. Hymns had an attraction for her from a very early age, and one day as she was looking in at the bookstore window she found a book of hymns laid open and read the hymns on the two pages with delight. She must, I think, have asked the price, for she ran home to her Mother and asked for a ninepence (12½ cts) to buy it. Her Mother willingly gave it to her and she brought it home in triumph. It was Jane Taylor's Hymns for Infant Minds.[12] A duodecimo copy printed on grayish paper with coarse woodcut illustrations, bound in thin pine boards, covered with paper of two shades of pink with a scarlet leather back with six gold lines across it at intervals. We had it in our nursery, I learned hymns in it and regarded it with no interest at all till Mother told me this story, and said that she had a sense of being infinitely rich in possessing not only the two hymns that she had learned through the window, but all that she had not yet seen, and that she always loved it and learned the rest of the hymns as fast as she was able, not to please her Mother but because she wanted to know them. This was a wholly new idea to me, that anyone should want to know them, and the fact that this was the very book that the story was about warmed my heart to it. I do not know when or how it disappeared. I haven't seen it for forty years. What would I give to have it back! It was the only book we ever had with pine boards in the covers. I have seen New England Primers bound in the same manner.

About this time it was said that a comet was coming and Mother heard somewhere that it would hit the earth and destroy it. Her Mother had custards for pudding at dinner and gave her two. She was happy indeed in this good fortune but for some reason asked her Mother to let her put one away in the under-closet for the next day. She understood at school in the afternoon that the collision with the comet was to occur the next day, perhaps that night, and the thought struck her that she mighn't live to eat her custard. The moment school was done she hastened home and enjoyed it to the last mouthful and had the serene consciousness that whatever happened she had at least secured that.

One Fast-Day she had time for reading; her inclination did not lead her to take her Bible nor her hymnbook, and she felt that was not Sunday either. Yet stories seemed to her not exactly the right reading for Fast-Day. She decided that a school-book would be not too pleasant and also improving. So she read her geography. She said that when she was first taken to church she used to amuse herself with screwing round such of the little banisters round the top of the pew [See Sketch] as were loose enough. Later she carried a piece of orange-peel in her pocket and consoled herself during the sermon by eating it. One day she had an orange and came into the keeping-room to say "Ma, may I keep the peel to eat in meeting?" She found the minister there, Dr. Kendall,[13] making a call. Her Mother, she saw, felt that he ought not to hear of such a plan, but it was already said, and Mother was beginning to feel frightened when he comforted both by smiling and saying, "I see that that practice is not confined to my own pew." As Mother grew older and listened to the sermons she began to think to whom this admonition applied and that cap fitted, and to look at the people who she had decided needed the instruction to see how they looked under it. But it never crossed her mind to take a word of it to herself.

This I think was written in a letter to Edith when Mother told it to was not Sunday either. Yet stories seemed to her *19*. not exactly the right reading for Fast-Day. She decided that a school-book would be not too pleasant and also improving. So she read her geography.

She said that when she was first taken to church she used to amuse herself with screwing round such of the little bannisters round the top of the pew ▦▦▦ as were loose enough. Later she carried a piece of orange-peel in her pocket and consoled herself during the sermon by eating it. One day she had an orange and came into the keeping-room to say "Ma, may I keep the peel to eat in meeting?" She found the minister there, Dr Kendall, making a call. Her Mother, she saw, felt that he ought not to hear of such a plan, but it was already said, and Mother was beginning to feel frightened when he comforted both by smiling and saying, "I see that that practice is not confined to my own pew.".

As Mother grew older and listened the sermons she began to think to whom this admonition applied and that cap fitted, and to look at the people who she had decided needed the instruction to see how they looked under it. But it never crossed her mind to take a word of it to herself.

me[.] One day the Governor of Massachusetts came to Plymouth to visit a gentleman there.[14] Mother knew his daughter and was playing on the beach with her that afternoon. The gentleman brought the Governor to take a walk on the beach, and they walked back & forth along it several times. Mother felt it her duty to show great reverence for the chief Magistrate so when they saw the gentlemen approach she stood up and as they passed, made her best dancing-school curtsey, her little friend following her example. The Governor and his host both took off their hats and bowed low in acknowledgment. By and by they came back and the little girls thought they ought to repeat their curtseys. Again the gentlemen uncovered & bowed. They now felt sure they were doing the correct thing and six times in succession these high civilities were exchanged upon the lonely beach.

When I was sick, which often happened in my childhood, I usually was kept in Mother's room and while she was cutting out work or cleaning up or dressing—whenever there was opportunity—she used to sing to me, almost always saying after each song "My Mother used to sing that to me." She sang to Mother a great deal. I know also that she spun yarn sometimes on the great wheel. Mother often too remembered the delight she used to feel when as she opened the door coming home from school she perceived by the delicious scent that met her that "Mother was frying doughnuts." Yet I can tell very little about Grandmother.

I intend to pin on here a scrap of her best summer-dress a pattern muslin.[15] Mother remembered seeing her dressed in it when she was going out to tea. But when Mother was six years old her Mother began to cough and to be an invalid; she was in consumption for ten years. She seldom went out to teas after that. I add here patterns of one or two of her working-dresses.[16] Mother and Aunt Lucy once found them and looked at them with "Oh! how natural it looks! How it brings her back!" Coarse as they are these calicoes were seventy-five cents a yard. Cotton was not manufactured in this country, and the war of 1812 made everything very dear. Grandmother always wore a cap tied round her head, not under her chin, with a black ribbon. "She was always sick and sad" Mother said. Yet one pleasant custom Mother often spoke of. Her Mother was a sweet singer and her Father was musical. Every Sunday morning her Mother used to comb & brush his hair, braid his queue and tie it with a black ribbon before he went to church, he meanwhile holding the hymn-book, and they sang hymns together. Her Mother always kept a girl till Aunt Lucy was sixteen and Mother twelve. Then their Father said it was time they should[17] learn how to carry on a house, sent away the girl and under their Mother's supervision they did the work and a neighbour, Mrs Richmond came Mondays and did the washing. When we visited the house together the fireplace reminded Mother of cleaning the brasses there, and she showed me the door from the kitchen into the keeping-room which she opened with her elbow to ask her Mother how to free her hands from the dough when she was making doughnuts for the first time. She said they often had for supper Indian hasty-pudding in bowls with milk or molasses to eat on it—nothing else. Her Father never allowed them to use both milk and molasses. He said it was "messing." He could not bear cheese. Whenever he went away he sent home cheese for the family to eat in his absence, but it never appeared when he was at home, and his wife always carefully washed the cheeseknife at once lest it should keep, or carry where he might perceive it, any taint of cheese. If the children said at the table they didn't like something he used to say "You have the privilege of going without, which I never had. My Mother used to stand over me with a stick to make me eat cheese till she was convinced that it always made me sick." He considered it very bad manners to speak with food in one's mouth, and if anyone asked him a question just as he had taken a mouthful, he would, with great composure, finish and swallow it in silence and then answer as if there had been no interval. He was engaged in commerce and had several ships. One was the Samoset, if I remember right, another, the Columbus, he took great pride in. She was built in Plymouth. Aunt Lucy and Mother one day when I was a child had a talk about the Columbus's having been an ill-fated vessel, the beginning of the end of their Father's life & work. I have forgotten why except that while she was building he walked backwards & fell into her hold and was hurt. These and the other ship for there were certainly three had figure heads, a painted Indian, a white bust of Columbus & c. And Mr. Hedge's[18] vessels were similarly adorned. The children after school used to say "Come, let's go down on the wharf and look at the images," that is the figure-heads on the ships, and Mother enjoyed greatly all these beautiful ornaments. It was so to speak, the Art Gallery. Mother remembered with delight the coming in of a ship every now and then, how her Father used always on such occasions to send up to the house a frale of dates, and how the bags of "chocolate-nuts" i.e. cocoa beans used to stand round the warehouse. In those days Plymouth Harbour was not filled up as it now is, the ships used to sail up to her Father's wharf. Her grandmother's house was the last one on the street, and a little farther down at the head of the wharf was the counting house. Her Mother used often to send her there to call her Father to dinner, an errand she enjoyed. "Pa, dinner's ready!" Her Father would come along with her, and as he entered the house would say "Well, Ma, what have you got for us today?"

Mother said he was the most dignified person she ever saw. He had very strong feelings and when he was indignant he would say "It makes my blood boil and my flesh creep!" He was a dyspeptic and by the Doctor's advice had bread for himself always *"green* with soda." Ill health took down his spirits, and he was apt to have an air of disapproval which Mother thought kept her Mother sad.

At school Mother had good times with the little girls. In winter when there had been a deep snow and it was drifted up to the fence, it was their delight to climb the fence at recess, stand in a row and then all jump down into the drift. She used to wonder after she grew up that it did them no harm. Of course their clothes got wet underneath yet they went in after recess and sat in them till school was done. In rainy or sloshy weather the children had no rubbers. They sat in their wet shoes summer & winter and, again, no harm came of it.

When a baby was born or any person died it was the custom for the children all to go in to see the baby or the corpse, the first was amusing[,] the latter was considered impressive, it would keep the children in mind that they must prepare for death. Mother of course went with the others.

There was a Watson family—tories—who lived on Market St.[19] in a large and handsome house. They had been rich but were now very poor, yet kept their pride and state. That is they could never make up their minds to leave their house or sell their silver, and they made it a rule to have the table in the dining-room set with a fine white table-cloth every day with all the silver and china ready for tea and the tall silver candlesticks with candles in them placed ready to light. But as there was no one to wash the table-cloths, no fit supper to place on the dishes, no money to buy more candles, the candles were never lighted, no food was ever set on the table, the family was never seen to eat. Plymouth supposed they did eat cosily in the kitchen.

The curtains of the dining-room were never drawn and it was one of the delights of Plymouth children to climb on the fence and gaze in the afternoon, after the table was set, at the handsome show of linen, silver & china and the imposing candlesticks. It had moreover a mysterious fairy-story-like interest.

She had a children's party. Her Mother allowed her to invite whom she pleased and she asked several little girls whom she liked from T'other Side (of the Town Brook, that is). Now Plymouth Society all lived on *this side,* and felt entirely above those on the other side. She heard presently that some of the little girls said "Liddy Jackson's going to have a party and she's invited all the rag-tag & bob-tail of Plymouth." This displeased her very much but dismayed her not at all. Her natural feeling was "So much the worse for those who say such things!"

She had a doll, but I only know it from her telling me with great interest of her doll's bed, its furnishings, its little high post bedstead with curtains, and that her Mother allowed her to have a corner of a chamber, where it stood with a doll's chair & table, making a complete little room for the doll. Later she used it in a corner of the kitchen for a family of kittens to sleep on. Her Father kept a hornless cow. She was named Buffalo and when she grazed in the back yard she used to like to look in at the kitchen door—would stand a long time with her head in. Mother was not afraid of her and used to clasp her arms round her neck and swing herself in or out, whichever way she was going. There was a beam across the ceiling called a summer[;] Mother never was tired of fancying how nice it would be to sit on if the room was inverted.

To show how different were ideas then from what they were twenty-five years later, I record a conversation[20] Mother heard among her aunts. One said she took a good bath on Saturday night. Another said that she considered that indelicate. She thought a woman should never have her clothes off, she had always slipped on the nightgown or chemise before she unbuttoned the other and didn't remember a moment in her whole life when she had had nothing on. Whether it was this Aunt or another one that had never been washed except her face and arms, I don't remember. Another said "But don't you wash your feet? I do." "Never! They have never been washed." The company desired to see how they looked, and the Aunt took off her shoe and stocking. Mother saw the foot. It looked red and shiny but not at all dirty. "How can you keep them clean?" "Why I always rub them clean with my stockings when I take them off at night." It was considered notable to make up the bed while it was still warm, and the good housekeeper before she put her gown on turned round, shook up her bed and made it, then finished dressing.

Election-day was to Mother in Plymouth, as it was to Father in Boston the glorious holiday of the year. Her Mother made Election-Cake, and there was almost always a children's party. Girls didn't go into water, but they often went in wading in warm days, and she among them.

In 1812 she and Aunt Lucy were sent to a boarding-school kept by Mrs Saunders and Miss Beach on the English plan, at Dorchester.[21] Here Mother found Miss Margaret Gourgas[22] of Weston who lived in Concord forty years not far from us and whom Mother cared for, yet never sought. Grandfather bought in Boston black beaver bonnets with plumes and (I think blue) broadcloth coats and new merino dresses for each of them, dressed them alike. He took them there himself and I think went to get them. They stayed there one year, and when they came home, Mother being now eleven years old, her Mother kissed her! The only kiss that Mother remembers her giving her.

One day Mother was looking in the glass and her Mother said

> While in the mirror, lovely maid,—
> You view the charms that soon must fade.[23]

I do not remember the poem, though I afterwards asked her to repeat it, probably many times, and she always could. It was to the effect that she ought to keep in mind that personal beauty couldn't be expected to last and she must undertake to fortify & purify her character that when a noble man should come she might be worthy of him.

Her garden began to interest her very much. No treasure seemed greater than new seeds & new roots for it. I don't know just where it was. Her love of gardens and gardening was always a marked feature of her character. She continued under all circumstances to have one, and a pretty and full one. Cats too she always cared for[.]

Her Uncle Daniel[24] who lived in the other half of the house had a large family of children older than Mother and Aunt Lucy. It seems to me even the youngest were older than they. I know there were three big boys when they were little, named Abraham, Isaac & Jacob.[25] One story she told of them was that their Father's horse was their care, and when he had a white horse they found that in the morning his haunches were all stained brown, so that it gave them much trouble to get them white and clean. They decided that he mustn't therefore lie down at all, and they nailed an upright pointed stick into the stall under him, so he could never lie down and had to stand night and day. Mother always felt badly about that. Abraham grew up to be her & Aunt L.'s & Uncle C.'s "Cousin Abraham," who after Uncle Thomas's death took all the care of their property and was as "honest as the sun." Isaac was the Father of the Abraham of our day who succeeded him as their business-man and kept them poor and uneasy.[26] Isaac has left a son Isaac, Jacob was Father of Mrs Lowe & Cousins Marianne & Lydia.

It was now the time of the war with England. One night news came that the British warships were coming to Plymouth. The men of the town, as I remember, met in Grandfather's Counting-Room to consult and make arrangements, and I think Aunt Lucy and Mother believed that their Father was made Commandant *pro tem.* I don't know how that was. They were waked in the night and told to get up and dress. Aunt Lucy in telling us about this said "They put on us our best beaver bonnets with plumes." These must be those bought for the boarding school[.] Their Mother with her night-cap, her best dress-cap and her bonnet on, brought out sheets and emptied the drawers in each room into them, or tied feather-beds up in them, and set all things, as fast as they were ready together, to go into a wagon which her husband was to send if there was time. If there was no time and firing should begin at once she was to take the children and run out behind the burying-hill carrying old linen, and there all were to scrape lint[27] as fast as they could. Mother enjoyed the excitement, and listened to her Father's voice giving orders down on the wharf. Nothing happened. Plymouth believed that those vessels started to come & attack her but learned that the alarm had been given[.]

When Mother was perhaps twelve a dentist came to Plymouth and her friends went to him to have their teeth cleaned. New and delightful adornment! white teeth! Mother asked to go too. Her parents did not consider it worthwhile, but they allowed her to buy a toothbrush. She found she could make her own teeth white and laboured at it till hers shown like the rest. She used to tell us this as an encouragement to be faithful about ours. She used to learn her lessons lying on a backboard or standing with her feet in the stocks.[28]

Plymouth, 12 May 1884[29]

So we came home to tea, and in the evening after I went up stairs Mother was treated to a game of Whist. Cousin Mary said the next morning "How much your mother enjoys Whist! and she plays very well too." On Saturday morning there was just time for a little walk before dinner. In May 1884, Mother being 81 we were in Plymouth and took a walk[.] We went alone and bent our steps towards North St. Mother did not as I expected march to the door of the Winslow house. It seems that she cares infinitely the most for that, and naturally her method is to come gradually to what she cares most about. She made for the gate of her Father's yard. She refused to go further "I can't go into *this* yard while I'm in pain. I feel too unwell today." So she showed me the steps where she went up and down all her days, the two apple-trees that were set out when she was twelve[.] "Oh, there is where I used to play hide & whoop with my kitten, Purry! I used to tear round from behind the house and hide behind the tree and she would come tearing after me, and *laugh!* If ever a cat showed laughter in her eyes she did; and then she would run away & hide in some other place, and I would run after her. The trees had little defences built round them just as little trees have now. But I think it used to look prettier here when there was neither tree nor bush nor this fence which was put up to protect them, only a green." Mother then went on to relate that Purry became the mother of Blacklegs and Squaller! How many times since

my infancy had I heard of these three pets of her youth! I was delighted
to have the locale of the game pointed out on the spot.

Her Father was a good business-man. He was in partnership with his
brother. Daniel & Charles Jackson was the firm.[30] Mother used to say
"Uncle Daniel put in half the original capital but did nothing further.
My Father made all the money and according to the agreement Uncle D.
always had half." Her Father was a strong Federalist and hated a
democrat. Cousin Edwin Cotton[31] told me how successfully my Grandfather smuggled and on a large scale, I had always believed he was an
exceptionally upright and honest man, and was very sorry to hear all
this. When I asked Mother about it she said "The Embargo interferred
with his commerce, and he thought it oppression and all wrong, and
that he had a right to disregard it." There was every year a time when
herrings came up the Town Brook in shoals. All the inhabitants caught
all they could and there was a law that a certain quantity *per capita*
should be given to every poor family in the town. Grandfather valued
this law & custom and was patriotically proud of it. About 1815 there
arose a scheme for having a factory, damming the Town Brook for
power was a part of it. Many gentlemen of Plymouth thought they saw
in it a great future for the town. Others and among them my Grandfather were conservative[;] they didn't believe in the proposed Factory,
they saw that it would alter the character of the town and my Grandfather on discovering the Town Brook plan became furious against
it. He said it was by taking bread out of the mouth of the poor that these
gentlemen proposed to enrich themselves, that the herring could never
come in again and the bounteous supply of provision for those who had
little beside would be cut off.

He spoke in Town Meeting. The war was waged indeed all through
the town with a vehemence and bitterness that opened lasting feuds.
But the Factory gained the day; the dam was built, the herrings were
shut out.

came into possession of the Winslow House.[32] His cousin Tom
Jackson had bought it, and furnished it handsomely, being ambitious,
and not considering sufficiently where the money to carry on life there
was to come from. He borrowed largely of Grandfather, or, I suppose,
mortgaged the house to him, and it fell into his hands before long. I
do not remember that Grandfather took any of the furniture to his
own house except the parlour-andirons & tongs & shovel which he used
in his own parlour, for by this time Uncle Daniel who for many years
lived in the West half of the house had moved into a house of his own
and Grandfather occupied the whole house and Uncle Daniel's keeping-
room was now Grandmother's best parlour. The fire-set returned to

the Winslow House with Mother & Aunt Lucy some twenty years later, and from there came to our house in Concord where we have used them in the parlour since 1836.[33] To return to Grandmother's parlour it had, Mother used to say "a lilac carpet and lilac chairs—Oh what would I give to see those chairs again!—and those two straight-legged round mahogany card-tables. Our house was not handsomely furnished. All the furniture was cheap—what my parents had when they were married before they had money. My Father always said he was soon going to move into the Winslow house and buy a thousand dollars' worth of furniture for it, as soon as he had time to attend to it, but at last he began to say 'Ma, by the time we get ready to live it will be time to die.' And so it proved."

Not so very long ago, in 1875 perhaps[,] Mother's cousin, Uncle Ward Cotton's daughter[34] came to see her. Mother knew that her Uncle Ward had bought the "lilac" parlour chairs, and she inquired about them. Cousin Sophia Whitney said that she had them and would send half the set i.e. four chairs and one arm-chair at once to Mother. They came. Mother had them in her own room the rest of her life. They are there now,[35] some of them just as they originally were except for age & wear (two of them Edith had "restored") but we could not but smile at Mother's calling the colour lilac. We have except the carpet all the furniture of Grandmother's parlour. Mother and Aunt Lucy were now growing up, Uncle Charles too was no longer a baby. I asked Mother one day just how they sat at the table[.] They ate in the keeping-room[;] the table was never pulled out but stood against the wall. Mother sat alone, facing the wall, her Father with Uncle Charles at his left sat on her right, and on her left her Mother with Aunt Lucy at her right. [See Sketch] They sometimes had a table-cloth, but often only the oil-cloth table-cover. The crockery was white with this blue edge, [See Sketch] just such as often we have now in pie-plates, but then they made dinner-sets of it, and Grandmother had platters, cover-dishes, tureen and pudding-dish of it. She had a Chinese tea-set[36] a very pretty one, which was used when she had company to tea. Mother had it later and my sister Edith has most of the remains of it. Mother gave her brother and sister each a share of it, however, and their children have it still. Her Mother always had a hand in the cooking, and everything therefore was very good, for she took great pains that it should be.

When gentlemen came to see her Father, Mother said he always first of all opened the sideboard and asked "What will you take?" There was rum and brandy and gin and wine. In the evening if they had company to tea it was the rule that when they rose to go Mother was to fill a glass of wine for each one, put them all on a waiter and carry it

the colour lilac. We have except the 34
carpet all the furniture of Grandmother's
parlour. Mother and Aunt Lucy were now
growing up. Uncle Charles too was no longer
a baby. I asked Mother one day just how they
sat at the table. They ate in the keeping-room
the table was never pulled out but stood against
the wall. Mother sat alone, facing the wall, her
Father with Uncle Charles at his left sat on her
right, and on her left her Mother with Aunt Lucy
at her right. They sometimes had a table-
cloth, but often only the oil-cloth table-cover.
The crockery was white with blue edge, just
such as often we have now in pie-plates, but then
they made dinner-sets of it, and Grandmother had
platters, coverdishes, tureen & pudding-dish of it.
She had a Chinese tea-set, a very pretty one, which
was used when she had company to tea. Mother
had it later and my sister Edith has most of the
remains of it. Mother gave her brother and sister
each a share of it, however, and their children have
it still. Her Mother always had a hand in the
cooking, and everything therefore was very good.
for she took great pains that it should be.

round while they were putting on their things, and everyone took it. Such an idea as that wine or liquors could harm any one never had entered anybody's head, and Mother I think never saw any drunkenness among her relations. Her Father had much business in Boston and business-friends there and on one occasion one of them came with his wife, a lovely lady, to Plymouth and spent the day with Mother's family. As they took leave the wife invited Mother to make her a visit in Boston and accordingly sent for her in winter to pass a week. Mother went. I know the house was on the corner of Bowdoin St[.] & Bowdoin Sq. but I have forgotten the lady's name.[37] I remember that the story of the visit was most interesting to me on the only occasion when I heard it. It suddenly rose to Mother's recollection one day not many years before she died, and it was like a novel to me, but I remember only one trifling point of it, her suffering in her paper-soled best shoes on the pavement one zero day that she went out with the hostess. She was about fourteen then.[38] She and Aunt Lucy were reading with zeal every book that came within their reach. The clerk in the bookseller's shop was one of Aunt Lucy's friends and took in her favour what seems to me a great liberty. Every book that came to the shop he at once covered one copy of with paper & lent it to her for two or three days. She & Mother diligently read and punctually returned them. Books were rare, two or three new ones a year besides standard authors were all that came to Plymouth.

It is time to tell of Mother's friends. Her three friends were called the Trio though she made a fourth because it was seldom that all four at once were together. They were Miss Betsey Davis,[39] Miss Mary Howland Russell[40] & Miss Sarah Kendall,[41] but I think it was later than this that they became great friends.

When I was in Plymouth in 1885 I made Mother show me Betsey Davis's house.[42] It was near Town Square. I never asked, but I think she was an only child. Her parents I think were rich. Mary Howland Russell was the daughter of Cap'n Russell. I don't know where he lived when Mother was a little girl,[43] but a certain Mr Joseph Bartlett[44] was rich and built a very handsome square three-story house of brick with a parlour on the right as you enter the front door so large that it received in Plymouth the name of "London." Just after he had moved in and when his wife and daughter Eliza Ann had just measured the windows to buy the curtains a young business-man of Plymouth came to see him very early in the morning. He was not up. The man insisted very earnestly that he must see him and see him at once, and finally Mr Bartlett allowed him to come up to his room. He said that he was at a point in his business where everything depended on his having ready money at once and Mr Bartlett, if he would lend him fifteen thousand dollars, could enable him to do just what he needed to do. Mr Bartlett thought he could trust him, but he said "You must consider that I cannot possibly afford to lose any of this. You must give me your word of honour that I run no risk, that you are sure you can return it immediately." "I do," said the young man "you can certainly have it back as soon as you want it," and Mr Bartlett gave him the check. The young man proved dishonest; it was not many weeks before Mr Bartlett learned that he should never have a cent back. The 15000 was his all. He had to sell his new house and hire a very small one and Mrs Bartlett & Eliza Ann took in sewing the rest of their days. The house was bought for a Hotel, and "London" became the dancing-hall of Plymouth. Later Cap'n Russell bought it and there lived his daughter Mary Howland till her death in 1865 I think it was.

Sarah Kendall was the minister's eldest daughter and lived on Leyden St did on N. St same side on North St. and on the same side[.][45] Among the books that made a great impression on Mother was Don Quixote[.] I never heard her mention any other not religious, so often. She read it when she was thirteen or fourteen and it seemed to her very funny. She mentioned several times that she was once lying on the bed reading it and laughed so hard that she had to roll to work off her infinite amusement. She felt that the bed wasn't wide enough, jumped down, and continued to read lying on the floor.

It must have been of her fourteenth and fifteenth year that she was thinking when she once told me that she and Aunt Lucy, when they went out in the evening, used to come home, go up into their room, put on thick shawls, and learn their lessons for the next day before they went to bed.

A trouble quite new began to rise in Mother's mind[;] it was the need of religion and suggested itself in every variety of form and she became full of questions which she remembered collectively always as "What is truth?" It seemed impossible to know and yet she must know. It made her very sad and often she had times of crying. Her Mother noticed it and asked what was the matter but she could only answer "I don't know." The church seemed to her anything but good or attractive. Her minister was good and a kind man but he did not in the least interest or help her by his preaching. He had for the long prayer many forms which he had written; her memory was perfect, she knew how many of them there were (sixteen, I think) and knew them all by heart. This I chanced to discover when she was near eighty, she began to recite a part of one, I forget why, which led to a talk about it and brought out this fact. She would not have considered it right, but I believe that then, if anyone had given her a cue in any one of them she would without effort or hesitation have gone on to the end. She knew who were the members of the church and knew very well what were their faults. She knew the Deacons, that they were all particularly wrong in one way or another, that one was guilty of a State's Prison offence though he had escaped, that another was heinously vicious and another dishonest. She knew also what the Church undertook to be, and seeing it so false, she could not hope for any help in that direction, and never, all her life long, entertained for a moment the thought of joining it. Jane Taylor's[46] writings helped her more than anything else. Once, much later, she dreamed of meeting Jane Taylor in heaven, and overwhelmed with gratitude, with affection and joy, she fell at her feet and cried and cried. That dream was so real it left as much excitement and content in her mind as if the event had really occurred.

Her Mother had ceased to do any work. She was far gone in consumption. She used to take a ride every morning "before the wind got out," which meant before it began to come from the sea. Every day the first wind was a land breeze, but at about half past ten or eleven the sea-breeze (which was not good for consumptives) superseded it. Grandfather who, as always, had much business in Boston had one regular boarding-house on Court St. where he always lodged. He owned the block on Court St. from no. 45 to 51 if I remember right, and other houses I forget where. In the summer of 1818 he was taken very ill there and Aunt Lucy was summoned to take care of him. She was nineteen. He feared he should not recover, and Aunt Lucy told the family afterwards that he several times tried to make her understand and remember details about his property and business. She was wholly uninterested, paid little attention, and never thought about it again for a long time. His most earnest instructions were neglected. After a week or two Mother came to take her place and stayed a week while Aunt Lucy went home to keep house for her Mother. She retained very pleasant impressions of that week. One day when the Doctor came he looked at her and said to her Father "Miss Jackson must resemble her Mother, I do not see that she looks at all like you." "Resemble her Mother!" cried her Father with a certain indignation—"far from it! Her Mother was a beauty. Liddy cannot be compared with her." When Aunt Lucy was ready to come back and Mother bade her Father goodbye he kissed her and said "You've been a good girl, Liddy, and have done for me all that you could."

He died a few days after.[47] Mother said it seemed to her a solemn occasion, but she felt no grief at all either then or when her Mother died, and reproached herself for it, but she could not feel any. It was in July. Her Mother's end drew on fast. Aunt Joa[48] came and stayed with the girls to help them take care of her. Uncle Charles was at Dr Allyn's at school. Her Mother was of a very timid and shrinking nature. She had never joined the church. Mother thought it was partly because after being "propounded" the person who was to join the church had to stand up in the aisle and "give their relation" of their experience, and if the church-members were satisfied that she had the proper sense of sin and of pardon and the witness of God's love to her in Christ sufficiently clear in her heart, she was admitted. Mother's indignation that such sinners as she knew the church members to be should think of being able to judge whether a saint might come to the Lord's table I have mentioned before. Her Mother, as far as she knows did not share it. She believes that her principal reason for hesitating till the last days of her life was that she thought she was not good enough. But after her husband died she sent for Dr Kendall and asked to belong to the church. She could not leave her room but she was admitted, and the elements were brought to the house and the Communion was administered to her. She also asked Dr Kendall to baptize her children, and he did. It was in their Mother's room. Dr Kendall knew very well that the eldest daughter was named for her Mother and the younger was Lydia, but he didn't know their faces and Mother was the taller, so he surprised Mother by beginning with her & calling her Lucy Cotton. She waited till he began to turn from her and then said "This is Lydia, Sir." He recognized his mistake baptized Aunt Lucy Lucy Cotton, and then came back to Mother. Mother wondered later to hear that he had said he was surprised at her self-possession. Why should she not be self-possessed?

The last night of her Mother's life she watched with her. Her Mother once opened her eyes and said "I can't tell you with what power and sweetness passages of scripture keep coming into my mind." There was little to do for her, but Mother was awake and attentive till towards morning she thought she would lean her head a minute on the bed. The next thing she knew there was a bustle and people talking. She had fallen asleep instantly and slept sound. Aunt Joa had looked in early and, seeing her asleep, had come to the bed[:] "the change had come." Her Mother was dying,[49] but she said "Liddy has been an excellent nurse," and Mother knew it was to defend her from being reproved or reproaching herself for falling asleep.

As I said, Mother had no sense of loss but the love of her Mother grew and grew all her life, and she often used to say "One can never get over having lost one's Mother." When Aunt Susan Emerson said "No matter who is left, the world is never home to you again after your Father & Mother die," Mother expressed entire assent. She had an enthusiastic admiration of both of her parents ever after I knew her, and often said "I want you to know my Father & Mother. I think you would enjoy them both. How I shall like to show them to you, if ever I am permitted to!"

After the funeral Aunt Joa stayed with the girls the two months before the house was closed and they went to Mrs McKeige's School.[50] These were two very happy months. Their Mother had died upstairs in the west chamber. They took her downstairs room and as no one was willing to sleep alone they [See Sketch] slept so; Aunt Lucy and her Aunt Joa in the usual way and Mother with her head out at the foot. "It did seem so cozy!" Mother invariably exclaimed when she thought of it. By day they were doing the sewing necessary before they went away. Every evening they sat in the parlour and just after tea they heard the gate click and said "There's Sidney!"[51] Sidney Bartlett for as Mother remembered it he spent every evening of those two months there. He and they were all three very bright young people, and readers. He was graduated, and had just begun to study law. They were distant cousins, had grown up together, and naturally they had very good times. At ten o'clock Aunt Joa would roll her knitting up and Sidney would say "I suppose it's time to go. I see Aunt Joa's putting her knitting away and I know what that means. Goodnight." The other Aunts knew of these regular visits and became alarmed. Sidney Bartlett's Father had been one of the founders of the Factory. He had been very hard & abusive towards Grandfather. They called on Aunt Joa and sent for Aunt Lucy to tell her they would rather see her in her coffin than engaged to Sidney Bartlett—"Why, your Father would turn over in his grave!"— I don't know whether Sidney Bartlett ever had any thought of marrying her, but they had always been intimate and suited each other as cousins entirely. Certain it is they were never engaged and the Aunts soon had the satisfaction of packing Aunt Lucy off to Jamaica Plain.[52]

The guardians counted that each of the children had fourteen thousand dollars. Whether it was at once or by degrees that the suspicions of fraud arose I don't know, neither am I sure that it was ever made quite certain that there had been any. But the day they heard of Grandfather's death in Boston, his partner's son[53] came over and demanded the key of the upper drawer of a bureau in the parlour where Grandfather kept his papers. It was given to him and he sat right down to it and was busy there all day long. In the days when the guardians remarked that they had been sure that Grandfather's property was much larger than it had proved to be, and that the books of the firm evidently had had the figures in them changed in various places, a sudden memory for the first time came to Aunt Lucy of her again after your Father & Mother die." Mother expressed [46] entire assent. She had an enthusiastic admiration of both of her parents ever after I knew her. and often said "I want you to know my Father & Mother. I think you would enjoy them both. How I shall like to show them to you, if ever I am permitted to." After the funeral Aunt Joa stayed with the girls the two months before the house was closed and they went to Mrs McKeige's School. These were two very happy months. Their Mother had died upstairs in the west chamber. They took her downstairs room and as no one was willing to sleep alone they ⬚ slept so; Aunt Lucy and her Aunt Joa in the usual way and Mother with her head out at the foot. "It did seem so cozy!" Mother invariably exclaimed when she thought of it. By day they were doing the sewing necessary before they went away. Every evening they sat in the parlour and just after tea they heard the gate click and said "There's Sidney!" for as Mother remembered it he spent every evening of those two months there. He & they were all three very bright young people, and readers. He was graduated, and had just begun to study law. They were distant cousins, had grown up together, and naturally they

Father's talk to her and she said "Why, I never thought! Pa told me to be sure above all things that no one went to the upper drawer of the bureau till the executors were ready to attend to his affairs. And we gave[54] that clerk the key the first thing!" And both she and Mother had heard him say after he had been taken into the business "I'm sorry to say I cannot trust that young man," and "I wish I could trust him, but I don't." Nevertheless fourteen thousand apiece was enough. The girls left their Father's house, never to return, the furniture was sold at auction but happily much of the best was bought by the Aunts, and they saved for the children the great black mahogany case of drawers that Grandfather bought at his Uncle Sam Jackson's auction, which has stood in Mother's room almost all her life long, the little cherry bureau which Mother thought her Mother bought when she was married, (and which Mother left to Edward's Ellen), the two mahogany card-tables and the parlour fire-set, the great lolling-chair (now in our red-room) in which her Father sat when he was tired, and the silver spoons. The little cherry bureau went with them to Mrs McKeige's and they had it in their room instead of a trunk.

This going to school was much more an era in their lives than the former time had been. Here they met girls who became real friends. Miss Margaret P. Forbes[55] was there, younger than Mother but very interesting. She told me once that she always wished Father could have seen Mother as she was that year "Cherries in milk is the only way I can describe her complexion." She attached herself to Mother and took her with her to see her cousins at Pine Bank[56] which Mother remembered as the most beautiful place. It certainly was when I saw it forty years later, and is still though much of its glory is gone. Alice Bridge of Charlestown,[57] Aunt Susan Jackson's elder sister was there and Mother lost heart at the first sight of her. No creature, she often said, had ever seemed to have such dignity, such beauty, such elegance. Alice Bridge and her friends Eliza Burling and Harriet Kinnicut became at once Aunt Lucy's and Mother's friends. They liked Mrs McKeige, they thought her a good and sincere woman but I think they did not advance much in learning. They studied French in a book called Dufief's "Nature Displayed"[58] and Mother valued it and felt she had really acquired something from it for she gave it to me to study all through my childhood and could not understand how it was that I took no interest in it.

Mrs McKeige opened the school every morning with a prayer first for the school and then for herself. I asked Mother to recite it for me, and wrote it down from her lips.

Mrs McKeige's Morning Prayer

Thou[,] O Lord[,] art my patience and my strength[.] Thou art the light of my countenance. Thou subduest the little people thou has committed to my charge.

Leave me not to myself one moment but grant me for the direction of others, and for my own salvation, the spirit of knowledge and piety, the spirit of peace and loving-kindness, and, above all, the spirit of the fear of our Lord.

Amen

She used to talk to the girls about manners, and Mother said "She impressed upon us that we were to be very exact and careful in un-dressing and in getting in or out of bed to do it in such a manner as to keep covered. 'You might show a leg!' she said." There was some point that displeased the girls very much, I can't remember what, some thing about the table I imagine, and Aunt Lucy asked to have it as they desired and the request was granted. Mother remembers one of the girl's haranguing one day and saying "The Misses Jackson have raised the standard of rebellion, and we will never let it fall," but this was putting it rather strong. They came home in 1819 to board with their Uncles & Aunts[.] I am sorry I don't know to whom they went first, nor where Aunt Lucy was married.[59] She had her Mother's silver melted up and made into spoons such as were in fashion then. She very much regretted this in later life. Both she and Mother longed to see "one of Mother's spoons."

Now began Mother's young ladyhood the long good time that she had in "dear old Plymouth." Betsey Davis[,] afterward Mrs Bliss and Mrs George Bancroft[,][60] came home from boarding-school and now she and Mother had such good talks, such happy times together as they had never had before. One day she came to see Mother and said "Lydia, I lay awake all last night, thinking we are twin souls." I knew very well what that meant when Mother told me of it. "And did you lie awake thinking of her sometimes?" I asked. "No. I loved her very much, but I don't think I ever lay awake thinking of her." Ever since I can remember Mother has talked of Mrs Bancroft with the utmost affection, and has even said "It seemed as if we had the same thoughts;" there is no doubt that she was nearer than all other friends, though after they were forty they never met but twice when Mother was invited to visit Mrs Bancroft, once in New York, once in Newport, and I believe Mrs Bancroft never came to Concord. Neither did they write to each other, except at those times.

Miss Russell was a friend who sometimes wrote, sometimes visited Mother, as long as she lived, and Mother sometimes stayed with her in Plymouth. This was a more useful-for-life friendship. She did not marry or leave Plymouth; while Mrs Bancroft did, and spent many years in Europe, living when in America in N. Y. or Washington[.]

But in these years of their youth they were together and Miss Sarah Kendall with them. Of her, Mother used to say, "She did not talk much herself, but had the power of making you talk your brightest and best when you had her for listener." There were six other girls, I don't remember certainly their names, Hannah, Eunice & Abby Hedge,[61] Eliza Ann Bartlett,[62] Mary Ann Stevenson, Jane Eliot, Betsey Morton Jackson[63] who with this trio which was really four made a nine which was really ten. All of them very earnest for intellectual culture, all great readers of whatever fell in their way. They made a Reading Society which met from house to house, and had a "newspaper" which they wrote and named "The Wisdom of the Nine."[64] There were two copies of it, both bound, though in manuscript, which belonged to two members[;] when they died the books passed to two other members. Mother & Miss Sarah Kendall were the last survivors and had the two books. Mother's copy was left to Mr Alexander Bliss, Mrs Bancroft's son.

The two hundredth Anniversary of the landing of the pilgrims was celebrated in Plymouth on 22 December 1820.[65] I never thought to ask Mother whether the 22*d* had always been observed or whether the undying blaze of enthusiasm for Forefather's Day which was always bursting forth in Mother's heart was first kindled on this occasion. Mr Webster[66] in all his youthful glory was the orator. The oration was noble, the greatness of the speaker was evident. The large audience of the gathered sons of the Pilgrims was kindled to a white heat. The dinner and the speeches were fine enough to correspond with the oration, and there was a Ball in the evening which no one ever forgot, the best ball any one could remember. Mother danced in one set with Mr Webster, and felt it a great, great honour. Then and for years after an Ode was written to be sung at the celebration. All these Odes Mother knew by heart and often recited to us. She boarded twelve years with Uncle Doctor and Aunt Cotton.[67] Uncle Doctor did the marketing. He liked poultry and as he kept seeing a fine turkey or chicken or duck he kept buying and bringing them home so that Aunt Cotton hardly knew how to use so much meat. I think it was in the earlier days before Mother came to board there that she had lost her daughter, Mrs Gordon. Lieut. Gordon[68] often came to see her and they sat alone together a great deal talking about Sophia. Neither of them felt like mentioning her to other people, but to each other they could say the whole. Some six years after Sophia's death Aunt Lucy asked Lieut. Gordon why he didn't bring a wife sometime to show Aunt Cotton and with *such* a look! he answered "Mrs Brown, I am not a marrying man." But at last he did marry again. Cousin Edwin, Aunt Cotton's youngest child, brought home from Maryland a beautiful young wife, named, I think, Louisa Watson.[69] Mother, and indeed everyone was charmed by her. She was not only lovely but there was an unusual interest attached to her; she was rich and an orphan, she came from a distance and with her Southern ways and accent seemed to the family a little foreign. All were very happy. She and Cousin Edwin lived at home with Uncle Doctor and when their baby was born it was given to Mother to hold. She sat by the fire with it watching and enjoying it, but soon became frightened about it, and it died there in her lap. The poor young Mother died too before the next morning. It was a grief that was ever new to Mother.

The year that she was nineteen she had the scarlet-fever. It was called the canker rash then. Uncle Doctor looked at her and said "Well you aren't complaining for nothing this time, you've got the canker-rash!" and he laughed. It was winter and it would be inconvenient to her Aunt to have her sick in bed. It was never thought of on either side. Mother lay in the keeping-room sofa all day through the whole sickness. She did not make a very good recovery, her head was hot ever after, and she never was so well in other ways. She read about Napoleon's never sleeping more than four hours, and many suggestions that sloth was a sin, that early-rising for prayer was the duty of a Christian, that it was ridiculous for anyone desirous of improving his mind and making the most of his time to waste hours in unnecessary sleep. Now she was earnestly bent on perfection and she made the resolve, 1[.] to sit up till one and rise at five; 2. to read only religious reading until eleven o'clock every morning; 3. to take exercise by adding to her dancing-steps two other performances, jumping rope and jumping over a cricket.[70] Now, her Uncle carefully took the fires apart before the family went to bed at nine o'clock. He considered that a necessity as well as a propriety in a house where all the deeds of Plymouth County were kept.[71] So that winter Mother wrapped in a shawl read without a fire from nine till one in the morning when she went up to bed, and forced herself awake at five in the morning. This troubled her good Aunt very much. She constantly, when she bade her goodnight, begged Mother to go to bed early this once. Mother became a dyspeptic, and so did many people at that time. She concluded that over-eating was the cause, adopted as her guide the sentence "The food you don't eat does you more good than the food you do,"[72] read with admiration of somebody that he made it a rule to leave the table hungry, read her Uncle's medical books and got out of them a complete theory of health and medicine. Her children feel that all this made the invalidism of the rest of her life. She also read about hydropathy,[73] about the importance of fresh air and loose clothes. So she used a cold bath and slept with open windows and never wore corsets but buttoned her skirts onto a waist.

She learned of Uncle Thomas that she had an income of about six hundred a year. He thought she ought to spend much less and lay up part of her money. This didn't at all agree with her views. She thought it all ought to be spent every year in a manner to do good to others as well as herself. The principal means of getting rid of it that suggested themselves were to dress handsomely with very fine and elaborate sewing and embroidery and she hunted up her poor cousins and all the people who had a genius for such work and set them to making pretty things for her.[74] One cousin who could knit fine silk knit & embroidered stockings for her, others made beautiful insertings and edgings, another worked in lace. She also took periodicals. The Uncle held back as hard as he could. Mother's lofty spirit was much fretted that she had to beg for her own money, but she was firm in insisting and kept her accounts accurately; her Uncle began to see her point of view and her talents for managing her expenditure and one day he said "Liddy's generous, but she's a good looker-out." Nothing could have described her better.

She had a decided taste, and inflexibly followed it, no matter what the fashion was. She hated scallops, tucks and ruffles and avoided them invariably. She made up her mind that there was a natural waist-line and never would have her waists made longer or shorter than that. She liked shawls & cloaks and objected to jackets. The colours that seemed to her beautiful were light blue and gray, but she wore very light pink sometimes and green occasionally. I don't think she ever bought a yellow or a purple thing for herself.[75] Her height, her beautiful carriage and handsome clothes soon made an impression, I have heard always of her beautiful appearance. No mortal ever loved society better. She was as quick and as keen as she could be and had a skill in repartee that has given me daily unspeakable amusement. It was simply impossible to catch her at disadvantage. Everybody knew that in Plymouth and Judge Warren and Sidney Bartlett loved to tilt with her. She loved to argue and there was a funny incapacity about her of seeing when she was worsted. When her adversary after a telling blow looked to see her brought low he always found her advancing against him with a cheerful confidence and a brandished sword, not having noticed that last, except as ground for another set-to. Dancing was always utter delight to her, the old-fashioned dancing. Waltzing had never been heard of in her day.

The mornings she spent in reading till eleven. Her garden always claimed much time in summer. She had no respect for sewing and made it a rule to have her sewing and mending done for her, but she always planned and cut out because she could manage with less material and could cut more accurately than most people. She used to sit down with her aunt often but I don't think she worked at that time.

Father used to say "All Plymouth is on its back at two o'clock." It was a town-habit which Mother observed as a matter of course to lie down after dinner. Then she dressed and went out. In summer evenings— and this Mother looked back upon as the loveliest of customs—everyone sat on the doorstep or in the dark at their open front-windows or walked up and down in groups stopping to talk here and there. There were no front yards. Every house was on the street, so that the whole society like one family met every night. This went on till eleven o'clock. The church bell rang every day at one at noon and at nine at night. Mother missed the nine-o'clock bell when she came to Concord. It always rang in Boston too, the one o'clock and the nine o'clock till 1850 or later & in Concord in early days. Mr Marston Watson[76] told me that when he was a little boy he sat behind Mother in church and her dress (in particular a swan's down cape) was a perfect delight to him, and, living not far from Uncle Doctor's, he was able to watch her in her garden.

Mrs Aurelio[77] told me that to her Mother appeared the most beautiful and exalted lady she ever saw[.] She dwelt just opposite to Uncle Doctor's and she found that she could arrange the shutters so that without Mother's seeing her she could stare at will and the picture of Mother among her flowers was the delightful one in her memory. She was then Lucy Goodwin. Mrs Parker who used to be a young girl boarding at the same house in Boston where Mother did for a time said that her idea of grace was Miss Lydia Jackson as she crossed the room in a white gown. Before I leave the subject I must mention a straw bonnet that Mother had trimmed with dark green. She got it in Boston and wore it to church. The next week Uncle Brown enjoyed very much teasing her with many remarks about that bonnet and the power it exerted, and by degrees made known to her that a gentleman had come to him to ask who was the lady who sat—in such a place—and who wore a straw bonnet trimmed with dark green, for he desired to make her acquaintance. Mother went home to Plymouth and after some weeks observed that at church there were many straw bonnets trimmed with dark green. It had so taken people's fancy that they must have the like. There was no other success so marked as that green bonnet's.

In Concord two people have told me that when "she walked out bride" (the old Concord & Plymouth expression for the first appearance of a woman at church with her husband after their marriage) she was beautiful to behold. "I shall never forget it!" said one[;] "I never saw anything so beautiful," said the other. "I lived in the house with brick ends, where Mrs Jansen & Mrs Barber live now, and I was at my front window when she and your Father came along.[78] I can tell you, now, every thing she had on. A straw cottage-bonnet trimmed with a very light pink ribbon, [See Sketch] a white silk shawl with a coloured, sort of cashmere, border and a blue-black brocaded silk dress." Both these ladies told me that both Father & Mother looked very handsome themselves. But to go back to earlier days. It was at this time that she was best acquainted with her Uncles and Aunts and I wish just to mention each. I incline to repeat a speech of Uncle Doctor's that Mother used to quote "I have often been called to a child made sick by cherries, never to one that had suffered from eating currants. I have often been called to a child who had been eating blueberries, never to one that had been made sick by blackberries." Aunt Esther's[79] girl was a black woman named Asenath and called Seny. I must tell Mother's early joke. In those days when children were sick they always had for a dose senna and something with it that was called manna.[80] The invariable pronunciation of it in Plymouth was Seny & Manny, as familiar a prescription in every household as castor oil is now. Once when Mother had been taking tea at Aunt Esther's Asenath and a colored man, her friend, walked home with her. "Who brought you home?" asked her Mother when she came in "Seny & Manny," replied she. Her Mother thought it was bright. Asenath had a pair of twins, and Aunt Esther, though their Mother was not married, was so glad to have babies in the house that she could not conceal her pleasure. "Very naughty of Sene," she said, in showing them to her neighbours, "but did you ever seen anything so cunning!" The little black creatures charmed Major Jackson no less. He always insisted on having the cradle in the keeping-room close by his chair. I never heard of them after they left the cradle.

I remember one story of Uncle Doctor that amused me. Aunt Cotton made herself some new nightcaps with a ruffle around them. When they were finished they proved to be so much too large that she couldn't wear them. It would be actually making them all over again to alter them. What should she do? She lamented and turned them over. "I'll wear them," said Dr. Cotton, "I'd just as lief." So he did, but one morning he forgot to remove the cap before he dressed. A boy came of an errand and knocked at the door. Uncle Doctor hastened out to speak to him. The boy could hardly do his errand and went home laughing to tell

made known to her that a gentleman had come   62
to him to ask who was the lady who sat- in such a
place - and who wore a straw bonnet trimmed with
dark green, for he desired to make her acquaintance.
Mother went home to Plymouth and after some
weeks observed that at church there were many
straw bonnets trimmed with dark green. It had
so taken people's fancy that they must have the
like. There was no other success so marked as that
green bonnet's.
In Concord two people have told me that when
"she walked out bride" (the old Concord (+ Plymouth) expression
for the first appearance of a woman at church with
her husband after their marriage) she was beautiful
to behold. "I shall never forget it!" said one "I never
saw anything so beautiful," said the other. "I lived in
the house with brick ends, where Mrs Jansen & Mrs
Barker live now, and I was at my front window
when she and your Father came along. I can tell
you, now, every thing she had on. A straw cottage-bonnet
trimmed with a very light pink ribbon
a white silk shawl with a coloured, sort of cashmere.
border and a blue black brocaded silk dress."
Both these ladies told me that both Father & Mother
looked very handsome themselves.

what he had seen—Dr Cotton in a ruffled nightcap tied under his chin. Twelve years Mother lived with them. Strange to say I don't think she ever stayed with Aunt Harlow and Aunt Joa who now lived together in the house on Training Green. I believe Captain Harlow was dead.[81] Neither do I remember her mentioning Uncle or Aunt Squire. I had never heard of them when Mother took me to see Aunt Squire in 1856 and was much surprised that there was such a relation. But she saw these other Aunts and Aunt Lydia Jackson constantly and by degrees came to understand that even Aunt Lydia Jackson, who never expressed a friendly sentiment and had a caustic tongue, was fond of her. Across Court St.[82] from Uncle Doctor's (which was a square brick house on the corner of North St. & pulled down before 1890 now the printing-office) lived Uncle Thomas Jackson & Aunt Sally[83] and in the half of their house furtherest from Uncle Doctor's lived Uncle William Jackson and Aunt Esther. Aunt Esther was a widow before she married him, she was a fine woman stately but most agreeable and always very good to Mother. Uncle William, Major Jackson, was famous for courtly manners. Aunt Esther liked and encouraged them and Mother considered it a fine show to see them come out of the house together and Uncle W. hand Aunt Esther down the steps by the tips of her fingers and liked to imitate her when I used to in her old age hand her down any steps. They had no children. Uncle Thomas & Aunt Sally had had one baby that lived but a little while, never any other. It was touching to Mother that Uncle Thomas always nevertheless addressed his wife as Ma, a custom that must have originated in the baby's life-time. The story that Edith loves about Uncle Thomas is that one day some niece, perhaps Mother,[84] inquired of Uncle T. about her aunt and he replied "Lydia's all beat out. A fly got into the house this morning and she has spent the whole day cleaning up after him." One morning Aunt Cotton looked out of the window and sad sight! beheld all her hens and the cock lying about the yard dead. Astonished she ran out to them. Not a sign of life in any of them. She was much grieved, but set herself to retrieve the loss as far as possible[.] The feathers were still good and she sat right down and plucked them, then had them carried out and thrown on the heap. The next day she was waked by the familiar sound of hens in the yard. She looked out and lo! a startling sight! there were all her hens without a feather on them walking about and wondering what had happened. She presently began to put two and two together. She had cleaned out her cherry-rum jug yesterday morning and thrown all the cherries out on the heap. This was the explanation! The hens had found the cherries.

Mother used often to say that when Uncle Thomas was carving a turkey, he would cut off its fine puffed front gouging out the stuffing within at the same time, put it on a plate and pass it to Aunt Sally to help, with "There Ma, there's your pudding."

Aunt Sally used to say "Charming hot." It had a most comfortable sound to Mother, and when I was sick and she brought me a hot flannel or a poultice or anything that should be hot, she always said "Here it is—charming hot," in the same tone her Aunt used. Another phrase she had, I don't know from whom she got it, was "proper good." I think it was her last word to me. I always loved it. It was only in sickness that it belonged. I don't remember it as a common word down stairs. In those years from 18 to 30 she was sometimes called "the living skeleton," she was so thin, and imagined she might die early, "but," she said, "my Aunt often said to me 'Oh! you'll be a stately old lady, yet.' "

She used to talk to us children about the wood-fire, instructing us in the Plymouth manner of building one—perhaps it is because my idea of it was formed on hers, but I think I have never seen any other half so good—and she often concluded with, "Uncle Thomas used to pile on the wood and make a glorious fire and forget all about it till it was burned down to coals. Then he would build up another. But at Uncle Doctor's the rule was to put on two sticks at a time every little while. The consequence was that at his house the fire was always just the same, and the temperature even, while at Uncle Thomas's the room was always hot or chilly." "Will you have some of this great-rorrity?" Uncle Thomas used to say when offering the rye and Indian Johnny-cake which he and Aunt Sally had every morning of their married life for breakfast.

Once, yes more than once, when Mother was telling her woes to me she charged me with a lack of sympathy that seemed to her even rude, and I answered that I was sorry for them and if I knew anything to do to help her I should joyfully do it, but I had ceased to be interested in hearing what I had already heard often. Mother said "Why when my Aunt Sally used to tell me her wrongs and her sorrows over and over again when we sat together by the fire, my sympathy was always as fresh and ready as if it was the first time. She was unhappy and I felt dreadfully for her. It made no difference that it wasn't new." I thought this was very sweet of Mother. Bright as she was and enjoying as she was she certainly responded much more quickly to pain than to pleasure, and her sympathy was invariably sure for any sorrow or resentment of wrong while it seldom had any flow towards the happy. Happiness didn't interest, didn't affect her. I never saw anyone like her in this. It was a most unlucky characteristic. Mother's Plymouth life was exactly to her taste, she loved perfection and exquisite order and with her small space of one room to care for and her command of her own time she was able to have it. Her garden was a delight to her and all passers by, she

had solitude & liberty to study, and at the same time she lived fully in
the town life, and had happiest intimacies with her own set; being surrounded besides by a society of friendliest Aunts & Uncles. There were
charities in which she had part. The young ladies devised two schemes.
One was to be a band of watchers and when some one was sick each
would watch one night in her turn, and a second time when her turn
came again. Mother tried this once, was sick after it, and dared not try
again. Bold as she was about most things she was actually timorous
about her health. The other scheme was an infant school, a charity-
school to take the poor children off the street. This Mother took much
interest in, especially in the little trundle-bed provided for them to take
naps on. The idea was that the young ladies were to teach it in turn, and
perhaps they did begin so, but of course they soon found they must
have a regular teacher, and I suppose they only supported and visited
the school. Both these things Mother remembered with the highest
approbation and was proud of her set for originating them. I should not
omit to say that of her set Betsey Davis married Mr Bliss and later Mr
George Bancroft and lived in Boston,[85] Eunice Hedge married Chandler
Robbins, and Hannah Hedge married Mr Thomas while Abby Hedge
married Judge C. H. Warren.[86] I do not know who were the young men
of her set except Andrew & Nathaniel & LeBaron Russell & Cousin Edwin Cotton.[87] It seems as if all her Jackson cousins were older or
younger. She sometimes visited the Boylston cousins,[88] and others who
had married in the Old Colony, but she went often to Boston to stay
with Aunt Lucy and had much joy in Sophia who talked very early.
Mother used to tell her Mother Goose which pleased her infant mind,
but after Mother had once recited Jane Taylor's Nursery Rhymes[89]
"Thank you, Pretty Cow that made"—and "I'm a pretty little thing"
and "What cry to be washed, and not wish to be clean!" she perceived
that these were a grade higher and if anyone began to her one of her
old favourites in Mother Goose she would stop her (or him) with de-
cision "Don't sayd it!" One day, when she was older, and was saying a
hymn to Mother, she stopped at the line "As holy children do" and
said "I want to be a holy child. I want to go to Sunday-School." I don't
know whether she was allowed to or not.

Mr Brown had an Uncle, General Dearborn,[90] who lived on Milk St.
in a square wooden house on the right hand as you went down with a
long green front yard with trees in it, a beautiful place. I think it belonged to his wife—he was her second husband. She was always called
Madam Dearborn. This couple were always very kind to Uncle Brown
and his brother Nathaniel and to Aunt Lucy. They continually asked
them to dine on Sunday, always including Mother when she was with

them. This Mother liked extremely, she liked the people, especially Madam Dearborn whose elegance of manner made a great impression on her, and the long walk up to the front door with the grass and old trees on each side, as she trod it on summer noons, was a picture in her mind.[91] The house corresponded; it was old and handsome and the rooms were large.

In Boston it seemed as if she heard preaching for the first time. The family went to the Brattle Street church, (Mother always called it "Brattle Street") and there young Dr Palfrey[92] was just settled. He awakened, helped and instructed her. She had gone to church all her days, but now she began to love to go. The sight of the church as long as it stood was sure to affect her, she gazed at it with reverence and love and a sort of homesick longing to enter and find the old times there. If Dr Palfrey had been there I am sure she would have gone if ever she spent a Sunday in Boston, but he had left the ministry before I grew up at all.

Uncle Brown[,] Mother did not enjoy.[93] He was good to her and to all the family but there was no sympathy between her & him, he loved to tease her, and she thought he had towards her "a hectoring manner." But with Nathaniel she had natural sympathy and he was a religious man. The first modern hymn-book[94] was published in Boston and adopted in Brattle St. Church while Mother was at Aunt Lucy's. Nathaniel was delighted with it[;] he brought it home and read to Mother the many hymns which he liked which he had found in it and it was a happy Sunday afternoon to her. He died young, but not till after Uncle Brown had run away. He went out to Constantinople to see if he could find him.

When Mother was twenty-three she went to Wood's Hole and stayed three weeks with her "Aunt Parker."[95] I have mentioned the incident of "the snake under her skirts," and I believe it is the only little story that I know of that visit except that there she saw the rocking-horse which we twenty-five years later named Diamond and took a notion that it would be good exercise for her to ride it every day—almost as good as riding a real horse. So she bargained with Aunt Parker for it. She had a mahogany table which Aunt Parker willingly exchanged the horse for; and the exchange was effected by sea.[96] But though I can tell no stories about it, I know Mother considered this stay at Wood's Hole one of the most important and interesting occasions of her life. She spent much time sitting alone on the hill behind the house. The book she had with her was Scott's Betrothed[97] and she always had a feeling of awe and personal interest with regard to that story. It seemed to her that she entered into a new state in those weeks, and that dimly all her future was shown her

"Diamond" in the nursery of the Emerson House

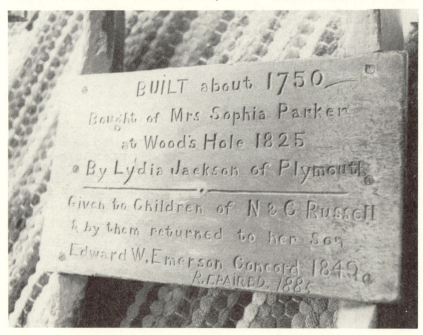

and she was mercifully prepared for all that was to come. She never could answer any questions on the subject, only said "I don't know how it was, it was different from any other experience. I felt all the time as if my Mother's spirit was very near me." But it was certainly one of the great seasons of her life.

It was after she had returned to Plymouth that another great event of her inner life came. She had always, perhaps out of rebellion against Watt's hymns, been a strong Unitarian. One day she had some religious talk with a man from some other town, I don't know who he was, but he said to her "You do not know Christ. I know how you feel about him for to me for many years he was as a root out of a dry ground. I saw nothing attractive in him; but now he is indeed to me the Bread that giveth life unto the world." Mother remembered these words a few months later. She always gave religion the first place but it seemed to her now that she was seeking God more earnestly than ever. It had been arranged that she and Aunt Lucy were to take Sophia and go together for a visit to some cousin, and this had been long looked forward to as a joyful vacation. But, as the date that had been fixed approached, Mother wrote that she could not go. Aunt Lucy was disappointed and indignant but Mother could not be moved. "I felt," she told me, "that there was a process going on in me that I dared not interrupt." I think Aunt Lucy went without her, and during the time that had been appointed for the visit the blessing fell on Mother's soul. I heard her several times in my life speak of it in the words "Christ was shown to me." Once at morning reading when I was perhaps eleven or twelve she spoke of it to us children more at length. Of the words I can only remember these "It seemed as though a curtain were drawn aside." "And what did you see?" I asked full of curiosity. "Remember, dear, there was no curtain; there was nothing that my bodily eyes could see," she answered, "I am speaking of spiritual things." Life was henceforth transfigured for her. The Bible was a new book. Its words now expressed what she felt and knew at first hand. "And it made a different person of me," she told me once, only once, "Aunt Cotton said she never saw a human being so changed." I suppose that it was after this—it may have been before—that she began to have a Sunday-School Class. This Class met in her room on Sunday evenings and was faithful and in earnest. Sometimes the girls talked to her, but usually she talked to them. She always gave them hymns to learn, and I know several of them thanked her for that thirty years after. When I taught Sunday-School I always thought it necessary to prepare my lesson, and Mother would always say "I never prepared a lesson[;] I always had so much to say that there was not time enough to say it in." She thought it was needless labour, but her way was hers, not mine, and I was not able in this case to adopt hers. This revelation of Christ came to her nine years before her marriage. I have mentioned all other features of the fifteen years of happy unmarried life first. Of course during these fifteen years two or three perhaps I should say five younger sets were growing up most of them well-known and dear to Mother, many of the girls her Sunday Scholars.

Uncle George Bradford[98] came to Plymouth to teach German, hitherto an utterly unknown tongue. Mother joined his class, so did most of her set. They learned German poetry (which Mother never ceased to repeat to me, and it always was delightful to hear her. I don't think anyone else ever heard it from her except Charley & Therchi)[99] and they read Wilheim Meister.[100] Mother was carried away with it. One other amusement I remember. She went to riding-school when she was in Boston and many years later, after she was engaged to Father she remembered that the Tucker sisters took lessons in the same class, and felt sure that she and Ellen[101] must sometimes have been in the ring together, but she had not particularly looked at them, and certainly had never asked which was which. She had two horseback rides in Plymouth afterwards. She often said "I used to ride on horseback," but I think this must have applied to riding-school principally for I could not make her remember any third ride outside.

She suffered from infancy the acutest anguish because animals suffered. I always thought it unreasonable, but she couldn't help it; she was made so. She magnified their sufferings and their power of suffering, and when I was little I believe it was just as she said and was aghast. She read me the poem called "The last dying Confession of poor Puss"[102] with an emphasis that carried it home and a sincere misery at the thought that I fully felt. She told me several stories of what she had seen herself of sufferings that I comfort myself with thinking were not lasting, but they seemed to her mind I might say ever present, such as this. Two stray cats appeared in the yard of the Aunt she boarded with one winter. Her Aunt did not wish to encourage them and would not feed them or let them in "And there they sat *screaming* with cold & hunger on the wood-pile, *with their fur blowing in the wind.*" There was a sharpness of despair in the tone with which she said this·that made me fully appreciate her concluding "I used to wish I had never been born."[103] A speech she habitually made was "I have suffered more from the sufferings of animals than I ever have from my own." But even to this religion brought peace at last. Perhaps in that same year when she was twenty three. The Lord made clear to her mind one day that he suffered in the sufferings of all his creatures and that he did not forget them, and made her able to trust them to his care. "I cannot always realize it," she used to say "but I remember that it was made clear to me once and it comforts me."

Uncle Charles went to Paris to study medicine, in 1828 I think it was. He came to Plymouth to bid goodbye to his relations and sat and talked with Mother all his last evening. She represented to him the care he ought to take not to forget his religion or take up a lower standard of life; but to grow in goodness as much as in intelligence; and what she said went to his heart. Years after, when he came home he thanked her and told her that it always seemed to him that that talk had forearmed him against much evil, and indeed had made all the difference and brought him home from Europe as innocent and as much in earnest as he had gone out. Later, when he announced to her his engagement, what was her joy to hear that it was to Susan Bridge, the little sister of her beloved Alice Bridge, now seventeen years old.[104] And when she came to Plymouth Mother said she was a most beautiful little creature; especially her exquisitely formed ancles and feet—people in those days wore dresses which now[105] would be considered short—made a great impression on Mother's mind. She was sure always to mention them when speaking of Aunt Susan young. Mother went to the wedding in 1834 and was exceedingly happy in her brother's marriage. On one Sunday afternoon when she was in Boston she went to Dr Barrett's church in Chambers St.[106] and had a seat at the side of the pulpit[.] [See Sketch] When she looked at the minister she was struck by his long neck, she didn't know a human being could have a neck so long. He began the service. When church was over she found herself leaning eagerly forward, and as she looked back on the whole dear & beautiful service and noticed that now she felt tired of her position she made up her mind that she must have taken it when the minister said his first words and had been too much absorbed to move from beginning to end. She inquired who the preacher was and was told it was Waldo Emerson. After this she saw him once walking in front of her on a Sunday going to church in his gown which fluttered in the wind. In 1829 little Frank Brown was born. Aunt Lucy was boarding and Mother came to board in the same house during her confinement. She earnestly hoped the baby would be a little girl and said she would have a good large tub of water ready to drown it if it dared to be a boy. But when Frank was three days old she said she wouldn't change him for all the girls in Christendom. It was at this time Uncle Brown had the broad new high post bedstead made which Mother bought of Aunt Lucy in 1835 and used as her own for the rest of her life. It seems to me that Sophia was sent to a convent of Ursulines in Charlestown this year or the next. One night while she was there the nuns who had locked her into a passage for a punishment forgot her and

On one occasion the Sunday afternoon when she [76]
was in Boston the went to Dr Badrett's church
in Chambers St. and had a seat at the side of
the pulpit When she looked at the minister
she was struck by his long neck, she didn't know
a human being could have a neck so long. He began
the service. When church was over she found herself
leaning eagerly forward, and as she looked back
on the whole dear & beautiful service and noticed
that now she felt tired of her position she made
up her mind that she must have taken it when
the minister said his first words and had been too
much absorbed to move from beginning to end.
She inquired who the preacher was and was told
it was Waldo Emerson. After this she saw him
once walking in front of her on a Sunday going to
church in his gown which fluttered in the wind.

she was not let out till morning. Mother thought that, altogether, the effect on her of her years at the convent was bad. She returned a quenched and timid soul; she had gone there lively and enterprising. Uncle Brown began now to talk of living in Plymouth. Aunt Lucy and Mother hailed the idea. They owned the Winslow house and would occupy that. I don't know whether it was for this or earlier that Mother turned her attention to furnishing her room handsomely. Spooner[107] was the famous furniture-maker of that day and Mother had him make her a centre-table, a bed-stead, a book-case, work-table, and a little cabinet intended to go under her tall case of drawers (from Uncle Sam's originally)[.] These were all handsome in form, well-made, and handsomely stained to imitate rose-wood (the wood was cherry) with a border of two gilt lines. Later and by a less skillful hand were made a smaller book-case, a bureau and some chairs (cane-seated) intended to match but really scarcely matching at all. She also had a sofa built, with carved legs. When Uncle Brown saw that, he inquired if Lydia meant to be married and this was intended for her parlour. He inclined to make a good deal of fun about this. Mother replied that it was for her room and she wished it handsome. All this furniture was certainly ready when they moved to the Winslow house, and a new carpet was bought, I am surprised that Mother should have chosen a green & white, but she did. I always thought it a beauty, but Mother said she was disappointed in it. On her large room in the Winslow house it looked like green dinner plates set regularly all over the floor. She had the room toward the sea, a great room, immensely high and large, and very handsome it looked with its new carpet & paper & furniture. With what joy Mother entered it. At last the dream of her Father's life had come in some sense true[;] his children had the hand-some furniture and were in the Winslow house. She needed no more be separated at all from her sister and the dear children. Her garden had been made this year behind that house and it was in full glory of marigolds, balsamines, four o'clocks and mignonette. Then came like a bolt from a clear sky the letter that brought the miserable confession of Uncle Brown. The bitterness of shame and sorrow that it brought to Aunt Lucy and Mother, and the sense of its utter irremediableness, the feeling that the children were now not only without a Father and probably without means to be educated but that they could never hold up their heads,—Mother could never express. Heaven itself was darkened and "her tongue clave to the roof of her mouth."[108] This was a heavier blow than she had ever imagined and she felt it to the uttermost. There could never be any brightness more. Sophia was thirteen. They told her what had happened. By and by she came and kissed her Mother and said, "There's something for you under the sofa-cushion," then left the room.

Her Mother looked; it was a little paper on which she had written "Dear Mother, I have a little money; I wish you would use it. It is on the mantel-piece. Your loving Sophia." On the mantelpiece she had left it, three dollars and fifteen cents, I think. There was a day or two of blackness and then light began to shine in Mother's heart and she found her way back to God. He showed her in a way that seemed to her amazing how fully he was able to care for them all to bring good out of evil, and a perfect peace settled in her soul. Aunt Lucy could not feel it but it brought her relief to read the Bible with Mother. They came nearer to each other than they ever had before the Bible-reading together became a daily habit and they found much consolation in it. After about a week Mother felt able to go out into her garden. She had left it a mass of colour, but the frost had come. Nothing was left but quantities of sweet-alyssum blooming white among the blackened remains of the other flowers. It seemed to say to her "The peace of heaven remains though earthly trusts fail." From that moment she loved the sweet alyssum, and I am sure Edith & Edward will remember as I do that it was always in our garden. Mother's friends and Aunt Lucy's came to them with the kindest sympathy. Uncle Thomas and Uncle Charles were outraged and indignant[;] both of them had lost so heavily. The Boston newspapers had a kind word[;] they said that Mr Brown had for many years been a merchant and had proved so upright that everyone had learned to trust him; his sudden fall must have been due to an unusual tangle of misfortune, or something of that kind. There was much consultation and overhauling of accounts and it was finally decided that Uncle Thomas, who could afford it should take his losses, that what property of Aunt Lucy's was left ought to go to Uncle Charles a young doctor just starting in Boston. This would almost make up what he had lost. Mother[,] who had lost less than he[,] agreed to share it all with Aunt Lucy, and by letting half the Winslow house they would receive rent which would help them along. Mother at first supposed she should do well to try to earn more and thought of seeking a post as a teacher, but after it became certain that there was a little income left, enough to enable them to keep one girl (at nine shillings, i. e. $1.50) a week she gave up the plan. Her beautiful room was still hers and all in it. Aunt Lucy I believe did not have to sell her furniture. Mother did not fail to mention to Uncle Thomas that she was glad she had spent her whole income, against his wishes, for if she had had more principal instead Uncle Brown would have borrowed it and where would it be now?

There is a little story of Frank Browne[109] (he changed his name to Browne) which Mother used to tell us that must be of this date. He had been sick and had nothing to eat and was naturally very hungry when

he began to get well. The first day he was out of bed he was longing for
dinner and they went down promising to send some right up. For fear he
should catch cold Mother charged him to stay on the hearth rug till she
came back. His Mother got his dinner ready and sent it up before anyone else was helped. When they came up after dinner there on the table
in the middle of the room stood the plate untasted, untouched! "Why
Franky! What's the matter? Didn't you want any dinner?" "You told me
not to go off the hearth rug, and I couldn't reach it." Mother thought
this obedience ranked with Casabianca's. With 1834 Father appeared in
Plymouth I think it was in this way. He had been acquainted through
his Uncle Sam Ripley's wife,[110] from earliest years with her brother[.]
Twice Father preached in Plymouth, and I think it was in the same year
as the lecture, 1834.[111] Mother did go, to tea perhaps, to the Russells' and
saw him both times I should think. She was introduced to him is remembered & told in that house. On the first Sunday evening of his preaching
one of her friends came to see her and said "I've been wanting to talk
with you all day. I wanted to know how you felt to hear your very own
ideas preached. What Mr Emerson said was just what you always say."
On the second Sunday Mother was so lifted to higher thoughts by the
sermon that she hurried out of church as soon as it was over and home
lest anyone should speak to her. She found that others were of the same
mind. People came out and separated without a word. Everyone in
Plymouth was now enthusiastic about Father, and all Mother's friends
and Sunday Scholars came to her to have outpourings about him and his
Uncle George Bradford who heartily admired many ladies in his Plymouth Class wished Father to see them and arranged that he should
lecture in Plymouth. People were invited to Captain Russell's where
he spent the night to meet him. Mother for some reason didn't go, as I
think I remember. But the lecture had charmed her,[112] and his teachings,
and she regarded him with reverence as an angelic being. One day as
she was going up the stairs of the Winslow house she saw a clear image
of herself dressed as a bride walking down those stairs with Father to
be married. It struck her as most shocking, and yet she did not feel to
blame, for such a thought had never entered her mind at all. It would
have seemed to her a great impropriety to have such ideas. She stopped
indignant and said aloud "I have not deserved this!" and she knew she
was innocent. So she banished the thought and forgot it. On the 26th
of January a Sunday evening, she beheld Father's face, very beautiful,
close to her gazing at her, just for a moment. Then it was gone. The
next afternoon, Monday, 27 January, she was lying on the sofa in the
parlour when the mail was brought, some one brought her a letter and
went out. It was in an unknown hand. It was Father's letter asking to

marry her. She was utterly amazed. How could he condescend to her? And then how little he knew her! She laid it before Aunt Lucy who cried for joy over it, and felt that Father had chosen right[.] Her interest, and the affection that she showed surprised Mother and won her warmest gratitude. Mother "gave her answer with much thought and prayer." She asked Father to come and talk with her on the subject. He came at once, of course. She shut her eyes while she told him that she foresaw that with her long life wholly aside from housekeeping she should not be a skillful mistress of a house and that it would be a load of care and labour from which she shrank and a giving up of of an existence she thoroughly enjoyed and to which she had become exactly fitted, and she could not undertake it unless he was sure he loved her and needed her enough to justify her in doing it, and many questions she asked him. In his letter afterwards he refers to "that catechism with the closed eyes." It was settled that day. She was telling him something and was afraid it was uninteresting, and asked him. He answered "Uninteresting! It is heaven!" and his eyes seemed to her to be like two blue flames. He went. Mother afterwards thought that when his face appeared to her he must have been writing his letter to her. The news was told in Plymouth the next day and the happy sympathy of all her friends came to her in wave after wave of love and gladness. Mrs Bliss heard it in Boston and walked the room unable to sit still for a minute or to do anything but keep saying "My Lydia! My dear Lydia[!]" At last she sat down and wrote her a letter which was one of Mother's most precious treasures. The tremendous manner in which she loved Father was always as astonishing to me as the coolness with which she treated him. Her excitement during her engagement whenever a letter was coming from him, it was twice a week, I think, was uncontrollable. She shut herself up as mail-time approached and it seemed as if it would never come. Aunt Lucy on these days sent early to the mail and told the boy to hurry back, and carried straight to Mother the letter which she had to read a long time before she could call the eager Aunt Lucy to hear about it. And this lasted some ten years after she was married. She pitied Grandma who watched for the letter too and was disappointed that she must wait for it so long, but it was utterly impossible for Mother to open it in the presence of another person it must always be with locked doors, and she must read it many times, get used to it, and recover from the excitement before she could carry it into Grandma's room. In Plymouth it was an impropriety for any lady to go to the Post Office, but if she had been in the habit of going every day as we do in Concord, she couldn't have gone when a letter from Father was coming. During her engagement when she felt most strongly that to be married was the greatest earthly bliss she called one day with Aunt Lucy upon an old lady a great invalid whose daughter Elizabeth took very good care of her, and this old lady said "Only think—only think! What a *mercy* that Elizabeth never was married!" Mother gazed at her in utter astonishment. How could she be thankful that her daughter had missed this unspeakable privilege and had instead what seemed to Mother the not very desirable lot of nursing a sick old woman? She told me of this when I was a little girl with a good deal of the same feeling. After she was eighty she often said that she had come over to agree with the old Mother and would laugh to me as she repeated her exclamation "Only think—only think! What a mercy that Ellen never was married!"

In March or perhaps in February Mrs Bliss sent for Mother to visit her in Boston and this was a glorious fortnight, all Mrs Bliss's cousins, the Sturgises,[113] two of whom Ellen and Caroline became very dear friends to her, all Aunt Lucy's old friends, and many of Father's came to welcome her. Mrs Bliss had a party for her Father who was living in Concord was near enough to see her often and I think his brother, Uncle Charles Emerson came to see her. Her brother Charles was married and living in Hanover St. and I think the first baby, Alice, was born while Mother was at Mrs Bliss's. Insert here letter from Miss Sarah Clarke to her brother.[114]

Last evening I was invited by Mrs. Bliss to meet Miss Jackson en famille, and I had a very good time. James, I think she is almost equal to Mr. Emerson, though very different; quite equal, if I knew how to rank them; as remarkable among women as he among men. She is a singular looking person, and to my thinking, very handsome. Her eyes are somewhat like lamps, and the expression of her face is that of a beaming soul, shining through. Then, while she talks, she thinks; and you see it. Her movements are free and graceful; she is a soaring transcendentalist; she is full of sensibility, yet as independent in her mind as—who shall I say? Margaret Fuller.

Let us return to our Lions.

Miss Jackson said she wanted to find Peter (Schemihl?). She had it, and sending it to be bound with some Unitarian tracts, the binder made a mistake, and put them all into one volume; so poor Peter was pressed down with the weight of these and became lost, substance as well as shadow. Somebody said, "You must not undervalue Unitarian tracts;" "Oh, no," said she, "I respect Unitarianism, for without it we should never have had Transcendentalism. That was a foothold." "It was terra firma," said Miss Peabody;[115] "And nothing else," said Miss Jackson "cold and hard, with scarcely a firmament above it." And so the conversation wended, with alternate merriment and seriousness; as Mrs. Bliss said, like a mountainous country, sometimes we were on the hilltops, rejoicing in sunshine, sometimes in the deep valleys, darkened by the shadows. That is the way she describes Miss Jackson's conversation.

I have heard in Plymouth a few remarks from the days of the engagement. For instance Miss Priscilla Hedge says Father once came on horseback[.] Another person told me that all Plymouth was on the watch, when he came, to see him & Mother come out of the house together and one day some eager lady asked of her friends "Do you suppose those two people have ascended? I'm tired of waiting for them to appear." Mother hoped Father would consent to come to Plymouth to live, but he said he thought she must follow him to Concord where there weren't so many eyes— "In Plymouth you can't even take a walk without its being known to the whole community." Father's Aunt Mary Emerson[116] now signified that she would come to Plymouth to visit Aunt Lucy and Mother. So Aunt Lucy invited her. In the course of the forenoon after her arrival she called Aunt Lucy and said fresh fish was a great luxury to her. Now Aunt Lucy's dinner of a roast of beef was already in train, but she felt that manners required that she should put by the beef and get a fish. So she did, and when they sat down to dinner and Aunt Lucy helped Miss Emerson to fish it was declined. Aunt Mary said she never tasted fish. She said later in explanation that she "supposed that on the coast there was nothing but fish to eat and thought she would set her hostess's mind at rest." But when it came to be dinner-time her exalted resolve had melted. She enjoyed making people uncomfortable and here was a glorious chance. When Dr. Kendall learned that Miss Emerson was in Plymouth, the sister of the late minister of the first church in Boston, and step-daughter of Rev. Dr Ripley of Concord he came to pay his respects. He found Mother & Aunt Mary in the parlour.

Presently rather to Mother's surprise Aunt Mary left the room and in a few minutes Mother saw her through the open door behind Dr Kendall beckoning & smiling, inviting her to come to her. Mother excused herself and went out. "Come, my dear, leave him, and come take a walk with me!" Mother of course refused and went back to the venerated old man, perplexed at conduct quite new to her, which when she fully understood she regarded with indignation though not unmixed with amusement. After a day or two Father came for a night and the next day Aunt Mary drove away with him.[117] The next letter from Father broke Mother's heart. It accused her of sentiment of which she was not guilty of valuing herself too highly and imagining that she was able to judge others. What could it mean? There was an explanation finally that showed her what innocent remark of hers had been

been twisted out of its meaning.[118] In later times Aunt Mary said "I spent the whole time we were riding to Concord in trying to make Waldo give you up, and ran you down in every way I could. I cannot bear to lose my nephews and I did the same when Charles was engaged to Elizabeth.[119] I tried to cure him of caring for her." There came a day when after a long talk with Mother Aunt Mary exclaimed "Heaven forbid that I should hurt such feelings!" Indeed Mother always won the victory though in this case slowly. In her first meeting with all the new relations she was in a state of lamblike innocence. Love and the love she had met on all sides lately and most of all the sense of God's light perpetually shining on her soul had lifted her into a state in which she had forgotten all the littlenesses of humanity and she came full of peace and love without a fear of criticism or thought of how she should impress *them* to see the family at Concord. She liked them all and with Aunt Lizzy[120] she had a most beautiful talk. She could not call Father anything but Mr Emerson, which he did not like. He had asked her several times to call him Waldo, but she could not. This day they were alone in the "little parlour" at the Manse[121] and Father gave her a ring, an old one, recording the death of his great-uncle Waldo, and said "Perhaps if you will look in it you will find the name you should call me by." Mother looked, smiled, and said "I do! It says *Mr* Waldo Emerson!" She always contrived to get the upper hand! I think Father was disappointed in the effect she had on his family. Naturally they didn't want him to marry, and their will was not toward her. What Father admired in her was "her air of lofty abstraction, like Dante," and it is quite possible that she wore that on that occasion. I have seen her wear it at times when no other mortal would, times when one would naturally expect her to be fully occupied with the people about her and it drove me to distraction. Yet it was only one side of her, and the indifference which it seemed to show was no part whatever of her character. After people knew her well they enjoyed it. It was very characteristic and very very funny. The visit was over, Mother had admired Grandma and felt a genuine sympathy with Aunt Lizzy. She liked Uncle Charles, but she didn't know him yet. But the unutterable joy of her engagement had somehow undergone a change. It was perhaps not to be considered but it was felt. She hesitated, but Father was absolutely firm. It was decided that they should live in Concord. Mother told him Aunt Lucy and the children were dependent on her. He said they should still have the use of all her income and Aunt Lucy should come to Concord and live with them. Mother bought Aunt Lucy's furniture of her for a thousand dollars from her principal. There was no money to buy a trousseau. Mother had all her dresses looked over and

restored a little or altered to fit the fashion. She thought she had under-
clothes enough to last a year or more. In this year of 1835 came three
of those remarkable Sortes Biblicae[122] which Mother found. There
was some hitch, some difficulty about their arrangements that disturbed her profoundly and she was much upset by it when she came
to her Bible-reading. The first words her eye fell upon were "Sit still,
my daughter, till thou see how the matter will fall."[123] She accepted
these words at once and felt ready to keep quiet and wait. A house in
Concord had finally been settled on, the one with brick ends, next to
the Minot Pratts', where Capt. Richard Barrett lived so long and where
the Merwins are now. Mother was pleased with the account of it. All
things were now settled[;] the wedding was to take place in the
autumn. But soon Father wrote in some despair. I forgot what prevented, but they could not have that house and there was no other
empty in all that part of the town. They wouldn't marry till they knew
where they were going to live. The wedding seemed to be indefinitely
postponed. This was hard to bear. Mother full of grief got her books and
began her reading. She opened her Bible and saw "Furthermore I tell
thee that the Lord will build thee an house."[124] It seemed a direct message
and comforted her once for all. Before long Father thought of the
"Coolidge house," a house and barn (and doghouse) that Mr J. Tem-
pleman Coolidge had built for his brother Charles in 1828 and which
Mr C. C. had lately left. He looked at it and concluded to buy it, our
own dear Bush where we have now lived sixty years.

It was the 200*th* anniversary of the settling of Concord on Sept. 12*th*
of that year. Father was asked to give the oration at the celebration.[125]
He consented, and wrote to Mother that as soon as that was over he
should come to Plymouth for her. The 12*th* was Saturday. He should
reach Plymouth at noon Monday 14*th* and they would be married in
the evening. Now Mother and Aunt Lucy began to consider the wedding. First the dress. Mother's white muslin was eleven years old, but
still whole and very pretty. Its sleeves were old-fashioned. The style that
year was what is now, enormous puffs. So they had new sleeves added
and the dress was like this. [See Sketch] I believe we still have most of
it though unhappily dismembered. Mother's head was very small her
hair, dark brown a little gray, and very smooth she still did in a twist,
as she had all her life, but since she wore a high comb, a very handsome tortoise-shell one which while she was rich she had had carved
on purpose for her she filled in the space between it and her head with
false curls. [See Sketch] This always seemed to me as immoral as painting. How often have I discussed it with Mother! Always in vain. I never
could make her see it as I saw it. She told me that once the subject

sleeves were old-fashioned. The style that year 94
was what is now, enormous puffs. So they had
new sleeves added and the dress was like this. I believe
we still have most of it though perhaps
pity dismembered. Mother's head was very small
her hair, dark brown a little gray, worn very smooth she still
did in a twist, as she had all her life, but since
she wore a high comb, a very handsome lovingly
one which while she was rich she had had
caused on purpose for her she filled in the
space between it and her head with false curls.

; This always seemed to me as immoral as
painting. How often have I discussed it with Mother!
Always in vain. I never could make her see it as I
saw it. She told me that once the subject came
up at a boarding-house table in Boston when she
was present, perhaps at the house where she came to
receive little Frank. The gentlemen objected, the 5th Jonesia
ladies defended it. At last the gentleman opposite
her said "I know at least one lady who never
wears false hair," and he bowed to Mother. "The
curls that I have on at this moment are false,"
answered Mother. "Oh after that, how could
you go on wearing them?" I cried, "I should think

came up at a boarding-house table in Boston when she was present, perhaps at the house where she came to receive little Frank. The gentlemen objected, to the practice[;] the ladies defended it. At last the gentleman opposite her said "I know at least one lady who never wears false hair," and he bowed to Mother. "These curls that I have on at this moment are false!" answered Mother. "Oh after that, how could you go on wearing them?" I cried, "I should think th'at the sense that you had shaken the man's confidence in the genuineness of ladies would have cured you forever of wearing anything false." "Not at all!" responded Mother gaily. "It is a matter of adornment. You don't think it wrong for people to put lace or ribbon or flowers on for ornament. Now I think it is better taste to ornament the hair with hair than with ribbons or flowers, and there is no falseness in it if you are ready always to acknowledge it." Indeed I think Mother thought the man might consider women more true because they did not wish to conceal the falseness of the hair, than if they had simply kept to their own. "Your Father doesn't object to it," she continued. "When after we were married he saw the curls on my bureau he said 'Secrets of the toilette, secrets of the toilette! Best kept out of sight.' If he had thought it wrong he would have had a great deal more to say." To return to the wedding-attire, Mother wore no veil, nor flowers, she had a pair of the stockings her cousin had knit and embroidered which were left. When Edith was married *she* wore them to her wedding.[126] The company to be invited was next considered. Uncle George Bradford was the only friend on Father's side to come. Dr Kendall of course was to marry them. Mother's relatives were innumerable. Her cousins were almost a roomful and few of them were near friends. The only way to do was to invite no one but Dr Russell and his sister Mary Howland (who should stand up with them) and all the Uncles & Aunts. Then all their friends & cousins and the Sunday Scholars were asked to drop in in the evening and bid Mother goodbye.

I have not yet mentioned Cousin Phebe Cotton. She was the widow of Josiah, eldest son of Uncle Doctor. Her name had been Phebe Stevens.[127] Her husband was a sea-captain and soon after her marriage sailed away and the ship never was heard from. She supported herself by taking in sewing. Mother never thought of her without exclaiming "O my dear Cousin Phebe! How I long to meet her in the other world! She was a true Christian." Once or twice I asked questions about her. Mother said she used always to say when they met "Well, Cousin Lydia, how do you enjoy your mind?" Once when they were talking about good works Cousin Phebe clasped her hands tight to her breast and exclaimed "It's all *here*! If the fountain is right, here, they come so naturally!" On the Saturday before the wedding I think it must have been, she came for a last talk with Mother which was as full of sympathy as it could be. When she left she took her hands and smiled with glad anticipation, saying "How happy you will be! How you will love to hear his step when he comes home! How you will love to see him come in at the door!"

It is strange, but I don't know anything about that Sunday. I imagine that Mother did not 'go to church. But on Sunday evening her class was to come as usual. She knew, and they knew, that it was for the last time, and on both sides the parting was very keenly felt. She expected the eight or a dozen who usually came, but, to her surprise, all who had ever belonged to her class who were left in Plymouth appeared also, it seemed as if they would never stop coming in. There were thirty of them. All were seated and Mother sat down behind her table facing them. But she had nothing to say. Her mind was a blank. Naturally, she turned to her Bible, hoping it would suggest something to begin with. She opened it and read "O our God, wilt thou not judge them? For we have no might against this great company that cometh against us; neither know we what to do. But our eyes are upon thee."[128] This filled Mother's mind to overflowing with instructions to communicate. All that she had longed to say came and ordered itself aright and she talked to them without a break till the hour was over; and then came the most affectionate farewells. (This was the third of the Sortes Biblicae I spoke of.) "And my Rebecca—oh dear child!—my Rebecca stayed after the rest had gone and cried and talked to me," Mother often said. This was Rebecca Bartlett, who with her brother Robert were very dear to Mother and religious.[129] They afterward visited her in Concord, I think. The next morning was the wedding-day it was dark and rainy. Mother who always noted portents felt very sorry. At about four in the afternoon Father arrived in a chaise. I didn't hear, and do not know where supper came in that day. It may have been at six, or earlier. I cannot arrange in my mind any hour of it, but I think Aunt Lucy couldn't have omitted it. This is the plan as I heard it. All were to be dressed and ready at seven. The company was expected to arrive before half past and Father & Mother as well as Aunt Lucy and the children were to receive them. The sofa stood behind the door and Mother thought she and Father should sit there conversing with the Uncles & Aunts till 7:30 when Dr Kendall would advance toward them and they & the Russells would rise for the ceremony. Alas! dear Mamma never valued punctuality, at least not enough to attain to it. According to her account she and Father sat talking in the parlour (and I always thought it was straight on from four) and the talk was so interesting that she never thought of time till she, or he, or someone else discovered that it was already seven. She hastened up stairs and hastened to dress; Father probably also dressed but he was expeditious in such matters. As Mother dressed, she saw that it had cleared up and the sunset was golden. Like any other bride she rejoiced and thought "At evening-time it shall be light[.]"[130] Father succeeded in being down in pretty good season, Uncle George Bradford was the only friend on his side, he was there Mother's Aunts & Uncles arrived, Dr Russell and his sister; and Dr Kendall; all was ready, it was half past seven, but no bride. Father couldn't stand it, he started up stairs to ask when she was coming. He met her on the landing and behold! exactly as that vision had presented itself to her, months ago, they were going down stairs together to be married! They liked their wedding and Dr Kendall's prayer, and, presently after, the room filled with all the kind friends and cousins, and from Dr Russell's plan of the Winslow House I con-clude that Father & Mother stood before the fire-place to receive. Mother had one wedding-present, "a standish," that is two inkstands on a bronze oblong stand, from Betsy Davis, which always was kept either in the parlour or guest-chamber, and is good and whole as ever after being used sixty years. Much later in 1839 she received another from Mr Thomas Carlyle, Guido's Aurora, which has hung over our parlour sofa ever since and hangs there still in 1896[.][131] The next morning they set forth in the chaise for Concord Cousin Abraham Jackson, Father of the Abraham we knew, helped her in and drove into our yard about five or six in the afternoon of 15 September 1835. Mother had never seen the house before. In those days it was con-sidered an impropriety for a lady to go to see her house-to-be before she was married. She and Aunt Lucy had packed all the furniture except what was actually necessary for the wedding and sent it in two great cart-loads to Concord a week before and Grandmother Emerson had moved into the house with Nancy Colesworthy a cook who had formerly lived with her and who came to live with the new-married pair and they had to some degree unpacked the things and tea was ready though as there were no plates at all, (the plates having been kept back, I suppose, for the cake & wine after the wedding though I never happened to ask about it) they had to use saucers to eat from the first day. Father was sent to buy pot-hooks[.] Uncle Charles Emerson was also there and made part of the family till his death eight months later. I must now make a little disquisition on the house.

I have drawn without accuracy a plan of the domain as it was when they entered upon it. The front yard was fenced away from the East Yard and from the space "behind the house" as we always called the

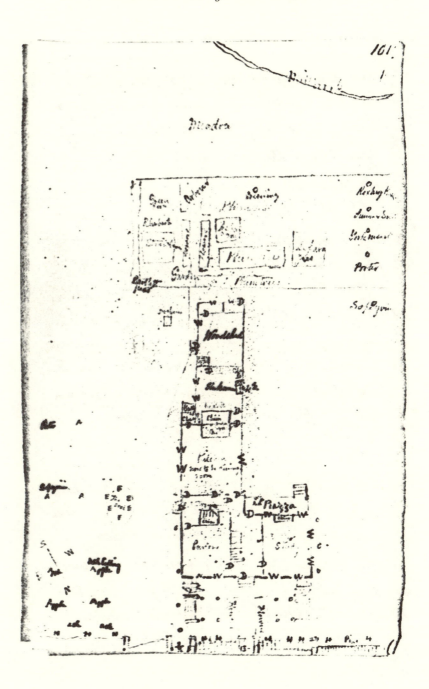

I have drawn without accuracy a plan of the 102
domain as it was when they entered upon it. The front
yard was fenced away from the East-Yard and from
the space "behind the house" as we
always called the West side by a
fence like this. There was a row
of nine horse-chestnut trees along
the fence between the yard and the road. The turnstile stood then as now beside the horse-gate. As to
other trees beside the horse-chestnuts I am not sure that
there were any, but they at once had four elms and
two fir-balsams set out in an oval in the East Yard.
I think Aunt Lucy said Uncle Charles Emerson
superintended that, and the other fir balsams, eight
in the front yard, four in the East Yard and three
behind the house must have been set at the same
time. I think it was in 1837 that Dr Hobbs of Waltham
brought up a hayrigging-load of young trees and set
them out with Father and a man, making "the grove"
as it was called, and really was, when we were
children, behind the house. In the front yard were
set besides the horse-chestnuts and the fir-balsams
two catalpas an ash, a pine and a hemlock.

West side by a fence like this. [See Sketches] There was a row of nine horse-chestnut trees along the fence between the yard and the road. The turnstile stood then as now beside the horse-gate. As to other trees beside the horse chestnuts I am not sure that there were any, but they at once had four elms and two fir-balsams set out in an oval in the East Yard, I think Aunt Lucy said Uncle Charles Emerson superintended that, and the other fir balsams, eight in the front yard, four in the East Yard and three behind the house must have been set at the same time. I think it was in 1837 that Dr Hobbs of Waltham brought up a hayrigging-load of young trees and set them out with Father and a man, making "the grove" as it was called, and really was, when we were children, behind the house. In the front yard were set besides the horse chestnuts and the fir-balsams two catalpas, an ash, a pine and a hemlock. It is hard to imagine how it could have held so many trees, but they were little, and low, too. For I distinctly remember seeing Miss Caroline Sturgis, sitting in Grandma's room, draw Miss Minot's house.[132] Not a tree, even then—perhaps 1844—lifting its head between that and us. The house was an L house with a long wing running out from the L. The Coolidges had used its three large rooms downstairs as Parlour, Dining-room and Kitchen, and had the Sink-room beyond the kitchen. Father took their parlour for his study. It had frescoed walls, so innocent! so funny! Whenever you tear off wall-paper you will see. The views are in India-ink and consist of a shed and a tree, or a house and barn and several trees. In the largest space is even a meeting-house! The study had six windows, two north, two west, two south. The front entry had at its south end a door opening onto the same piazza which, moved farther out, is still there. The Coolidges' dining-room (now our red room) became Mother's parlour, and Mother put there the buff cambric curtains made for her room in the Winslow house, with a new carpet of two shades of red crimson. This was the only new carpet[.] It has been in use ever since, more than thirty years on the room it was bought for, two years in the study and twenty-three in the den. Mother always preferred plain colours, I mean things all of one colour, and she was successful in finding this time what she liked; the carpet, though of two shades, was, on the whole, plain crimson and the paper was cream-colour, watered, on a satin ground, with a crimson border round the ceiling. The handsome furniture she had had made for her room, the large looking-glass, the centre-table, book-case and low cabinet, stained rosewood, with a border of gilt lines, the sofa-with-carved-legs, covered with red moreen, and a sewing-chair covered to match, (this was a chair she had had copied from one of Mrs Bliss's which she admired) the red parlour

rocking-chair from Aunt Lucy's parlour, which still stands by our
parlour fire and the mahogany card-table and work-table which have
stood in the dining-room now more than forty years, and a set of
hair-cloth seated mahogany chairs all went into this parlour—now our
Redroom—and when all was in place and the fire lighted on our
parlour andirons which had formerly graced Grandmother Jackson's
parlour Uncle Charles Emerson looked round the room with admiration, and said it was a gem. He rejoiced much in Mother's taste. It
agreed with his own. And Mother was delighted with her pretty
parlour, and happy in his sympathy and approval. No doubt Grandma
and Father were equally contented but I do not remember hearing their
remarks. The green and white carpet from her room in the Winslow
house went into the dining-room.[133] Aunt Lucy had a pair of matched
mahogany dining-tables, one went into the front entry and one into
the dining room. There was a set of quartette tables and they were
distributed in the three downstairs rooms, as well as the rest of the
haircloth-seated chairs. In the study was set up a funny Siamese-twin
kind of coal stove [See Sketch] which was ineffective and troublesome.
The rest of the house had only open fire-places. Father's own furniture—
his contribution to the house—seems to have consisted of his rocking-
chair given him by his sister-in-law Margaret Tucker, probably in
1829 the chair in which he really spent his whole indoor life, his cabinet
of drawers, his tall book-cases with cupboards below, a table with
leaves, stained red, his bachelor bedstead, which has been in the den
these twenty-three years and is especially Cameron Forbes's[134] and the
green rocking-chair in the dining-room, which was Ellen Tucker's. The
bachelor bedstead went upstairs into the room over the kitchen for
Uncle C[harles]. C[hauncy]. E[merson]. who slept there all that winter,
the red-stained table, I think. The green rocking-chair took at once, and
permanently, its present position. The rest, as immediately and as
permanently, was placed where it now stands. What was originally the
study-table I do not know, perhaps it was his Mother's dear old black
mahogany dining-table. In my earliest days the table in the study was
covered with a red and white cotton-damask cloth, and it was a large
square table. I remember when Mother bought at an auction-store to
replace it a handsomer one[;] perhaps it was in 1846 or 7. This remained
the study-table till 1854 when Mother moved the parlour furniture
into the study, the rosewood table & bookcase and the sofa; and the
study-table moved out and has been ever since the front-entry table.
To Grandma was allotted the room over the study, Mother took the
next room, over her parlour, the nursery was to be for Aunt Lucy,
and Uncle Charles E. took the room over the kitchen. There was no

And happy in his sympathy, and approval.   105

No doubt Grandma and Father were equally contented
but I do not remember hearing their remarks.
The green and white carpet from her room *omit in reading* in the
Winslow house went into the dining-room. Aunt Lucy
had a pair of matched mahogany dining-tables, one
went into the front-entry and one into the dining
room. There was a set of quartette tables and they
were distributed in the three downstairs rooms, as
well as the rest of the haircloth-seated chairs.
In the study was set up a funny Siamese-twin
kind of coal stove ▥ which was ineffective and
troublesome. The rest of the house had only
open fire-places. Father's own furniture *— his contribution to the house —* seems to
have consisted of [1] his rocking-chair given him by
his sister-in-law Margaret Tucker, probably in 1829
the chair in which he really spent his whole
indoor life, [2] his cabinet of drawers, [3] his tall
book-cases with cupboards below, [4] a table with
leaves, stained red, [5] his bachelor bedstead, which
has been in the den these twenty-three years and
is especially Cameron Forbes's and [6] the green rocking-
chair in the dining-room, which was Ellen Tucker's

guest-chamber. Grandma had been keeping house for Dr Ripley, and was to go to New York to spend the winter with Aunt Susan and Uncle William. I cannot quite understand how things were for she could not have been at our house the first week or so as this story proves. Aunt Lucy and the last load of furniture from Plymouth arrived—the load first, for it was unloaded but not unpacked or placed. Before the stage arrived with Aunt Lucy, came Mr Rodman and his wife to make a call.[135] They were on a driving journey in their carriage. Father intoxicated with the joy of having a house of his own, and wholly green and ignorant about housekeeping felt an ardour to use his house and exercise the power of being hospitable, which he had almost for the first time, and insisted on their staying all night. They cheerfully accepted the invitation, and he hastened to tell Mother who was indeed aghast. There was a room, that is Grandma's room, into which the newly arrived furniture had been shoved, and that was all. Aunt Lucy came. Mother showed her to her room which she had spent the day in making as pleasant as she could. Aunt Lucy was tired with the journey and moreover a clear sense had come to her that this day ended her career as head of her house and Mother of her children. She was so sad she could do nothing but cry. Mother felt deeply for her and longed to sit down with her and try to cheer her, but could only tell her about the guests and run first to see about tea and then take Hitty, the second-girl, whom she had brought from Plymouth, to the room over the study, unpack the furniture and move it into the entry. By this time they had to stop for tea. She took Mrs Rodman to her own room to get ready for tea. After tea she and Hitty, and even Nancy, had to take hold, unroll a carpet of the Winslow house, lay it down on the room, & tack it round the threshold, then move in some chairs and a washstand and dressing-table, then put up a bedstead and find bedding for it. They worked as fast as they could but it was half past ten before Mother could invite her guests up. Mrs Rodman told her she had brought nothing with her and must ask for night-clothes and brushes—everything. Mother brought her best nightgown, left from former days, it was getting old but it was handsome.

Grandma[136] had not yet moved to the house and remained at the Manse till Mother had furnished the house. When she came she brought the furniture for her own room, which has always remained in it. In January Miss Harriet Martineau[137] with her companion came to stay for a few days. This visit gave Mother great pleasure. Miss M. was very deaf, but they had good talk together nevertheless. Uncle Charles was a delightful inmate. Aunt Lucy told us he was full of fun— "*How* he used to dance around the table in this dining-room in his camlet cloak!" Mother said "Your Father has never laughed since he died as he used to make him laugh." Grandma always called Father "my son" instead of by his name, probably because he was a minister, and Uncle Charles would sometimes say to her as he saw him coming in at the gate "Mamma, here comes your son." Once, in speaking of these days, Mother said "My mind was so full, so occupied, with the greatness, the solemnity, of marriage that all other things, the housekeeping & c., were as nothing." Another time she told me that on a cold day Father[138] brought his papers into the dining-room where she was sitting and where it was warm and worked there. There came in callers, and sometimes the members of the family came in; and always when they went out of the room and she & Father were left alone they looked at each other. How pretty, and how natural! But Mother spoke of it with pleasure to Aunt Lucy, and Aunt Lucy told her it was selfish, and unkind to the friends who had just left the room.[139] I hope Mother did not believe her. Much record of these months may be found in letters and in Father's journals. I shall omit all I have learned from them and only put down what Mother told me. She was preparing her garden. I believe she had only the two beds beside the front walk which was then a gravel walk. She found there a rose bush left by the Coolidges with a tag on it marked "Charles Duval" the parent of half our rosebushes at the present day and of many in many towns which Mother has given away. There was also a Boursault[140] at the front gate which in 1860 or about that time was moved to the Bulkhead-corner of the house and in 1890 was for the first time allowed to climb. Then it began to prosper mightily and is now, 1896, almost up to the nursery windows. Mother brought with her from Plymouth a pink Damask rose from her Grandmother Jackson's garden which she had had in her own for years, double & single white English tree roses, and blush roses. All these have increased and one of Greatgrandmother's pink Damasks, being beside the East door, has of late years taken to climbing on the house & porch. I think it will rival the Boursault. Four other kinds were numerous in our garden in my childhood that have since disappeared, the "marbled rose" a bright red that faded purple, the "York & Lancaster," variegated, the glorious crimson velvet yellow-centered "Grand Duke of Tuscany" and the red, neat, miniature "Duke of Burgundy." I do not know whether Mother brought or found these or bought them later. Nor the Petite Hundred-leaf, which still survives. I think she brought the flowering almond, the Missouri currant and the flowering raspberry.

I don't know where I have heard that the neighbours came to call and some of them said they would never enter the house again. Poor

Mother had received them with her far-away manners. But certainly dear Miss Minot who lived opposite was always on most affectionate terms with her. Mrs Hersey Goodwin, whose husband was Dr Ripley's colleague, & came from Plymouth, with her sister & brother, Mr & Miss Mackay[141] were friends from the outset. Also Mrs Nathan Brooks.[142] Her [friendship] with Mrs Nathan Brooks was always satisfactory, she admired her as a house keeper and a wife, they were equally ardent in the Anti-Slavery cause, and equally interested in politics as far as they related to that. Further, when spirit-manifestations began it was equally interesting to both.

Mrs Thoreau and Miss Sophia[143] were also friends, but the relations with Mrs Thoreau had amusing features, Mrs Thoreau both liked her and didn't like her, loved to put out a claw and inflict a scratch when she saw a chance, as, when Mr Thoreau had written Mother a grateful and affectionate letter, and she said to his mother "I don't deserve it[;] he sets me higher than I am," Mrs Thoreau replied "Well, Henry was always tolerant."

Father bought a horse and old chaise in 1852 and in 1853 a second hand Rockaway which had long been used in the Livery-stable. Mother went in it to the Anti-Slavery society. As she came in, one of the ladies said "Was that *your* Rockaway, Mrs Emerson[?"] "Yes," answered Mother gaily, "I've set up my carriage." "I've often seen Mr Staples[144] driving the prisoners to court in it," said Mrs Thoreau. Mother often said it was a typical speech. Aunt Lizzy constantly came to the house with Uncle Charles and oh! how Mother loved her! Father took Mother to Waltham to see his Uncle Ripley's family. Alas! with no success. In 1856 Aunt Ripley said to me "Your Mother is grand! When I first saw her, I couldn't bear her. But now I think she is a noble woman."

Father was preaching in Lexington I think it was this year. He used to go over in a chaise and Mother always went with him. She loved to hear him preach. Of course, Everyone did, but *what* was it to her!

One day, as they returned the autumn foliage in a swamp was so glorious that they got out and gathered branches. When they got home they found it was poisonous dogwood. "We ought to have been poisoned to make a good story against breaking the Sabbath," Mother said, "but we weren't."

They were invited to a party, and went. Mother, who had always dwelt in aristocratic Plymouth, was astonished when she recognized, in the first gentleman who made his bow to her as she entered, the butcher who supplied her with meat. Judge Keyes, who was then a boy of fifteen, liked her looks and at once invited her to dance.

So she danced her first dance in Concord with him, with the Grandfather of Ellen & Florence & William & Raymond, her dear grandchildren. I think this party was at David Loring's.[145]

She & Father both hoped for children, Father so much that Mother could not bear the idea which grew upon them both that they should have none. It was therefore the greatest joy when she was able to tell Father that she believed a baby was coming. He kissed her and said "I hail the little new being."

Mother had a Sunday School Class as she had had in Plymouth. I have heard four of them tell how great a blessing it was to them, Mrs Edward Hoar, then Miss Elizabeth Prichard, Mrs Rockwood Hoar, then Miss Caroline Brooks, Mrs Saunders, then Miss Mary Ball, and Mrs Stephen Barker, then Miss Jane Whiting. Deacon Tolman's daughter also, Abby Tolman.[146] Mother of course loved them all, and she always spoke of these, and of everyone who had belonged to the class with the greatest affection. She used to say "Abby Tolman, dear child! When she was dying, made them burn her blank-book which she used to write in 'for fear that if they read it after she was dead they would think she was better than she was.'" Teachers' Meeting, to which Mother, Uncle Charles and Father seem all to have gone, was usually a very interesting occasion and Mother's talk was always appreciated. I have heard it spoken of. They met sometimes at our house.

Aunt Lucy told us that one Sunday the minister, Mr Goodwin[147] I suppose, did not appear at S. S. All were seated & waiting. Then Uncle Charles arose, "took off his Camlet cloak, walked up to the pulpit and opened the school, making such a beautiful prayer—do you remember, Lydia?"

"Oh *yes!*" said Mother with much feeling. This story impressed me very much. What young man of twenty-six or seven have we ever seen who had no intention of entering the ministry who could or would do this? In March they began to be anxious about Uncle Charles's cough. Nothing did him any good. The Doctor said he must go to the South. He went to New York to his Mother about the first of May; they were to sail for Porto Rico, but he seemed too weak. On the 6th, I think it was, a letter came asking Father to come at once and bring Aunt Lizzy. He was lecturing at Salem,[148] but as soon as the lecture was over he joined her and they set forth. They arrived the 9th of May, too late. That morning Uncle Charles had felt so much better that he wished to take a ride so he & Grandma went out in a hack. Uncle Charles when they came home got out, walked up the steps of the Fourth St. house and to the stairs, but sat right down on them, fainted, and never revived.[149] They had the funeral at N. Y. at Uncle William's.[150] The coffin was placed in the vault under a church, temporarily. I cannot understand why. In the course of time they undertook to get it to bring to Concord but, as the story was told to me, there had been an epidemic in that parish, which had carried off many, and many coffins had been placed in that vault. The silver coffin-plate was considered always the perquisite of the undertaker and was removed. There were no means of identifying the coffin and the search had to be abandoned.

It had been planned all winter in Concord that Uncle Charles & Aunt Lizzy should be married the next September and should come to live with Father & Mother, so, perhaps in April, the carpenters were called to build them a room & dressing-room over a new parlour which was to be theirs. And Aunt Lizzy's piano was to stand on the S. side. She was asked to measure her piano and bring the measure that the carpenters might plan to set the S. window so that the piano might have room enough to the right of it. She did, and Mother and she were stretching the string against the wall when Aunt Lizzy cried, "It is of no use. It *never* will be!" This impressed Mother as real phophecy, afterwards. At the time she only thought it was natural that the future should seem too good to come true. So the parlour became our parlour. The room upstairs, which opened by a door into the wall of the landing of the front stairs, Mother called the Prophet's Chamber because of this text "Let us make a little chamber, I pray thee, on the wall, and let us set there a bed and a table, and a stool and a candlestick and it shall be when he cometh to us that he shall turn in thither."[151] Her own parlour was now vacant and was turned into a guest-chamber. It kept its own carpet, and from it was called the Redroom. The new parlour had a red & yellow carpet, the red pinkish the yellow almost a drab. A new hair-cloth sofa was, I think, bought for it which is now in the Study. Perhaps from its position, it did not tease us in the parlour as it always has in the Study. Father used to say it was "handsome in form, but it appeared to have elephantiasis," which, he explained to me, meant great enlargement of the feet—a disease. Almost never has gentleman or lady sat on that sofa and risen to bid goodbye without falling a prey. The sofa extends its giant left foot in such a manner as neatly to catch the caller's right heel as he backs with his parting bow, which is thus ruthlessly destroyed; the victim just saves himself from falling, the sofa is elated with a grim triumph and Father and I are filled with indignation at its conduct, shame that we cannot prevent it and compassion for the guest. To me that sofa is associated with the last days of Father's life; he lay there the three days before he went up stairs for the last time.

Mr Ogden Haggerty sent from Europe two engravings of a Madonna by Correggio to Mr S. G. Ward,[152] asking him to frame them, one for himself, and one for Father, and deliver Father's, keep the other and send the bill to him. Father told me this and that Mr Ward had had his own framed comparatively cheaply but the one for us with the best gilt frame and plate glass. "It was the act of a gentleman," he said, if I remember the words right. This hung in the parlour and, seeing it from my infancy, I always in my own mind called a mackerel· sky "cherub's heads" and was surprised when I was ten or twelve years old to find that the world had another name for that appearance. Moses in this picture has a little glory on each side of his head, so arranged, I suppose, with reference to the fancy that he had horns. I always supposed them to be long ears, and having heard that asses had long ears called these asses' ears. By the time I got to be 7 or 8 I began to ask the questions which had always puzzled me and asked Father who was the man with asses' ears. He was much displeased, I couldn't understand why. At last he found I knew no better and was quite serious, so he explained to me the picture. Later Mr Sam Ward gave him the Endymion which is a Roman sepia of a relief on one side of a staircase in Rome. Aunt Lizzy saw it there and told us what was the subject of its companion-piece on the other side of the staircase. It seems to me as if she had said "in the Capitoline Museum."

——— . . . . . ———

Grandma & Father & Aunt Lizzy came home from New York, this must have been the beginning of Grandma's actual living with us. Aunt Lucy moved, I think to Mrs Thoreau's.[153] Aunt Lizzy came to stay a month with Grandma & Father & Mother. "Her heart was so sore," Mother said. The firbalsams must have been there for Mother also said "Our trees all round the house were full of birds, it seems as if we never had so many. Again, they seemed actually to blossom birds. Your Aunt Lizzy sat at the window and watched them. She said it seemed as if Charles sent them." One day she said "And Lidian what am I to do with this passion for children?" Her nieces & nephews had the full benefit of it and are grateful. Mother was very sick most of the summer[.] She told me her face was set, looked like death, and no one thought she could live. Father, alarmed, consulted Dr Bartlett[154] who encouraged him and said he "had never lost a case." Father said "It does not seem just that the Mother should have so much pain and suffering and the Father none." And Dr Bartlett answered "She is re-paid. She has the pleasures of lactation." This always seemed to me a funny speech, a regular Doctor's speech.

I think that this summer Aunt Lucy brought Mr Thoreau to our house. He was early interested in his Mother's new boarder and her knowledge of poetry and literature and flowers. One day a bunch of violets flew in at her window bearing with them a poem by Mr Thoreau who was out in the yard. If I remember rightly she brought the poem to Father who liked it, and that was the beginning of Father's and Mr Thoreau's friendship.[155] The reason I believe it to be 1836 is that I have always understood that it was in their first year that Father & Mother kept chickens.

The miseries of her hens were ever present to Mother's mind. First she was tormented to think how cold their poor feet must be in the night. They slept on a long roost in the barn cellar which was open on the South and Mother thought the frosty night air must come on them with full force. So she went out and wound the roost with list,[156] the woollen would feel comfortable to them. How glad she was for their sakes when spring came! But too soon they showed such zeal in digging all the roots and seeds out of her garden that they had to be shut up. Mother's heart was now oppressed with a sense of the weariness & cruelty of their imprisonment, if she was a hen she should feel it a flagrant act of injustice and tyranny. Mr Thoreau then made some neat little cowhide shoes for them which fitted well and were tied tight round their slender ancles, so that at least they could promenade about the yard[.] One of these shoes remained in our garret till the fire in 1872. But ever new sorrows about the hens kept coming. They showed a desire to sit perpetually and the cure proposed was to keep them in barrels with water under them so that they couldn't sit and *had* to stand. Then to kill a chicken to eat was to murder a defenceless creature dependent on her care and as to the cannibalism of eating it, she was incapable of it. They gave up keeping hens. Though they must have done it once later, for a hen-house was built in the top of our shed, still there, to keep them in in winter.

In the autumn Aunt Lucy decided to spend the winter in Plymouth. As soon as she arrived every one fell upon her with "What *did* Mr Emerson mean? He said 'the arrows of Fate stuck fast in Lydia!'" It seemed that all Plymouth had been so mystified and its curiosity so provoked by these oracular words that they had never been forgotten. It was indeed an absurd answer of a bridegroom to the friends of his bride, yet to me it seems amusingly true and natural. In Plymouth she had been quite free from the little difficulties & failures of a housekeeper. It was her nature to take them with a curiously exaggerated view of their importance and to expend on them an amazing amount of indignation and shame. Father, who was comparatively easy and light by nature, looked on puzzled & surprised. He called her Asia,[157] for no New Englander that he knew of had ever possessed such a depth of feeling that was continually called out on such trivial occasions. There was no bluster about it but a tragic, yea awful reality. Mother was evidently an Oriental. "Your mammy has no sense of measure," he often observed. He constantly spoke to us of Mother as "Your Mammy," it is an ugly word, but it wasn't in his mouth. Aunt Mary had always called her nephews her Sirs, and the nieces whom she liked Queeny. Father, adopting it from her, usually called Mother Queeny, but for the first few years he also often used Asia. When he went to New York with Aunt Lizzy he saw his first nephew little William Emerson jr. not quite a year old and came back to tell Mother what a glorious little fellow he was with his fair skin and fine dark eyes. "We will set up a blue-eyed opposition," said Mother, but found, with some grief, that Father considered it presumptuous to hope for a child half so fine.

One day Father was going to Waltham to Uncle Ripley's and Mother having heard that one of Aunt Ripley's friends had a newborn baby advised Father to call upon it, for he had perhaps never seen a very little baby. When he came home she eagerly inquired "Did you see the baby?" "Yes," he replied with disgust, "it was nothing at all! It had neither hair nor teeth!" "But when his own baby came," Mother went on when she told me this, "it was quite a different story. He was only astonished that it had hands and feet." Mother's fourpost bedstead which she had inherited from Aunt Lucy had two sets of curtains[;] one was white dimity with ball fringe and one was coffee-coloured chintz with bright flowers. I suppose that she had used the chintz, but, when the time of her confinement drew near, she rigged the bed in all its white magnificence and put up white dimity window-curtains with fringe, to match, at her four windows. Grandma and she admired the fresh and handsome appearance of the whole room. But by & by up came Father. "What is all this?" he asked, and said it was too much parade. "So I took them all down and packed them away," she said, "and without any grief at all. 'Husband knows best' was my creed in those days, and I really thought he did. If he saw that it was unwise to have them, I didn't want them. The next time Mother came into the room she stopped, looked round surprised, and said 'Where are your curtains?' 'Waldo thought I had better take them down.' 'Why, my dear! You are very good!' said she. Aunt Lizzy afterward told me that I mustn't regard him as an oracle for my department; he couldn't be expected to know anything about the housekeeping. She thought I ought to have kept them up and probably he wouldn't have noticed them again,—very likely would have come to like them."

The baby came, his little head was all out of shape and he was indeed an ugly sight but Father could see only his perfections.[158] Aunt Lizzy hastened down to see him and brought him a rattle of silver bells with a mother-of-pearl handle. What should he be named? "Waldo," said Father, "the oldest son should always be named for his Father." Mother had thought he would of course be named for Uncle Charles Emerson. So had Aunt Lizzy. "I don't care anything about the baby now," she exclaimed with tears, "I never doubted that his name was Charles." But Father was immoveable, the eldest son should always be named for his Father. Little Waldo's head soon came right and Aunt Lizzy was not slow to learn to love him for his own sake. I thought Aunt Lucy had gone to Plymouth, but she hadn't, for she told me that Dr Ripley called and desired to see the child. She brought him down; Dr Ripley laid him on his knees, rolled him out of his blanket onto his face and proceeded to push down his little lownecked slip towards his shoulder-blades. Aunt Lucy thought Dr Ripley thought something was wrong about his attire and anxious & expecting to be mortified she drew near saying "What is it, Sir?" "I've been told," said Dr Ripley "that the child of this couple would probably have wings; and I'm looking to ascertain whether they have sprouted." He satisfied himself that they had not and returned the baby. In the course of time Father & Mother took Waldo to church and Dr Ripley christened him. He wore on the occasion the christening-dress of his Uncle Charles Chauncy Emerson for whom he was not named, and I believe his contemporaries Hersey Goodwin[159] & Elizabeth Cheney were christened with him. Aunt Susan Jackson gave him the silver cup Edward used, and Mrs Bliss gave him the one Edith used.

Mother had one lesson in housekeeping from Grandma which she never forgot, but it was most gently given. When Grandma was helped to meat one day she said "Is it lamb?" "Yes." "No I thank you" said Grandma, "I'm a little tired of lamb. I think we've had it rather often lately." Mother felt badly, she searched her mind, and could not recall having ordered beef. The moment she left the table she sent for the butcher's book. All up the last page was an even column leg of lamb

leg of lamb

She turned back. There was another whole page of it. She found that whenever she was asked what she would have from the butcher she had mechanically made the same answer. She at once began to set her wits to work. She read the Cook's Oracle[160] she visited the butcher's cart, she discovered that it was a good plan to ask the price beforehand, and soon became a good judge of meat and had variety, and smaller bills too. She was indignant at the butcher's tricks, at his calling anything at all over a pound a pound and a quarter; and at his invariably bringing in a pound or more over & above what she had ordered. On one occasion when she was sick in bed she found he had committed an unusually great sin of this kind. So she had him sent up to her door and talked very plainly to him through the crack, ending off "It isn't the money value that I care for, it is that I will not consent to be cheated." "Oh don't be afraid I shall lay it up against you," returned the butcher very pleasantly "I make it a rule never to lay things up." "Lay up!!!" cried Mother, amazed, "That is not what I am considering. What I say is that I will not allow you to cheat me." "I never lay things up," repeated the butcher, withdrawing. For forty years Mother stoutly withstood & endeavored to checkmate all the butchers & force them to honest dealing, but with limited success, for she always had a bill, and that gave them an advantage. Mother had a Concord man helping her in the garden, I think his name was Peter White. In the course of their talk Mother said something which caused him to suddenly turn round and stare, and stopping with his foot on his spade he informed her "Mr Emerson had seventy thousand dollars with his first wife and twenty thousand with you! I guess he's got enough." Mother concluded that all Concord regarded them as rich and very mean.[161]

I feel as if from this moment I shall have nothing to guide me as to the time when things happened and though by much labour in looking over letters and putting down memoranda I could straighten it out very much I have none of the letters here, and perhaps never shall have time, so they may be in most unchronological order.

Both Father & Mother were hospitably disposed, they had two guest-chambers and when Grandma went to N. Y. they had three, and many people besides their invited guests came to see them and were asked to spend the night. Nancy Colesworthy, the cook, said one day, "I'm going to put a poster out at the gate 'This House is not a Hotel.'[162] for folks to see when they come in." Mother's excellent Hitty was followed by a new chambermaid named Harriet who was very plain, and Nancy made merry about her want of beauty which seemed to impress her more powerfully than the rest of the family. Hearing someone speak of burglars she said "You needn't be afraid of anyone's entering this house. If I wake up and hear them trying any door, I'll light my lamp and look out of the window. I guess I'm ugly enough to scare 'em away by the sight of me. But if they don't run then I'll tell them I've got a sister in here as much uglier 'n I am, as I am than the rest of the world then if she should look out they'd say, like the Queen of Sheba, that the half hadn't been told 'em." Father & Mother loved to remember these smart speeches of Nancy and were sorry that no more had been preserved. She was a bright and sharp character and amused while she often displeased them. She never was reconciled to Mother and was very trying. Mother said "I did not treat her as she should have been treated. Non-resistance was a part of my Christian creed, and I carried it further than was wise. One day the study-door was open and your Father heard one of the servants answer me back impudently. Out he came, but she had already got away. "Lidian, send that woman instantly out of the house." But I told him I didn't mind it, I knew she was only out of temper and she would obey finally. I used to make excuses for them, I didn't for a long time see that I ought not to allow them to misbehave.[163] I think if I had managed Nancy as I ought she would never have gone away." I had heard Mother say these last words several times in reminiscences of early days before, some time in my teens, Mother and I met Nancy in Boston on Washington St., the only time Mother ever saw her after she left her service or I at all. They shook hands very cordially. "I have always regretted your leaving us," began Mother. "I never regretted it, Mrs Emerson, not for a moment," said Nancy briskly. "This is my eldest daughter," said Mother, "How do you do? You look exactly like your Mother" said Nancy to me. Mother then asked her about herself & N. told her what she was doing, and they parted.

One Sunday morning Mother found her June pinks had just opened and were beautifully fresh and fragrant. She gathered a little bunch and carried them up to Grandma as a present, asking her to admire them. "Yes, my dear, thankyou, they are very beautiful, but, my dear! it is Sunday!" Grandma hated to be ungracious, but she could not have the Sabbath broken.

At the time she came to live with us she was sixty-eight. She was a little bent, Mother thought it was because she often slept in her chair in the afternoon, it being against her principles to lie down. This made her shorter than Mother, but Mother said she always spoke of herself as tall. Her hair was hardly gray, brown & soft & fine. She sat chiefly in her arm-chair in her own room. Her usual occupation was sewing, sometimes for herself, sometimes for Uncle Bulkeley her deficient son, sometimes for Mother. She always sewed Father's sermon or lecture together for him. I have not said a word about Aunt Mary M[oody]. E[merson].[164] since her visit to Plymouth. I don't know how soon she began to come to our house, nor how often, but she began her usual course of conduct and found in intercourse with Mother a sensation wholly new to her. All her relations were more or less afraid of her, but here it was diamond cut diamond. Father & Grandma trembled when Mother answered her back and enjoyed the combat; and were astonished and most thankful to find that it was pure pleasure to Aunt Mary to find a foeman worthy of her steel. How they did fight! The earth shook under them! But Mother proved quite to Aunt Mary's taste, and when they weren't quarrelling they were of one mind and really affectionate. I remember several set-tos, Aunt Mary growing more and more violent, and Mother undismayed and laughing at her shafts. In the third autumn I think it was of their married life Father & Mother thought they would have a party, a large party. It stood in Mother's memory, I should say, as the largest and most serious social effort she ever made. Whenever anything recalled it she would say "Yes we gave a great party, and dear Cousin Elizabeth Ripley came over from Waltham and spent the whole day in the cellar freezing the ice-cream!" Her gratitude to Cousin Elizabeth for that labour was always in her mind. I never heard any word of how many came, what they did or whether they had a good time, but, from my infancy on, I heard always of dear Cousin Elizabeth's goodness, and once Mother & Aunt Lucy told that Mrs Bridge, Aunt Susan Jackson's Mother came to it— or may have been boarding in Concord—and had with her a coloured woman who was to assist our girls on the great occasion, yet the force seemed wholly inadequate to Mother's and Aunt Lucy's anxious mind. When lo! by the stage, the coloured woman's husband came up to see her, and she proposed to Mother that she should engage his services. Mother did. He was a handsome mulatto and proved to be a trained waiter with fine manners. He took right hold, showed such skill & experience that the load of responsibility rolled at once off from her & Aunt Lucy's shoulders and the man was the ornament of the occasion as well as a Capital manager, so that all the family felt he doubled the grandeur of the party.

I know Mother took Waldo to Plymouth and I think Father went to bring her home, but no details of the visit are in my mind. Waldo had got to creeping round—I think 'twas after the Plymouth visit. He investigated the feet of the tongs. Mother ran, and found his hands black. She told him he mustn't touch the tongs and holding his hand open she struck his palm three times with her forefinger. He took her hand and struck her in the same way three times.

Mother asked Father for some money to buy a hat for Waldo to wear—he said they really could not afford it but she found at the milliner's a little hat which a carpenter's wife had ordered for her baby & then having carried home decided she could not afford it &

She had about the curtains. The baby wore the cap. She wanted a baby-wagon of course, but Father declared it absolutely could not be afforded; which was true, but Mother's sanguine friend always trusted that, later, debts could be paid. She thought it absurd to go without important conveniences. One day a letter came from Uncle William in N. Y. saying that little Willy had graduated from his baby-wagon, and was sending it as a present to his cousin Waldo — had dragged it onto the boat himself, and it would arrive in Concord directly by express. This seemed a godsend indeed. It came. This was its shape. A basket-body large & deep painted green, a glazed green cambric hood on willow hoops immoveable; with small wheels and a straight heavy tongue. Such was our baby-wagon and I think it was the only one in town for years. I don't remember seeing any other before 1845, say, and then the same thing, but lighter &

smaller, painted wicker with yellow   138
cambric hoods on larger wheels. The little
1855 covered buggies appeared — ten years later
1870 ten years later still the perambulator
1890 and now we have the wicker chariot.
When Waldo was two he got hold of a lump
of sugar. Mother told him not to eat it now
but carry it to the table till supper-time.
He started, but instantly she heard behind
her "the crunch of the dear little teeth on the
sugar." She turned round and asked him if he
had bitten the sugar. He held it out of her
sight and said no. Then Mother said he trembled
It was his first sin, and a sense of its dreadfulness seemed to fill the little creature, and
Mother was much, much, impressed; it was
to her as if she beheld the fall of the angels.
Aunt Lizzy one day was in the East entry
waiting for him to come down stairs, he
stumbled and fell down the last four. I
don't remember whether he cried, but she said

brought it back to be sold & the milliner sold it for less than first price & so Mother took it, and from her "rag bag" made out an outfit for her baby's first appearance in Plymouth[.]

It was 1837 the time of a great financial crash. They became poorer than before. Father was very anxious about making both ends meet. His spirits were never high about money matters, it always looked to him as if we should be poorer & poorer to the end. It became necessary to provide the baby with a winter-cap. Of course Mother desired that he should look well-dressed. Father said he would have to go without. Mother turned over her pieces and made him a very pretty one of black velvet. But when she brought him to be admired Father disappointed her by saying he didn't like it, he would seem to the humbler people in town better dressed than their babies, he ought to be dressed like the poorest. To this Mother could not for a moment agree. It seemed to her unreasonable; she no longer did as she had about the curtains. The baby wore the cap. She wanted a baby-wagon of course, but Father declared it absolutely could not be afforded; which was true, but Mother's sanguine mind always trusted that, later, debts could be paid. She thought it absurd to go without important conveniences. One day a letter came from Uncle William in N. Y. saying that little Willy had graduated from his baby-wagon, and was sending it as a present to his cousin Waldo—had dragged it onto the boat himself, and it would arrive in Concord directly by express. This seemed a godsend indeed. It came. [See Sketch] This was its shape. A basket body large & deep painted green, a glazed green cambric hood on willow hoops immoveable; with small wheels and a straight heavy tongue. Such was our baby-wagon and I think it was the only one in town for years. I don't remember seeing any other before 1845, say, and then the same thing, but lighter & smaller, unpainted wicker with yellow cambric hoods on larger wheels. The little covered buggies appeared [See Sketch] ten years later fifteen years later still the perambulator [See Sketch] and now we have the wicker [See Sketch] chariot.[165] When Waldo was two he got hold of a lump of sugar. Mother told him not to eat it now but carry it to the table till supper-time. He started, but instantly she heard behind her "the crash of the dear little teeth on the sugar." She turned round and asked him if he had bitten the sugar. He held it out of her sight and said no. Then Mother said he trembled. It was his first sin, and a sense of its dreadfulness seemed to fill the little creature, and Mother was much, much, impressed; it was to her as if she beheld the fall of the angels. Aunt Lizzy one day was in the East entry waiting for him to come down stairs, he stumbled and fell down the last four. I don't remember whether he cried, but she said he turned round, climbed up those four stairs and came down them properly. He wished to do what he did well. In helping him at dinner, someone was careless and let his squash lie partly over his potato. This made him cry till, finding he couldn't be stopped, Father carried him out to the front gate to look at the clouds. He came back serene but when Father put him down in the high chair and he saw the dreadful contiguity of the squash and potato again he broke forth afresh in screams. I don't know how it ended. Mother always told this as a proof of his inborn love of propriety. It used to entertain Father & Mother to hear Grandma say to him after meals "Now jump down, Waldo, Grandma is going to jump down."

Mother asked Father questions about his first wife. In one of his journals he says "I had a long, long remembering talk with Lidian about Ellen, which brought back that delicious relation."[166] Mother once told me that I was happy in my name, that she hoped Ellen was my guardian angel. "Your Father gave me all her letters to read. She was a holy creature, truly religious."

One night she dreamed that she and Father were together in heaven and they met with Ellen and she went away and left him with her. She told Father in the morning, and he said "None but the noble dream such dreams." Mother had her pretty plan and I believe it was a profound secret. One day in February 1839 she had got every inch of her house and all her possessions in absolutely perfect order, but the barn had been neglected, and the weather being mild she went out and cleaned that up too most beautifully. We had no animals[.] I don't know what was in the barn. That night about ten o'clock she sent Father for doctor & nurse and called the two girls telling them the baby had sent compliments and they must come and help get ready. I believe she had not yet put up the curtains that were resigned so willingly when Waldo was born, but this time she meant to have them. The chambermaid was much frightened and wanted to sit and cry, but seeing Mother so busy and delighted she at last took hold and the curtains went up with expedition.

When the baby was born at six the next morning and Father came to see it Mother said "Her name is Ellen," and he was as much pleased as she had hoped.[167] Mother had told the girls the night before what to prepare for the gala breakfast, and all hands went down to enjoy it at once leaving Mother quite alone and the baby wrapped up in an eider-down under her work-table on the floor near the fire. "And I lay there hearing all your cunning little baby-noises," Mother always concluded the tale, with a smile of delight.

But what actions! How funny, when there were four people besides the girls, to leave Mother all alone, and how extremely queer to put the baby on the floor! We shouldn't think of doing so now. These are my later reflections. Mother didn't make them.

I think it was in this year that Mr Jones Very[168] came to Concord. Mother sympathized fully with him; and Aunt Lucy and she often recalled together the pleasures of his visits. They used to say he had been indeed restored to a state of childlike simplicity and always there was some speech like this "How he sat there with a piece of gingerbread in each hand, so innocent and unconscious! and how beautifully he was talking!" I think Miss Margaret Fuller made her first visit and that Mr [Bronson] Alcott[169] came too in this year, and Mother found both very interesting. She retained through life much sympathy with Mr Alcott, they were very good friends. She had visits from several of her Plymouth friends quite often in these times too. Once Mrs Captain Russell[170] the Mother of Miss Mary Howland Russell came and showed much interest in the house. Mother took her all over it, and let her see how and where she kept everything, and Mrs Russell not only approved but told her she had never seen a house in such order in her life. This compliment did Mother's very heart good, and she never forgot it. Whenever she spoke of it she said "And Mrs Russell was a capital housekeeper herself."

Father still belonged to the Cambridge Association of Ministers, and they met at our house I think three times, the last time in 1847. Mother used to relate that there were twenty of them who came to dinner, and the first time it met, three or four of the young men undertook to rise early and *walk* to Concord. They arrived about nine, very hungry, and she had to turn aside from dinner-preparations and get them a breakfast. "And I didn't mind in the least. I thought all these things pleasant in those days. I was able to do it and enjoyed it; but now! I wonder how I ever got along!" she would usually conclude.

Waldo was getting old enough to learn lessons, Grandma had taught him to read. Mother invited Cousin Mary Russell from Plymouth to come and spend a summer and teach him. She had a little school in an old shop building which stood between Sam Hoar's house & Mrs John Brown's;[171] and the Cheneys, the Lorings, the Goodwins,[172] Henry Frost, and Ellen Shattuck[173] I think, went to school to her as well as he. This is the time Father refers to in Threnody[174] "The school-march, each day's festival[.]" Cousin Mary was a most agreeable addition to the household. I think she stayed two years. *I* can remember being sorry when she went. On one occasion Waldo was to stay with the cook while the family were at church[175] on Sunday afternoon. He cried, when told of it, and explained "I do not want to go with Mrs Hill! Because she has red on her face and red on her arms, and she eats at a table which is not painted" (that is not mahogany) "and she is not beautiful." After dinner when it was time they said to him that he must be a good boy and remember that Mrs Hill was always very kind to him. "Yes," he said, "I have prayed a little prayer and now I think Mrs Hill beautiful." One day he said to Mother "Will you tell Ellen to hush? She makes such a noise that it makes my horse's head ache." As Mother once found him gazing at a spider crushed in the crack of a door she supposed he had just such feelings as she had at the sight and was picturing to himself the awful moment to the spider when he found there was no escape. So she hastened to comfort him, telling him the death was doubtless instantaneous and that she hoped the spider was now happy. The next time that we were sent out of doors together we reappeared almost immediately. Waldo with such an air of energy and importance and I looking so full of joyous anticipation that Mother said "Where are you going Waldo?" "Ellen has found a bug and we're going to make him happy?" "How?" "We're going to shut him in the crack of the door." Mother opened my hand and found a small beetle which she put out of the window and told us he would like that better. Once Waldo being out of the room I knocked down his house of blocks. Immediately he opened the door, saw what had happened and his face portended vengeance on me. Mother said I picked up two blocks as weapons and started for him, which made him laugh. Another time Mother heard me scream and looked in to see what was the matter. "Ellen got pushed," he said. One of our girls took him to see her Mother who gave him some cranberries. "I don't know whether Mamma would like to have me eat them," he said, and he didn't but they thought he wanted them very much.[176]

For five years Mother said she and Father were getting more & more married all the time, they were as happy as it was possible to be. Once she spoke of one of the letters he had first written to her and said he had expected more than she had proved to be. "You are worthy of any letter that could be written to you" he answered. Now began what Mother called Transcendental Times. Either now or earlier Father gave up family prayers. Mother and Grandma mourned together, and together read the Bible and a hymn for a long time. I remember that. Mother had always felt as if Father's & her religious views were the same, and, she said, had become "unconsciously warped" herself by him. Now it was clear to her that he was not a Christian in her sense of the word, and it was a most bitter discovery. All sorts of visitors with new ideas began to come to the house, the men who thought money was the root of all evil, the vegetarians, the sons of nature who did not believe in razors nor in tailors, the philosophers and all sorts of come-outers.[177] Mother's receipt-book is a sort of confirmation to the impression I received from her that she had a goodly family to cook for. All the receipts begin "take 3 pts. of sour milk," or "beat 2 doz. eggs[.]" They are all of three times the quantity that we have cooked since I had charge. She used to say "Poor Grandma and I were never half through eating our meat before the whole company of Grahamites,[178] having bolted their potatoes and squash and beans, were sitting looking hungrily for the pudding, which to them was the main dinner. Grandma was a very slow eater and it was uncomfortable for her."

One day a certain new light arrived in the morning, and in the course of conversation mentioned that he was going in the afternoon stage (which always went at three, I think) for he must be in Boston that night. In due time Father heard the stage approaching, and supposed his guest had told it to stop, but, as he showed no sign of taking leave, Father rose and said "Here comes the stage, I'll stop it for you." By this time it had passed. Father darted from the door, gave chase and caught it. [I]t stopped at last and the guest, who meanwhile had got his hat and was ambling after Father, ascended and departed. Mother who had watched all with sympathy and infinite amusement from her window, looked over the banisters when Papa came in and said "How you did run! You flew! There was zeal—and desperation—in it!" "Yes," laughed Father, "my running was like the running of Ahimaaz the son of Zadok."[179] "I could see that you were running for liberty—that you saw clearly that 'twas your only chance of saving the rest of the day, and tomorrow." Father and she always remembered it.

I should imagine that Mother somewhat overdrew the number and the queerness of Father's visitors but that Aunt Lizzy called them "Waldo's Menagerie," and she said to me after I grew up "Oh! when I looked into the parlour one day and saw him sitting in that circle,— it gave me a feeling of horror-men with long beards, men with bare feet"—

One gentleman said that his principles forbade him to use money, so that though he was in need of a handkerchief he could not provide himself with one. Mother got him one of Father's[.] Another who was spending the night came to Mother just after he had gone to his room to tell her there was a wasp on his bed. She went up with him and took it up on a handkerchief to throw out of the window. "Poor creature! Poor creature! Don't hurt him!" cried the guest. Mother thought his anxiety turned in the wrong direction.

At tea-time one night Mother offered one of these gentlemen a cup of tea "Tea! I!!" he exclaimed. The next minute Father undertook to help him to butter. "Butter! I!!" he exclaimed again.

One of the philosophers wrote after going away that he had fallen in love with a most estimable young lady and they wished to marry but she was in delicate health and they both were poor. Would Father send them a competence?

Another sent a letter setting forth that he needed more education but could not pay for it, would Father enclose to him the money? He "should like it the last of this week or the fore part of next."

I should say this kind of company passed away before long, and was succeeded by another set, among them people whom Father and Mother loved and enjoyed, people who were friends all the rest of their lives.

There were some who ceased soon to come but those whom I remember as visiting Concord often between 1840 & 1845 were Mr [Charles King] Newcomb, Miss Fuller, Miss Caroline Sturgis, Mr Alcott and Mr [Charles] Lane, and occasionally Dr Hedge, Mr William Henry Channing, Mr Caleb Stetson and once or twice Mr Sam Ward & Mr Christopher Cranch.[180] Uncle George Bradford and Mr Thoreau were always constant visitors.

The talk began to be of a kind which we can guess at from Mother's "Transcendental Bible," a document which pleased Father and which was mentioned often. I always in childhood dumbly wondered what it was that Mother would speak of by that name and Father called "The Queen's Bible." He always laughed when he thought of it. In their old age I one day discovered the paper. It is on a sheet of square paper written with pencil by Mother as she lay on her bed when she was staying one day at Uncle Charles Jackson's. She brought it home and read it to the circle in the parlour. I think it should come in here.

"Whole Duty of Man.

Never hint at a Providence, Particular or Universal. It is narrow to believe that the Universal Being concerns itself with particular affairs, egotistical to think it regards your own. Never speak of sin. It is of no consequence to "the Being" whether *you* are good or bad. It is egotistical to consider it yourself; who are you?

Never confess a fault. You should not have committed it and who cares whether you are sorry?

Never speak of Happiness as a consequence of Holiness. Do you need any bribe to well-doing? Cannot you every hour practise holiness for its own sake? Are you not ashamed to wish to be happy? It is egotistical—mean.

Never speak of the hope of Immortality. What do you know about it? It is egotistical to cling to it. Enough for the great to know that "Being" Is. He is quite content to drop into annihilation at the death of the body.

Never speak of affliction being sent and sent in kindness; that is an old wives' fable. What do you know about it? And what business is it of ours whether it is for our good or not?

Duty to your Neighbour

Loathe and shun the sick. They are in bad taste, and may untune us for writing the poem floating through our mind.

Scorn the infirm of character and omit no opportunity of insulting and exposing them. They ought not to be infirm and should be punished by contempt and avoidance.

Despise the unintellectual, and make them feel that you do by not noticing their remark and question lest they presume to intrude into your conversation.[181]

Abhor those who commit certain crimes because they indicate **stupidity,** want of intellect which is the one thing needful.

Justify those who commit certain other crimes. Their commission is consistent with the possession of intellect. We should not judge the intellectual as common men. It is mean enough to wish to put a great mind into the strait-jacket of morality.

It is mean and weak to seek for sympathy; it is mean and weak to give it. Great souls[182] are self-sustained and stand ever erect, saying only to the prostrate sufferer "Get up, and stop your complaining." Never wish to be loved.[183] Who are you to expect that? Besides, the great never value being loved.

If any seek to believe that their sorrows are sent or sent in love, do your best to dispel the silly egotistical delusion.

If you scorn happiness (though you value a pleasant talk or walk, a tasteful garment, a comfortable dinner) if you wish not for immortal consciousness (though you bear with impatience the loss of an hour of thought or study) if you care not for the loss of your soul (though you deprecate the loss of your house) if you care not how much you sin (though in pain at the commission of a slight indiscretion) if you ask not a wise Providence over the earth in which you live (although wishing a wise manager of the house in which you live) if you care not that a benign Divinity shapes your ends (though you seek a good tailor to shape your coat) if you scorn to believe your affliction cometh not from the dust (though bowed to the dust by it) then, if there is such a thing as duty, you have done your whole duty to your noble self-sustained, impeccable, infallible Self.

If you have refused all sympathy to the sorrowful, all pity and aid to the sick, all toleration to the infirm of character, if you have condemned the unintellectual and loathed such sinners as have discovered want of intellect by their sin, then are you a perfect specimen· of Humanity.

Let us all aspire after this Perfection! So be it.

Abstract of New Bible"

When I found this I brought it down into the Study and read it in the evening to Father and Mother. Father laughed all the way through and said "Yes, it was a good squib of your Mammy's." Mother at once fell into the strain of it and made a few remarks on those views and those times.

But to return to the company of which I was speaking, Mother really valued, and had some intimacy with, Miss Fuller and Miss Sturgis, and Mr Newcomb even more; and Mr Alcott, Uncle George and Mr Thoreau were to her near personal friends. The other gentlemen she liked very well but they cared especially for Father. Miss Fuller brought Miss Anna Barker[184] once. Father had seen her and was delighted that she was coming. He told Waldo that a Beautiful Lady would arrive tomorrow—said so much about it that Waldo and Mother were worked up to great expectations.

They met her in the East entry when she came. She exclaimed, "Is this little Waldo? Really?" She stooped to kiss him, but he backed. "I'm afraid of the Beautiful Lady. I'm afraid of her curls," he said to Mother after Miss Barker had gone into the redroom. That visit was occupied chiefly in walking and driving and Mother lost most of it.

In 1841 Mother waked to a sense that she had been losing—had lost—that blessed nearness to God in which she had lived so long, and she never regained it. Her religion was still the foundation of her life, but its fulness was gone.

"She gleaned a berry here & there
But mourned the vintage past"

As I have said before, she was always more sensitive to suffering than to happiness, now this became more true of her than ever before. She read the papers faithfully and their pro-slavery tone made her hate her country. She learned all the horrors of slavery and dwelt upon them, so that it was as if she continually witnessed the whippings and the selling away of little children from their mothers.[185] She joined the Anti-Slavery Society and remained a zealous member till Slavery was abolished.

Her health was worse than before, her old griefs and anxieties about animals returned. I shall a little later enter upon the subject of her sad thoughts once more, and to me it seemed that for the next thirty years sadness was the ground-colour of her life, but it was not unrelieved.[186] Many rays of kindness and gratitude illumined her path. Father often rejoiced her weary spirit. I remember one pretty story which she told me. One day when Miss Fuller had been staying with us and departed in the stage Father said to Mother

> "Happy—happier far than thou
> With the laurel on thy brow—
> She who makes the humblest hearth
> Happy but to one on earth."[187]

that seemed to Mother very sweet.

Again, when Aunt Lizzy had invited our household to spend the evening at her house to hear Miss Jane Tuckerman[188] sing, (and, Mother, as usual, not being ready in season, they went off without her), as she came crawling after, weak and forlorn, and reached Squire Hoar's gate, Sarah Hoar, now Mrs Storer,[189] ran out to meet her, threw her arms round her and kissed her. It was heavenly balm to her. She never forgot it. At this time she made acquaintance with Miss Sarah Searle of Brookline, a Swedenborgian lady[190] who came very near to her heart and gave her more sympathy and consolation than she had had from anyone for a long time, a Christian who knew what real religion was, so that they understood each other's language. I think it was at her suggestion that Mother took up Swedenborg, read some of his books and for many years regularly the New Jerusalem magazine. She made a visit to Plymouth and carried me. She was delighted there to find that a set of the young ladies had "made a paction[191] 'twixt themselves" to reduce each her expenditure to $100. a year that they might give all the rest of their income to the Anti-Slavery Society, and that some people had given up rice and sugar & molasses because they were products of slave-labour. She returned prouder than ever of her native town, "good old Plymouth." In this year 1841 she seemed so feeble that Aunt Lizzy thought she ought to make a journey. Aunt Lizzy offered to go with her (I believe to pay all the expenses) to Staten Island to stay some weeks with Uncle W*m* and Aunt Susan Emerson. On the way they stopped at a tavern to dine and as they walked into the parlour Mother found a picture looking at her which made her start. It seemed to her a good portrait of her Father. It was a head of Gen. Andrew Jackson. Aunt Lizzy was a most affectionate and attentive companion, and the journey and visit did Mother good.

Then she had as much delight in her babies as most Mothers. She took Waldo and me to Boston to Aunt Adams's once. Aunt Adams pronounced me the cleanest baby she ever saw, "as clean as ice," and gratified Mother infinitely. Waldo standing beside her and gazing round at the handsome parlour, finally smiled to Mother his sense of its beauty and said "How glass their Knobs are!"

He, assisted by Mr Thoreau, was engaged at home in making me a watch and had various glorious plans for my delight. He meant some day to build me a house with "interspiglions," which was something very stately and attractive evidently in his imagination[.] No one knew exactly what the word meant; it was of his own invention. He moreover planned a clock for me which he said when it struck would "be heard all over the house, all over the yard, all over the world," and he seemed to be listening in his imagination to its strong tones. He had been, Mother thought, much like other children till he was nearly five. Then he seemed wiser and more angelic all the time. In the October, I should think it was, of 1841 came the first travelling daguerreotypist to Concord. Mr John Thoreau offered to take Waldo to have his daguerreotype taken.[192] It needed in those days a blaze of sunlight which made Waldo frown; otherwise it was good. Father, Mother and Aunt Lizzy also went and had their likenesses taken. Mr Wm. Ellery Channing,[193] I know not how, possessed himself of Father's. I have never seen it, but he gave Edward a cabinet-photograph of its head and I have it. Mother's and Aunt Lizzy's were very bad and they rubbed them out. I never saw them either. Ten years later, when daguerreotyping had advanced and the plates were much smoother and better, Mother had Waldo's copied, and the copy I still have. We had both it and the original till Edward who was accustomed only to photographs and little knew the nature of the daguerreotype, seeing it dusty, removed its glass and wiped it with a soft cloth. He was dismayed to find no trace of Waldo left, only a bare silver plate.[194] On the 21 Nov. Father told Mother he was going to Boston the next day. In the morning she said she thought he would be welcomed by a new baby when he came home. He had to go, though he was very sorry to leave her. At five o'clock in the afternoon Edith was born.[195] When Mother heard the stage stop, she said "Part her hair and brush it before her Father sees

By permission of the Houghton Library, Harvard University

Waldo Emerson

her." "There isn't any to part," was the reply. Edith was a beauty with the fairest rose-leaf complexion. Her Aunt Lizzy was enchanted the next morning, when she came to see her, and on the following day brought the Misses Prichard down that she might exhibit her to them. What was her disappointment to find the baby had turned bright yellow! It was some days before she Edith recovered her pretty colour. The day that Mother left her room after this confinement, she came out into the upper front entry. The first thing that met her eye was the dust thick on the frames of all the pictures there. She at once inferred that her whole house had been neglected and looked frowsy and forlorn, and that the girls had been unfaithful. There was company in the house, had been when the baby was born, & ever since which made such a state of things more grievous. She began to cry. Aunt Lizzy came in & finding her so unhappy asked anxiously what was the matter. Aunt Lizzy heard very kindly and understandingly, and then said "But, Lidian, think! How transitory these things are!" and Mother was at once able to rise above it by the help of this wise and tender sister.

Mother had a dream which she told to Aunt Lizzy suggested by the difficulties she experienced with her housekeeping. She thought she had died and was in her coffin which had been deposited in the parlour all ready for the funeral, but the room needed brushing up and the chambermaid and nursery-girl came to sweep it. Mother felt the hour for the funeral fast approaching and was dismayed to see the girls stop sweeping, lean on their brooms, talk and get into a frolic quite regardless of the flight of time. At last she could stand it no longer, she sat up and said "The people will be here in a few minutes! Make haste! you can hardly get the room swept before they come!" Her anxiety waked her. Aunt Lizzy when we were grown referred to it,—"Just as you sat up to dust your own coffin yourself at the last minute in your dream, Lidian,"—"No, no," said Mother, "I didn't dust my coffin"— and she told over the dream, which otherwise I shouldn't have known of.[196]

There was great difficulty about finding a name for Edith. They wished to name her Ruth for Grandma. Grandma would not consent, she did not like the name. Father then wished to name her Asia for Mother. Mother would not consent, she did not like the name. At last Sophia Brown suggested Edith, and that suited everybody's taste. It was a name then almost unknown. Mother always told us Edith was far the most charming baby she ever had, the prettiest and the cunningest. Her nurse Louisa Snow called her her gold robin and often exclaimed as she held her up and admired her "There never was a baby before!" Mother called her Dovelet and White Dove, as she had called me her Angel Pussy. Grandma and Father also appreciated Edith's unusual charms. I remember standing beside Waldo, looking at the baby in the cradle with him, he on his knees, the cradle at the foot of Mother's bed, which then stood with the head to the W. wall of the room. I think this is my earliest memory of him. There are only two more, viz. once I remember running about with him and Bingo, our little dog, in the East yard, the other is after he was already sick with the Scarlet Fever seeing him sitting up in the trundlebed in his night gown, unwilling to take the castor-oil. He had gone to church with Father the Sunday before 23 Jan. 1842. It was the first Sunday the meeting-house had been opened after being remodelled. Mother thought he had caught cold there which made the fever so severe. I believe it came on the next day. On the 27*th*, Thursday, he was delirious. Mother left him to take a little rest but they came for her saying he called her persistently. He didn't recognize her, but the sound of her voice quieted him. Doctor Bartlett was there and she asked him if he would soon be better[.] "I had hoped to be spared this," was his answer. Mother understood. She had not thought before of losing the child. He died some hours later. I was already coming down with the fever, and Mrs Keyes, Annie's Grandmother[197] came right to the house and offered to take charge of me. I was "screaming most discordantly" Mother said but Madam Keyes sat down by me saying "I want to tell you about a little kitty" in such a sweet & cheering tone that I concluded to keep still and listen. She kept me amused or asleep all night. They told Mother afterwards that the day of Waldo's death Dr Bartlett walked from patient to patient making gestures of despair, thinking of Waldo, he was so sorry for Father. That night as the baby lay on Mother's lap by the fire in her room she kept stretching 'way over to look at something behind her little head and smiling most brightly at it. [See Sketch] There was nothing there but the bedstead. Mother hoped it was the angel Waldo smiling to his innocent little sister still able to see him. Another time a few days later I started and listened and asked "What was 'at 'at said Ah?" "I didn't hear it," said Mother. "I fought it was an angel in e corner of e room."

Some school-children knocked at Aunt Lizzy's door to ask "Did you know Waldo Emerson died last night?" It was a sharp blow to Aunt Lizzy. She came at once to Father and Mother. Waldo's face as he lay dead had an expression Mother said "as if he were taking a long, long look into Eternity." They were at dinner the day of the funeral when the door from the front entry into the dining-room opened and dear Aunt Susan Jackson came in with such a look of sympathy as

that I concluded to keep still and listen. 160
She kept me amused or asleep all night. They
told Mother afterwards that the day of Waldo's
death Dr Bartlett walked from patient to patient
making gestures of despair, thinking of Waldo,
he was so sorry for Father. That night as the
baby lay on Mother's lap by the fire
in her room she kept stretching
way over to look at something behind
her little head and smiling most
brightly at it. There was nothing there but
the bedstead. Mother hoped it was the angel
Waldo smiling to his innocent little sister
still able to see him. Another time a few
days later I started and listened and asked
"What was 'at 'at said Ah?" "I didn't hear
it," said Mother. "I fought it was an angel
in e corner of e room".
Some school-children knocked at Aunt Lizzy's
door to ask "Did you know Waldo Emerson
died last night?" It was a sharp blow to
Aunt Lizzy. She came at once to Father
and Mother. Waldo's face as he lay dead
had an expression Mother said as if he

broke Mother down. Aunt Susan had just lost her little Susy. Everyone mourned with them and gave them the sense that their loss was understood and shared. Miss Margaret Fuller had felt like Father that this child had been born to lift higher his fellow men.[198] She could not get over it that he had died and I was left. He was buried in Doctor Ripley's tomb, but after our lot in the new cemetery was bought Father removed the coffin there and had him buried with his family. He said he had looked into the coffin but he said no more.[199] I have omitted one story. When Dr Ripley died he looked majestic & noble. Waldo, taken to see him walked round & round the couch, and at last asked "Why don't they keep him for a statue?" Mother said when he liked to see anything he would gaze and keep winking and by and by a slow smile would come. I asked Mother whether God wouldn't be willing to stay alone with the angels a little while and let Waldo come down and play with me.

A mile further from Concord on our road lived Mr Edmund Hosmer, a farmer of the oldest Concord stock, who became a friend of Father's. Each interested the other every time they met. He had[200] ten children, four sons. The youngest boy was five, Waldo's age. Father & Mother liked his face, they began to wish they had him and considered very seriously asking Henry Hosmer of his parents and adopting him as their own, but they did not. Mother went often to see Mrs Hosmer, who, unassisted, was doing all the work for the family of thirteen (for her husband's insane father, himself a great care lived with them) and making thirty pounds of butter a week to sell. Mother asked "What *do* you do when the two-year-old and the year-old and the little baby are all crying at once?" "I have to *let* them cry," was the answer. At one of the evening Conversations Mr Alcott was holding at our house he proposed that Mr Hosmer should do—I forget what—and, to Mother's surprise, Mr Hosmer answered, "I couldn't do it, I don't have time. Mrs Hosmer has nothing to do, perhaps she would."

But on another occasion when Mr Lane, who was exhorting the company to study and meditate that their souls might grow, turned to Mr Hosmer and said, "You ought not to spend your days ploughing behind your oxen. You ought to withdraw into solitude & cultivate your mind," Mr Hosmer's reply, "I don't know what Mrs Hosmer would say to that," made Mother forgive him for his former remark. Mother was much interested in all the remarkably bright and strong children of this couple. She gave them books every New Years, and invited them into her garden, and they all loved her and brought her bouquets of the rarest wild-flowers, which bouquets always seemed to me the most beautiful things I ever saw. They say now that they used to come right into the house, run up the E. stairs and knock at her door, and feel proud and pleased that they didn't have to knock at the outside door. They picked berries in summer and she used to buy them. Their affection for her as long as she lived was a comfort to her. There was a school house across the road from us till 1876 or perhaps later. Lizzy Weir[201] says Mother used to ask one of the school-children after school to take her baby out and she often heard one of the Hosmers, or some other child, say, "I'm going to draw the baby." It seemed to her a most delightful amusement, and she longed for the privilege. At last she thought, "Why not try?" and with her heart beating went over & knocked at the East door. Louisa Snow, Edith's nurse, came down. "Can I draw the baby?" Lizzy asked wondering at her own presumption. To her relief Louisa at once said yes, and asked her up into the nursery while she got Edith ready. Lizzy had never seen Mother[.] While Louisa was putting on Edith's coat Mother came in. It seemed to Lizzy that one of the Immortals had floated into the room. "I never had imagined anything like her," Lizzy said, "she seemed a vision." Mother was at once throned as a Goddess in Lizzy's mind, and her seeming pleased that she wanted to draw the baby an amazing indulgency. From that moment Lizzy and all her family became a part of our life. Mother loved them and they one and all loved and looked up to her. One of Lizzy's sisters says that after her first visits to our house Mother seemed the natural resource in case of difficulty and to this day when she has a bad dream of being pursued by man or beast she always runs, in it, for our house. Lizzy was engaged, after Waldo's death, to lead me to school (for I was three and in those days children began school at that age). She tells me it was trying work for I was strong and wilful. Aunt Lizzy told me that one morning Lizzy Weir knocked at her door and asked her to please see if she could get Ellen along for Ellen wouldn't stir. Aunt Lizzy followed her till they reached me seated in the road.

One morning one of the babies a little over a year old escaped from the nursery all naked and of course trotted—more probably staggered—right across the upper East entry and into Mother's room while Father was shaving. He was in ecstasies at the sight. "Oh! waves of marble! waves of marble!" he cried. "See what you lose by not dressing your children yourself!"

He used to be very sportive and poetical always when he was upstairs with Mother. I saw in one of his journals "A man needs a wife to be silly unto," and he fully enjoyed the privilege himself. I remember he once broke forth

> "How beautiful in the morning is the human race
> Getting up to breakfast"—

and there stopped short, his inspiration not carrying him further. When Mother had waited a minute and saw no more was coming, she took up the strain

> "Head foremost tumbling
> Out of bed, grumbling
> They wash their face and neck first."

It charmed Louisa Snow when she first came to our house to hear Father call in the East entry. "The dinner waits, O Queen!" and Mother answer[ed] "One moment, O King, and I will come."

Mother one night thought she was making too many impatient ejaculations as she was trying to clear up her room and go to bed "I scold because I's cold—ice-cold!" she apologized.

Miss Margaret Fuller at this time held Conversations[202]—I think in the forenoon—in Boston. Mother liked to go, and the stage left Concord at 7. She loved to recall that she used to get up before light on those winter mornings, jump into her tub of cold water and take a fearfully cold bath, and be dressed and ready to go in that 7 o'clock stage.

When the snow fell thick on the fir-balsams and we looked out at it from the nursery-window they used to say to us "Oh the white rabbits have come! See, there is one on every bough," and the upper boughs used to look very much like white rabbits. The outline of Fairyland woods against the sky used to be [See Sketch] like this and was pointed out to us—"Don't you see it looks like some ferocious monster plunging through bushes?" Indeed it had an active-looking line. This that I have drawn looks sleepy. I think the upper part of the hill was covered with pines, and there were round-topped deciduous trees on this side of them.

As one approached Mr Heywood's house from town two of his great elms struck Father & Mother as forming a mighty mastodon. I never could be made to see it, but "the Mastodon" used to be spoken of in spring as "Coming in sight," as "perfect today" as "better than ever." "Did you look at the mastodon as you came along?" This perplexed me a long time. I think I was in my teens before it was so explained to me that I understood. The Fitchburg R.R. was opened in 1844. They used to talk about it with much interest and cheerful anticipation. Later the tone changed and I heard words shocking and sad. I asked at last, "Father what makes the railroad grow worse?" Everyone laughed and Father assured me that it hadn't, that they were talking of accidents that had happened on other railroads. I put this in because it was at

When the snow fell thick on the fir-balsams
and we looked out at it from the nursery-
window they used to say to us "Oh the white
rabbits have come! See, there is one on every
bough." and the upper boughs   used to
look very much like white.   rain's.
The outline of Fairyland woods against the
sky used to be
like this and was pointed out to us—Don't
you see it looks like some ferocious monster
plunging through bushes? Indeed it had an
action-looking line. This that I have drawn looks
sleepy. I think the upper part of the hill was
covered with pines, and there were round-topped
deciduous trees on this side of them.
As one approached Mr Heywood's house from
town two of his great elms struck Father & Mother
as forming a mighty mastodon. I never could be
made to see it, but "the mastodon" used to be
spoken of in spring as "coming in sight", as "perfect
today" as "better than ever". Did you look at the

the same time and caused me the same wonder as the mastodon, about which I have not quite finished. The people who talked were Father, Mother, Grandma, Aunt Lizzy, Uncle George Bradford & Mr Thoreau. Who discovered the rabbits, the monster and the mastodon I don't know, I imagine Cousin Mary Russell saw the first for us and that Mother discerned the other two. She was always quick to notice effects of light and shade that made a figure. Many a time she'would call us to look at profiles made by the shadow of a valance. Aunt Lucy sometimes reproached us children for our light and silly talk at table. "It seems such a shame!" she said, "When I think of the conversation I used to hear at this table when your Father and his friends did the talking, it seems as if I could not bear the change. It was always the finest till you rose up to usurp it." We saw that this was true, yet it did not seem our fault. It had come about of itself.

Mother always had a New Year's visit from the school. At least though I don't know when the invitation was first sent, I imagine that it was in 1836 on the first New Years. In my earliest memory the children and teacher came and knocked mightily at the East door, Mother went down followed by Louisa Snow both carrying cake baskets with little books and candy images in them and a basket of apples. As Mother opened the door the children with one voice shouted Happy New Year! and Mother answered them, then gave each child a candy image, a book, & an apple she standing on the threshold. In forty years there were changes. I remember their coming into the East entry sometimes, sometimes into the dining-room, for the last twenty years into the parlour. The books changed finally to papers of sugar-plums, pewter things sometimes to pencils, but the candy-images never changed, nor, of course the apple. Mother usually made an address against bird's-nesting or tormenting kittens or some other thing which she hated to have them do. Often they sang to her. The children enjoyed these times as much as she desired. How many grown up and even elderly people have told me that it used to be a festival which marked the winters! This was never omitted. But when the school moved away to the Emerson School the custom died.[203]

Whenever Mother's garden looked to her unusually gay with flowers, she used to send the teacher an invitation to bring the school over to walk in the garden as soon as lessons were done. She of course wasn't always ready, but they waited at the East door for her and when she came they followed her round the walks. Those children who loved flowers liked this particularly, I have often heard this mentioned too. And all of them were pleased with the little event because it was out of the every day course.

One of Mother's talents was making something out of nothing and there was room to afford it great play. Her house must be handsome and her children must be well dressed, these were necessities to Mother's mind while Father considered both as less important. Every rag of remains of her days of fine dressing was used in one way and another with great ingenuity till there was nothing left of it. Every garment by judicious alterations could be made to serve a second term. So whenever Mother saw an opportunity she spread out the wearing out things and the stores in the bundle-trunk and devised intricate plans, having Louisa Snow and her successors & often a seamstress at hand to baste as fast as she could arrange the pieces. This was more or less perplexing and nervous work, it took time, and space too, and it was usually interrupted just too soon, just before the scheme which at last was clear before her mind could be "materialized," as people say now, by actual cutting and basting. Something perhaps was accomplished, but another hour would have made her able to leave the work ready for the seamstress to go on without her. It must be bundled right out of the way and wait till a convenient season, when, practically, her part had to be done all over again. This Mother never could endure with philosophy, it seemed everytime as if it was a trial she had never experienced before. To our infant minds this serious tragedy which we couldn't understand was very painful. One day Aunt Lizzy came to see us and meeting me down stairs asked "Where's your Mother?" "Oh, she's fixing her rags," I answered with a heavy sigh. Aunt Lizzy was amused. She told Mother of it, and Mother used often to quote it. Bad as this was it was slight compared with the carpet-business which began when our first strong old-fashioned carpets wore out. I don't know whether Mother didn't know there were professional carpet-women or whether she felt we couldn't afford to get them. Mother attended to every piecing personally, and she suffered extremely over it, too, for many years. She often had a feeling of satisfaction when the work was accomplished. "There, the house is all carpeted now and will look well for a year at least, and I've saved your Father a good many dollars. I believe most housekeepers would have thought those carpets fit for nothing but burning." Almira Flint[204] the daughter of one of our Concord farmers came to sew for us and told me afterwards that Mother taught her how to do many things by telling her how, and simply expecting her to do it; she made her a carpenteress, an upholsteress, a paper-hanger, a dress-maker. Almira had naturally a true eye and a skilful hand, a spirit also that hated to give up, so she wouldn't say I can't, so she and Mother were always triumphant together over many successes. And then Almira having papered a room for us went home and papered her Mother's parlour. Every economy and skill that she learned of Mother she used at home.

Kate Sally, a seamstress who lived with us five years, was married when she left us. She had six children. One day twenty years after her marriage she said, "When one of my children wears out a coat; I always think 'Oh dear! I wish I had never lived with Mrs Emerson! Then I could throw it away. I don't want to fuss with it!' But after I've made it over into a little coat just as good and strong as a new one, I say 'Well, I'm glad I lived with Mrs Emerson, and learned how things ought to be made over.'" Economy was natural to Mother. She wished everything to serve all the purpose it could. She was, as naturally, magnificent and generous. Aunt Lizzy was right when she said "Your Mother should have been an Empress. She could have spent millions and spent them wisely. She never would have wasted a cent." She was not an anxious person and felt as certain that we should come out solvent as Father felt uncertain. Accordingly when she saw, and her eyes seem to have been always sure to see wherever it might be, a piece of solid mahogany furniture that was just what she wanted selling cheap at second-hand she hesitated not to buy it. Father would groan, but it always could be paid for, and it gave her real content ever after. Often Father came to like it and praise it too. I am glad she did this. It seems to me it was worthwhile. Her economy did not lie in going without. Father owned that that was his kind of economy, the only kind he could believe in or imagine. To her economy was a large science with many intricate and minute ramifications. She knew she was practising a vigilant and severe, yea an active and inventive economy in all departments of her housekeeping and it grieved her that Father far from appreciating it really thought her recklessly and even cruelly extravagant. One of her rules was, "All the Indian meal & rye which you can put on your table, in such a form that your household will gladly choose it, saves just so much Graham meal & flour which cost twice as much." This is no longer quite true, as flour & Graham are less expensive than in her day. Another was, "Never use rice where Indian meal will do, nor macaroni where rice will do." Another was "There is no need of throwing any clean crumb away. Everything can be utilized." Mother's mind was inventive, she knew a little chemistry, and never failed to catch the chemical ground of every kind of cooking. Accordingly her mind easily noted the correctness, the folly, and the trivialities that appeared in each receipt as she read it, and she accepted the first, rejecting or changing the others. We believe she never used a receipt as it was given to her, she instantly devised one based on it that was more economical or better or easier. At first she wrote out her own receipt-book, but, ever after I was old enough to know, she made up every receipt afresh every day. These were usually wise and good, but there were points which she would have modified if she had had experience in the actual cooking.

Though she hated them, she bought when the time came that she had to buy for us, remnants of coarse cotton-&-wool delaines and we were dressed in them. They seldom suited her taste, but if she did find a pretty one she was very happy over it. We never had a cotton dress nor white stockings, except for best after we began to wear colours, nor a cotton apron, and Mother didn't have them herself; a calico, a cambric, a muslin, didn't come into the house in ten years, because they needed washing. In winter we had blue merino best dresses once or twice, and Aunt Susan Emerson sent us a plaid dress apiece at New Years when I was six and again when I was twelve. The year I was eleven she sent Mother and each of us a beautiful woollen barege. I have always remembered mine as one of my handsomest dresses. In winter our doors had laths wound with green baize nailed round them to batten the cracks; and to make a further rampart against the cold, a four-leaved green baize screen some six feet high was set up round the table in the dining-room and always stood there in winter. An air-tight stove was invented at last. I think Mother, who liked inventions, must have bought one immediately for Grandma's room, then one for the nursery, I think we had one there by 1840. In 1844 or 5 she bought one for every room in the house, gave up open fire-places and Father was comfortable for the first time in his life. He always hated cold. They didn't carefully shut the outside doors, the East door and the Front door stood open and Mother who didn't mind cold at all and believed that fresh air meant not only health but wits had all the doors inside the house and all the chamber windows open at night even in winter. She made it her last care to see that both the kitchen doors were open so that the blast might[205] tear freely down the front stairs, the East stairs and the backstairs and that kitchen, dining-room, parlour, redroom & above all study might get a thorough airing all night. How often have I heard her exult in the thought of the pure atmosphere she thus provided for her family! It did very well when five airtights began early every morning to raise the temperature. But in 1852 we had a furnace. Deluded that we were, we expected now a paradise of warmth and comfort. Mother sold several airtights[;] the others were put in the barn. Father kept his in the study. Before we had suffered through one winter, all the airtights left were in place and active service again, only the parlour & dining-room were without. We were never very comfortable in those rooms either on cold days. Still the outside doors were freely left open. In the autumn of 1867 Uncle William came to spend the winter in Concord and often called on Father. After the first of November he made it a rule to close the front door behind him when he entered, then to march through the entries and close the East door, after which he would remove his hat and go to the Study. He usually opened conversation by advising that our doors be kept shut in this savage weather. At first we smiled at his views but they gradually prevailed, and now it seems to us a self-evident first necessity to keep the doors shut if we want the house warm. Mother's nocturnal practice of airing it continued in full force six or seven years longer. In 1878, I think it was, a cook complained of it to her and said it was something frightful to come down from her cold room to a kitchen colder still, that she shut it up tight every night and left a fire hoping to find it would keep warm till morning, but always found both doors open and a draught of outdoors air through. Mother perceived the reasonableness of Margaret's complaint, and ceased to open the kitchen doors, but otherwise made no change. She slept with two windows open all winter till the last winter of her life, when her nurse found she no longer thought of it, and gave her less outside air. Mother's hands were always so hot that she left a door-handle warm just by turning it. I have often known in this way that she must have just passed through a door I was opening. In 1842 or 3[206] the Hawthornes came to the Old Manse, just married, and Mr William Ellery Channing married Miss Ellen Fuller[207] and came to live in a little red house next below us on the same side of the turnpike, now painted white and owned by the Bulgers. These two families became friends, the husbands to Father, the wives to Mother. Uncle George Bradford was at Brook Farm and through him, I think, Father made the acquaintance of young Mr Charles Newcomb. Mother never could get over her gratitude to Mrs Ellery Channing and Mr Newcomb because they espoused my cause. She often said "Mr Newcomb was your first friend; he said to me one day, 'I think you are unjust to Ellen. She has her good qualities.' " I went to school to Mrs Channing for a year, and so did all the children who used to go to Cousin Mary Russell. I remember accompanying Mother when she called on Mrs Channing who was tending her first baby and that Mrs Channing said "We plunge her into stone cold water every morning and she comes out as red as a little lobster." This was quite in accordance with the ideas of those times. I think Mother admired, I know I did.

Madam Keyes who had taken care of me in the scarlet fever remembered me once by asking me to come spend the afternoon with her.

Many years later we had some little children at our house to tea and Mother said some rich cake must be made for tea. I scouted the idea; but Mother said "When you went to spend the afternoon with Madam Keyes you told me with smiles when you came home that you had 'had sponge cake and *prefers* for tea' and I was very much obliged to Madam Keyes for pleasing my little girl with such good things. It *is* worth while." "But what were prefers?" "You meant preserves."

I must put in here the party that Father & Mother gave to Mr Webster. I believe someone else had planned to have one and sickness or something prevented, the invitations being all out and the refreshments prepared, and it was transferred to our house—some such impression is in my mind. Mr Webster was in Concord, it was court-week. My distinctest image of our parlour in those times I took in that night seated on a stool on the hearth rug before a blazing fire all dressed in my white gown, as I waited there alone for the family to get through tea. I think if it had not been for that solitary opportunity for contemplating it I should scarcely know how it looked. This party was an interesting one to everyone in the house, and Mother, who still loved & honoured Mr Webster as she had since the 1820 Plymouth Oration, considered it a sight most beautiful, most memorable, when he gave his arm to Grandma and came across the room with her.

In the summer of 1844 my trundlebed was in Mother's room and Father waked me one morning the 10*th* of July by coming and sitting down on it. I remember how the sun was shining into the room and the exact figure of the chintz on his bed. He asked me if I remembered my little brother Waldo. Of course I did. "You have been without any brother since he died, but now God has given you another little brother." I at once began a course of questions and ascertained that this brother was a newborn baby, that he was down in the redroom with Mother, and that I couldn't see him till I was dressed. But when Edith and I were both dressed and tried the redroom door, it wouldn't open. Someone looked out of the dining-room and said we couldn't see the baby till after breakfast. After breakfast the redroom door was as unyielding as before. Edith & I took hold of hands ran across the entry as hard as we could and bumped against it. I don't know what good we thought it would do, but we tried it a second time, and then someone opened the door and invited us in. The blinds were all shut, we couldn't see our brother as well as we should have liked to, and we weren't allowed to get hold of him. I know just how he looked. He was a brown little boy, not half as little as I hoped, but quite satisfactory nevertheless. Edith and I were presently sent up to the nursery.

Father wished to have him have his name, but neither he nor Mother wished quite to call him Waldo. Father said he would name him for Uncle Edward but give him Waldo for his middle name.

We children were brought up very well as to obedience. Mother's rule was "They ought never to think it possible to disobey" and we all loved and needed approbation, so that mere displeasure was a punishment. Mother who knew all the poetry she had ever seen by heart, used to be always saying Original Poems & Nursery Rhymes by Jane Taylor to us and Miss A. A. Gray's and Mrs Follen's poems for children, and all the Odes that had ever been written for Forefathers' Day at Plymouth.[208] When she played with the baby she used a rhyme one of her Uncles made when carrying round his grandson and his toys

> "Ride horse, ride lion, ride moolly-cow
> Ride man, kadark, puss, ride bowwow."[209]

When lately I questioned her on this second line she said "kadark" meant a hen and that the man was a wooden man. Another nursery rhyme, that had a tune, she learned from Frank Browne's nurse

> "Once there was a little dog
> That lived in a hole
> He lifted up his little leg
> And scratched against the wall
> His Father said he should be burnt
> So did his mother too
> He was condemnèd to be burnt
> With a fallal lallal loo!"

There was another with a tune, I don't know where it came from, which I never tired of hearing—

> "Away we went to wedding
> Up to Uncle Lumper's
> There were men & boys
> And women without numbers
>
> In came Uncle & Aunt
> And in came sister Keturah
> In came fiddler John
> And sawed away like fury

Turn your —— —— man   (perhaps right
And turn your partner again   hand man I've
Turn your middlemost man   forgotten)
And now you're right again."[210]

I don't think she ever used Mother Goose, though we always had it
and read it and got the nurse to read it to us. No children ever knew
it better. Dear Grandma always recited two to us, no three. "There
was an old woman tossed up in a blanket."—and "Boys & girls come out
to play"—and finally, "Rockaby Baby upon the tree top."—Mother used
to sing the Cradle Hymn to the tune of Greenville to us, all through.
She never omitted verses. We all duly learned Twinkle, twinkle, little
star,[211] and I was taught to say every morning

> "Now before I run to play
> I must not forget to pray
> To God who kept me through the night
> And waked me with the morning light"[212]

I am sure there were more verses but I don't know now what they
were.[213]

We were not taught "Now I lay me"—I learned that from the nurse
who took care of Edward. Mother used to come up to my trundle-bed—
For fear posterity shouldn't know what a trundlebed is I insert a
picture of ours. [See Sketch] It ran in under the nursery bed I have
turned up a corner of the counterpane of the latter to show you the
whole of the trundle-bed. At night it was pulled 'way out. After it was
made in the morning it was pushed in, quite out of sight. I slept in it
alone, till Eddy needed the crib out of which Edith moved to the trundle-
bed, which we slept in together till I was ten.—Mother used to come up
to me to hear me say my prayers and my evening hymn, and then pray
for me, every night after I had gone to bed, long before Edith slept
with me. When she came she had her prayers and hymn to say too.
When we were very little Mother began to have Sunday readings and
I think also daily readings with us. Chiefly hymns & the Old Testament
stories, but she used some other books which were not very interesting
to us. I believe she avoided the New Testament, for I found it new
to me when I began to read it to myself. Not that she kept us in
ignorance of it, for I knew the story of it. She told that I was much
distressed when she first read me about the Crucifixion and cried, and
said more than once "But I didn't want them to treat him so." This

We were not taught "Now I lay me —
I learned that from the nurse who took care of
Edward. Mother used to come up to my trundle-bed
— For fear posterity shouldn't know what a trundlebed
is I insert a picture of ours. It ran
in under the nursery bed
I have turned up a corner
of the counterpane of the latter to show you the
whole of the trundle-bed. At night it was pulled
way out. After it was made in the morning it was.
pushed in, quite out of sight. I slept in it alone,
till Eddy needed the crib out of which Edith
moved to the trundle-bed, which we slept in together
till I was ten. —— Mother used to come up to
me to hear me say my prayers and my evening
hymn, and then pray for me, every night after I
had gone to bed, long before Edith slept with me.
When she came she had her prayers & hymn to say
too. When we were very little she began to have Sunday
readings and I think also daily readings with
us. Chiefly hymns & the Old Testament stories, but
she used some other books which were not very
interesting to us I believe she avoided the New
Testament, for I found it new to me when I began
to read it to myself. Not that she kept us in
ignorance of it, for I knew the story of it. She told

I don't remember, and I think it was not the Gospel-story but a hymn in Hymns for Infant Minds. And I can recall hearing the story read from the Bible later, when perhaps I was ten, at one of our morning readings, and that it was in its particulars new. I think she did read us about the birth of Christ, and his being with the Rabbis in the Temple, and the raising of Jairus's daughter, and in Acts she read us about the Angel's opening the prison for Peter. She had no plan of keeping the New Testament from us, but she seemed to think the Old Testament stories were the children's part of the Bible. I think so too. Sunday was then kept rigidly the children of these days would say, but Father & Mother considered it kept only sensibly and easily, while Grandma thought it not strictly enough observed. I had no playthings out on Sunday; the baby, of course, had[.] I don't know whether Edith remembers having hers but I imagine not. I was brought up to keep Sunday fitly by having tasks enough to occupy me. Every Sunday I was to learn a hymn. Most of them had five verses of four lines, sometimes they had six. After I was sure I could say that smoothly I was to review another. As I advanced in years I had two to review, finally three. By the time this grew easy, the task of writing out the idea of the hymn in prose was added, varied sometimes by rendering one of Mrs Barbauld's[214] prose hymns into verse. These were my solitary labours. I was expected to begin to learn the new hymn after breakfast to see if I could learn it before church-time. I was to return to it or the reviews between church and dinner. After dinner I was to go on till all was done, when, if Mother wasn't ready for us, I might read "a Sunday book." The Sunday books were Pilgrim's Progress, Mrs Barbauld's Hymns, Mrs Sherwood's stories Lucy and her Dhaye & Henry and his Bearer,[215] a religious story called Henry Langdon, the Child's Book on the Soul[216]—not good for anything and the Sabbath School Teacher's Aid. Later Anna Ross[217] and Ruth Lee were added. When Mother was ready for us I had to recite my hymns new & reviewed and the other children theirs. Then she read to us, and as we grew older she was apt to read to us one of Jane Taylor's Contributions of Q.Q.[218] and she read more from the Gospels. She used to say to us poems—one on the Sermon on the Mount beginning "'Tis but the daystar's earliest glance" and "It is the Sabbath Day, in the wide fields I am alone"[219] and occasionally "Among green pleasant meadows"[220] less often still "The morning sun rose bright & clear, On Abraham's tent it gaily shone."

—— • ——

In 1851 Grandma broke her hip and was thenceforth confined almost wholly to her room. After this we always had Sunday reading there, and Father often came to hear our hymns too, which added much to our pleasure.

I am trying to show what was Mother's method in the religious education of her children, to have them made familiar with many hymns, and with all the interesting Bible stories. To accustom them to hearing some serious writing read aloud to them regularly, to make it a habit to omit play on Sunday and have it a day devoted to church and religious study at home. When Eddy got to be perhaps three or even earlier perhaps she began to read aloud to us when we were all in bed Mrs Barbauld's prose Hymns,[221] and often a story-book of a religious character. I think we all remember with most interest a book called Mary and her Mother.[222] The Mother told Bible stories to Mary. This was not always done, for I remember as if it continued a long time the practice of singing before we went up stairs Miss Taylor's hymn "Now condescend, all-loving King, to bless this little throng," we used to sit on our three stools round Mother and sing it with her to the tune of Auld Lang Syne. She had a little blue book of morning and evening prayers for children, and I think she read one of those prayers. When I went away from home for three months at the age of ten she gave me Ellen Tucker's bible and told me to read a dozen verses in the Psalms every day. I did, but I wasn't old enough; it was a ceremony. I think I had never read in the Bible before. When I was sixteen and went with Father to spend a Sunday with Mrs Ward Mrs W. said to me "I take pains to educate my children religiously. If they were to be mathematicians they would have to study arithmetic and algebra for years; if I wanted them to speak languages I should have them begin early to learn grammar and acquire vocabularies. If I neglected to lay these foundations I couldn't expect them to turn out when they were grown up as I had planned and wished. It is the same with religion, they must have an early and large & thorough education in religion if they are to be religious people by and by." I don't know whether Mother ever put it before her in this distinct form, but it is evident that she did labour from the beginning to educate us in religion. Again I think she was wise, most wise. I thank her.

She sent us early and constantly to dancing-school, but she never put us in the stocks[223] nor had us practice our steps every day, as she used to do. I do not remember that she taught us manners, except to say Thankyou. Grandma, as I remember, gave me what teaching I had before I went to Staten Island, where Uncle William and Aunt Susan gave me a little more. But one admonition was always on Mother's lips, "Don't make unnecessary motions!"[224] and she told us of a little

girl who resolved to be perfect, and began by sitting up straight."
Two other exclamations we heard daily "Don't *tickle*" which meant
giggle, and "Don't bicker!" To this last Edward learned to answer "We
aren't bickering, we are conversing on various subjects."

We certainly were taught to lay things straight[;] Mother used to
tell us that if we left our clothes lying carelessly about or had an extra
blanket uneven or in wrinkles on the bed "the angels couldn't come
to us." This phrase was so frequent in her latest years that I think it
must have been an early fancy repeating itself in her mind all her life.
She told us that she had often got up in the night remembering that she
had left a large book on a smaller book, to place the larger where it
belonged, i.e. underneath. She often said "I have a carpenter's eye. I
know when anything is a hair's breadth off the right line." I remember
her constantly complaining that the carpenter who had built the new
parlour was no good workman "There isn't a straight line in it." How
often has she cried out desperately "Put that vase in the *middle* of the
table! It ceases to be an ornament, and becomes mere litter when it
stands an inch or two out of position." In the same way she was most
uncomfortable if a piece of furniture was not exactly placed in the
middle of a space, or under a picture evenly. A candlestick or shell on
the corner of a mantelpiece must be over the pilaster as if it were its
continuation.

She could draw flowers very well and design patterns for embroidery.
Edith has had several of her designs worked, and one engraved on our
pie knife. She could also draw a very pretty paper-doll. She had great
facility in rhyming, and sometimes would take a fancy to talk in rhyme
or in Hiawatha metre, and would go glibly on for a long time.

I think in 1845 Uncle George Bradford spent the winter with us
and took a school in Concord, and it must have been in the autumn of
that year that Mother decided to have a Governess for us and took Miss
Sophia Foord of Dedham,[225] who was of one mind with her & Father
about us. We were to touch neither egg nor meat, we were to have a
pail of cold water dashed over us every morning, we were to be made
active & hardy, trained to write a diary and taught sewing as well as
lessons. To all this Miss Foord attended zealously, and we children all
liked her. I was an early convert to all these ideas.

But Mother found this was not relief enough she felt too weak, too
miserable, to keep house at all. So a housekeeper was proposed and in
the spring of 1846 Mrs Goodwin with four children took the house
with leave to have other summer boarders there. We were to keep
Mother's room, which became our nursery, the Redroom, which Mother
& Father took for theirs, and Father was to have his Study and Grandma

her room. Mrs Goodwin was to have our Nursery, the Prophet's Chamber after Uncle George who was in it went away for vacation, and the wing, except Miss Foord's room which she still retained. But Mother with that housekeeperly ambition which was always mighty in her at once set out upon a tremendous upheaval of the whole house to have everything "as clean as hands could make it," to make over every carpet, to penetrate to every dark corner and bring all things to judgment, a piece of work equal almost to moving, even a strong and quiet housekeeper would have found it hard, especially pushed up to get through at a fixed date not far off. Of course Father thought it foolish, so did Miss Foord, Grandma understood it better. She looked on sorry, Father in dismay, Miss Foord with pronounced disapproval. Mother soon fell beside the way, but there was nothing for it but to get up and go on. The tragedy darkened every day, it was terrible, and the way it was regarded by her family greatly embittered it. One day as she lay spent & moaning on the sofa Mrs Richardson who was sewing for her for dear life drew near. Mother opened her eyes, Mrs Richardson was actually crying with pity for her! Mother was comforted more than she could have believed. That one person on earth cared for her sufferings lightened them at once. You may be sure she felt unending gratitude to Mrs Richardson thenceforth.

Mrs Goodwin was to furnish her part of the house and that was empty and clean when she arrived but Mother's task was not quite completed.[226] She must have a day of reckoning with Miss Foord, and finally asked her how she could see her overworking so sadly and sit down at leisure to read an interesting book or go out to take a pleasant walk. Miss Foord said "Because you are disquieting yourself in vain. I know that carpets are useless luxuries, and many of the cares which weigh so heavily on you come from a love of style and ornament which is simply worldly and ought to be denied. I should be false to my principles if I took hold to help you minister to your own vanity." "Vanity! Good heavens! Are decency and order vanity?" cried Mother astonished. Well they argued away about it for some time, with good results. Mother found that Miss Foord had really withheld her assistance from principle, not from indifference or selfishness, and Mother convinced her that a carpet was positively useful and on the whole saved labour as everything kept cleaner on it than on a bare floor. So Miss Foord helped sew on the carpets. It took Mother all summer to recover from her labours, and she found too that so large a family and so many more children made an increase of care for her in keeping the entries & doorsteps and parlour free from litter, this care seeming to devolve always on her, for Mrs

Goodwin with all her children and the boarders was very busy attending to the providing and the chambers.

At least in this time she made several new friends, Mrs Goodwin herself, and among the summer-boarders Mrs Paine, Mrs Martha O. Paine (a lady who always attracted us children to her room, told us delightful stories and contrived to give us lessons in behaviour which really told. Mother had visits from her for years after), and dear 'Mrs Hemenway[227] and Lotty constant and beautiful friends as long as they lived. By this too Mother's nephew Frank Browne became acquainted with Mrs Goodwin's daughter Lizzy whom he married.

Our barn was now very useful. As I have said we had no animals and we used the west end down stairs for a school-room. It was white-washed, very white & clean. Lizzy & Abby Alcott, Lizzy & Barry Goodwin,[228] and Caroline Pratt of Concord all came to Miss Foord's school there for a whole year, indeed I think a year & a half. A chimney was put in in the autumn. Upstairs Mrs Goodwin's servants slept while she had boarders, and she and her children had our servants' rooms, her Father the South room which we call the blue room. Mr Lane[229] came one Sunday in the summer, and proposed to hold a conversation in the barn. I remember Miss Foord, assisted probably by John & Lizzy Goodwin, hung great bunches of red poppies & green asparagus on the white walls, and it looked so festive and pretty that I thought the conversation might be interesting and attended it very willingly—to be disappointed. I think everyone in the house was there, and Mother too.

Every summer, beginning about this time we had huckleberryings. Mr Thoreau would come and say he knew where they grew thick, and Father drove a carryall with Grandma & perhaps Aunt Lucy or Mrs Paine or other guests & Mr Thoreau drove the hayrigging with Miss Foord, all of us children & our Mothers and the servants. We started immediately after dinner and came home to tea. These were joyful times, Mother liked them too. Grandma, Father and Aunt Lucy never picked, they strolled about or sat in the shade, and Mr Thoreau walked hither and thither to find the best places for us, where bushes were loaded, and he & Father would cut off amazingly full ones and take to Grandma. Mother always picked, and sometimes Father would put handfuls into our baskets.

It was this year that Uncle Ripley left Waltham and moved to the Manse. Up to this time Father & Mother had gone every year to dine at Waltham with them on Thanksgiving Day. We children didn't know anything about that day[.] In the next summer 1847 I remember two nights of great joy. Eddy cried and couldn't be got to sleep and Father

came up into Mother's room (our Nursery then) and carried him
round and round the room singing him nursery rhymes improvised for
the occasion, two verses ended "Goodnight to Mr Minot's barn," they
grew funnier and funnier and I lay in the trundle-bed and laughed[.]
"Goodnight to Cousin Pelly, goodnight to laughing Nelly," sang Father.
(Cousin Pelly was Mother's cousin Experience Cotton, always called
Pelly) I'm sorry that I remember not another word. Eddy certainly cried
no more he was too much flattered, being carried round by his Papa
and too much interested in the lullaby, but happily he wasn't sleepy,
it was a good while before his little head dropped and my joy was not
of cruelly short duration. Another night was when the room was full
of musquitoes and he & Mother came up to kill them. Father was very
frolicsome and funny, he had a new and ingenious story about each
one he slew. Again I was perfectly happy. But I only remember a single
speech because I didn't understand it "There was a hart of grease!" he
cried after a pat on the wall. "And here's another stag of ten!", another
pat. I asked what, and Mother explained to me. "I have slain him with
the edge—not of my sword!—of my towel!" Father cried.

Mother now began to be a great homeopathist, a little medicine-chest
appeared on her bureau. The squills and paregoric[230] with which we
had formerly been dosed when we were sick disappeared forever. She
had soon four or five medical books and for forty years was diligent in
consulting them and selecting remedies for her own ailments and those
of all her large clientele of dependents & semi-dependents.

In the autumn of 1847 Father went to Europe, Miss Foord left us,
Mrs Goodwin also. Mr Thoreau came to occupy the prophet's chamber.
I remember Mother sometimes said "Mr & Mrs Alcott and Mr Thoreau
went with me to the ship to see your Father off. I didn't shed a tear,
but Mrs Alcott wept convulsively. I wonder what she thought of me."
Mother *didn't* cry. I think she never did. I have heard her many times
wish she could.

I believe it was that winter that Mother had the jaundice, which
she always spoke of as the most trying illness of her life.

We children went to school to Anna Alcott at the Alcott's house. The
barn rooms were no longer used. There were two old French people
from Canada of the humble sort, Colombe[231] and his wife Lisette, to
whom Mother decided to let them for the winter. They came, but in
the spring they departed. Grandma could never say Lisette she always
said "My dear, since you went out, that—that Gazelle has been in to
see you."

The next tenants were an old Mrs Clark who used to knit our stockings, and her son Adolphus who, I think, didn't lodge there, but came

for his meals. Mrs Clark used to amuse us children by coming in and asking for things always with the formula "Mrs Emerson, I suppose you hain't got any wormwood among your yarbs" or "any old petticoat that you've done with, have you?" and Edith long owed her a grudge because one day when she supposed Mother hadn't any spare rocking-chair, Mother gave her one which she had previously told Edith she might consider hers.

In the summer of 1848 Father came home, and now we began life as a regular family. No one after that lived with us, as Miss Foord or Uncle George or Mr Thoreau had before ever since Eddy was born and Edith could remember. Eddy[,] this reminds me, when learning to talk called Uncle George Brad and Miss Foord Foord, and Uncle George laughed and said "Now sir, if you could put those two names together, you would get mine." The next year as he was creeping round under the table in his pantalettes—we children were brought up in the days of pantalettes—he said "Mr Thoreau! I did bite your pantalette-loon." I will draw the costumes we children wore. [See Sketch] Never have been fashions so ugly as those prevailing at the period in which we grew up. Our best pantalettes were white but the every day ones were like our dresses. Neither we nor any children wore white round our necks except in our best dresses. Edith and I were usually dressed alike, but I have put on her the long-sleeved tire (Mother said it ought to be spelled tyer, but I like tire better) which we each possessed a few of, but the usual tire was short-sleeved and low-necked. Edward's little dark blue twilled cotton & wool sack (Edith says it was merino) was cut at the waist behind and had a fuller skirt[.] [See Sketch] We were all bony little creatures, Edward & I had long necks and sloping shoulders & large bones. Edith's bones were smaller and she was always better-looking and hadn't so long a neck, also her ears were set closer to her head and her hair was from the beginning thick and of a remarkably beautiful quality. Mother liked the half-high neck for our dresses—I like the modern ones, but those of 1840–48 I hated and hate—and she always had our short sleeves come down to our elbows and hitched them up with a button. Our mates wore shorter sleeves and we groaned in ours. When Mother's taste was formed pantalettes touched the instep, so ours always did but those of the other girls at school grew shorter by degrees. We all liked ancle-tie shoes but my feet grew speedily longer than the largest-sized ancle-ties, so I wore them only for a few years. Edith, who had them made for her when she could find none ready-made, wore them till she was married. Mother often took Eddy to Boston with her when she went shopping and when he was four and had just donned his first fawn-coloured trousers she brought him home in a pair of blue lasting boots

Me, when learning to talk called Uncle George Brad and Miss Ford Ford, and Uncle George laughed and said "Now sir, if you could put these two names together, you would get mine." The next year as he was creeping round under the table in his pantalettes — we children were brought up in the days of pantalettes — he said "Mr Thoreau! I did bite your pantalette-toon". I will draw the costumes we children wore.   Never have been fashions so ugly as prevailing at the period those in which we grew up. Our best pantalettes were white but the every day ones were like our dresses. Neither we nor any children wore white round our necks except in our best dresses. Edith and I were usually dressed alike, but I have put on her the long-sleeved tire (Mother said it ought to be spelled tyer, but I like tire better) which we each possessed a few of, but the usual tire was short-sleeved and low-necked. Edward's little dark blue (Edith says it was merino) twilled cotton & wool sack was cut

201

201

at the waist behind and had a fuller skirt 202.
We were all bony little creatures, Edward & I
had long necks and sloping shoulders & large
bones. Edith's bones were smaller and she was always
better-looking and hadn't so long a neck, also her
ears were set closer to her head and her hair was
from the beginning thick and of a remarkably
beautiful quality. Mother liked the half-high
neck for our dresses — I like the modern ones,
but those of 1840–48 I hated and hate — and
she always had our short sleeves come down to
our elbows and hitched them up with a button.
Our mates wore shorter sleeves and we groaned
in ours. When Mother's taste was formed pantalettes
touched the instep, so ours always did but those
of the other girls at school grew shorter by degrees.
We all liked ankle-tie shoes but our feet grew
speedily longer than the largest-sized ankle-ties,
so I wore them only for a few years. Edith, who had
them made for her when she could find none ready-
made, wore them till after she was married. Mother
often took Eddy to Boston with her when she went
shopping and when he was four and had just donned
his first ~~short~~ trousers she brought him home

in a pair of blue lasting boots with black patent leather heels and toes. How pretty they were! And they just matched his blue sack. Those boots were admired by everyone in the house. He had several pairs before they were given up. Mother was utterly delighted with them.

It was at this time that we had our first Irish servants. Mrs Margaret Casey was our cook, and her sister Mary Bannan was chambermaid. They were very good — lived with us a year or two, and Mother valued them. They decided to go to New York and left us.

Father began to give lectures in the West and when he was gone Mother once had her Cousin Pilly to stay with her and once a Miss Bartlett from Plymouth who was a skillful knitter and knit for Edith and me, also for Aunt Lucy our knit jackets which served us till they were outgrown & for Edith & me little netted german worsted cravats which we wore round our necks as tippets they were white with coloured borders Edith's yellow mine crimson, for Mother a netted miniature scarf white barred across with a few blue stripes. Mother always kept it and called it "my fascine" "About this time the old strawberry-bed in our garden was changed to flower-beds and hazel...

It will remain

in the shape Mother then had it cut into. It 204
was the centre of the N.E. corner of the garden
and she gave Edith & me each a bed of it as
our own [diagram] She had removed all the plants
from the [diagram] front-dooryard and from the oval
bed in the East Yard into the garden, Aunt Susan
Emerson had sent her some new kinds of roses,
and Mr Wheildon had given her his Juliet rose
and the dark red one which Mother christened
Ethiop Queen; her bulbs had multiplied and she
began to buy a few tulips and hyacinths every
winter which blossomed in the house, were put
into the garden in the summer and by the
second year bloomed there and usually continued
to prosper there. She had multiplied all her
shrubs and her currant-bushes, her garden began
to be fine and please us children very much.
Also the cherry, plum and apple-trees showed
symptoms of bearing. In these early fifties Father
and Mother enlarged their borders. very much.
In 1847 Father bought of Deacon Cyrus Warren
the lot East of ours and had it set with
apple & pear trees. A little later he bought thirty-
five acres of woodland on the other side of the
pond. Then in 1849 he took a man, James Burke, who
204

[See Sketch] with black patent leather heels and toes. How pretty they were! And they just matched his blue sack. Those boots were admired by everyone in the house. He had several pairs before they were given up. Mother was utterly delighted with them.

It was at this time that we had our first Irish servants. Mrs Margaret Casey was our cook, and her sister Mary Bannan was chambermaid. They were very good—lived with us a year or two, and Mother valued them. They decided to go to New York and left us.

Father began to give lectures in the West and when he was gone Mother once had her Cousin Pelly to stay with her and once a Miss Bartlett from Plymouth who was a skillful knitter and knit for Edith and me, also for Aunt Lucy our knit polka-jackets which served us till they were outgrown & for Edith & me little netted german worsted cravats which we wore round our neck as tippets[;] [See Sketch] they were white with coloured borders Edith's yellow mine crimson, for Mother a netted miniature scarf white barred across with a few blue stripes. Mother always kept it and called it "my fayaway[.]"[232]

About this time the old strawberry-bed in our garden was changed to flower-beds and made over[.] It still remains in the shape Mother then had it cut into. It was the centre of the N.E. corner of the garden and she gave Edith & me each a bed of it as our own[.] [See Sketch] She had removed all the plants from the front dooryard and from the oval bed in the East Yard into the garden, Aunt Susan Emerson had sent her some new kinds of roses, and Mr Wheildon had given her his Juliet rose and the dark red one which Mother christened Ethiop Queen; her bulbs had multiplied and she began to buy a few tulips and hyacinths every winter which blossomed in the house, were put into the garden in the summer and by the second year bloomed there and usually continued to prosper. She had multiplied all her shrubs and her currant-bushes, her garden began to be fine and please us children very much. Also the cherry, plum and apple-trees showed symptoms of bearing. In these years Father and Mother enlarged their borders. In 1847 Father bought of Deacon Cyrus Warren the lot East of ours and had it set with apple & pear-trees. A little later he bought thirty-five acres of woodland on the other side of the pond. Then in 1849 he took a man, James Burke, then bought one cow, then another, then the pasture on the other side of the brook, having tried sending the cows to our pasture at Walden, and found that so distant as to be most inconvenient.

—— • ——

I remember well the grief and indignation with which Mother read Mr Webster's speech of 7 March 1851[.] I keep the anniversary still every year.

I think Edward & Edith will wish that I should mention that in the spring of 1847 Mr Thoreau sowed our heaterpiece[233] with buckwheat. It yielded a fine crop, and the next winter we lived on buckwheat. Mother liked it, she thought it was better for her than anyother flour. Let·no one imagine that we ate it in buckwheat griddle-cakes solely, or chiefly. Mother had it made into bread, muffins, johnny-cakes and, with plenty of raisins in it into steamed loaf puddings, it was, in all these forms, our staple diet. I like it myself, no one spoke against it and it was not till years afterwards that I learned the sentiments of the rest of the family, when one of the children remembering those days expressed the strong-est hatred of the buckwheat diet, the other chiming in heartily and Father said "Yes I think I may say that a buckwheat pudding is the poorest." He once said "it tasted like the roof of a house"—which was true if one judges by the taste of rainwater from the roof.[234]

When Eddy was five years old he had a cold and seemed sick and Mother undressing him herself at night found him all red and knew it was scarlet-fever. It seemed a fearful thing for Waldo had died of it at five. She ran down to the kitchen to send James for the doctor. He, alarmed by her alarm made a rush for his hat almost before he straightened himself from sitting, and it did Mother's heart good that he felt frightened too. But Eddy, and Edith who had it too, got through very comfortably. How little people feared spreading contagious dis-eases then! This was at Christmas-time and we were invited to a Christ-mas-tree at Mrs Rockwood Hoar's. Mother and I dressed in her room, where our scarlet-fever patients were, and went straight to the tree where Gary & Sam[235] were with all their and our little friends, never thinking of harm, and I never heard that any followed.[236]

In 1850 in March Mother was invited by Mrs Bancroft to come to New York and make her a visit.[237] She took with her the Precious Lamb, as she always called Eddy and he was sufficiently liked to content her. She used to say to him as she always had to us Miss A. A. Gray's poems for children, and about a year before this it was discovered that he could recite

> "A gentle hind and her young fawn
> Upon a summer's day"[238]

one of the prettiest of them, from beginning to end. Mother's heartfelt tones reproduced in his innocent baby-voice seemed, to me certainly, and, as certainly, to all the family, apparently to everyone, the most captivating music. We were always asking him to recite it to people, and I remember when we three went on an errand to Miss [Jane] Whiting, our teacher, on a Saturday morning I made him say it to her & her Father & Mother. He had in the course of the year enlarged his little stock and could say several from his Picture-&-Verse-Book, especially "Dear Pigeon on the house-top, say-"[239] simply wonderfully. When Ralph visited his Aunt Margaret Forbes one Sunday she said "Tell his Mother, I've experienced religion. I have heard Ralph recite

'God who madest earth and heaven'."[240]

So might anyone exclaim who had heard Edward's rendering of the reply of the pigeon. He said these pieces in New York to Mr & Mrs Bancroft, and they listened with appreciation. To Mother it was renewing her youth to be again with Mrs Bancroft[;] it was as if they had never been separated. They couldn't get through talking.

Mrs Bancroft went shopping with her and having strongly advised her to buy a grey watered Irish poplin dress & cashmere shawl, helped her to choose a beautiful one which cost forty dollars. Mother loved that shawl, it exactly suited her taste; she wore it constantly, and in the course of the next forty years wore it all out, nothing was ever more absolutely reduced to its lowest terms. Mrs Bancroft was in mourning and wore a cap which pleased Mother better than any she had ever seen. One of its details wasn't quite to her fancy, she used it in general however as model for the cap which she devised and which her family and everyone else like to see her in all the rest of her life.

Aunt Lizzy had bought all Miss Bremer's novels as they were translated into English[.] "The Home" was one and "The Neighbours," "The President's Daughter" another, I forget the names of the rest.[241] She lent them to us and Aunt Lucy read them aloud. Mother read extracts from them to us children. She was charmed with them and when Miss Bremer came to this country she herself planned to have a visit from her. Father was not at all interested, but he was willing. She came, and stayed I think two days, and with her brought Mr and Mrs Marcus Spring and their son Edward.[242] I remember she asked Father if he had not a friend, a very remarkable man who "lived altogether on troots and roots and fruits." This for a moment perplexed Father, till he perceived that she had not mastered th and meant truths, when he laughed and was charmed with the sentence. "Very good!" he cried "Yes, Mr Alcott is truly described by that." She gave to Edith a charming Chinese tumbler who turned somersets for us for many years and to Eddy a Farm. Some of its sheep are still in existence. To Mother she gave a book of hers in existence which she said was her own favorite "The Bond-maid."[243]

In 1852 Kossuth—Louis Kossuth, the Hungarian patriot—who was in exile for having tried to free his country from the Austrian yoke—came to this country, hoping to raise money enough to help the Hungarians to fight once more for independence. Everyone was much interested in his cause and in his personal part in the rising, the newspapers of the day were full of him. In every city he was welcomed, crowds were eager to hear his story, the best citizens received him and he spoke in public, the tickets being a dollar apiece and the buyers receiving with each ticket a Hungarian bond handsomely engraved and with a full length likeness of him promising that the Government of free and independent Hungary would redeem it with a dollar, in case it ever existed. Concord was as eager to hear Kossuth as Boston was, he was invited to address us and accepted the invitation. Mr Keyes brought him in a barouche from Lexington where he spoke in the morning and he spoke in the Town Hall. Father was appointed to welcome him. He was to have come on Friday 7 May, and that day Mrs Sam Hooper and Mrs Tappan came bringing Alice Hooper to hear him.[244] Mrs Tappan was the dear Miss Caroline Sturgis once so often at our house, always so kind to me who had told me and read me such beautiful stories and had drawn such beautiful pictures. I had not seen her for many years, and it was wonderful to hear her own voice again and recognize all her ways, for Mother called me right down when they came to amuse Alice. I don't think I did. I listened only to the talk and gazed at beautiful Mrs Hooper whom I believe I had not seen before and at Alice's pretty clothes and my dear Mrs Tappan. I had heard about Kossuth more or less, but this talk quite stirred me up, and I began to regret as the others did that something had happened so that his coming was deferred. When they went, Mother made them promise that when he did come they would come again and dine and go with us to hear him. I began to ask about Kossuth and found Father valued him. He brought home from the Atheneum two books about him and Hungary, one by Mr C. S. Brace and one by Mr F. Olmsted[245] and showed me the pages to read. Aunt Lucy was reading them to Mother. It turned out that Kossuth could come on Tuesday, May 11th, and Mrs H[.] & T. would come too. Grandma, confined to her chair, was yet reading every word about him and so much devoted to him that people spoke of it and Mr Mackay[246] brought her a framed engraving of him which was hung up in her room. The day came; and at noon Mrs Hooper and Annie—not Alice—and Mrs Tappan. I had some time alone with Annie and found that she knew all about Kossuth and was

"Hungarian Fund" bond

all enthusiasm for him. It was the greatest good fortune that she was
going to hear him this afternoon, and I quickly imbibed from her the
first feeling of the kind I had ever had. We all went in the afternoon to
the new Town Hall. Mr Wheildon[247] had lent his great Gobelin Tapestry
of Fame and it was on the wall over the platform. Father made the wel-
coming address[248] and Kossuth answered in a speech which everyone
thought was as good as it ought to be. I remember one sentence "The
conservative is like a child who has a hole in his apron, who puts his
finger in the hole and conserves the hole." The audience laughed. Once
he turned to Father and said "What is your word for Outerreich." "Os-
trich," suggested Father. "Oh no, no! Outerreich?" Someone recognized
what he wanted and said Austria[.] He thankfully accepted it. I know
they both referred to Concord Fight, and that Father quoted

"The mighty dead
Hear from the dust the tread of Liberty."

As we came out from the Hall after, what I believe it was to many, the
great experience, I heard a lady say "What a glorious afternoon—those
two great souls greeting each other!" Father hastened to find Eddy and
brought him, followed by us all, to the depot to see Kossuth off. Father
said to him "I have brought my little boy that he may have your blessing." He shook hands with Mrs Hooper & Mrs Tappan, and Annie—
she had said "Oh don't you wish you could shake hands with him!"—
with Mother and us children and stood on the back platform as the train
bore him away. We went home to tell Grandma all about it. Mother said
in the evening that it was the anniversary of Grandfather Emerson's
death and that she could not tell whether it was that or this day's event
that had so stirred Grandma who seemed much moved and had exclaimed
when she went in "This day, my dear, this day!"—but went no further.
   Sunday had meanwhile become in many respects altered. We still
learned each our hymn every Sunday but reviews were no longer
exacted.[249] After breakfast we usually went out into the garden with
Father and visited its trees, then out into the pear-orchard and not seldom
this round took all the time before church. It was a most domestic and
happy progress from tree to tree. In the year 1848–9 the first year that Miss
Jane Whiting taught us Lydia Hosmer (Dea. Cyrus Hosmer's daughter)
had won 37 Approbations, that is cards signifying that for one week she
had had no miss in lessons or mark of any kind against her. Dear little
Edith had striven week after week in vain for one Approbation. One
week her hopes rose high for till Saturday morning not a question had
been too searching for her, she had been neither late nor absent and

had kept every rule faithfully. She and all her family were all excitement and anticipation. But just as Miss Whiting was taking the last
report, Henry Frost, who sat behind her, sharpened his pencil and as he
looked at its perfect point, he desired to use it. He reached over and
pricked Edith's neck. She started and involuntarily cried "Don't!" The
Approbation was lost.[250] She and I went up to plead with Miss Whiting
that this might be excused. But Miss Whiting very wisely said. "I am
as sorry as you are. It certainly was no sin, it was only an inattention—
that is just what it was. You must learn to have your attention to rules
so faithful that you don't break them for any sudden surprise. The value
of an Approbation is that it can be won only by work and exact keeping
of rules. If I excused mistakes it would cease to be valuable." So the card
that week had on it one inattention. The next week Edith won her
Approbation, and I think two more in the year. But Lydia Hosmer won
thirty-seven; and when Father found one of his young pear-trees Louise
bonne de Jersey had sent up a shoot 3 ft[.] long he christened that
tree "The thirty-seven Approbation-Tree." This brings me back to the
subject of our Sunday march through the pear-orchard. Father told us
all about each tree and we talked to him, and when fruit was ripe we
picked it up and ate as we went. We were all together, and all enjoying
each other's society, our land, our trees, and the sunshine. We often
prepared a dish of fruit with leaves & flowers to carry to Mother when
we went in. We all three went always to church with Mother and I came
home with her. The children went to Sunday-school. After dinner came
learning our hymns. Mother went to church in the afternoon. When she
returned we recited them to her, she read to us, and we afterwards sang
with her three or four hymns. For a long time the only tunes we used
were Bonnie Doon, Auld Lang Syne, Missionary Hymn, Watchman, tell
us of the night, Greenville, Shirland, Peterborough and America, but
it never occurred to us that it was a scanty stock. At four Father called
us to go to walk with him, at first usually to Walden, but as we grew older
the walks lengthened we went round the Pond, to the Cliffs, to Baker
Farm, to Copan, to our Saw-Mill Woodlot or rather to a little Waterfall
in it, to Flint's Pond, once certainly round the Five-mile Square. After
tea we had a family evening till Aunt Ripley began to come. This was
a very easy and happy Sunday to us all, and when we wanted hours of
solitude we found space for them. Mother sometimes took a Sunday-walk
with the family and enjoyed it so much that she went the next week and
the next. But a stormy Sunday would break the habit and she might not
try it again for a year. We *always* went, in rain & snow, great heat or
fierce cold[.]

In 1852, I think it was, Father while lecturing in the West[251] had a letter from Professor Nichol[252] who I think was from the University of Edinburgh saying he should like to come to call on him while he was in Boston. Father when the letter was forwarded to him wrote advising Mother to invite him to come out to dine and get Mr Channing to come help her entertain him. Mother accordingly did so. Both the gentlemen accepted the invitation. On the appointed day Mr Channing duly came but not Prof. Nichol. A note by the night's mail apologized for his absence, and asked if he might come on another day. Mother wrote saying that day would be convenient to her & asked Mr Channing. The day arrived, Mr Channing was on hand, but no Prof. Nichol. At night another note explained his nonappearance and set a later day. Exactly the same experience was repeated, but this time a telegram came during dinner to say that he had found on reaching Concord N. H., that we lived in Massachusetts, and he was sorry but had no other day to give. Mr Channing wrote to Father that he & Lidian had eaten together with all ceremony three legs of mutton in honour of Professor Nichol, but had caught no glimpse of that worthy, who seemed to be apocryphal.

Mother was very skillful in the use of language, 'not like Father because she thought much about it. It was natural to him to think of it as in itself an interesting subject, and he was quick to feel any beauty or any clumsiness of expression—besides, the managing of language was the business of his life. This was quite different from Mother, who never thought at all on such subjects, nor paid the slightest attention to the style of anybody's speech or writing. She had a very large and varied vocabulary, probably because of her perfect memory and her constant reading, and her deep and powerful feeling brought it out in quite fresh forms continually. Yet she had plenty of stock phrases, anyone who has lived in the house with her will be sure to recognize as old familiar friends "ingenuity of mischief!" "main strength and ignorance," "mind the main chance," "abomination of desolation!" She always called the pig "the unmentionable animal." She read when a child a story translated from the French to this effect. A little girl was playing in the park and her Mother gave her a bunch of fine cherries. She saw another little girl eyeing them & offered her half. The child refused but the heroine insisted on her taking them, saying "Whatever we possess becomes doubly valuable when we are so fortunate as to share it with another," and the little girl's goodness told her to take them.

Very soon after, the heroine's Father lost his property. She was already invited to a party and had accepted, but now couldn't go, as she had no money to buy her dress. A large box was left at the door containing a complete costume for the party, on which lay a card inscribed "Whatever we possess becomes doubly valuable when we are so fortunate as to

share it with another." At every crisis of the heroine's life, the very thing
which she needed came to her just in season, with the same words. At
last she learned that it was a princess, one of the King's children to whom
she had given her cherries. The words of this little heroine were always
repeated to us if we didn't wish to divide[253] our possessions, or share our
pleasures, and Mother often used the famous sentence, when she wished
to bestow. Another, used in the same way, was "Nothing is too good for
Dr Robbins[.]"[254] That came from this story. Dr R. was the old Plymouth
minister, and when he was visiting as pastor some of the families of
Indians who lived in Plymouth woods, a squaw offered him a cup of tea.
He said he should like it. She brewed it & got a teacup then called to
another squaw to sweeten it. That one brought the molasses-jug and
put in a little, "More, more!" cried the squaw. "No, there is plenty,"
said the other "its good enough!" "No! More, more!" insisted the first,
"nothing is too good for Dr Robbins!" Mother always said that was the
spirit of *true* generosity. "Out of the way, or I shall jump over your
head!" was an admonition very frequently bestowed. "Mystery of mysteries! where have my scissors gone?" she would cry when she had laid
her work down on them, as she was planning & cutting. Her usual exclamation was "Ye Powers!" sometimes ["]O ye Powers!["] or ["]Ye Powers
above!["][255] No one knows where it came from, she didn't herself. When I
asked her she said so. She seemed hardly to know that she did use it. Eddy
loved to hear it and aspired to appropriate it, but he kept finding too late
that he had allowed a fine occasion for saying it to pass without remembering to bring it out. Uncle Charles Jackson's troubles Mother felt very
keenly. First the treachery of a student whom he took with him on one of
his state surveys, and who stole his papers and published them as his own,
or something which made that impression on my childish mind. Uncle
Charles suffered much on the occasion and Mother with him. Then came
the ether discovery. Mother was full of interest, then the Morton
fraud,[256] followed by years of controversy which stirred her indignation
continually. Mother wrote sheets & sheets of big letter-paper on this subject to many men who she thought needed only to read her statement
to be convinced and to espouse his cause. Father was very good to her
and to Uncle Charles, he always exerted himself to gain for him allies
and supporters. The failure of her expectations with regard to her letters
cost her the most vehement displeasure and wounding disappointment.
Year after year this trouble really gnawed at her heart. She never could
for a moment listen to Aunt Mary's view "What matters it by whom the
good is done?" She felt that justice demanded that the right person should
receive the gratitude of his fellowmen. She and Uncle Charles were

constituted exactly alike in this. To both it was a grief that could never be set aside.[257] to see, and the religious darkness which made the rest seem intolerable.

Grandma had broken her hip in 1851. Cousin Charlotte Haskins came in the January of this year, I think to be an older daughter to Mother, and when Grandma had this accident she took the care of her[,][258] and was a cushion of comfort to poor Mother for one year. Then her niece Lois Chamberlain took her place, sixteen years old, pretty and dutiful, a pleasure to the whole family, but too soon called home by the sickness of her sister. Next Grandma had an Irish attendant who was a further source of exasperation to Mother. When Grandma first met with her accident, her two surviving sisters, Miss Betsey and Miss Fanny Haskins came at once from Boston to see her. Aunt Betsey was already broken. As Aunt Fanny led her into the room she asked "Sister Fanny, who is this poor sick lady?" "Why, Sister Betsey, it's our dear Sister Ruthy Emerson!" Still as they proceeded across the room Aunt Betsey repeated "Sister Fanny, who is this poor sick lady?" "Why, Sister Betsey, it's our dear Sister Emerson!" They had now reached Grandma who with emotion was stretching her arms toward them, and Aunt Betsey chimed in "Why it's our dear Sister Emerson!" All three wept together.

When these gentle and innocent Aunts had last visited us, I think it was their only visit at our house—Mother believed they had never before ventured outside of Boston—when Mother accompanied them at night to their chamber, Aunt Fanny put the lamp on the floor and looked under the bed "I want to see, my dear, that there are no toads or snakes under us, you know." Some little time after their visit came the news of Grandmother's brother Thomas's death. It was a regular practice in our church then, no doubt was in all churches, and had been since the days of our Pilgrim Fathers to "send up a note" when any member of your family died, to be read before the long prayer, which ran as follows: "John Smith and wife desire your prayers that the death of a daughter may be sanctified to them for their spiritual good."

Grandma asked to have a note sent up, and Father wrote it. At church that day the minister read it, "A member of this church desires your prayers that the death of a brother may be sanctified to her, and that God may graciously sustain her under her own advanced age and infirmity[.]" Aunt Lizzy came home with us after church to see Grandma, as she often did, and stayed to luncheon. When she came down to the table Father asked her whether Grandma's note had been read. "Yes," said Aunt Lizzy, and then, breaking down, she went on "I think to every one who knew Mamma it came like a breath from heaven!" It was always to me very pretty—her sudden tears when she cared much.

In this year we heard that Miss Fuller or rather Mme. Ossoli was coming home. Mother was delighted. She and Father looked forward to her arrival with the greatest interest. I remember well what a shock to them was her death, and how constantly every detail they could gather was talked over. Father sent Mr Thoreau at once to Fire Island Beach to learn all he could and to collect whatever remained of her possessions. When he came home he had written out carefully an account of his days there, all he had seen, heard & gathered. He read this diary to Mother, Father and Aunt Lizzy in Grandma's room as soon as he came home, and I was present.[259] It seemed so hard to Mother, that it shook her faith. Could a tender Providence have ordered this loss of the whole family just as they were entering the harbour after safely crossing the ocean, longed for by so many friends? She went to her room, opened her extract-book remembering that in it was a hymn of Cowper's which contained the words

"we and our affairs
Are part of a Jehovah's cares"[260]

As the book opened, she found her thumb was on these words, and that circumstance made the hymn speak to her more consolingly, more convincingly. It enabled her to accept the wreck as the intended conclusion of the lives of the Ossolis.

In 1853, Nov. 9, Grandma was eighty-five years old. In the first year after her accident she was well enough at Thanksgiving to be brought down in one of the white Windsor armchairs and to dine with the family. She also walked with crutches almost every day, attended by Cousin Charlotte or Cousin Lois through Mother's room, into the nursery & back for a month or two. I think that again in 1852 she came down at Thanksgiving, for Thanksgiving since 1848 was held at our house, and the Ripleys, Uncle George Bradford and Uncle Charles's family, also Uncle Bulkeley Emerson,[261] always came. She had a whirl[.][262]

Immediately after her 85*th* birthday Grandma was taken ill, and they watched with her at night. Father lectured I think in the neighbourhood in the evening of the 15*th*.[263] Aunt Lizzy & Cousin Elizabeth came to watch with her, and saw before morning that she was dying. She Aunt L.[264] climbed on the bed, and sat down by her, leaning on the pillows that propped her up, put her arm round her, and with the other hand held her hand, and Grandma died quietly without rousing—she had been unconscious more than twenty-four hours—. Aunt Lizzy didn't stir, but sat there till day-light still holding her hand and thinking over all her life in this world. They laid Grandma out and covered her face.

When after breakfast they went in to see her and removed the face-cloth, they were almost startled at the radiance of her face, it seemed as if joy shone in it. The next day she looked simply peaceful. But Father saw her before the light faded. I was in Lenox. When I came home to stay I inherited her room. I have so far made no remarks on the relations between Grandma and Mother, but I think all will see them in what I have written. Mother was not, and knew she was not, an ideal daughter-in-law to Grandma for she never sat down nor sewed, nor was sociable, and Grandma could not believe in lying down, nor understand Mother's distresses, no nor her kind of economy. Hers, like Father's, would have been going without. Yet Grandma loved her, they loved each other, they had religious sympathy, and sympathy in important points though none in detail. Grandma was invariably gentle and affectionate though undemonstrative. It must have grieved her that she spent all her days shut up solitary in her room, because Mother must be always planning or writing or doing something which made it impossible to have anyone but assistants with her. But Mother always naturally went to Grandma to report her visit anywhere, even to the shops, showed her everything she did &c. and carried her fresh flowers whenever she came in from the garden. As far as she had time she was with her, and many things, indeed everything that could be read or told or showed to amuse her, was always brought to her room after her accident.

On the Fourth of July 1853 or 4 I don't now know which, Mother considered our country wholly lost to any sense of righteousness, and hearing that there was to be some celebration of the Day, and seeing flags going up, she asked Father's leave to cover our gates with a pall. Father smiled and consented. So she got a quantity of black cambric, and made a great show of it on our front gate and gate-posts. I think the children were a little mortified, but Mother said it did her heart good to express her feelings, and she thought Father quite approved. "Your Aunt Lizzy didn't like it, she said it was silly, but I am glad I did it." she ended.

From early times, perhaps since I was seven, every time Mother was particularly miserable I used to offer to help. She always replied, unless Aunt Lucy was in the house "Yes, you can read to me." This was an ever new disappointment to me. Of course I could read, but that affected nothing whatever. Accordingly since that was what was ordered I did read, and, when I wasn't reading, very soon Edith, and, much later, Edward read instead. Mother wished to be read to every moment except when she was writing, even when she was working in the garden. It bore this good fruit at least that it made me read many books, and made reading as natural as breathing to us all three. It was an excellent secondary education for us. This I didn't discover however till I was forty, I should think, but I groaned less than at first as I came to see that it had a soothing effect on her.

It was the same when I took a share in the housekeeping. I wished to take the whole, have the satisfaction of feeling that I had lifted Mother's load and the glory of being a real housekeeper. I only had the charge of the second-work and the ordering of the bread and cake and fruit, the vegetables, puddings and pies. It was more than I could suddenly master to do that, and gradually I became convinced that not only Mother was better able to manage the rest, but that it was good for her, and I needed a longer apprenticeship than I had supposed.

Mother at this time became interested in the manufacture of currant wine, she had all her currant-bushes bearing their best, and not caring for jelly she used all their crop for wine; rows of jugs in the nursery and the cellar were filled. This on the chemical side was a most beautiful experiment and study, and her dear sanguine mind thought it would save buying wine and cider. Then she went on to making wild cherry wine, and wild grape wine. Most of the jugs turned out rather ill, but she utilized them as cider for the Thanksgiving pies for a year or two. A few proved good enough for Father to like the beverage. We children all remember, too, various terrific scenes of bursting jugs making a report and plenty of devastation of paper, carpets and sometimes clothes; popping of corks too at midnight and fountains playing to the ceilings, notably one of wild-cherry in the nursery where Edward slept. After the second year, Mother ceased to make wine, but for ten years she was active in brewing, raising hops and celandine, gathering and drying them, collecting when she occasionally walked in the woods all the pyrola she could find, and buying sarsaparilla of Mrs Cook and others who knew where to get it.[265] Big pails she 'bought to boil them in, the house was scented with them and the jugs were ranged in her closets, on her hearth, and in the cellar. Father & her nephews liked her small beer, which flattered her very much, and she drank it herself and believed it did her much good. She liked bitter tastes and put quassia[266] in one brewing. Well pleased with the result, she offered some to Aunt Lizzy who took it expecting something good. One taste and she set down the tumbler with an expression of horror,—gazing at Mother. Then she burst out "How could you, Lidian, how could you? Why didn't you warn me?" "Warn you? Why I thought you'd like it." "Like it! It is dreadful! The bitterest thing I ever tasted." Aunt Lizzy seemed as much hurt as if Mother had struck her, and Mother was surprised.

One funny point in Mother's character was her feeling about the sick, especially in contrast to Father's. The sick were to Mother's mind rather enthroned. Every thing new, fine, handsome she inclined to put away "for the sick." New blankets ought to be saved to use in sickness. If we had any good fruit, she would say "It's too good to eat. It ought to be sent to the sick."

In 1857 a thousand dollars came to Father from Ellen Tucker's estate. He and Mother who were tired of the twenty years' leaking of the roof of the prophet's chamber, which had become Edith's room, decided to take it off and raise a square room over the parlour for themselves, with an attic over it for a Den for Father to retire to away from the household and callers. He fancied he should like it better than his Study.

Mother's old room now became Edith's, and Mother entered upon her large and pretty new room with a plain blue paper and a gray carpet to suit her taste, and two large south windows. They, however, were rather thrown away on her. She always spoke of "the sun, my enemy." She said she felt worse and worse every day till noon, and about four in the afternoon relief began to come, when she felt better and better till at midnight she was bright and well. Cousin Sarah in a letter about Mother said "She ever bloomed brightest in the evening." It was funny, though lamentable, sometimes, to see what a time she had walking up in town in the afternoon when the sun was low, and she passed continually from shade to sun—there used to be apple-trees all the way. She evidently felt that each time a ray fell on her the sun had made a thrust at her and hurt her. She would cry out, then come into shade objurgating the sun, till another burst of sunlight would make her cry out again. Oh! "It seems as if he was doing it on purpose to tease me!" Oh! On entering her room when the sun was shining in, she would wince and say, "Shut out that dreadful sun!" She loved rain and howling winds, and snowstorms, "because it makes it seem so comfortable indoors."

I ought to have told before this that Mother often had what she called little fevers, when she had the doctor and kept her bed for a week or two. The Doctor would come and say "Well, Mother, what's the matter?" "Oh, one of my little fevers." "You do look like time in the primer!" he responded, and inquired into her symptoms. "I've been doctoring myself with homœopathy and am already a great deal better than I was last night. You don't mind my going on with it[,] do you[?]" "No indeed! Take the whole box, bottles and all!" The next day he would say "You look as if a breath would blow you away! If 'twas any one else I should say you wouldn't live a week, but as it's you I guess you'll pull through this time."

Mother had from the beginning taken immense interest in mesmerism, in phrenology, in astrology, in Rochester knockings, in mediums, clairvoyants, table-tippers and in planchette.[267] She must at once witness all such proceedings, employ all such agencies, have her horoscope cast, her head examined and letters fingered by diviners. Father also must go to the phrenologist, to please her; and she carried the place and date of his birth to Prof. Lister the astrologer, and had his horoscope cast. She however strictly forbade any word about the future. The descriptions by Lister and by Fowler,[268] the phrenologist, of both her & Father remain to this day and are rather true and highly entertaining. Father thought very lightly of all these occult sciences; still, Mother said, he always liked to hear her account of her adventures when she had consulted clairvoyants, or attended sessions of mediums or table-tippers. So did we children though we regarded this whole class of interest with distaste and dread.

For several years table-tipping was rather a constant amusement. Mrs Nathan Brooks[269] had a brother Mr Augustus Merrick who excelled in it, and Mrs Thoreau and her daughter were often present at Mrs Brooks's, as well as Mother and Aunt Lucy to see what he could do to obtain news from the other world. Miss Bridge a dress maker was also a medium. They sometimes met at Aunt Lucy's, once or twice at our house, when I shuddered to hear the thumping of the table's feet in its gambols, and all this was a kind of social life to Mother—took her away from her housekeeping, her worries and her sad thoughts.[270] I have not yet spoken of these thoughts which were the heaviest cloud of all, and made the dungeon in which she suffered for so many years. They were the natural result of her character, her temper and her principles. It was her character to desire actual solid truth, her temper was combative. (Mrs Cabot spoke most truly when she said of the pastel portrait of her "The failure in it is that she looks resigned. Now *that* she is *not*. She never was resigned for a moment in her life.") Further, her memory was perfect. Finally, her principles were that she ought to forgive. Every injustice, every slight, every wrong to her that anyone was guilty of lived before her mind and caused her permanently the same resentment that she felt at the first moment (unless the sinner had expressed a sense of his misconduct's being misconduct, which inevitably blotted it out. Now unhappily most of the offenders held the view that begging pardon was unnecessary, and others didn't know that their speeches had been reported to her.) She ought to treat these false friends well, but it wasn't true to do so. She ought to forgive. How could she forgive, for they considered wrong right, and wrong that hurt her so terribly? She read the Bible, she read every work on forgiving that she could find. She consulted Father, and he said no one should be forgiven while he persisted in his wrong course. But, as Father said of himself, "his vials of wrath were soon emptied" and troubled him very little; he never could have any guess of what Mother's were to her. She asked him whether she couldn't set forth her views of their actions to those who had so troubled her, but he said "No indeed." She studied this question year in and year out, her poor mind was all worn to deep & hopeless ruts, the deepest ones of course in her natural sensibility now morbid and exaggerated, those in the intellectual part, which had never yet led anywhere, only a little less deep. Through sleepless nights, in church, at work in her garden, even in company she laboured at this problem in her heart. It was made worse by a natural trait, uncorrected by education or experience, inability to see both sides.

Her sorrows seemed irremediable, her lot hopeless. Think of that, when actually blest with everything the human creature could desire, as she certainly was! When I first saw the proverb "It's a long lane that has no turning," it caused me to wonder whether my Mother would ever see a turning in her's, and gradually I came to hope with some confidence that she would. I can't say that there ever was any turn that one could see, it was so gradual that no one ever noticed it at any point, yet it is certain that before 1870 she suffered much less both in mind and body than she had up to 1850 and 1860.

Mother visited Aunt Susan in Plymouth—the house where she was born in 1853[271] with Edith and again in 1854 took Edith & Edward to Plymouth and boarded for two or three weeks, had very happy times seeing her friends, and was pleased that the children should become acquainted with her beloved town. Undoubtedly these visits distracted her attention a little from her troubles and did her some good. In these two years there were rose-shows in Concord. This was something delightful to her. She hastened to carry and arrange all her roses and discovered at the Show, quite unexpectedly I think, congenial souls in Judge Hoar and Mr Wheildon, who also loved and brought their own roses, and these three went round together examining every flower.[272]

Our Cousin Phebe Ripley gave us children music-lessons, and whether in that way she & Mother met more than the rest of the Ripley cousins, I don't know, but she was the one who first came much to our house. She always gave Mother a good time. Aunt Ripley began, perhaps earlier than this, to come every Sunday—we found her sitting on the parlour sofa after tea—and spend the evening. In 1854 Cousin Phebe was in Europe and the best letters imaginable came from her once a fortnight. Sophy came, certainly every other Sunday with her Mother, to read them to us, a delight to us all which we shall never forget.

Finally Sophy came every Sunday evening. Uncle George too when he was in Concord. Mr Channing about this time began to take tea with us on Sundays. He too spent the evening. In 1855 Mr Sanborn[273] came to Concord and usually walked in on Sunday evening. Our Sunday evening party was very agreeable, Mother liked it too, and every year it enlarged for a long time. I should say a dozen people were pretty sure to come, year after year, and often there would be twenty or more.

In 1856 Mr Agassiz was to give a lecture in Concord on the 20*th* March[274] and we asked Mrs Agassiz and Ida to come with him, and Annie Ward. I should say that this was the beginning of Mother's enjoying company again in a natural way. For a great many years she had only had Father's company whom she had got in the habit of regarding from the housekeeper point of view, as people for whom everything must be done very beautifully, and much trouble taken, so that her work must be set aside, but who would probably not regard her as anything but the housekeeper. But dear Mr & Mrs Agassiz were friendly and she had a day as happy as the rest of us did. And this experience kept being repeated till finally we children were able to add a cheerful ending to the sense impressed on us all our lives "Mother dreads company" and feel "Mother dreads the company before they come, but as soon as she sees them she enjoys them, and she loves to think of their visit afterwards."

In 1857 we had six or seven girls come for a week and Mother talked with them a great deal. Especially she talked Anti-Slavery to them, and it seems that it was a doctrine new to some of them, for Aunt Ripley told me afterwards that they had said to her "Only think, Mrs Emerson says"—and gave her an account of Mother's views. Aunt Ripley thought it was brave of Mother to set them forth clearly before the children of people who were pro-slavery and held high position in the world. But Mother would have been surprised to hear it called brave, it was a thing of course.

Mother and Father were faithful attendants of Anti-Slavery conventions, lectures &c. and Father gave lectures in New York and Boston Anti-Slavery courses. Mother had several friends made on these occasions, Mr Wendell Phillips, Mrs George R. Russell, Miss Lucy Goddard, Mr & Mrs George L. Stearns.[275] Dear Mrs Russell invited her several times to her house, so did Mrs Stearns, and Mrs Stearns and Mr Phillips often came to our house. With them she would hold pow-wows refreshing to her very soul, together they would pour forth their indignation and their forebodings, and blast with every epithet of contempt the South Side Clergy and the treacherous statesmen.

We children were growing up. That was one element in the turning of Mother's lane. We were becoming more available not only as readers but as assistants and companions. Our good times were somewhat reflected on her too.

In 1857, I should think it was, began her acquaintance with the John Forbeses.[276] They invited her and Father and me to Naushon. We all had a very good time. It was on this visit that Mother took a ride on horseback which I shall mention later. [Edith's comment: Father went in 1857—All were asked in 1858 together with choice of 2 weeks[.] Father sent Edward[,] me the first week & took Mother & Ellen the second.] Captain John Brown[277] came to Concord, more than once, and once stayed at our house. He told us that sheep had each its own physiognomy and if he had five hundred sheep he should know the moment he looked in its face if a strange sheep joined his flock, or, in other people's flocks, if he saw one of his own he always recognized it. When I was present he was talking on peaceful subjects, his conversion, and stories of things he had seen and known, very pretty stories—not about slavery.

Father had a double cousin, sister of Cousins Sarah & Charlotte, Cousin Rebecca Hamlin who when she was left a widow became a Shaker and went to live at Harvard with the Community there.[278] Her little daughter Mary grew up there, a Shaker. Once they came over to our house to see Cousin Charlotte.

Cousin Rebecca died and a year or two later Mary wrote to her Aunt Charlotte that she and a young Shaker named George Whiting were engaged and wished to go away to be married, had made up their minds to do so, when one of the Eldresses said that Sister Rebecca Hamlin's spirit had—I think it was at some table-tipping session, for the Shakers were spiritualists at that time—come to say that Mary was meditating a project which made her unhappy and that she begged the Eldress to expostulate with her and get her to abandon it. So, when Cousin Charlotte came to Concord, she told Mother about it, and Mother said "We will go right over and bring Mary away." On Saturday noon we set out in the carry all, I driving Dolly, Mother and Cousin Charlotte behind, and arrived at the Shaker Village about four o'clock. We drove up to the Office of the "Church Family," and were kindly received by the sister in charge who sent for Mary. I don't know whether Mary had said we could spend Sunday, or whether that was arranged after our arrival. A brother took the carryall and in due time we were shown to our rooms, through long entries without a thing in them, the floors of new yellow paint varnished and looking as if they were hardly walked on, and the rooms also shining yellow without carpets or curtains with a plain washstand, a plain table, two or three old-fashioned wooden chairs, and a bed with all its sheets, pillow-cases and counterpane so blued in washing that they were blue rather than white.

Mother had her nap and then we went down to tea. Mary visited us at the office, I don't remember that she went at all to our chambers, nor that she sat with us at tea. We did not eat with the Community. Their dining-hall was in another building. We had a table to ourselves and the sister who waited on us entertained us. Various elders & eldresses called on Friend Emerson's Wife, and had reminiscences of his visit some years before,[279] and some of them remembered Aunt Lizzy with affection she had visited them when her Father who was their lawyer, going to see them on business had taken her there. I remember she had made the acquaintance of a sister who loved to observe the stars and longed to know astronomy, and Aunt Lizzy after she came away sent her a Celestial Atlas. Some months later as she was riding in an omnibus two Shaker ladies got in and sat down opposite her. Instantly one of them leaned forward and clapping her hands upon Aunt Lizzy's knees cried out in ecstasy "You dear creetur, you dear creetur! It's you yourself! Oh how glad I am to see you! That Atlas about the Stars is the very best thing that ever was!" It was the astronomy-loving sister. I think she had died before this time when Mother, Cousin Charlotte and I came.

All the Shaker ladies were pale, all had either two or three black front teeth or none, all had on caps alike of course, beautifully done up but blued so much that they were blue rather than white. All were dressed in dark sober colours and had on a little shawl, either white, fawn-colour or gray. They began to be very depressing to me. While Mother was talking with the callers, Mary got a chance to talk to Cousin Charlotte, and she told us after we went upstairs that George like Mary had grown up in the Church Family, but about the time her Mother died he had been sent over to live with the South Family, and the separation revealed to both that they could not live without each other. So they came to an explanation, and as George was by nature a machinist and inventor and the Shakers had already accepted and profited by several of his improvements he felt sure he could make a living in the world, so they had planned to go quietly away and be married, when the messages from her Mother's spirit, and the laments and entreaties of the elder sisters who loved her made it uncertain whether she would do right.

Cousin Charlotte encouraged her, Mother too, and Mother soon made a direct request to take Mary with her. They were displeased and said Mary could do as she chose, they would not interfere. Mother now made an advance into the enemy's country. "She must not go away empty-handed. She has worked and has been useful to you for years. She ought not to be dismissed with nothing to show for it, she ought to have clothes and money provided." And to this Mother stoutly adhered, till they agreed to her taking all her own clothes and then to giving her some new clothes and a new dress. Mother said it mustn't be a Shaker gown, it must be plenty of new cloth, of such a colour as she liked, to make a world's dress of. This also they promised, and I think a few dollars in money. Mother wished to take her straight to Concord, but it was finally settled that George ought first to go out and find his place in the world, and then come for Mary, which certainly was wise.

On Sunday the Church Family had no service, I don't remember why. They took us over to the service of the South Family. This Family sat round the room and after the sitting service they rose and danced, singing hymns meanwhile, without any instrumental accompaniment. Each hymn seemed to be two verses long and was repeated more than once. I remember one,

> "Oh the beauty of Zion!
> See his branches shining there!
> Oh the beauty of heaven!
> See how the children grow there!
>
> All who are faithful here below
> Shall obtain a home there.
> Ye the obedient, simple and true
> Shall be freely crowned there!"

We dined at the Office of the South Family and while the sister was out of the room I said "I wonder how they feel while they are dancing." She heard me and rushed in, saying "I'll tell you how we feel 'Oh be joyful, and dance before the Lord'! that's the way we feel."

Having returned to the Church Family Mother found a gentleman—perhaps it was Elder Myrick Holden—waiting to see her. So she sat down with him, and another and another came in. Indeed they didn't stop. Mother sat in a corner far from the door. I sat opposite the door. All chairs were soon filled and many men were standing, several just outside. Presently a brother tiptoed into another room and brought two chairs, these were at once occupied and more and more were brought till the sides of the room were lined, and still other men arrived and whispered "I thought I'd come in and hear Friend Emerson's Wife talk."

Mother's nearer neighbours answered her and asked questions, nevertheless she did most of the talking. She gave them her views on marriage, that people were meant to marry, that they could be better and happier married than unmarried. One of the Shakers said "That is true, or would be if people were good enough." "Oh yes, if people only were good enough," Mother exclaimed. "The reason we object to marriage," said the Shakers "is that it is so high a state that the fallen creature is not worthy of it, is not capable of it. We hope to be raised by this life to a holiness in the next that shall enable us to enter into perfected marriage there." This statement pleased Mother very much, she told them she fully agreed with every word of it, yet it did not seem to her that this view should make them object to marriage, but should only lead them to make it high and holy here, that it might be only more so in heaven. She inquired whether they read Swedenborg and finding that they had not she gave them his teachings on "Conjugial Love." Next she learned that they had not heard of Coventry Patmore, and set forth the story and doctrines of the Angel in the House and the Espousals.[280] They expressed a wish to see it, and Mother promised to send them the books.

As the audience increased, for it was becoming really large I looked now and then at Mother to see whether she perceived that had any. I couldn't tell. She seemed entirely occupied with her interlocutors.

At last she said she was going up stairs, and with some difficulty made her way through the crowd. I asked her when she lay down whether she knew all those people had come to hear Friend Emerson's Wife talk. "Yes. When I saw they wished I should, I thought I would use my opportunity and hold forth to them. I hope you weren't ashamed of me."

After tea we took a walk from one settlement to another and round the buildings. Mary was with us. She said "George is coming" and pointed out to Cousin Charlotte which he was. She had some grass in her hand. After we passed it was in his. We were only four ladies when we set out, but very soon we were eight, and the procession grew. Those who joined us were chiefly young women Mary's friends I suppose, each seeking an opportunity to tell Mother or Cousin Charlotte that she wished to abandon the Community.

For twenty years afterwards we would occasionally meet a lady who would say "Don't you remember me? I had a talk with you when you came to take away Mary Hamlin from the Harvard Shakers. Yes, I used to be a Shaker. I've come away,—and so have a good many others."

On Monday morning we bade farewell to our new friends and came home.

Aunt Lizzy was going to Europe for the first time[.] Everyone was glad, she was just the person to go. Mother, always looked upon eider-down as one of the most desirable of possessions, it carried so much warmth, took little space, and weighed nothing, so thinking that was the best present she could give to Aunt Lizzy she decided to make her a little eider-down comforter. Aunt Susan Emerson some years before had given us a brown & white checked silk morning dress of hers which was made into a dress skirt for me and then for Edith to wear with a basque waist. There was enough left of it still good to make a case five feet long and two wide which Mother divided into rather narrow runs which she filled with down. After it was sewed up she put on each corner one of the little brown and white sewing-silk tassels which had adorned the waist of the dress when Aunt Susan wore it. When it was finished it had a modest elegance of expression that delighted Mother and her daughters, and it felt as soft and light and rolled into as small a bundle as Mother had hoped and she carried it to Aunt Lizzy. When Aunt Lizzy came home she said "Lidian, let me confess on the knees of my heart, that I have always rather despised eider-down, and when you brought me this little comforter I felt as if it was the kind of fussy thing that well and active people didn't need. But when I was cold in my berth I remembered it and put it on, and what a comfort it was! then and all winter! In the first place it was of a size that just fitted my berth, and then it was so small I could easily carry it round with me. When I went to cold galleries I wore it under my cloak and it warmed my shoulders and warmed my heart. I came to regard it as one of my chief treasures, and now, I have made my confession, and I thank you for giving it to me." This, of course, was a speech most charming to Mother, and after this when other near friends went abroad in winter she delighted in making for them a little eider down. The first time she came to our house after her return Aunt Lizzy again made Mother happy by saying, as she stood looking round the parlour, "I haven't seen in all my travels a prettier or pleasanter room than this." How Mother treasured that assurance! Aunt Lizzy had come as long as Grandma lived very often to see her and would stop into Mother's room for a call. Afterwards one day Mother said "You don't come half as often as you used to." "No, for there is no longer any centre in this house. I was always sure of finding Mamma in her room and ready to see me, but I may find you so busy that I shall interrupt you, or gone to Boston or out, in your garden or elsewhere." But she never left off coming, and how much of joy and comfort she usually brought with her! She had al-ways pretty little stories to tell, as, for instance, that she had bought a doll's bedstead for a child and if I remember right was making a mattress & pillows for it and Miss Martha Munroe,[281] returning from her morning errands down town, came in, saw it with the quickest interest, and exclaimed "All it needs to be perfect is a little feather-bed!" "Yes, but it had used up my materials & my energy to make the mattress and pillows. I have decided that they will have to suffice for it," said Aunt Lizzy. "You just let me make the feather bed. I have a piece of ticking and some feathers that will be just the thing!" and Miss Munroe having taken the measure, hastened home and brought back at noon the most perfect miniature feather-bed! "That was just like Miss Martha Munroe," she ended, "the eyes open to see where she could please and help, and the cheerful sense of power to do with ease any exquisite handiwork." Aunt Lizzy as long as there was a baby at our house used to tell beautiful nursery-stories, as about a mouse who desired to get some one "to sew on my beautiful long *tail* again." And, when we were a few years older, tales from Gammer Gretel.[282] All our lives she continually brought funny accounts of children's sayings and doings, and indeed there was no end to her charming talk and all its beautiful subjects[.] Her epitaph truly says "In her unfailing memory all things excellent and beautiful lay in exact order as in a royal treasury, hospitable ready to instruct and delight young and old." Mother could sometimes complain to her of things that troubled her and obtain sympathy, or light on the case, and it seems to me she was the one person to whom she could.

It always seemed to Mother wholly wrong that Aunt Lizzy had never invited her to a meal in her house, and after feeling badly about it for some years she asked her how it had happened. "Why it isn't my house, it is my Mother's," she said, "and Mother feels much aggrieved on her part that you have never asked her here. Therefore she does not invite you." A most unexpected turning of the tables! Mother also, more & more shocked at Mrs Hawthorne's asking Father several times to her house when there were other ladies and omitting her altogether, finally asked her "Why do you so?" and Mrs Hawthorne answered "you are such a great invalid it never occurred to me that you *could* come." "Yet I have often invited you and you have seen that the company was sometimes large. If I am able to have much company, why should you suppose me unable to enjoy the refreshment of going out?"

To return to Aunt Lizzy, she was not only a sister to Mother in coming to see her, in being the best friend to tell everything to on our side, and on her side to interest us with all her talk, not only making all our acquisitious presents or purchases doubly valuable by her caring to see and talk them over, and especially all letters that came, but she came, like a good fairy, to tell Mother, when she was going to New York, that *undersleeves,* a thing we had never heard of, had come in fashion, and to bring her three pretty pair to wear there. And when Mrs

Bancroft invited Mother to Newport Aunt Lizzy brought three or four yards of real lace to add to her equipment. The Mechlin lace was her present from Europe[.][283] On occasion of Cousin Mary Simmon's wedding she drove over to Waltham with Father and Mother, she alone on the back seat sewing all the way to finish Mother's dress for the wedding. She had praise for all Mother's household achievements when she approved of them, but she did not always approve. Sometimes she even blamed and, as Mother thought, unjustly, but this made us sure that when she praised the praise came from her heart. That September Miss Mary Howland Russell wrote from Seconnet[284] inviting Mother to come and spend a fortnight with her there as her guest. Mother had settled into the habit of thinking she couldn't go anywhere, but we all said she should and she got off at last to our great satisfaction. In two days I wrote to her and my letter crossed one from her saying the place was beautiful, the air in itself seemed to make her well, everything tasted good, she had had good nights and was having beautiful talks with Miss Russell and found most agreeable new friends. How we did rejoice! And wrote our congratulations to send in the morning's mail. They went. In the afternoon the R.R. carriage drove into our yard. We ran to the window. Mother was getting out—and there was her trunk with her! How dreadfully we all felt! Our glorious bubble burst so suddenly! "What has happened?" we all cried, for Father had seen her from the study window and we all had run to meet her. "Why Ellen said in her letter her Father had caught a cold and I knew no one would know how to take care of him, so I came right home." I cannot convey the utter misery of that moment to me and all of us. There was nothing to be done. Mother had given up her visit and closed the door behind her. We could not send her back. Father's cold was nothing—already well. That it could have in the slightest degree alarmed Mother I had never had any reason to suppose, no one had ever thought of a cold's doing anyone harm before, that I could remember. Edith went to school in Cambridge a few weeks later than this, and had the privilege of boarding at Mrs Charles Lowell's.[285] Mother had immense interest and pleasure in getting her ready to go and in her letters which gave us the account of all her happy seeings and doings. Edward was now fourteen, I was going to school with him at Mr Sanborn's school, and his language so amused the family, and was so catching that Edith said when she returned in the spring she was dismayed to find everyone, even her respected parents, talking slang.

We had seen at Naushon for the first time a Moderateur lamp with a china shade casting the light down, and I, two years before, had seen the Ward family sit down together every evening to be read aloud to by Mr Ward while Mrs Ward and the girls sewed. *We* had never sat together in the evening, Father had retired to his study, Mother to her work upstairs, we children might be with her or each in a separate room. We counted that if the 4 or 5 other lamps we now used were put out every evening we might afford to burn a Moderateur, so we bought [See Sketch] one[.] Father graciously granted our request to read aloud to us till 8 o'clock & we began to have family evening putting out the other lamps when Moderateur was lighted, and *that,* when we lighted them to go to bed. The next year kerosene was introduced and we bade a joyous farewell to other oil. Father always trained Edward & Edith to speak their pieces at school well, and me too while I went to Mr Sanborn's school. One afternoon he was teaching me to speak Childe Dyring[286] and could not in any way get me to give the right sound to

> "'Twas lang in the night & the bairnies grat
> Their mither she under the mools heard that.

Mother was lying on the study-sofa with her eyes closed, I doubt whether she was paying much attention to the lesson. Father suddenly said "Here's your Mammy—she'll be sure to say it right! Queeny,"—"What?" said Mother, opening her eyes with a start.

> Say, 'Twas lang in the night and Bairnies grat
> Their Mither under the mools heard that."

And Mother instantly said it with such truth as left Father's rendering nowhere and made him laugh right out with joy. It was pure nature with her. Mr & Mrs Bancroft sent an invitation to Father and Mother to go to Newport. How glad we were that Mother would go! I remember very little about this visit. I know Mr Alexander Bliss[287] was there with Father and Mother. I remember that Mother had the old joy in talking with Mrs Bancroft, that Mr Bancroft was interested in roses, (they were his, not his wife's) and took Mother out to show them to her and tell her all about them, and that the beautiful lawn, the surrounding beautiful lawns and fine houses, the Cliffs and the Cliff-walk and the sea seen from it and from the windows, that all these were seen and admired by her. In fact the whole visit was good.

They also went to stay with Miss Sarah Clarke[288] at this time, or another summer, which was another week of unusual health and happiness. They both always cared for Miss Clarke, Father sometimes said she ought to be called Santa Sara. Mrs Helen Hunt,[289] the poetess, H.H. was her guest at the same time, and became a friend, with whom

Mother I had never had any reason to suppose, &
no one had ever thought of a cold's doing anyone
any harm before that I could remember.

Edith went to school in Cambridge a few weeks
later than this, and had the privilege of boarding
at Mrs Charles Lowell's. Mother had immense interest
and pleasure in getting her ready to go and in her
letters which gave us the account of all her happy
doings and sayings. Edward was now fourteen, I
was going to school with him at Mr Sanborn's
school, and his language so amused the family,
and was so catching that Edith said when she
returned in the Spring she was dismayed to find
everyone, even her respected parents, talking slang.

We had seen at Nauchon for the first time
a Moderateur lamp with a china shade casting
the light down, and I, two years before, had seen
the Ward family sit down together every evening to
be read aloud to by Mr Ward while Mrs Ward and the
girls sewed. We had never sat together in the evening;
Father had retired to his study, Mother to her work
upstairs, we children might be with her or each in a
separate room. We counted that if the 4 or 5 other
lamps we now used were put out every evening we
might afford to burn a Moderateur, so we sought one.
Father graciously granted our request to read aloud
to us till 8 o'clock. & we began to have family even—

both Father and Mother kept up intercourse till she moved to Colorado.

There was a time when frolicking began in our household and I suppose it must have been about this time. Father was always ready and now we were old enough. We had almost always, after we once began, very funny times at the table, but I think Mother held quite aloof from it at first.

One day I was reading aloud Mr Sears's book Regeneration[290] to Mother and when I stopped I asked her whether he was living. She said yes, he was minister of Wayland. Wayland was only 7 miles off. Why shouldn't we go over to hear him preach? We went, the next Sunday, and his preaching seemed just what we wanted. So we went almost every week. It never crossed Mother's mind nor mine that this must be uncomfortable for our own new minister.[291]

In April, as we were driving home we discovered Walden woods were burning. Edward was sure he could make better speed than Dolly and the carryall, and he ran all the way to the churches to give the alarm, then hastened back to help put out the fire. He had had nothing to eat since breakfast, and he wasn't sixteen. When he came home hot & exhausted at about five in the afternoon he naturally ate a good dinner, and was something that was perhaps in itself not good for him. He came down the next day with his typhoid fever. The doctor came. Mother inquired after the medical visit was over and she and the doctor were still sitting in Edward's room whether our minister had spoken as he ought about the sins of our Government. The doctor thought he ought not to speak of them in church. They soon started an argument. Edward beckoned to me and said arguing distressed him, he wished I would see whether they wouldn't move into another room. This was the first light I had on two points 1st that Edward hated arguing and 2d that Mother loved it better than any other amusement. Ever after, both these facts were clear to me and received abundant illustration I could discourse a long time on this fever of Edward's, but that is not about Mother, so I will return to her. Mother had begun to call Mrs Sanborn her dear eldest daughter, and she said she didn't know anything about the Old Testament, so Mother undertook to read the book of Genesis aloud to her and several of the girls we liked. I remember its beginning with enthusiasm, and that the familiar words never seemed so beautiful and it was one of the times when Mother's voice sounded most charming to me. But it cannot have gone on many weeks. I don't know what put an end to it. From the beginning of her acquaintance with her to the last Mrs Sanborn brought Mother more joy every time she saw her than anyone outside of her immediate family.

From 1860, on, Uncle William's family came to Concord to spend the summers. This made a new era for us children, it was having second parents and three delightful brothers; especially happy was the summer of 1862 when Aunt Susan stayed all summer at our house and we had the rest of her family every now & than, one or two at a time. But I do not recall that it made so much difference to Mother.

In 1861 when the war broke out Mother felt nothing but gladness "This is the beginning of the end of slavery," was the first word she said to me when I met her in Boston (I had been away from home.) Edward was then seventeen. He hoped at eighteen to go to the war, but Mother always said "not till the slaves are freed." She used sometimes to go to Soldiers' Aid Society, but her low esteem of sewing kept her at home, and when she found that the bandage-department valued English pins, she set herself to buying those and bringing them to the ladies. Our managers were very exact, never sent a garment that was not well made, and as to bandages they had a certain bandage stitch very superior, allowed no knots and insisted on firm fastening-off. Mr Reynolds[292] tested their strength & rolled many on the machine[.] Miss Martha Bartlett had a machine to roll them on; when rolled, they were pinned with Mother's pins, stamped Concord, Mass. and packed. It is really incredible the fame those bandages won. We heard about them more and more as long as the war lasted; from all sorts of sources, tales such as this. A Concord man was having an ugly wound dressed, and heard the surgeon exclaim when the nurse brought him the bandages "Thank goodness! they're Concord, Mass. bandages. They are always perfect and they have a pin in them that will work!" Of course the man wrote this home when he was able and we were all proud and took more & more pains with them. When every old sheet in Concord had been made up and sent, people began to sacrifice their good ones, and Mother, greatly elated, saw to it that the supply of pins never failed. The Sanitary Commission authorities sent thanks for our superior bandages, and every army-surgeon that met any Concord citizen was sure to speak of them with praise.

Edward went to College but had not recovered entirely from the effects of his fever, and in six weeks came home unable to go on. That winter he had a job in a surveyor's train doing some measuring-off at Mt. Auburn, and in the spring Uncle Adams sent him to California with a party headed by Dr Anderson,[293] a physician and a botanist, a superior man, who was to travel across the plains from Omaha to Nevada, emigrant-fashion, on horse-back and with a wagon. Edward made this journey. I should like to tell all about it, but it isn't about Mother.

In the course of this summer the President said he should issue the Emancipation Proclamation on the next New Years Day. The fortune of war seemed steadily against the North at that time. Charley Emerson, hearing of the defeat of Banks in the Shenandoah Valley had gone to his Father determined to go, and backed by his eldest brother William had wrung from him a consent to his joining the 7*th* Reg. of N.Y. which was to go on garrison duty, and several of Edward's schoolmates were already gone. He came home hoping to be allowed to go too. Poor child, he was burned dark brown on Western plains and on a three weeks voyage, and he was so thin it seemed to us all that the parlour-door opened scarcely three inches to let him in. His parents were frightened by his looks—as Wm Emerson jr. said of him "His cheeks looked the cheeks of sixty rather than sixteen." He couldn't go to war. But he picked up a little at once and was considered fit to try college again, and there he grew strong so that when he came one day to dine at home and Mother offered him her beer saying "It will be good for you in your present low condition," it made him, and all of us, laugh.

He never stopped trying to get leave to go to the war, and the slaves being free Mother gave her consent, Father too; and when he was off at last Mr Forbes waylaid him and said to him. "I am not half the man I was, since Will went to the war. If Malcolm should go too, I think my usefulness would be ended. You are your Father's only son. I leave it to you to judge whether your Father's services to your country or those that you could offer would be of most value."[294] And dear Edward gave up his heart's desire just as he had at last attained it, and came home to the friends he had just said goodbye to, and told them he would not go. How grateful were Father & Mother to Mr Forbes!

It was amusing to us when we came to notice it that the family were Freshman in feeling when Edward was a Freshman and actually became Sophomore when Edward was a Sophomore. Mother had all her life declaimed to us against hazing as a dastardly and even criminal practice and in the year 1861 she felt it more vividly than ever. In 1862 Edward's former class—as he had dropped a year—were Sophomores, and I think he and Tom received only one hazing visit which was not very severe, but Mother was of course indignant. In 1863 Edward himself told of their visits of some classmates to the Freshmen, and when he related their experiences all of us, even Mother, laughed at the funny schemes of the Sophomores and wondered that the Freshmen should be so terrified, so weak and compliant. Not a word was said about the atrocity of terrifying them. Yes the Family all went through College *with* Edward, he brought us on Saturday nights all the experiences, the fun and the songs.

We now come to a further turn in Mother's lane. Aunt Susan Emerson said to me one day[,]²⁹⁵ "Your Mother, I am convinced suffers much more than she need, for want of sufficient food to properly support her. A good many years ago, when your Grandmother was spending a winter with us, and I was very feeble and growing more so, the Doctor told her that my digestion was all out of order but that I needed nourishment, and two mouthfuls of something appetizing that was a surprise given me every quarter of an hour through the day would probably restore me, and your Grandmother at once did exactly what he said. One time 'twas a little scrap of hot buttered toast, another time 'twas a spoonful of good broth, another time 'twas two broiled oysters. It took much ingenuity and a great deal of time and trouble, but because there was one person in the world who cared enough to have me live to be willing to do that for me day after day I was made well. You don't take any care of your Mother. I am sure, if you did, you could help her very much."

This was a new idea and I saw it promised well. I was besides much affected by those words "cared enough to have me live." As I went home I thought over what I could do. Mrs Hemenway²⁹⁶ had lately taken me to a cooking-class where I had seen a lesson in broiling steak and, further, the preparation of what the teacher called a *"tisane."* She beat up an egg in a tumbler with a little salt then got some one to drip water from the spout of the boiling tea-kettle drop by drop upon the egg, she still briskly beating it, till the tumbler was nearly full of what one might call a smooth yellow milk. She told us that the weakest stomach would welcome it, and it was sure to do good. I resolved to begin with this. First on reaching the house I ran up to Mother's room. She, in a paroxysm of nervous distress, was violently pacing the room, looking wild & wringing her hands. This alas! was only too common a state of things. I ran right down, prepared my tisane successfully, brought it to her and told her what Aunt Susan had said. At first she would not pause in her walk, but the sense that Aunt Susan had felt for her was grateful to her and that I had taken the pains to make something for her made it necessary to have the manners to accept it. Besides, starving nature at once perceived the attraction of food. She approached me, said she shouldn't dare to take it, she was not well enough, but she would taste it as an acknowledgment of my attention. She tasted, she drank a little, she actually sat down and while inquiring into its composition, she sipped at it till 'twas all gone, I watching to see if it had any effect. How happy I was to see all the agony not only over but forgotten! She calmly said it was time for her nap, asked me to read to her and went to bed and to sleep. Of course I pursued this course, not once in 15 m[inutes] but I made sure that at meals she did eat, and thought of things to use when she had not and using all my wits was able to get Mother to eat more and more. The other children, of course too, took hold, and when we were in the house it seldom happened that Mother had those terrible times again. She learned to believe that food was not poison, she gained flesh and grew pretty having often a lovely colour in her cheeks like sunset on snow. How proud of her beauty we became!

Mrs Richardson who used to come to the house and make Mother's caps & bonnets for her learned to watch them very narrowly when they went out of her hands, for Mother would take them up to try on, and forget them instantly (as it says in the epistle of James) after having critically surveyed them in the looking-glass.[297]

She didn't take off the fresh cap or the new bonnet, but would, almost surely, make straight for her bed and lie down, wholly regardless of its welfare, unconscious of its existence; though to Mrs Richardson or any bystander it looked as if her intention was to ruin it. Mrs Richardson assisted by a chorus of all present, would cry "You've got the bonnet *on*! Don't lie down in it!" and Mother would laugh, quite pleased with her sin and take it off.

There was one peculiarity about Mother's dressing very amusing to me and vexatious to her which was new, and which neither she nor I had practical philosophy enough to trace to its cause and prevent. It was this; her skirts, almost invariably, as they went on, got a twist which caught the hem in the placket so that it hung out as a tail, and there was a festoon below in consequence. Whenever I came into her room while she was dressing I found her thus adorned and straightened her out. It always made us laugh. I, "There it is again!" Mother, "Ye powers! A sight for men and angels!" she would cry, or "Mystery of mysteries! how came it there?" She had also a wondrous faculty for catching the door-knob or the bureau knob both in placket & pocket, and was continually brought up short by this means as she hastened hither & thither[.] This she never could endure. "That *dreadful* knob has caught me," she would wail, "As if I wasn't suffering enough before!" She sometimes gave orations on the subject full of fun and fury, but one of the most impressive to me was her innocent and unconscious remark one evening "I have had a good day today; I have felt remarkably well all the time that I wasn't caught in knobs."

Father every night when he came upstairs was sure to sing the praises of his children, but he wished to impute his pride in them to Mother so he usually began "You think your son Edward is"—&c and ended with, "Mrs Dowd[298] thinks just the same about her Johnny." "So does Mr Dowd!" Mother would retort. By degrees parental satisfaction acquired in our family the name of Dowdism, and when Father repeated any proud remark of Mother's he said "Mrs Dowd says"—

Father, as he grew older, began to lose his hair in patches, but some months after a patch had been bare the hair would grow again on it though falling off somewhere else. He took in his youth a dislike to what he called "the unending ablutions" of his tidy brother Uncle William and always made short work with washing[.] One night after he came upstairs Mother who was searching her homoeopathic medical book cried out joyously, "Mr Emerson, Mr Emerson! I have found the very medicine for you! Listen to the symptoms which are mentioned as pointing to the need of it. 'Irritability of temper, aversion to ablutions, falling off of hair.' Don't you want to begin the cure this minute?"

In 1862 came Edith Davidson to be my daughter[.][299] She was ten years old and remained till she was thirteen when her Mother went to house-keeping and wanted her back. Mother had on the whole little to do with her while she was in the house though she enjoyed Edie's hearty interest in the hymns she read to her & me every night after we went to bed, but while I was in Fayal Edie, who remained all her life a part of our family, often saw her at Edith's[,] read to her, talked with her and thenceforth was a daughter to her[,] too.

Another turn in Mother's lane, and quite as important, was that Mr Horatio Woodman and then Mr James T. Fields[300] asked Father to give courses of lectures in Boston and took all the charge of them, hiring hall, selling tickets &c. and various friends old and new, Mrs George R. Russell, Mrs Tappan, Mrs Bartol,[301] Mrs J. T. Fields and others wrote to ask him and Mother to come after the lecture and spend the night, and Mother went—had good times, made friends, and life began to be more interesting. Father usually went to Boston to Parker's Hotel[302] a day or two before, that he might shut himself up alone with his lecture and write uninterrupted. On the day of the lecture she followed and went up to his room in the Hotel. She always said "I think your Father loved to have me come. He always seems as glad to see me as if he had been homesick." On one of these occasions Mother was going to bring a trunk with her, and before he went he said "The best way will be to send a carriage to meet you at the train. I'll do that." "But how will the driver know me?" "I can tell him to look for a tall thin lady, dressed in black, with a white face and her eyes fixed on the distant future." Whether he did give this description I don't know, but the driver pounced on her unhesitatingly. Certainly these words of Father's caused us children to look at Mother in the street for her general effect, and it is true, the whiteness of her face shone in her black bonnet to a great distance[.]

In the last year of the war Storrow Higginson sent his Colonel (who had then no acquaintances in this country to visit in his leave of ab- scence) later Gen. S. C. Armstrong[303] to Edward with a letter of intro- duction and he spent the evening and night at our house. Father was away, but he took to Mother instantly and told her all his story. He said he had come from the Sandwich Islands to Williams College and when the war broke out he "volunteered at once as a soldier, simply because he liked to see fair play. Somebody had got to go, and it ought to be young strong fellows like himself who had no family ties rather than men who were husbands & fathers. This was all very well till he went into his first battle. Then he couldn't see any reason why he should stand up there to be shot at" and it troubled him. He wasn't sure that he cared enough to prevent the South from seceding to give his life for that. "But the moment the emancipation of the slaves became the question it changed his feeling wholly. Now there was a principle behind him whenever he stood up to be shot at. For their freedom he was willing to lay down his life." That visit of his was a romance to us all and we loved him ever after.

I think Father's nephews had grown up without knowing Mother very well, though they had been so much at the house but in 1863 William brought his friend Abraham S. Jackson of New Jersey to stay a day or two with us, and I should say that for the first time William devoted all the time that she was in sight to talking with Mother, he seemed to discover her. They got at once onto politics and public affairs and while Mother was a hot & fiery radical in such matters William was conservative. He loved to argue as well as Mother, and she—not to lose the joy of combat—instead of going up to her room after dinner lay down on the parlour sofa and continued the discussion. Edith and our cousin Harriet Jackson, Edward & I went out to play crocquet. By and by William's Mr Jackson came out and exclaimed "It amuses me so much to hear William and his *ant* argue, I could roll on the floor with *laffing!*"

From Wayland we had brought home two white kittens, one with yellow eyes like topazes we named Topaz, our Kate Sally called her the tuppuz-cat, she grew up into an ordinary cat with coarse white fur, ordinarily clean, the other named Milcah kept her soft fine coat always white as snow, was beautiful and graceful more than any other we have had and was remarkably large and intelligent. She used to look very handsome stretched on the grass by the front door in hot days. One of her eyes was light yellow the other light blue. They belonged to Edith but all cats belonged to Mother. When her breakfast was carried up they accompanied the bearer if they had not preceded her. They at once jumped up on the bed and paid such devoted attention to each mouthful she took that she threw one on the floor to draw them off. Both great creatures bounded down, but if there was only one piece the one that didn't get it was back again in an instant. This became very entertaining to Mother. She loved to see them sitting before her all earnest and alert and the jump off and the jump back each amused her. [See Sketch] It often too tired her, and certainly interfered with her getting her breakfast. A great deal of the time as she went about the house and always in the garden they were following her about, not, as she truly said, from affection but in hope of the loaves and fishes. She always gave them a ten o'clock supper and as that hour approached they were more and more devoted. When she passed our doors or through our rooms after we went to bed the tarumpa tarumpa of eight cantering paws accompanied her, and she used to cry out with nervousness and impatience "Oh if these cats would only let me alone I could live! Yes Topaz, Missy will! Missy knows, Milcah! I wish I had never begun to feed them at night." They added much fun to the family life every day. Once Mother brought home from the shop a roll of batting and laid it on a couch of Aunt Susan Emerson's which was at that time in her room, with a pile of work. Its end was toward the door. Presently Topaz came sauntering in; she instantly descried this round white—I suppose she thought—face of some strange animal,—cat possibly, and was filled with indignation. I think we were all present, and Topaz's reconnoitering and final charge upon the enemy were one of the funniest little dramas ever seen. Then the sports of Topaz & Milcah together were daily exhilarating. One day I jumped into the middle of Mother's room with a shout—I forget whether I was pleased or angry—Mother, startled, screamed loud & long, Milcah sound asleep in the rocking-chair waked in affright and tore frantically up the back of the chair to escape she knew not what. Her great weight tipped over the chair, it banged on the floor, she spit violently, tried to run ten ways at once, at last made up her mind and vanished like a streak of lightning. Mother now screamed with laughter, and so did I. The thought of it has made us laugh ever since. We had another domestic comedy soon after not less exciting. Edith had a parrot which was a member of the family to whom we owed many gay moments out-of-doors and in. She slept in her cage but spent her days on a perch which was moved about with the family. She could get off it, and often did. At Thanksgiving we have always dressed the rooms downstairs with hemlock over every picture and the

threw one on the floor to draw them off. Both 251
great creatures bounded down, but if there was only
one piece the one that didn't get it was back again
in an instant. This became very entertaining to
Mother. She loved to see them sitting before her all

earnest and alert and
the jump off and the
jump back each amused
her. It often too tired
her, and certainly
interfered with her getting
her breakfast. A great
deal of the time as
she went about the house and always in the
garden they were following her about, not, as
she truly said, from affection but in hope of
the loaves and fishes. She always gave them a
ten o'clock supper and as that hour approached
they were more and more devoted. When she
passed our doors or through our rooms, the
after an overt to bed
tarumpa tarumpa of light cantering paws
accompanied her, and she used to cry out
with nervousness and impatience "Oh if these
cats would only let me alone I could live!
Yes, Topez, Missy will! Missy knows, Milcah!" I
251

parlour & dining-room looking-glasses and the hemlock stayed there all winter. In those days there was no bay-window in the dining-room, the windows were like the red-room windows and had curtains. One winter Sunday we had just returned from Sunday walk and had come in to the dining-room fire. It was near tea-time, the lamps were lighted, Mother was down and stood at the pier-table between the windows with her cake-boxes open on the table, cutting cake to fill the cake-basket for tea. Suddenly rose such a combined shriek and squawk as brought us all, confounded, to our feet; something heavy & clawy with rustle of plumes too had fallen on Mother's head in a smart rain of hemlock leaves & boughs, bounced thence to the edge of the open trunk-cake-box and thence to the floor, and Mother had screamed mightily. It was Polly, who certainly not less amazed & terrified than Mother had also cried out to heaven & earth[.] By the time any of us had got our wits together to inquire what was going on she was travelling swiftly along the wall under the sofa, calming her excited nerves with repeated exclamations of "pretty!" and as we took in what had occurred, the whole family, and Maggie the girl who was setting the table, were doubled up with laughter. Polly, mistress of all she surveyed while we were gone, had left her perch, climbed up the window-curtain and settled herself in the hemlock boughs over the looking-glass, where probably she had taken a nap, but reviving with the light and the company, she had undertaken to chassez out to the end of one of the boughs, which of course her weight pulled right out, and from her proud height she had fallen oh! how unexpectedly! into depths of dismay.

Once we asked our seamstress, whom Polly loved, to teach her a new speech and for several days we kept the parrot covered dark in her cage and the seamstress who was at work beside her kept making the speech. But it was of no avail. Father asked Kate whether Polly had said her lesson "No," said Kate, "but she made a beautiful offer to say it." Father often spoke of this as a most typical Irish answer.

In 1864 our James Burke who had lived with us eleven years went to a young married man, John Clahane,[304] who had lately moved to Concord from Lincoln, told him he was going to Boston and asked him if he would take his place and work for Father till he came back. John agreed to do so. When Father went out to look at his trees, he saw a strange man at work. He accosted him, asking where James was, John told him what James had asked of him. "Oh, very well!" said Father supposing James would be back at night. He did not come for many days and then only to ask whether Father was pleased with John and say that he himself had given up field-labour and was working in a lamp-factory, and John stayed with us twenty-eight years, dying only seven or eight months before Mother did. John was all this time perfectly devoted, faithful and pleasant. He made our interest his own, and used to say when Mother would tell him she might want him to come bring her home late tonight "Any time, Mrs Emerson. I'll be ready when you want me."

In 1865 Edith was engaged, and never was a family better pleased with an engagement than ours, Mother as much as the rest. It seemed to me quite individual and unlike other people that Mother said over & over again that summer when she or we were rejoicing in it "Yet a great sorrow is often a greater blessing than a great happiness."[305] Her mind seemed to fall in that direction. The getting Edith's wedding outfit was naturally an immense pleasure in every detail. Mother boarded for those weeks in Dorchester with Mrs Increase Smith[306] and two of those weeks Edith and I were at Mary Higginson's house in Boston by her kind invitation. Mother came to town as soon as she had had her breakfast and we went round all day together shopping. It was a happy time and Mother all the rest of her life used to look back to it and say "Wasn't it pleasant?" For her dress to wear to the wedding she got a black silk with satin dots and said it was the last silk she should ever buy, it would last her the rest of her life. This was the first time she said that in buying a black silk. I think she said it on some dozen later occasions. This dress being made in due season was put away till the wedding. Mother always counted it one of the greatest escapes of her life that the day before the wedding it chanced to occur to her to try the dress on, it seemed always very remarkable to her that it had. She couldn't get it on, she tried again. What was the matter? On examination she found the right sleeve had been sewed into the left armhole, and the left into the right. "And what could I have done at the last minute? I had no other dress. The last one was old and shabby." Now there was time to attend to it. I wonder whether any family ever had so much pleasure out of preparing for a wedding and the wedding itself as we did that time. From beginning to end we enjoyed every minute to the utmost, and I am happy to say there was no old shoe business and the rice-throwing had not then been invented. When all was over Mother found the caterer had scraped all the ice-cream from the plates into a pudding-dish. She seized it and said "I wonder if the horse wouldn't like it." She carried it out to Dolly in the East yard, and Dolly seemed to fully appreciate the luxury. "She likes it, she likes it!" cried Mother as she stood holding the dish till Dolly had taken the last drop went on, "Dear Dolly! Did you have a wedding-feast too? You should! Yes you should!"

Edith's house and the visits to her and from her were as delightful to Mother as to all Mothers. The next year Edward was graduated and went immediately to Burlington Iowa to see if he could be found useful in the C. B. & Q. R. R. office. Mother packed his trunk for him, it was his 22d birthday. The next morning before he started came a telegram from Will announcing that Ralph had come.[307] Father's voice broke as he read it. We rushed up to tell Mother who of course rejoiced greatly, then Edward bade her goodbye. I drove him to the train and we started early that we might stop to tell the news to Aunt Lizzy (who at once, when we left her, went into her garden, gathered all her white July lilies and went round to give each of her neighbours a stalk of them with the announcement) then to Aunt Lucy at Mrs Thoreau's. She cried for joy. I went that day to stay with Edith and a week or two after Mother & Father came to see the baby. Mother laid him in her lap. "Why don't you kiss him?" I asked astonished. "I want to wait till I begin to love him," said Mother. That always seemed to me very funny. She loved babies and was utterly devoted to Edith's in particular, I cannot understand how she could help hugging him at once. Then Father came up. He hugged him as I desired but he had forgotten how to manage a little baby, and was most grateful when I showed him how, having[308] lately learned myself and retaining a clear remembrance of the difficulties. As soon as Father had properly placed him both baby and Grandpapa were happy. That summer Mother had a very long sickness I thought she couldn't live; very likely I had no reason to think so, but I did. At last however she began to improve and in October was walking out again, and when I, beside her, shivered in the frosty gale, she said, "I enjoy it. I love to drink in these 'gallons of good October'!" She took a class in Sunday School of girls of sixteen and went to Teachers' Meeting at Mr Reynolds's[.] She enjoyed both. At Christmas-time Edward came home pulled down with malaria and remained at home till spring. He took a S. S. class and went also to Teachers' Meeting. These were Mr Reynolds's happiest days, his Bible-Class of young people was large and to the Teachers' Meeting on alternate Sunday evenings came many grown-up people besides the teachers. At one of these meetings Judge Hoar who was often there, in a tone which sounded to Edward's sensitive ears like an attack, asked Mother a question. Edward's soul died within him. "He knew," he said afterwards "that Mother could defend herself and would enjoy doing it," and there would be an argument in which he himself should be cruelly interested for Judge Hoar would say things that would sound to him sharp. Mother, also foreseeing an argument, kindled up to the onset and sparkled with satisfaction as she got her lance in rest. She thought

By permission of the Houghton Library, Harvard University
Lidian Jackson Emerson

for a minute just what was her opinion and out it came clear and fully stated. "Thankyou, Mrs Emerson," said the Judge, "that is exactly what I hoped you would say. I agree with you." Edward felt as one does when one dreams one is falling off a precipice and wakes with the fright to find one's self in one's quiet bed. I am sorry to say Mother soon gave up her class. She said she was not strong enough to sit up another hour after church was over.

In 1867 I was sick and Mother took all the care of me. People in those days never thought of nurses. I seemed to improve for several days, then I grew worse. All my relations Aunt Susan, Uncle William and Aunt Lizzy were disturbed and I remember Mother's indignation as she said "They all talk to me and blame me as if you were their child and I was taking care of you for them, and it was my fault that you are worse. I should think it might occur to them that you are my child and it concerns me more than it does them that you are sick!"

It was in this summer that Aunt Ripley died.[309] And Aunt Lucy, who had been boarding in the house Aunt Susan Jackson now lives in, moved to Mrs Beal's the house now called the Wright Tavern. Aunt Susan Emerson lived in Miss Angelina Ball's house,[310] and invited us and Aunt Lucy and Aunt Lizzy to spend Christmas-Day with her & Uncle William & Charley, and Cousin Charlotte who also lived with them. At dinner Uncle William said "We have some good sparkling cider, wouldn't you like some, Mrs Brown?" Now Aunt Lucy highly prized any acid drink and the "sparkling" sounded very good, and she said yes. The cider was brought. I think Charley was sent down cellar for it, and it opened with a fine pop. Uncle William filled Aunt Lucy's glass, then offered the cider to Mother who refused, to Aunt Lizzy who accepted, and then all round the table, but no one else said yes. Aunt Lucy said afterwards "Oh how thankful I was that your Aunt Lizzy drank some cider too. I should have felt like sinking into the earth if it had proved to be brought and opened only for me." I told Aunt Lizzy and she said "Yes, I was sure it would be much more comfortable for her if at least one other person joined her." It always seemed to me a most Christian act in Aunt Lizzy, it showed a watchfulness to serve that the plan instantly suggested itself to her, before she knew certainly that the other five or six would all refuse. In the evening Uncle William read to us Milton's Christmas Hymn.[311] I believe that was the first time, and every Christmas since it has been read when we have been in Concord. The next Christmas how were we scattered! Aunt Lucy, Aunt Susan and Uncle William dead, Charley in Europe, Cousin Charlotte in Brooklyn, I in Fayal.[312] In February Aunt Susan and Aunt Lucy died within a few days of each other.[313] Aunt Lucy was buried from our house. Miss Fanny Prichard[314] stayed after her funeral and said to Mother "You must feel that a great deal of that natural affection which is so necessary to us has gone out of the world for you with your sister[.]" That is true and Mother did feel it. We felt it too, though not so much. Mother often exclaimed "To think that your Aunt Lucy is dead! I cannot take in that it is true." It seemed to us children the greatest blessing that her weary comfortless days were over. But Aunt Susan's death was sad, she was loved and needed by husband and children, and to Edith and me she was a second Mother, every visit to her was a new pleasure and her counsels and instruction had been of value to us from early days. Uncle William broke up housekeeping. He & Charley went to N.Y. to live with Haven, who was married the next June and Charley wrote, "Susy is as gay as a lark about the house and twice as pleasant." Uncle William before that began to have difficulty of breathing and after a summer of much suffering died in September and was buried from our house. He saw little Edith at the time of Haven's wedding, Edith had them in N.Y. and brought them to see him. He looked on them affectionately, smiled to see Ralph, who was nearly two, pull out big books from his bookcase, and said "He's a fine little boy."

A month after his death Charley had gone to Paris to study medicine, and about a month after that it was decided to send me to Fayal.[315] The day I sailed, Mother, when she opened her Bible found it spoke to the occasion as it used to long ago "Truly this is a grief, and I must bear it," she read, "My tabernacle is spoiled and all my cords are broken, my children are gone forth of me. . . . there is none to stretch out my tent any more and to set up my curtains."[316] Edward, I have neglected to mention, was living this year in Milton working in Will's vineyard on Quincy Hill, so that my departure left her and Father for the only time in their lives without a child in their house. The mention of her curtains especially pleased Mother for it was always my business to "set them up" again on her bed when they had been washed. After a week or two Edward came home and having chosen the medical profession went daily to Boston to the School, returning to sleep and recounting the interesting things he had learned to the parents in the evening. They were most agreeable to Mother. When Father went to the West to give lectures Mother & Edward went to Milton and were there a month[.] Mother had a good time there and Ralph & Violet who were one and two years old used to sit before her on her bed while she ate her breakfast exactly as Topaz and Milcah used to, watching her and hoping when she came to her banana, which they called belladonna, that they should get slices, nor did they hope

in vain. When Father returned from the West she began housekeeping
again, and when I came home in May 1869 Will & Edith and the
children and Edward came too and we had a joyful week together. It
was about this time that Mother, who had for several years acknowl-
edged that a perpetual contemplation of the wrongs she desired to
forgive was not leading to forgiving, and that other subjects of thought
would be both more agreeable and more wholesome, seemed to begin
to act on that conviction a little, and to see that she was having a good
time in the world. She joined more in the family fun, and upstairs
with me she frolicked more and more often[.] In the following year
May Alcott founded a club which was for young and old, her parents
and herself, and invited Father & Mother to belong. It was to meet
every other Saturday evening, hear an essay read and then discuss it.
Father & Mother joined it and liked it very much. I presently began
to hear from all the members how beautifully Mother talked and how
much pleased Father always looked when she was talking. Ten years
before I had heard that Mrs Nathan Brooks said the world little knew
how much Mr Emerson owed to his wife, that he would have been a
different man with another woman; and I had listened and thought
it over often and wondered how much truth there was in it, certainly
the little world that I lived in did not seem to me to set Mother's worth
so high. But in these ten years I had gradually opened my eyes first to
her beauty, then to her courage, then to the high pure atmosphere in
which she dwelt, later to the amusing and more slowly to the excellence
of the amusing traits of her character. The undue distress at all sorts
of little things which had always tormented me began to seem funny,
indeed I had learned that life with her was as astonishing and as
funny as a farce, looked at in one light, in another light it was a
privilege to know a being so simple so innocent and so tender. More
and more tributes to her charms henceforth kept coming to my ears,
"Why is it," asked a visitor to the club one night as she went away
with her hostess, "that we always hear of Mr Emerson and never of
Mrs Emerson? It seems to me that she is quite as wonderful as he."
The Prichards told me that an Englishman who had seen her at the
Club said "I never saw before so many of the points which are said
to mark[317] blue blood united in one person as in Mrs Emerson. I
watched her all the evening and counted them over." This was Mr
Wm I. Knapp[.][318] Mother's descent was nothing remarkable, her
ancestors on the Jackson side had always lived in Plymouth and, so
far as she knew, had been comfortable reputable people; on her
Mother's side all, except her great-grandfather, had been ministers,
but she had never heard anything of them beyond the story or two

that I began with, till we got back to the John Cotton for whom Boston was named.[319] Nevertheless we were much pleased and so were the Prichards with this remark of the Englishman and, besides this, he had been charmed with Mother's talk. Once or twice I myself went with her and heard her remarks at the Club. She did seem in her element, she looked animated and talked very well, all she said was sincere and real, and her voice never sounded prettier.

In 1871 Edward came home from the Medical School sick. Father had just gone with Will & Edith and the Forbeses, as Mr Forbes's guest to California and Edith's three children Ralph nearly five, Violet three and Cameron almost a year old had come to stay with us. Edward's disease proved to be severe varioloid and was followed by abscesses, and our second-girl Sarah Jones a strong young Englishwoman proved never to have been vaccinated and had the small-pox in the natural way. The town was quite alarmed. It was the only case there had been within its borders for fifty years at least. We became as separate from the world as if we had gone to a desert island, except that Aunt Lizzy and Annie Keyes came every day to visit us in the yard and the doctor came all the time and Miss Bartlett with him. Our kind friends sent baskets of food to the gate. This was a great mercy, as our cook had taken to her bed in terror. Mother, the children, their nurse, and a little girl from Milton who assisted her, the cook and I were all vaccinated and no harm came to any of us. Lizzy Bartlett, the Doctor's second daughter, went to Boston having made a vow not to return without a small-pox nurse to help us. It got to be three in the afternoon. She had seen many nurses, but all promptly refused to go to a case of small-pox, and she began to be afraid she could never go home, when she thought of the City-crier's office. There she found a woman who said "Certainly! If the Lord sends you small-pox you'd get it if it was corked up in a bottle ye was. And if he doesn't you won't, no matter what you do." So Lizzy brought her to us, and she was simply perfect. She took all the charge of Sarah, did all her washing, was always cheerful and strong and ready to do what was needed. Mother always said that was the happiest spring she ever passed. There was no one to do any housework, but very little was necessary; we were out in the yard in pleasant weather having a beautiful time with our dear babies, and the weather was heavenly. The whole world and its responsibilities being removed, there was time for play, for reading to Ralph & Violet. Mother was never in the least an anxious soul, and I don't think she noticed—I did, but it didn't thoroughly frighten me any more than her—that Edward looked and spoke exactly as William Emerson did when he was in consumption. He was out of bed and down stairs and

Sarah to the Doctor's surprise had begun decidedly to improve when Cameron's birthday came, his first birthday, and Edward went with us to a picnic at Fairyland to celebrate it. He rode however in the wagon with the dinner[;] the children & I walked & dragged C.'s wagon. Finally Sarah got well, the house was fumigated and the happy day came when Will & Edith & Father drove up to the gate. To my surprise there wasn't a ray of gladness in Father's face. I drew Edith off and asked her if anything was the matter "Why Ellen! Well, I suppose you are so used to it you don't see it so much—but Edward looks as if he were going to die. Of course Father is miserable." The next day she & Will took their family home and the next they sent for us all and for a surgeon whom Edward valued, and he found the abscess inside his ribs which was pressing upon his lungs, and slowly slowly, he recovered, but in the course of that year he was twice again almost at death's door. He went in August to Germany to continue in Berlin his medical education. Two weeks before he sailed he asked Annie Keyes to marry him and she happily consented so that he went away a joyous, not a heart-broken, lover. On this occasion Mother though she had the highest opinion of her son said to Annie "If ever you have any quarrels I'll side with you against him, through thick and thin." Father had given to Mother when they were engaged a diamond which had been Ellen Tucker's and asked her how she would have it set. She said "as a little pin"; so he took it to the jeweller's and left that order. It [See Sketch] came home in a regular gentleman's shirt pin, such as were worn in those days, and Mother said nothing but never used it. It had been 36 years in her upper drawer, and now she gave it to Edward who had it set in an engagement ring for Annie. We told her that when her eldest son was engaged she must carry on the custom and give it to him, but she said she wouldn't agree to that, she should have to like the girl very much to feel willing to give up Edward's diamond to her. Edith had built her new house at Naushon that summer and we had all gone down to see it together. Mother was much interested in it, and Aunt Lizzy was with us. Then there were the dear children; yet she was unusually sad through that whole visit. Now Edith sent for me to come again by myself. With me arrived the letters Edward had sent to tell of his engagement and he & Annie were at once sent for to spend one of their two weeks there. Don was born while they were there, and was eight days old when Edward left poor Annie & sailed away.

In the following January Will & Edith took all four children and their nurse, with Miss Caroline Leavitt[320] to mother the children when they should be settled for weeks at a time while their parents travelled round, to Europe. Mother felt, as she expressed it, that they were "all going to

was the matter "Why Ellen! Well, I suppose you 266
are so used to it you don't see it so much — but
Edward looks as if he were going to die. Of course
Father is miserable." The next day she & Will took
their family home and the next they sent for us
all and for a surgeon whom Edward valued, and
he found the abscess inside his ribs which was pressing
upon his lungs, and slowly slowly, he recovered, but
in the course of that year he was twice again almost
at death's door. He went in August to Germany
to continue in Berlin his medical education.
Two weeks before he sailed he asked Annie Keyes
to marry him and she happily consented so that he
went away a joyous, not a heartbroken, lover.
On this occasion Mother though she had the
highest opinion of her son said to Annie "If ever
you have any quarrels I'll side with you against
him, through thick and thin." Father had given to
Mother when they were engaged a diamond which
had been Ellen Tucker's and asked her how she
would have it set. She said "as a little pin"; so
he took it to the jeweller's and left that order.
It came home in a regular gentleman's shirt
pin, such as were worn in those days, and Mother
said nothing but never used it. It had been 36
years in her upper drawer, and now she gave

be drowned like a batch of kittens," she could never understand how anyone dared to cross the sea. But to her relief and surprise, not only Edward but all this large party crossed in safety, and every week we had the joy of letters. Father more than Mother enjoyed these. It made him happy to have the children see places and people he remembered. Mother's time for rejoicing came when Edward at Berlin found her dear Mrs Bancroft, Mr George Bancroft was at that time our ambassador at the German Court. Edward took pains to write fully to Mother of his visit to her and of her talk.

In July 1872 while the children were still abroad came our fire. Father was waked by its crackling and called to Mother, who was then sleeping in the redroom, in a voice which terrified her, she thought he must be struck with paralysis or something quite as dreadful and hastened upstairs. When she found nothing more was the matter than that the house was burning her heart was light at once. She put on (some short down skirts over her nightgown,) a black alpaca dress and her mantilla and bonnet which lay in the redroom as she had gone out the night before doing some errands, and tried to think what she wanted to save, but nothing in particular occurred to her, the house was already full of neighbours carrying everything out. She thought she would go up into my room, for I was in Beverly Farms, to see if she could save something of mine, but Mr Staples[321] stopped her on the stairs. "Go right down, Mrs Emerson. It's as much as your life's worth to come up. The roof will be falling in." "There's a camphor-trunk under Ellen's bed, full of shawls," she said, happening to remember it, and she congratulated herself that she did, for a man at once ran into my room and brought it out. She almost immediately stepped on her dress, and it tore where the deep facing was sewed on. Then it drooped there and directly she trod on it again and it tore further. When dear Annie Keyes arrived she was a forlorn sight with the bottom of her dress hanging round her feet (and the short down skirts over her night-gown showing.) Annie's first act was to pin up her facing and then take off her own long waterproof, put it on her & button her up in it, so she looked respectable again. It rained at first but held up later. What Mother did, she didn't clearly remember, there was nothing she could do to much purpose, but she didn't want to go away and she & Father stayed by till the fire was stayed. Then Mr Keyes took them home in his wagon and they breakfasted with the Keyeses, who begged them to stay, but Cousin Elizabeth Ripley invited them to the Manse, that was an old home to Father and of course they went there. That very afternoon came Mr Lowell and Nina from Waltham and invited them to return and stay with them. This delighted and touched them both. But the Manse

seemed to Father the only place, and there they remained. Mr Lowell
& Nina stayed to tea, and Nina says that Mother said she did not feel
the whole pathos of the fire till she saw—or heard that someone else had
seen,—Nina is not sure which—the procession of homeless rats starting
across the field into the wide world. "However," she added, brightening,
"there is this consolation. They are sure to find a home somewhere!"
"Why, Mrs Emerson, what cruelty!" cried Nina. "Cruelty, no, pity!"
returned Mother. "I mean how cruel to those people whose houses they
invade," said Nina. But Mother was not easily brought to think the
people need mind if the rats were only at ease. At Judge Hoar's suggestion, a room in the Court-house was offered to Father for a study
and there all his books and papers were brought, in utter confusion of
course. Every day he went there, both morning and afternoon. I went
to help him set up the book-cases, but everything, books & cases, were
so dirty with rain & smoke & sand, besides the dust that was on them
before the fire, that cleaning was the first necessity. We did get things
wiped and Mr Harry P. Richardson came in one day and gave us immense help in the heavy work. Mother used also to come in. These
weeks at the Manse were a pleasant holiday to her. She loved Cousin
Elizabeth and Cousin Mary, and she often looked back afterwards to
that time as a sunny interval and mentioned the visits to Father's room
at the Courthouse in particular as good times. Father soon grew sick
and he and I went to Waterford where he recovered. On 12 Aug. Will
& Edith landed in Boston and by Cousin Elizabeth's invitation came to
the Manse with the dear little four bears. How interesting it was to go
down to the burnt house with them! And how they enjoyed Cousin
Elizabeth's good cooking after living at Hotels so long! They declared
that we must go to Naushon as soon as they had opened the house there.

It was while we were at the Manse that Mr Lowell came again and
brought Father a check for the thousands of dollars that his friends
sent when they heard of the fire and I remember how Father's voice
broke when he read the list. And on a later day Judge Hoar came on
a similar errand.[322] Father said he did not see how he could accept so
much "I don't know what you can do about it," said the Judge, "it is
in the Bank to your credit. The best use you can make of it is to go to
Egypt with it." And he left the new bank-book when he went.

We all went to Naushon and saw the unpacking of Edith's trunks.
She had at Mother's desire chosen for her in England a fine cashmere
shawl to succeed the old standby bought in New York with Mrs Bancroft, and a new velvet cape for winter. She had besides brought her a
black silk dress as a present, all made up, and she showed us on the
Paris dressmaker's bill that it was entered as Robe de Madame Mère.

For me she had brought a whole wardrobe—it no longer made any difference that all my clothes had been burned. Now I was going to Europe with Father and the fine new outfit was of more importance and value than if I were going to stay at home.

It was arranged that we should return to the Manse to make ready there for our departure and that Mother should remain there a week or two after we sailed, then go to Edith for the winter. In that week or two that Mother stayed behind with Cousin Elizabeth, Cousin Mary & Lizzy Simmons[,] William Simmons returned from Germany bringing his wife with him.[323] The family gave her the kindest welcome and Mother threw herself heartily into it and, delighted to see a lady who could only talk German, a language that had sweet associations since the German Class of Plymouth days, listened eagerly to all she said and felt herself fortunate in belonging in this chapter of the Manse family-history.

She went to Edith before Thanksgiving, and at Thanksgiving Edward surprised her by coming home, so that she had all her family with her except Father & me. In January came the sixtieth birthday of Mrs Forbes and Mrs Watson and Mother and Sarah Dougherty, Edith's cook, made "four kinds of cake in one pan" as Mother expressed it for the birthday party. This little achievement she looked back upon with content for a long time. This winter she wrote to us very good letters, not so good however as those she wrote to me at Fayal, those were the best she ever wrote, Mary Watson said they were the best letters I had. I mourn whenever I think of it that they were burned in the burning of the house. In spring she and Edith began the refurnishing of the house Bush which Mr Ralph Emerson, architect, and Mr Cutler of Bedford,[324] builder, under the superintendence of Annie's Father had restored better and more convenient than before. This refurnishing was one of the pleasantest experiences Mother had. There was money enough and time enough and Edith as much interested and as ingenious as herself as a coadjutor. They went shopping together, or one stayed in Concord and sent measures while the other gathered patterns in Boston, and not only were they going to restore the old home to look just like itself only somewhat spruced up and improved, but it was to be all ready for Father & me when we should come back from Europe.

They had many triumphs in finding just what they wanted and many amazing successes in matching things, every day the task advanced, and when we landed all was done but final touches. Judge Hoar had roused the town to gather at the depot and meet Father, and had asked Judge Russell, Collector of the Port of Boston, to hinder our getting home before the 3 o'clock express. We had anchored in the stream too late to enter the port the night before but were ready to go ashore right after breakfast when Judge Russell came on board and said it wasn't advisable yet. He sat down and talked with us two hours. I saw that we should lose the eleven o'clock train and made several rises to go, but he calmly told me all our baggage was not yet out, he would let me know when the time came, and at about one he gave us leave to depart. So we reached Concord when all was ready for us, found the whole population, horse, foot, wagons, babywagons and schools all in array at the depot. One carriage, bristling with little Forbeses and Edith and my daughter smiling behind them, drove close by as Mr Keyes escorted us to a stately carriage drawn by two horses, and so all in procession we went along the old streets. It was a warm day, May 28*th* 1873, and all the trees were in their spring green. We drove into the East yard and Mother met us at the East door.

First we all went out to the front gate together, and Father thanked Concord for its friendly greeting then we all returned into the house, Father & Mother Edith, Edward and I, Will and the four children, Annie and my daughter, and began a progress all over it with overflowing pride and admiration, indeed it took days to hear the history of the papers, the carpets & curtains the collecting and polishing the furniture and restoring each article to its place.

Then the story of the great town demonstration was full of charming particulars and Will & Edward were enchanted to hear of the faithful interposition of Judge Russell. Next came the unpacking. Joyful moments!

Mother's room had been improved in the rebuilding by slightly increased height, the addition of the Oriel window, and a handsomer mantelpiece. Her blue paper was lighter than the last and the carpet was a prettier gray and had a blue border. The old secretary which she bought of Aunt Lucy had been destroyed in the fire but Edith had found for her at an auction-store a fac-simile of it, which stood in the old place. The old highpost bedstead had been badly scorched, its sacking & furniture burned, but there it stood newly polished, with curtains wonderfully like the old and new duck instead of sacking. The old black case of drawers which Mother always spoke of as the Juggernaut stood as of old in its alcove. She called it the Juggernaut, she once explained, for two reasons, first it was her idol; second, it was so heavy it was as much as your life was worth to move it. The drawers above the shallow drawer were all devoted to Father. His clothes were kept there from the beginning. Mother said to me as she put his shirts in one day, after reviewing them. "I have been a good wife to your Father in one way. He never has gone to his drawer at any time without finding there what he wanted. I have looked out to have the new set made before the old set failed, and the summer things and the winter things put in good season."

Certain pieces of furniture Mother didn't like had been changed for what she liked better, her rocking-chair which Mr Lawman the Plymouth carpenter had made for her of a chair which she bought of Aunt Cotton was here in the new room, her old bureau and work-table. All looked fresh and handsome. When Uncle George came on Sunday to tea we took him up to see the room. "It makes me want to say Do you expect to 'live alway' here?" he exclaimed, "or as the parishioner said to Dr Beecher[325] when he had a new oil-cloth for his entry, 'What! all this and heaven too?' "

We have never got through with feeling most appreciatively the improvements upon the former house, the square light china-closet between the front entry and kitchen, the pleasant bathing-room above, which took the place of the dark & cramped ones we had before, the bay-window of dining-room & nursery, and the dining-room alcove, the improved closets, and the square roof which gave such a good large den & high light garret.

Up to the time when the house burned Father had used a hat-tub with cold water for 18 years as his morning-bath. He used to call it "the *invairi*able," for he was vain of it and of his constancy in taking it even in winter—he was fifty before he ever thought of a daily bath. He often said "I know of nothing which so conduces to self-righteousness as the *invairi*able[.]" At one time he had for weeks the company of a spider which had crawled into his sponge as it hung out of the window[.] The spider was in swimming all the time Father took his bath, every day. Father didn't trouble himself about him. Father left the sponge in the water the spider we suppose landed on it & entered one of the holes of the sponge didn't mind the second-girl's squeezing it, nor its wetness all the morning as it swung in the wind[.] At any rate he was always on hand to bathe with Father, who made charming speeches about him at breakfast. After our return to the house Father used the bathing-room.

One night Mother was waked by forlorn mewing. She was up & exploring in a moment. She found on the piazza a kitten a month old, thin & dirty. She brought it right up to her room, got a saucer of milk and held it in her lap smoothing its wretched fur while it drank. Father seemed much interested. "I heard, over Acton way, that there wuz a Mis' Emerson what was kind to cats down in Concord" he remarked, "so I thought I'd come. I'm glad I did." Mother next made it a little nest of cotton wool to be soft to its infant bones and brought down a box of sand, which she had up garret.[326] No sooner did the kitten see this than she proceeded to make use of it. Father actually sat up to see, she seemed such a baby. "Poor little shing! Did it know how to empty its little bowels!" he cried. His sympathy enchanted Mother. The next day she chloroformed her poor sick little guest.

In June, on Midsummer-Day, we had a reception. We desired to show our tidy new house and we were sure our friends would like to see it. Two days before Ned Bartlett and Sally French[327] were married and Uncle Charles & Aunt Susan, John and his wife and Lidian came to the wedding and stayed with us.[328] That was Uncle Charles's last visit to Mother. Lidian stayed to the reception, he and Aunt Susan went home, she meaning to return the next day, but instead she telegraphed to Lidian to follow, Uncle Charles had fallen down in his study and remained unconscious. Mother was anxious about him but we had our reception just the same. Lizzy Bartlett helped us get ready my Sunday Scholars and my friends were marshalled in Committees, one to show people over the house, one to take them to the garden, one to invite them into the dining-room, one to wait on them there. We had also ushers. Mother & Father and I stood still in the parlor all the time. It seemed to us very pleasant. Lizzy Bartlett thought it did to all.

The next day Mother went to see Uncle Charles. He was conscious but could not talk any intelligible language, he made some new words and used old ones out of their meaning, and as days went on it was evident that his mind was deranged. He never recovered. The trustees or corporation of the MacLean Asylum[329] at Somerville voted to receive him and keep him without compensation as a recognition of his services to the medical profession; and this did Mother's heart good.

He lived there for several years. Mother & Aunt Susan visited him when the authorities said he could bear it. She said he recognized them and was always overjoyed to see them. He called Aunt Susan Alice and Mother, I think Lucy and talked to them eagerly all the time they were there, but they could understand nothing.

Mother always believed that it was suffering about the ether-discovery that brought on this Coesion of the brain. He was only 67. She never was easy about him, she feared he was homesick and unhappy; and then what was it that he seemed so earnest in telling them?

In July of 1873 little Edward was born at Naushon[;] Will named him for Edward, much to the content of all our family. Edith always called Ralph & Edith "the children," the next division of the family, Cameron, Don and Edward, was called "the boys." I think Mother did not go to Naushon this year, nor see this new baby till he came home to Milton three months old.

Mother saw several coloured photographs on porcelain and was delighted with them. She thought of the daguerreotype of Waldo and carried it to a photographer in Boston who readily undertook to have it enlarged and painted. He had a lock of Waldo's hair, and instructions not to emphasize the frown and to have the dimity ruffle round the neck less tumbled. When it came home Mother was well pleased with it, though she had hoped it might be better still. At dinner-time she brought it down and laid it on the table between the windows as she passed. She had never said a word to Father of this enterprise, and wondered whether he would recognize who it was. The success was complete, lovely! After dinner Father walked toward the window and seeing a morocco case on the table he opened it and straightened himself back to look at it "Oh!" he cried out with emotion, "What?—Where?—Who?" and fled to the Study for his glasses. I suppose he undertook successively to ask "What is *this?* Where did it come from? Who did it?" He hastened back, and looked at and looked & looked. "Yes," he kept saying "Yes,—yes." Then he wished to hear all about it, and got the daguerreotype to compare with it. "It was a good thought," he said.

I think it was earlier than this that Miss Mary Howland Russell died in Plymouth, the first of Mother's trio, who had been the most constant of them all, partly because she remained at home and was accessible. For a long time she had not been in Concord but Mother had visited her at Seconnet and in Plymouth, and they had had sweet converse over books and all other subjects. Mother went to Plymouth to her funeral, she was as near as a relation. She was very good to us children. I went to Cambridge to school two years. Each year she sent me a hundred dollars, so that I might feel at liberty to wear pretty things and do what might cost money, and when Edith went to Cambridge for a year a hundred dollars from Miss Russell for her promptly arrived. This went to Mother's heart. After she died her nieces sent to Mother her new black silk winter cloak. It was exactly to Mother's taste, she looked beautifully in it, and whenever she had a new winter cloak afterwards she had it made on its plan. Mrs Nathan Brooks too died. This made a great difference to Mother. And now Mrs Thoreau was in her last sickness. As I have said, Mrs Thoreau both liked Mother and didn't like her; she had always enjoyed making covert thrusts at her, but now that she saw her end near Mother was the person she wished to talk with and sent for. Mother went, and they had a true love-feast. After her death her daughter, Miss Sophia, went to her cousins in Maine.

Will Forbes was and had been ever since his marriage made him acquainted with our circumstances striving to bring Mother's cousin Abraham Jackson to render an account of his stewardship. "Abraham is exact and careful but he is dilatory" was a constant word in our house, alternating with an occasional note of distrust. Mother owned the Winslow House and a wood-lot called Owl Swamp in Plymouth, and an undivided sixth of the Court St. property. Sometimes she got a rent, sometimes only a few dollars with a message from Cousin Abraham that repairs had taken the rest, or the tenant wasn't quite ready to pay. Will never rested till he succeeded in selling the Court St. estate for enough money for Mother's sixth & Frank's sixth which were paid into their hands to be each 16,000 dollars. At about the same time she sold her most beloved possession, the Winslow House[330] to Dr Briggs, who had married Miss Mary H. Russell's youngest sister Lucia, for $2000, so that now she had 18000 of her own—more than her Father left her.

Will also attended to the publishers' paying Father some four times as much for his books as they had hitherto given him, and though Father was no longer able to give lectures and earn, we were now rich, we had more money than we needed, so that Mother's whole income came into her own hands to spend, and she was able to do many things that she had wished to do. Her garden at once was improved by the addition of new roses and lilies and tulips. Mother knew many cases of the difficulties & humiliations to which men had exposed their widows by not making a will. She always was begging Father to make a will but he seemed unwilling to undertake it. In the summer of 1874, I should think it was, he took me with him to New Hampshire for a little journey. We crossed Lake Winnipesaukee on a steamboat. Leaflets were scattered on its seats with an appeal to every man to make a will, showing that the widow must in most cases be impoverished and dependent on her children, if her husband makes no special provision for her. This made an impression on father. Soon after our return, he sent for Mr Thayer,[331] and inviting Mother and me into the Study he began in earnest upon the will, and every clause was submitted to Mother's approval, Mr Thayer explaining the bearing of it, so that she understood it all and was entirely satisfied. Edward was to have the book money, which would lessen her income just so much, but as she had property of her own which gave about as large an income as the books, now given away, but available for her use; she said she liked that entirely.

One day as I came home from the post-office I saw our cow standing mooing aloud & continuously in the Minot lot, I approached. She was bewailing her bossy born dead and lying on the grass before her. Mother heard the lament and opened her window. "What is it, *dear* Mooky?"—she always called a cow Mooky, not Moolly. The cow again lifted her voice, Mother caught sight of the bossy, and I told her it was dead. "Yes! it is dreadful, it *is* dreadful, Mooky," cried Mother. "Your beautiful baby is dead! I don't wonder your heart is broken." The cow seemed to listen, and to welcome the condolence. She looked at Mother, and again and again poured forth her grief, Mother ardently responding, till John came and carried away the calf, the cow following.

She used to tell us, after working in the garden, that she was having a most romantic experience[;] we had no cat of our own, but *a* cat was ever with her though unseen, mewing and mewing, not in distress, but expressing the utmost devotion & confidence. Sometimes she would cross the garden and though she did not see her wooer follow, almost instantly from the nearest leafy covert sounded the insinuating mew. If I went out into the garden Mother would point and say "My coy kitty is under there"—where there was a tangle of grapevine perhaps. "She is telling me her heart is empty, she wants someone to love. I assure her she may love me and I will love her." The leaves trembled and a gentle mew would be heard "Tis kitty! Missy will! You've made a friend!" Mother would cry, as she dug away. It was more amusing every day. At last the invisible princess resolved to step forth from her covert. She allowed one golden eye to peer from among the leaves, then two, and finally came frankly to Mother's side. She never entered the house but was always on hand in the garden. She was one of the ugliest cats I ever saw.[332]

Edward was a house-pupil in the Massachusetts General Hospital and came home occasionally with most amusing stories. He and one of his mates were obliged to leave the Hospital because they altered the treatment of a sick baby who they were sure was dying under the system to which it was subjected. They disobeyed orders, used their common-sense, succeeded in restoring him to health, and were dismissed. Edward passed his examinations, received his degree, came to Concord and entered into partnership with Dr Bartlett. He had already bought his house. The 19th of September, 1874, he was married, but all summer we had him at home and found it an immense convenience to have a doctor in the house. He assumed the care of Mother's health thenceforth. He was no friend to homeopathy, but Mother never thought of giving it up.

I do not remember when the Dumb Animals Society[333] was founded; Mother felt that in its coming into existence the world took a long step forward. She was one of the Vice Presidents as long as she lived. She subscribed for perhaps ten copies of its paper which she sent to young friends and to the schools, she bought bound volumes of it annually to give away. She once told me that she herself wrote articles to be published in it. I have long regretted that I did not follow this up, learn which they were and secure those numbers in which they appeared, for they did appear.

On her birthday, a neighbor brought her a present of two Maltese kittens.[334] We named them September and Twenty. September lived with us till the next summer and was all the time admiring Father. If Father was in the garden September sat near with lifted head gazing in his face. If he was in the dining-room and September could get in he would immediately assume the same attitude of rapt contemplation. This is all I remember of him but Twenty was with us for years. She had kittens, two of whom were allowed to grow up, one was a stalwart black cat. Mother kept them all well fed. We now had as many rats as before the fire I think more than ever we had. I met one on the East stairs, the corners of several doors were gnawed off, there was a hole in every closet, they were at work gnawing their way into mine. One evening Mother and I were shutting up the house, the lamps were out except one (turned low) in Mother's hand. As we entered the Study she started, then smiled and said "Why! I thought I saw a kitten." I at once suspected the truth and asked where. "I fancied it ran along the sofa." I hastened to close all the doors. "What's the matter?" "No doubt it was a rat." "What are you going to do? Oh let him alone! Poor fellow." Seeing me obdurate, she entreated me to let her get away, which I gladly did, and then I brought in Twenty, and lighted the lamps. I got a cane and soon brought the miscreant to light and drove him across the floor. Twenty saw & followed. He reached a corner and seeing her near, he crept above the mopboard, then looking over his shoulder made a few remarks which caused her to stop. I poked him down with the cane. He again crossed the floor, Twenty following doubtfully, and when he came to the corner he did exactly as before. Twenty now went to the door of the Study, sat down and waited for me to let her out. I went for her black son and brought him to assist her, but now I could not find the rat. So I went to bed, having dismissed the two cats[.] Early in the morning I went to the Study and found all the doors closed as I left them. It was evident that the rat had not escaped as I had thought the night before, through some hole; the woodwork round the door was shockingly gnawed. I called John Clahane and brought in the black cat. After long hunting in every part of the room John with a pole pushed out the rat from behind the high book-cases, he ran across the room, the cat after him, but a single word from the rat sufficed to make her abandon any idea of interfering with him. We went to breakfast leaving her in charge. I knew she would like to get away, so I closed every door & window except that the one nearest the parlour was open a little way at the top. You wouldn't think a cat could get out there even under desperate circumstances, but after breakfast she was gone! We brought in Twenty and the other kitten, closed every avenue of escape, John took his pole and poked thoroughly behind the bookcases, we moved the furniture; we made sure the rat was not there. Had the black cat jumped out of the window with him? We departed, cats & all. Father sat down to his papers. At dinner time he told us that as he was quietly at work the rat fell down the chimney but the moment it saw him it scrambled up again. "Poor creature!" cried Mother "how frightened he must be!" Father said he had left all the doors & windows shut. John, shocked at the conduct of Twenty & Co.[,] had told me his kitten was a fine mouser, so I went right over to his house to borrow her. The children agreed to bring her, and I went back to the Study and looked up the chimney & poked along the top of the fire back. I brought down a half a doughnut and two pieces of toast. "The wretch has been here before," I said to Father, Look at his little hoard of provisions!" and my wrath increased. But in a moment I noticed that they were quite fresh. I thought a minute and hunted up Mother "Have you put something up the chimney for that rat to eat?" "Certainly I have—a half a doughnut and some scraps of toasts; I hope he has found them." I told her I wondered at her. "Isn't it hard enough for him to be kept anxious and frightened a whole night and day without being hungry too?"

The kitten was brought. She was lonely & homesick and sought consolation on Father's knee. He did not like cats, I never knew him to hold one before, but he held her all the afternoon and nothing further was seen of the rat. When Father was ready to go to the P.O., later, I had a letter to carry and said I would go too. We decided the kitten had better go home to stay while we were gone and sent her off, carefully closed the study, and started. I found I had left my letter, ran back for it, forgot the rat and didn't shut the door! So it escaped in our absence and Mother was devoutly thankful. We used poison finally and got rid of our rats in that way; but while we still were suffering under their reign, Mother, in answer to something that was said, declared that she felt the warmest interest in every creature under her roof. "Not the rats!" I said[.] "Certainly I do, in all their concerns, in them and in their little families," she answered.

One of the most amusing and continually unexpected effects of her love for animals was that whenever a story was told in her presence in which any dumb creature appeared as an accessory, so little that no one else remembered that it had been mentioned, Mother, who perhaps did not notice the point of the tale, was sure to inquire how that animal was affected. I wish I could remember an instance, they were ever-recurring but I can't recall one.

Robins gave her endless trouble. They are great at worrying and complaining. One day when we were all out in the strawberry-bed they gathered round, scolding us & making such a noise that Edward indignantly exclaimed "Let us hope that in a better world the birds will learn to keep their temper,—not to give way, as they do here." Edward was irritated and disgusted with their senseless clamour. On Mother it always had a more serious effect. Not only did it deafen her and weary her nerves, but she must believe, she was convinced, that it was made for sufficient cause. Four promising and tenderly loved young robins had been eaten by a fierce cat or carried off by cruel boys, or perhaps a nest built by weeks of devoted labour, as dear to the owner's as her house was to her had been pulled down, or a beautiful blue egg which to a robin's heart was as precious and important as her own Eddy or Edie in the cradle had been stolen. These wrongs must be searched out and redressed. She would rise from her nap—I cannot set forth strongly enough the distress on account of the screamers, mixed with an equal amount of vexation at the personal trouble they gave to her, wasting her afternoon by destroying her rest, and a foreboding that they or other robins would do the same thing every day all summer with which she hastened to dress and go out into the yard. The robins redoubled their cries and flew wildly hither & thither. But what could she do? Till she came out she felt as if she could go straight to the spot. But among so many tall trees how could she guess where was the ruined home. Often she had to return baffled to her room. Sometimes she found a young bird in the grass. Then she would put it in a cage on a tree hoping its parents would come and feed it through the bars. Sometimes she took it into the house. In every case it died, and then she was relieved.

If the uproar was out in the road she would go over and question the school-children; and when from her window she saw a boy climb a tree, or any stoning of a tree going on, she hastened forth to ascertain that no bird or squirrel was molested.

When we were old enough to assist and to observe we collectively learned, and the knowledge made ever after an immense increase to Mother's comfort, that half the robin's noise meant apprehension, not actual mishaps. We saw and pointed out to her that Topaz had only to stroll through the grove, or Father to visit his pear-trees, to excite an absurd commotion. Mother once came in saying that she had just been out to the currant-bushes under the Porter apple tree and the robins had all screamed "Murder & devastation!"

She loved to throw out food for the birds and especially for the jays in winter. She put spoonfuls of Indian hasty-pudding on her window-ledges as well as crumbs for them, she thought that on the ground snow would cover it, but on the window-ledge the jays could always get at it. They could and did, never seemed afraid of our movements in the room so long as we did not come to the window, and allowed us a fine view of their plumage. In the night the pudding would freeze and at daylight the hungry jays had to hammer off crumbs of it with their beaks. Father was waked every morning by their determined rapping, and watched them with great satisfaction as he dressed.

By and by it occurred to Mother that they would like raw corn and oats, and John brought her a pailful from the barn which she scattered all over the ground under her windows. She also threw out Graham bread. Before long, grey squirrels from Sleepy Hollow came to help eat up her bounty and she loved them as well as her jays.

Whenever we had a calf we had sad times. Mother insisted that it should never be separated from its Mother while it lived; but when it was killed the cow mourned day after day and not in silence. Mother heard and sympathized with every tone. She often exclaimed "Why was I born to live in a world where every animal must be cruelized?" Another calf was kept separate from its Mother, but Mother desired that it should be allowed to nurse four times a day. This kept both cow & calf calling to each other. Always the coming of the butcher for the bossy made Mother most unhappy. Before long we learned never to mention that a calf was expected, that one had come, nor anything connected with it. John kept them out of the cows' sight, taught them to drink their milk and we had very little lamenting, and unless Mother saw the butcher come she knew nothing of their existence.

In 1875 we had a great Centennial commemoration of Concord Fight. How the whole town did work for six months beforehand to prepare for it! I never imagined anything like it. Edward was a doctor then and busy with his patients, but every minute he could get he with one Committee was deciding what & where the explanatory signs should be, and the street decorations, and with another consulting about the pedestal for the Minute-Man, and the arranging the procession. Every night for hours in a certain cellar he helped to letter the signs. He exclaimed again and again " 'Time and the hour wear through the roughest day', sometime it will be the 20*th* of April!" Mother and I were having the first grand house-cleaning since we went into the house two years before. I cannot remember why we had so much to do, but there were carpets to make over, and we were possessed by the spirit which moved in all the town and exacted that every inch of everybody's domain should be at its sprucest. I remember clearly feeling every night too tired to go to sleep and saying

> "I'll just lie down and ache awhile
> And rise at five and work again"

How many houses were painted and how many fences were built new that spring!

We were to have Mr & Mrs Geo. W*m* Curtis, he was to be the Orator, and Mr & Mrs James R. Lowell, he was to be the Poet, at our house, and Effie Lowell was coming. Edith & Will and the children came, and my daughter with Edith Hemenway & Nelly Cabot and I think Eugenia Oscar & Lidian Jackson. We had too Mr Theodore Lyman who was to be a marshal.[335]

Our house was ready and in shining order to suit us, the town was all in festive array with its signs in place, its triumphal arches up and a gorgeous display of bunting. The 19*th* was to come on Monday the guest would arrive Saturday night. President Grant & Cabinet & ladies and bands of music came, and Governors of States with their staffs. These stayed at Judge Hoar's. Our guests arrived except the Lowells who wrote to say that if there was a Poem they would come Monday, but as yet none was written. I desire to lecture endlessly on this subject, but it isn't about Mother, so I will turn only to her and say that she had a most happy time with her guests; Mr Curtis was an old friend of more than thirty years, Mrs Curtis & Effie & Mr Lyman were new.

She could not go to the exercises on Monday but we, like every one else, were to keep open house; we had made cake & Charlotte Russe, and cooked meat, and Edith brought more, and made sandwiches and added her store of silver and her waitress to the dignity of the dining-room. Mother admired the table, all handsomely set, and the viands were as good as she could desire. The day was desperately cold, windy & black. She stayed in the parlour and received, assisted by a good fire, and she had so many guests all so thankful to get warm and have something to eat that she had a festive day. Mr & Mrs Lowell arrived at the Tent near the Battle Ground and the beautiful poem was delivered by Mr Lowell but then they cruelly drove right back to Cambridge, in the carriage which brought them, and didn't visit us at all. Father made a short address[336] at the unveiling of the Minute-Man, I don't think it was much more than five minutes long. Mr Curtis's Oration was beautiful. I thought it a great triumph that he gave it all and kept throughout a large audience attentive when the circumstances were so against him, the tent flapping and the people shivering in the biting blast.

That summer Cousin Charlotte spent with us. Who would have thought it? She turned out to be a great arguer. She was devoted to the Episcopal Church and Mother had many faults to find with it. I don't think she had been with us for a day before the combat began, and it never slackened. When Mother's breakfast went up Cousin Charlotte went in to read to her while she was eating. Perhaps the first word she read would lead to a little talk and this to Mother's attacking the church. They argued till Mother was dressed and ready to visit the grocer and butcher. Cousin Charlotte accompanied her to carry on the discussion. They returned so eager in it that they could scarcely part to take off their things. There was usually then a truce till after dinner, but the moment Father had gone to his study, at it they went again, hammer & tongs. This went on every day all summer. Mother had never in her life before had such a chance, and Cousin Charlotte seemed to enjoy this variety of intercourse quite as much.

The long lane had completely turned. At the Club Mother had made friends with all the people she had known slightly hitherto, she had actually become a belle and was invited out all the time[.] With the social life, her spirits rose, her ill health passed away, and she became a happy person. I remember the text that came to her as she dressed for her wedding and felt that now

"At evening-time it was light."[337]

Father was losing, losing, his powers, continually, though gradually, but Mother almost never noticed it, and he was always happy and a most entertaining companion. We all three had perfectly delightful times all day every day.

Mother had been a whist-player in her youth, and as long as Aunt Lucy lived whenever a whist-player chanced to visit us, Mother would get Almira Small[338] to be the fourth and they would have a game of whist which would do Mother good like a medicine. She now found that the Alcotts loved whist and she went sometimes to have a game with them. One night she made a mistake as to where their front stairs began and walked off the top stair shooting straight to the bottom as a rod would and didn't hurt her at all. The Alcotts flew to pick her up and were astonished to find her scarcely jarred, very glad to begin at once on the Whist. She used to say Whist appeared to her so wonderful a game that she could hardly believe a human being had invented it, she felt that it must have been a revelation from heaven.

This summer Edward's little eldest boy was born, and named William for the revolutionary Grandfather. We all went to see him on the first day of his life[.] First Father & I, before breakfast, then after church Mother and Aunt Lizzy, my daughter, his Aunt Flory Keyes and I. He had lovely red cheeks. As we stood looking at him Flory said "The last baby I saw didn't have a real little nose like that, it had a flat place between its eyes and "—Aunt Lizzy interrupted her with "You didn't expect this baby would be without a nose because ordinary children don't have them?" she seemed to feel as Aunt Mary had when she exclaimed of her nephews "*These* children are born to be educated!" That darling little boy only lived three days. He was buried from our house.

Mr [James Elliot] Cabot had made us happy by consenting to help Father with the proof-reading of Letters[.]³³⁹ He would come and stay a day or two, arrange papers for the printer and go away, then come back when the proofs came. His visits were as refreshing to Mother as to Father. At meal-times and in the evening, when she was present, book-work was not in hand and we used to have fine talks.

Once, when he was there, company was coming to dinner and we had no second girl. I was as busy as I could be and far behindhand too. Mother came down, like an anxious housekeeper, some time before dinner to see what might be wrong, a habit of hers I never took the least comfort in but I could not break her of it. The dining-room was dusty and there was no fire. "Oh how forlorn!" cried Mother, "dust, thick! on everything, and no fire!! Oh how cold it is! I'm frizz!" and she shuddered. Mr Cabot who was working at his table by the window, rose at once "Wouldn't you like to have me build a fire?", he asked. It did seem as if it would be invaluable assistance and a saving of time to me, and I said yes. He stood still a minute then briskly left the room and before I had finished dusting it he had the fire blazing.

The next day I saw the fireplace in his room was empty. I knew there had been one laid ready to light, but evidently there had been no burning. Then I saw. When he had risen to make the fire he found he had no materials and didn't know where to look for them. He thought if he asked me it wouldn't be half so real a help; so, in that minute that he was standing, he searched his mind as to what he could do to evolve kindlings and small wood, and remembered his own room. This I consider a most lovely and instructive story, illustrating several moral & practical points

1 "Be helpful where thou livest"
2 You aren't so very helpful when you keep asking How? Where?
3 "Where there's a will there's a way"

and by this deed he comforted Mother's very heart.

In 1876 Father and I went to the University of Virginia, and to the Centennial Exhibition in Phila.[340] and Cousin Sarah came to stay with Mother while we were gone. Before we came home my donkey, whom we named Graciosa for her native island, arrived—she was a present from Father to me and Mr Oliver chose her and sent her from Fayal.[341] Mother never saw her without saying she should like to ride her often, but I think she never took more than two rides, it seemed an effort to mount when it came to the point. When she rode both those times I led Graciosa; it was necessary, for Mother actually was more pleased with a ride as an opportunity to give an animal the satisfaction of having its own way for a while than for any other reason. When she was at Naushon in 1858 she took a horseback ride with Mrs Forbes and two young people. They rode smoothly along till they came to the woods, when her horse snatched a mouthful of leaves, then another and finding the reins slackened, stopped to browse. Presently Mrs Forbes turned round and called "Mrs Emerson, where are you?" Mother thereup urged the animal to join the company and they did, but presently it spied a good oak-tree and stopped again "Yes, you shall have a good luncheon now," said Mother. Mrs Forbes rode back to her. Mother's horse now began to push into the woods towards an attractive tree, almost scraping Mother off under a bough, Mrs Forbes and the others raised a warning cry, Mother turned round with a happy smile "I let him on purpose. I'm not afraid. I love to have him enjoy himself." Mrs Forbes said to the gentleman "What shall we do? Mrs Emerson has lost all control of her horse!" and asked[342] me whether Mother knew about guiding a horse, which rein to pull.[343] I assured her that she did; and went to Mother and reasoned with her. I could not make her see that she was spoiling everybody's ride. "Let them go on, and I'll follow slowly. Horsey is having a beautiful time, and I love to have him." I do not remember how it ended. I imagine Mrs Forbes presently turned the party homeward.

Mother hated to have a spider-web swept down if there was a bunch of eggs suspended in it, and when she found one in her own room she would zealously protect it. Once she was taking up some rose bushes to give away and found a spider in one with a nest. She carefully set the bush out again lest the spider should lose her little family. She

Ellen Emerson with sister, Edith, on Ellen's donkey Graciosa

really felt badly when she disturbed an ant's nest in her digging, and she could not bear to have a wasp killed.

Edward's little Charles was born in 1876 on the 3*rd* of July. Annie was glad he was not so patriotic as to come on the 4*th* and be a thorough Centennial boy, but I don't know why. Edward and Annie brought him every week when they came to dine and Mother took much comfort with him.

In 1877 Aunt Lizzy came to spend a month with us, with her niece Lizzy Storer.[344] Strange that it had never occurred to us before to have a visit from Aunt Lizzy! This was a great & joyful occasion to everyone of us. She already had had the cancer, of which she died, cut away once, but she was at this time comfortable, and we had beautiful talks and drives and reading, and we were sorry when the month ended and she went to Mrs Storer's. Mother's sleep at night was of an interrupted or fragmentary nature. She was always waking up perhaps cold, when she would rise not only to put more coverings on her own bed, but on the children's or because of sudden rain or wind to attend to the windows, or because of discomfort, when she would light her lamp and resort to her homeopathic books and medicine-chest, or she would simply find herself broad awake and meditate on her sorrows and perplexities. At such times housekeeperly cares suggested themselves and she would rise to visit the dough in the kitchen and put it in a warmer or cooler place, and find many other little things that needed attention. Plans, errands, orders meanwhile crowded into her mind. Sometimes she wrote them down and pinned the memorandum on the middle of the bathing-room door for me. Let me write here one which I found lately that I had saved written in Dec. 1881

> Dear Ellen, at this witching hour
> It cometh over me with power
> Tomorrow we must have to tea
> Rev. Mr & Mrs Chan*ey*
> > Midnight
> P.S. No no I see it may *not* be
> on Sunday, (but upon Fridayee)
> Because we'll have no Margery
> > One o'clock
> P.S. 2*d* Or this Thursday shall it be?

One day I chanced to fix my eyes critically on the bathing-room paint. Why!˙What an assembly of flies there must have been on the middle of the door, a place four or five inches in diameter dotted all over! It proved to be the scars of Mother's midnight pins. I wondered that I had not noticed them before, and showed them to her. She was shocked that she had so marred her woodwork.

Very often she visited me to give me her directions or consult me about matters. We had very confidential intercourse on all sorts of household subjects in the night. Edward used to remonstrate with Mother and say she ought not to visit me after I went to bed, and the month that Aunt Lizzy was with us when I slept in the Den, Aunt Lizzy in Edith's room could hear every time she mounted the garret stairs, and attacked Mother finally with very earnest words adjuring her never to hunt me up in the night, but Mother turned a deaf ear to both. "I never found her asleep in her life, and it is necessary to attend to things when I think of them," was always her answer. Certainly it never disturbed me and I often enjoyed the interviews.

Speaking of Mother's pins I remember her funny habit of throwing them always on the floor when she undressed, a nervous impatient action of which she was unconscious, and which when we mentioned to her she stoutly denied. "I *always* put them on the pincushion."

I think it was this year that Mother found that Miss Sophia Andrews, an Englishwoman who had settled in Concord, could read aloud continuously and would like to, so she engaged her to come every day; sometimes she was in Mother's room ten hours a day and reading most of the time. She always read till ten at night. She was very deaf, and that gave rise to many funny scenes that made Cousin Sarah & me laugh interminably. It was common to hear Mother calling from her bed "Stop a minute, please, Miss Andrews," and quite in vain. Miss Andrews read loud & clear so that we in *our* rooms could hear every word, and Mother exerted herself in vain. If we ran, Mother would say, "Stop her *for mercy's sake! Somebody* stop her! if you can." Often no one came to the rescue, and Mother had to get up and cross the room to her.

Aunt Lizzy, when she saw her reading, said "I can't tell you how relieved I am to find this poor little lady domesticated here. I have seen her passing by and she seemed rather lonely & forlorn, and I have been uneasy about her. But under your Mother's wing she is safe."

Mother often exclaimed "What a special Providence she and I are to each other! She can read on & on, and is glad to, I don't know what I should do without her. And really I don't know what would become of her without me. She has no money, no faculty, but now she is sure of one good meal a day, and a little stipend."

Miss Andrews added a new & very different figure to the funny life in Mother's room. I know some little incidents, but not the thousandth part have stayed by me, of the delectable situations, always common, and now so comically set off by the action conscious & unconscious of this new element.

Mrs Cabot began to come with Mr Cabot, Mother had a new and dear friend in her.

Emma Lazarus[345] to whom Mr Ward had introduced Father in New York sent him her poems which he liked and he used always to see her when he went to New York. She wrote and invited him to come to Newport. When he wrote to refuse, he asked me to send her an invitation to come to Concord. I refused. Mother heard the conversation and asked what he wanted. The moment he told her, she said, "I'll ask her. You can invite her from me." So he did, and Emma came.[346] She began to ply Father with questions. This seemed to me ill-advised and I told her it was of no use. "I know what I am about," she said, her eyes sparkling with fun. She seemed to feel she did get what she wanted, if not what she asked.

On Mother she turned the same fire of cross-examination. This Mother liked, liked very much. It was amazing to me to see how many more questions each of her answers seemed to suggest to Emma; and pretty soon I became much interested in Mother's answers. I felt as if I had never before known half as much about her as Emma was eagerly dragging into light. Perhaps Mother had the same interest too, for

"Water in the well will come
Only the while 'tis drawn therefrom."

That autumn we had a Sunday-School Convention in Concord and never did Mother enjoy an occasion much more. We had at our house Mr & Mrs Howard N. Brown, Mr Weston, a minister from Plymouth or Kingston originally, whom Mother had known in early days, Mr Edward P. Gibbs from Athol, Mr Edw. H. Hall, Mr W*m* H. Channing, Mr & Mrs Tiffany and Mr & Mrs Hussey, of the ministers, and Mrs & Miss Endicott and some two other ladies of the teachers, also Mrs Bradford Bartlett. We had beautiful talks at home and beautiful meetings at the church, and beautiful weather. On the second day more people came to dinner. Dinner was a little late, we had only one waitress, and to expedite matters I rose to brush the table. Mr Hall jumped up too. "Oh let me brush the table. I should like to see how it feels!" and he did. Mother was much pleased with his act, and often mentioned it afterwards.

In 1878 little John, Edward & Annie's third son, was born at Milton, at New Years, while Mother was there. Exactly like his aunt Edith, he came into the world with the loveliest complexion and rosy cheeks.

Exactly like her, he was bright yellow the next day. When Mother and I came home and I was telling Edward with enthusiasm the charms of the baby, he said "Oh! You mean the new baby? Oh I don't care about him! I thought you were talking about Charles!" Edward couldn't be in Milton as he feared Annie, (on account of other patients he had charge of with catching diseases) might take harm from him. She came back with both babies when John was three weeks old, and adopted Philip, Flory's motherless baby, who was six weeks old. That winter she had three babies who couldn't walk. The next winter Charles still crept, and there came one proud day when C. was creeping after her into the kitchen, and, thinking he made more noise than usual, she turned around to see three enchanting boys creeping in procession! One had been trying before, but one had suddenly discovered that he could, and had followed when he saw the other two set out. Another day as she was bringing C. & J., both, down stairs, she was afraid John might throw himself over backwards and told C. to put his other arm round him—one was round her neck,—John responded, and they came down an embracing trio all smiling with pride and affection. In the spring of 1878 Aunt Lizzy died on the 8*th* of April;[347] we were sent for to see her when it was evident that death was near. I went twice and never had more valuable talks with her. Now all the friends Mother had had from early days in Concord had died except Uncle George and Mr Channing, not a lady was left of those she found in Concord. Oh yes! Mrs Edmund Hosmer was, and Mother once or twice went to see her, but she lived at a distance and Mother seldom got so far. Their greeting was very affectionate, but Mrs H. talked little[.] Aunt Lizzy was a loss we never can get over. She was the most near, dear and important friend to Father and to Mother both, and whatever happened we always wished at once for her to tell her about it. She left to Father, and to each of us, a hundred dollars. Edward put his into a horse, Edith hers into a sun-dial, I use[d] mine as principal, Father with his bought him a beautiful little spy-glass of unusually high power, which gave him great pleasure. We could distinctly see the four moons of Jupiter with it. I think it was this year that Mr & Mrs Bancroft wrote to invite Father and Mother to come to Newport again. Father gladly went, but we could not persuade Mother to accompany him. She declared herself too old and too feeble to make visits.

When however Mrs Cabot invited us all three to come to stay with her at Brookline, and again when Nina invited us to come and make her a visit, neither she nor Father saw the least difficulty in the way. They came with all their hearts, and happy happy times were both of those visits, remembered with joy ever after.

In 1879 Waldo was born and named for Father, though Ralph had been named for him. It gave Father great pleasure. He was sorry that Edward did not like to name a son for him. In April, little John Emerson died. I had always had remarkable pleasure in him. That summer once more Father, Mother & I went to Naushon together to stay with Will & Edith. Everything was delightful but Mother was again as sad as night. One day when I was pushing to know what was the matter, Mother finally said she couldn't think of any cause, yet she could not resist the weight of melancholy that pressed upon her. I remembered only too well that it had been the same in 1873. Some time after, Nina told me that a gentleman whose family were down at Cape Cod told her he couldn't stay there. "Why not?" "I don't know how it is, but always when I'm there I *feel*"—"As if you should commit suicide?" Nina ended for him. "How did you know?" he asked, surprised. "Because it always makes me feel so."

When I heard that, it explained to me Mother's state, and I told her. Thenceforth she refused invitations to Naushon, for perhaps nine years. Father and I went alone.

Dean Stanley's[348] visit[349] with two friends was a great event to us. Mr & Mrs Cabot came too, and Will and Edith; and Mr & Mrs Reynolds & Judge Hoar dined with them. Mother had good talk with Dean Stanley and loved him. He told her about Lady Augusta.[350] Judge Hoar begged him to stay and preach in our church; he said "no other had such claims, he thought it might justly be called The Westminster Abbey of America." But Dean Stanley had engagements which took him away.

The Summer School of Philosophy[351] was started at Mr Alcott's old house. Louisa [May Alcott] had named the place "Apple Slump"; she did not love it. Her Father did. He called it The Orchard House. Mr & Mrs Emery[352] of Quincy[,] Illinois, whom Father liked very much, and with whom he had stayed, years ago, when he lectured in the West, moved to Concord and settled, for that year, in the Orchard House. Mr Emery was chairman of all the sessions of the School, which was held in Mr Alcott's old Study, the room on the left hand of the front door. Mr William T. Harris[353] of St. Louis was one of the teachers and lectured that year about Hegel, Dr Jones[354] of Jacksonville[,] Illinois lectured on Plato, and there were many others, some who gave courses, and some who gave one lecture.

A great many ladies and gentlemen came to attend the school in earnest, and twice as many more came for a week or two or three. It was a sensation to see the procession of votaries of divine Philosophy marching for more than half an hour, morning and afternoon, past our house, going and coming.

A most unexpected thing happened. Mother found the lectures exactly to her taste, and was unwilling to lose one. She gave up her afternoon nap, if necessary, that she might go, and almost every morning she breakfasted in haste and appeared at the morning session. Father went with her sometimes, but to him it made a great difference who lectured; Mother cared so much for the subject of the lecture that she wished to hear even the less agreeable speakers. She made many new acquaintances, several really won her heart Mrs Denman & Dr & Mrs Jones. She desired to have them to tea, and did have two or three tea-parties. That first year I believe the School did not meet in the evening and Mother, who had been used all her married life to Father's having "Conversations" for Mr Alcott, that is his inviting as many friends as he could find to come after tea and hear Mr Alcott talk, invited the philosophers to have conversations at our house.

Then she and I had much inviting to do, and where we invited one, that one begged leave to bring from one to four more, so that the company of twenty or thirty planned, proved to number seventy or eighty. One night Edward & I, having brought down every chair in the house, were reduced to bringing divans, and finally even the washbench. That summer I learned how many chairs we had. Seventy. I never was present at these conversations that year. I think people liked them though, for they continued very popular, & populous, and Mother sometimes joined in the talk. People rejoiced when she did.

The regular rising and regular walking to & fro, the new interest and the extremely social life she won great benefit from. I was as sorry as she when the six weeks were over.

The Prichards[355] began more and more to be a part of our life. Cousin Elizabeth had a houseful and was too much needed at home and too busy to come very often to our house. Uncle George came every Sunday evening, and usually Mr Channing took tea with us on Sundays. These and Mr & Mrs Sanborn and the Prichards were our chief friends, also Miss Martha and George & Lizzy Bartlett. We used to say Mother had six beaux. Whenever Father did not go with her to any party one of the six always walked home with her. These were [1]Mr Alcott, [2]George Bartlett [3]Mr Sanborn [4]Mr Jas. L. Whitney,[356] one of the Librarians of the Boston Public Library, who boarded with the Prichards, [5]Mr Charles Williams, a lawyer, who lived in Concord, and [6]a Mr Wentworth who boarded at Miss Barrett's[357] for a few years, but proved to be a bad man and disappeared.

In 1880 little Ellen junior was born at Edward's[.] We had had nine grandsons and till now only one granddaughter and we were delighted indeed. I met little Charles with three or four violets in a basket in his hand. When I asked whether they were for our baby he said "Not *ours.* She isn't yours, she is *my* baby. They are biodets for my baby." And before she was six weeks old he died of croup. After having had three sons Edward & Annie were left with none. It seemed as if the name was not to be carried on. Mr William Henry Channing, who had christened Edith & Edward, had christened Charles, and, when he came this summer to attend the School of Philosophy, Edward asked him to christen little Ellen, and he did. Mother & Father, Mr Channing, Cousin Sarah and I went to Edward's, and baby was christened in the parlour. Of course the Keyeses too were there. The School this time was as interesting to Mother as before, and again there were conversations at our house, on Sunday evenings; the School had evening lectures during the week. Josephine Loughead[358] from Philadelphia came with a letter of introduction to us from Mr Henry James,[359] and Mother took to her at once, liked to have her come where she was cutting the cake or attending to other household business, though in general she objected to having a guest come at all behind the scenes, so that Josephine became a frequent and most welcome visitor. Mrs Jones and Mrs Denman of the ladies with whom Mother had made friends used to come to see her. Mr Harris took Mr Alcott's house, bought it, and settled in Concord. The Emerys had left that house and moved to the Main street. They were building a house.

Cousin Sarah spent every summer with us, (except that Cousin Hannah came instead in 1878) after she once began in 1876. She hastened into Mother's room as soon as she waked and read to her the Psalms for the Day. When Mother was dressed they walked out together, Mother always had errands. I think she went almost every day to the butcher's and it is surprising how many other shops she went into. Mr John Brown[360] was the Agent in Concord of the Society for the Prevention of Cruelty to Dumb Animals, and Mother occasionally went to present cases to him. He never was interested to hear; gave her little satisfaction. If she smelt the slaughterhouse, as she did too often when the wind was South, she visited Mr Derby that very day, and if he did not prevent her getting a whiff of it the next day by immediate thorough attention, she looked up the select men and complained of him.

The sight of any utensil of unusual size was sure to attract her into the tin-shop, and whenever I saw one displayed I learned to expect to see it next in our kitchen. That was a curious trait in Mother. I wonder why she liked big dippers and pans; and whether she knew herself that she invariably bought them. She made it a rule to patronize every new shop; she said it was convenient for a town to have two or three of a kind, and the man who was just trying to get a foot-hold needed as much custom as possible. So when she first went in she told the man she was glad he had made the venture and she intended to buy of him quite as much as she did of the old established shop. How often she was indignant when that older shop persistently undersold, to drive the new-comer away, and how faithfully she then avoided the old shop and gave and begged her friends to give custom to the new!

But this is a parenthesis. I was telling what a comfort to her Cousin Sarah was. After dinner Miss Andrews came to read but as soon as Mother had her nap she was likely to go into the garden to work and Cousin Sarah went with her. Often Miss Andrews (and a stool for her to sit on while she read) went too and Miss Andrews would read in the garden while Mother weeded, transplanted and tied up, Cousin Sarah assisting. After tea Miss Andrews went home if Cousin Sarah was there.

In one of Cousin Sarah's letters to Mother she says "It is so much joy to be in your room with you that I am willing to bear the frequent thrusts at the Church I love so much," which shows that Mother treated Cousin S. as she did Cousin Charlotte. I didn't know it till I saw that letter, for she did not argue like her sister, but bore thrusts in silence.

We were getting acquainted with the Emery family. We went to tea at their house and Father as well as Mother had a good time. We invited Mrs Emery and her sister Anna McClure to spend the day and Miss Caroline Leavitt and Mrs Sanborn were all so happy together that Mrs Sanborn invited the same company, then Mrs Emery did. It became a habit among us to spend a day together several times every year, and we called ourselves "The Cheerful Companions[.]" All the Cheerful Companions had the greatest reverence and affection for Mother.

In the autumn of 1880 on our blessed Violet's thirteenth birthday, was born her baby-sister. Never was a family more blest. We would rather have had her a birthday present for Violet than born on any other day of the year, and she was a little blonde girl who showed herself through her short life to be of a most sociable and cheerful disposition. I suppose since she was not a month old at Thanksgiving that she and her Mother did not come.

The New Years of 1881 was a proud one to Edith and Will, with seven children, I remember the baby's coming down into the parlour. But Edward & Annie had only one, of four. I don't know whether it was this New Years or one a little earlier that Edward was telegraphed for by the Bartletts on the morning of Jan. 2*d* 1878 to come home for Dr Bartlett had pneumonia and was worse. Edward went by the first train and took care of his last days which were very few. We went home to his funeral. He was a dear Doctor and friend; had made every illness we had had in a great degree a pleasure because we only had daily visits from him on such occasions, and his visits were always interesting and consoling, often most lively. I think this must have been earlier than 1881, perhaps 1878.

At Edith's the measles set in, and through January and February the children had them successively. In March they had diphtheria and Waldo and his nurse came to Concord to Mother and Father. He was two years old and how happy they were to have him! The children at home Ralph, Edith & Don recovered from their illness, (Cameron & Edward were at Mrs Forbes's) but the precious little sister was taken with pneumonia and died.

The whole family went to California the next month and insisted on Edward & Annie and little Ellen's going too.

It was in this spring, while they were gone, that the Harvard Students acted the Oedipus Tyrannus of Aeschylus in the original Greek. The Faculty were all interested, and the University put all its force into making the presentation perfect. The newspapers had articles on the subject daily, perhaps, for weeks or even months beforehand. Father became very much interested. Mr William Goodwin Greek Professor,[361] Mother's and Father's friend from the days of their first coming to Concord, when he was a little boy, perhaps six years old, son of Rev. Hersey B. Goodwin, Dr Ripley's colleague, now with his Uncle and Aunt, Mr & Miss Mackay, with whom he lived, invited us all three to come spend the night and to see the Greek play. We were all more than happy, and Father was eager to go. Yet by a woeful chance one of the confused seasons came to him on the way, and though he went to the play and sat beside his friend Dr Furness,[362] and every outward advantage possible was given him it was in vain. He came to himself after we returned to Concord, and said "When are we going to see that Greek Play?" but Mother fully enjoyed both the Play and the visit, dear Mr & Miss Mackay and Mr Goodwin and Amy & Hersey. Hersey called on her in the morning and affectionately recalled all that she had done and said when he was a little boy in her Sunday-School Class. She was amazed to find he recollected it and that he cared so much for her, and of course thankful.

Again this summer came the School of Philosophy, this time already somewhat shorn of its beams. All the people who taught, the first years, were not there. Still Mother went regularly and Father occasionally. It seems to me that we had this summer another visit from Emma Lazarus who talked with Mother very interestingly, she had begun to care for her co.s as she called the Jews. She explained that this meant co-religionists. When she came the first time she did not love her nation, but now, she said, *now,* that Hotels would not receive them, and that they were persecuted in Russia, she was wholly & earnestly a Jew herself.

Mother had certain books which she read with such interest and which suited her so well that she never got through with them, but read them again and again. The first one that I remember was the Life of Rev. Edward Payson, the next was the Divine Drama of Civilization a very large book which she wore almost out, as to its covers, that is. Another was called "Plenary Inspiration," another, not quite so much valued, was named "Woman[.]"

A French volume by Mme Guyon called "Les Torrents," and her life by Upham were also very constantly in use, and when Dr Holmes's "Autocrat of the Breakfast-Table" came out as a volume I think she had it read aloud to her almost every year, even to the last.[363] She had a German Old Testament and two German copies of the New Testament, one of these last she kept in church under the pew-cushion. I think she liked to read these daily.

After the slaves were emancipated, she had no quarrel with Mr Reynolds, and loved to go to church. Father also liked him as a citizen; and, on the School-Committee, where he served with him for six years, he often said he was a Ulysses. In 1881 he was called from Concord Parish to be the Secretary of the Unitarian Association. Mother felt very sorry to lose him. She and Aunt Lizzy had often said to one another after church "Mr Reynolds is preaching beautifully now—and always!"

Mother had never ceased to love to go to church, she seldom missed either service, and now Father who had begun to go to church again,— it was to him a most agreeable change from sitting still in his study— became as regular as she. It pleased us to lock up the house on Sunday mornings and leave it empty because all its inmates were at church.

I do not remember any happenings of this year 1881 & 2 before Father's death. We were all three together and at home, I was principally with Mother till Miss Andrews came. Every evening I sat with Father in the Study and Mother often came too. Father was reading aloud to me the Light of Asia.[364] In March we had a tea-party, and invited Mr Bulkeley[365] already our promised minister, though still at the Divinity School, to come to it and spend the night. The party was given actually for the Emerys and two other families lately settled in Concord. It was very large and, as I remember it, the pleasantest we ever had. Mr Bulkeley's presence was a surprise to the guests and made everyone happier. Mr Emery and one or two gentlemen whom Father liked got away into a corner with him and gave him a really lovely quiet social evening, so that he enjoyed the party as much as the rest. After everyone was gone, while Mother and I were setting up the chairs Father & Mr Bulkeley stood by the parlour fire-place where the last coals of that festal fire were dying down and Mr Bulkeley expressed his joy & wonder that he was to have our parish, he said it seemed to him that he had drawn the highest prize, no other place was in his eyes so desirable.

On the 19*th* of April Edward was to deliver an oration to the Middlesex County Medical Society, and went to give it. It was his first public speaking. Father went out to walk in the evening and was caught in the rain. He returned and sat in his wet clothes; no one knew they were wet. The next morning as he came down to breakfast, he cried out and staggered as from a blow, just as we passed the rocking horse in the front entry. He stood still. I could not get any answer as to what, was the matter, but he let me lead him into the dining-room. I at first thought it was nausea, but it was not. He never had been able, poor man, to tell what was the matter when he felt badly, he had been sick so little that he had not learned to localize his bad sensations and did not know their names. Now he could only speak ordinary English a part of the time, often made up words. So there was no way to learn just what was the matter. Edward came, eager to tell him how the Oration had fared and nothing in the world would have interested him more, but now he could not understand.

He lay on the sofa all day in his Study, except that he came to meals but couldn't eat. In the evening he sat at the study table and tried a little to read. This went on for two days. On Friday night he for the last time took his fire to pieces, fastened his shutters and carried his lamp upstairs.

Mother took constant care of him all night both nights. On Saturday morning Edward said it was pneumonia, sent to ask Cousin Mary Simmons to come, and a trained nurse. Mother moved into Edith's room. Will & Edith came on Sunday noon and Edith stayed till Tuesday. On Tuesday noon she sent Ralph & Violet to see him and Ralph was so sorry to see his Grandfather so ill that he wanted to go right home and did. Violet was so sorry that she wanted to stay, and remained till Wednesday morning. At noon Cameron & Don came and climbed on his bed to kiss him as beautiful with their curls & red cheeks as the bunches of Mayflowers they brought him. It all pleased him. "Good boy!" he said, as each kissed him. Cameron felt so badly he wished to go right home and did; Don felt so badly that he wished to stay all night, and did. Father thought he was away from home and was all the time trying to get up and dress to go home. But once in a while we could make him recognize Mother's curtains, the furniture in the room & pictures, and, most convincing of all, Mr Cyrus Stow's[366] house through the window. Then he would say "Why yes! Here we are in Mamma's room, after all! I *am* glad." I went up to the Manse and saw Cousin Elizabeth who had received a letter from Dr Fanueil Adams of Waltham,[367] who had heard the oration and had written her a full account, with praise of its substance and form, the delivery, and Edward's voice. I came home and recited every word to Father who listened with the liveliest pleasure. When I ended I asked "Would you like to have me begin at the beginning and tell you all over again?" "Yes." The next time I came to him he said "Tell me about Edward." I did, and he liked it this time three times in succession.

Mother sat beside him on the bed when she could. The last day, he talked much to her, quite unintelligibly most of the time, but he said again and again "the beautiful boy." Mother imagined he was telling her he looked forward in dying to see Waldo again. He always smiled, rejoiced at the sight of her, when Mother came into the room. On Sunday & Monday Edith was with him most of the time and that was a comfort to him.

The last day Edward sent for Mr Channing, Mr Staples, Judge Hoar, Mr Sanborn, Mr Elliot Cabot, to bid him goodbye. They all came. To Mr Staples, to Judge Hoar, to Mr Cabot, he said some words sufficiently intelligible, he knew them and was pleased to see them. I don't think he was so clear when the others came. But when we told him Mr Cabot was there, his face shone and he exclaimed "Elliot Cabot! Praise!" Dr C.P. Putnam[368] came with Edward in the afternoon. While they were there pain seized him and they gave him ether, saying he would not come out of it. He lay unconscious till about nine when Edward called us together.

I had written and sent notes to Judge Hoar & Charley Emerson to tell them Father was dying and they came after tea and sat down in the parlour without sending word. Mr Keyes came too. Now, at nine o'clock, Judge Hoar came with us to Father's bedside, and Cousin Mary was there too. Mr Keyes & Charley did not come up. Judge Hoar went right to Mother, and put his arm round her supporting her while we all stood in silence. "He will breathe once more, perhaps twice," Edward presently said, and the second breath was the last.

Edward went down and told the others. They came up to look at him. Then all went. The church-bell tolled his age, and every one knew by that that he had died.

We all went together into Edith's room, for the time, Mother's room. It had been her room as a bride; she now sat there a widow. "I am a widow," she said, "I never thought of this." Edward consulted with us about the ministers for the funeral. Reynolds was in Washington. The next morning, April 28*th*, the world was white with snow. It seemed lovely when we saw it and right. It was gone before noon when Edith came.

I remember it all as a very beautiful time in our lives. The coming together of all our friends to us. The stories that reached us of the action of the Town of all the ladies' having a meeting and making black and white rosettes to hang on every door between the depot, the house & the cemetery, and the authorities having the church floor and galleries supported that they might be strong enough, the dear letters that arrived, the sense that all this gave us of everybody's interest in Father was most sweet.

Dr Furness came on Saturday, he had, of late years, spent some days with us every year and had become like a dear Uncle. His coming was a great pleasure; and, that evening, Judge Hoar brought the organist who was Tom Surette[369] and church hymn-books to consult about the choice of hymns for the funeral. Many hymns were read and the talk over them was most interesting. Mother was present and gave her attention and her vote. There was much housekeeping to be done, and our dear Kate, Mrs Rouse, came Friday night and with her Sarah Gately who had sewed for us for years, both full of affection & compassion for Mother and of mourning for Father and insisted on throwing themselves into all gaps, sweeping, sewing or washing; or dressing Mother or arranging rooms, and stayed till after the funeral, the greatest comforts they were! In five years they too were dead[.] I saw little of Mother I was so busy, so was Edith. Alicia Keyes stayed with her in Edith's room and read her Father's Essays. Dan French[370] came and helped Edward to dress Father in white, like a statue. All things in the domestic and in the church funeral were as we liked, and at the burial, at the end of a dark day the sun came out and gilded the trunks of the trees around us.

All our relationship from far & near were together at Bush at tea that night and we had delightful family talk. For instance, Cousin Samuel told how Cousin Hannah always wished to undertake every labour and go every errand so that her Aunt Phebe Ripley said Hannah's motto was, "But, howsoever, let me run," and Haven looked up and smiled saying "I'm afraid my little Helena has the same spirit. She always does the errands and helps the others on with their coats." And after tea in the parlour we had a cosy time, all thankful to be together, Mother, children and grandchildren, nephews, nieces and cousins. With the morning they all went. I think, since Edith and Will had to go the next morning, also, it seemed best for us children and Mother to sit up that night after others had gone to bed that we might read the Will together, so we all assembled in the Study for it.

When Father's will was read, Mother, who had forgotten all about it, was quite frightened lest she should be unable to get along without the book-money, and when she went upstairs gave way to distress. I told her she had been present when the will was made and had it all arranged exactly as she pleased, but this didn't comfort her "I didn't understand," she said, "or I never should have consented." I knew she had fully understood. I tried hard to remember what had been said, and at last I did bring it back that she was going to use her property's income, instead of what went to Edward. "Oh! Very well!" she said when I told her, "Then it is quite right, and I don't care a particle for any more," and we have found the income quite sufficient.

Mother wished to give up the blue ribbons of her cap but we all were decided in opposing that. There was no reason to mourn, and we none of us inclined to believe in wearing mourning so she retained them.[371]

A week or so after the funeral Nina Lowell and Mr & Mrs Cabot came to look over and clear up Father's papers that Mr Cabot might take them to write his life. While they were there, on the 14th of May, 1882 Alexander, Edith's youngest child was born. I went to see him and brought back the account of him to Mother who was of course most eager to hear. This visit of Mr & Mrs Cabot and Nina was full of pleasures for her. Sometimes the ladies were helping Mr Cabot in the Study, but sometimes they sat with her in her room, and the best of all was when we were all together[.]

For a while Mother liked to keep going to Father's grave, and the young ladies of the town made a plan to keep it dressed all the time that summer,—a new pair undertook the charge each week,—so that Mother was overwhelmed with gratitude finding it always so freshly and beautifully adorned, and asked for a list of the ladies, which she read with great interest, and always kept. Before the year was over she said she thought it was a mistake to keep visiting the grave, she did not believe Father was there, nor did she wish to associate the grave with the thought of him. So she ceased to go.

Cousin Sarah remained with us that summer and we asked Mr Bulkeley to board with us. His coming, and his Ordination in July, were to us most interesting events. His Mother died on the day he was ordained. He adopted Mother in some sort and talked to her a great deal, not only about his affairs, but they had religious conversation.

On Thanksgiving Day after his sermon, which pleased Cousin Sarah who went to church with me, he went to Cambridge to Mr Warren's, and we had a quiet little Thanksgiving with Cousins Sarah & Hannah (whose little granddaughter Edith Bardwell was with her) and Edward & Edith's families. Edith brought Alexander a beautiful baby six months old, and I think Florence must have come too, just one month old with her funny nodding plume of long hair.

Mr Bulkeley was married in January and he and Miss Warren begged hard that Mother would come to the wedding but I am sorry to say in vain. She loved them both and felt that they and their children belonged to her.

After this we had in succession Miss Worcester two years or less, Miss Sage three years, and Miss Legate[372] the last three years of Mother's life, all dear friends to her and me, all giving her daily pleasure and enjoying all that she enjoyed with her. She used to like to recite to them her store of poetry; especially as a Sunday recreation. They appreciated the beauties of her character and laughed with me at the funny incidents of every day.

Mother often walked to Father's grave and then from there to Mrs Sanborn's and home again. That must be three miles, and it did not fatigue her in the least. If she went into the garden to work before dinner she surely refused to come in to dinner. I, for a long time, used to labour to make her come. But I soon found that she always did come in, quarter of an hour late, and lay down on the sofa "for the sake of your company," she would say.

Then I would get her plate prepared and ask her to come to her place and eat a little just for company, and she would come quite naturally and dine with us. Sometimes Mother liked walking better and better the farther she walked; sometimes her whole desire was to get home. If as might occur, we met one of her friends who joined us she no longer wished to go home but lengthened her walk for the pleasure of company.

In 1884 Cousin Mary Watson invited us to spend a week with her in Plymouth, I think 'twas in April.[373] We had all sorts of pleasures. Cousin Mary & Lulie[374] sat with her while she ate her breakfast, at the other meals she saw all the family. In the evening she had a blissful game of whist. Her walks along the familiar streets were most interesting to her, she took me to her Father's house, to her Grandfather Jackson's, to the Winslow house. We went to Mrs Hedge's to tea, and to Miss Mary H. Russell's house to see her niece. She showed me her Uncle Doctor's house and Uncle Thomas's & Uncle William's. We went to see Dr Kendall's daughters, and Mrs Tolman who once had been a Sunday-scholar, and Mrs Bartlett another. Also Mrs William Russell who had been one of Aunt Lucy's mates. Her house was very handsome, and

Mr Watson once went about with us and showed us many elaborately-finished ancient interiors.

While we were gone this time our John Clahane's wife died, leaving eight children the youngest a baby. Our Kate Sally, Mrs Rouse, soon after spent a week with us and mourned much over this death, "the mother's leaving all those children that she loved so dear." In three months dear Kate herself died of the same disease.

One Monday morning, 26 May 1884 Charles Prescott[375] told me on the Mill-dam that Edward & Annie had a son. I hastened to the house, and there sure enough was a stout little fellow looking like the first baby; William; none of the rest had. We were overjoyed; Annie said Edward had supposed he was willing to have a third daughter and was himself surprised to find how glad he was to have a son.

When June came he & Annie and all three went to Richmond Mass. and spent a week with us on their return in September. In this week fell their Tin Wedding-Day and Mother's birthday came the next day. This made one of the most glorious family festivals we ever had, full of surprises. Edward & Annie & family dined with the Keyeses. Edith & some of her children came at noon. We invited all the Keyeses to tea and they kept the secret well. Annie came home, put her babes to bed and was amazed, when she came late to tea, to find the long table and her family, all but Alice & Prescott. Yet no thought of tin arose in her mind not even when the infant Alexander (2½ years), going to bed while we were at tea, gave her his tin present first. So when she entered the parlour and saw the shining pans and pails it was great fun to everybody. Hardly had she seen all when Aunt Susan's family, the Bartletts, Cousin Elizabeth & Sophy & Lizzy Simmons marched in with tins & poems, then Prescott & Alice. We had a joyful evening, and last of all were surprised by Edith with an ice-cream supper.

When all the guests were gone there was still much ice-cream left. I carried it over to John's. The house was dark, all were gone to bed. I stood under the eaves and called distinctly and aloud. "John! Are all the family asleep? Is it too late for them to eat some ice-cream?" Instantly from the eaves above me in all voices of man & boy girl and baby came a simultaneous and decisive "No" with a discernible note of joy in it.

"I'll set it down on the steps," I said. The next day was Mother's birthday, she was eighty-two. We gave her her presents. Then came a photographer and took a photograph of her with Waldo & Alexander and Edward's little three. In the evening we surprised her with a great tea-party. She knew nothing about it till when she rose from her nap at half past five we brought out her "Ball-dress." "Not that," she said. "Yes, put it on to go down and see your friends," and we brought her down to a parlour already full. Judge Hoar, after presenting his congratulations, said he could not stay to tea; and asked her to accept from him the basket of peaches in the entry. Mother had a very happy birthday.

I asked Annie whether William talked. He was four months old. "No he never makes any noises, except when he cries." The next day, Sept. 21*st*, he began, and was so delighted with the new accomplishment that his oration lasted an hour or two without stopping. As I came home from church I heard his pretty voice, ran in to see, and behold he was hard at it, and talked to me in the loveliest manner as long as I could stay he was lying on the bed in Edith's room. I think he went on all day.

I date from this autumn Mother's old age of eight years; a decay as slow and even in its advance as Father's had been. For some years after this she walked as well and seemed as bright, but it became necessary to take care of her at night, and I soon was so tired that we had to have an attendant, so that I could sleep. It was at Christmas that she came, Miss Brown.[376] And she remained nearly a year. She played whist and so did Miss Mary Sage who was with us then and whenever they could get a fourth player Mother had happy evenings. Indeed whist was more and more a resource for her henceforth.

When we put up the green at Thanksgiving Mother who in old times put up the whole, but early relinquished that business to us children, always retained the charge of dressing with it the parlour looking-glass. Sometimes when she had been sick she would say "I must wrap up and go down just long enough to do that" and of late years she would say "*I* must do the parlour-glass," but now the time had come when she dared not stand so high up for fear of falling.

Every summer she took up bulbs to give away. This year she sent by me the various bags of them to the friends to whom she had promised them with instructions to each about setting them out. She ended with "Tell her the sooner they go into the ground the better. They are industrious cattle and will immediately set about making roots."

There was one nightly scene which made us laugh then and we still laugh when we think of it. Our dining-room window-sashes are long and the bump and shriek and groan as they go up and again as they go down, really make much and ugly noise. Every night, after tea, we open them to shut the blinds; each window opens & shuts, that is the din is repeated four times, Mother was usually talking, lying on the sofa. The first window goes up, Mother starts & screams. "What is that?

Oh it's that window." It goes down. Mother makes up a face. The second goes up, again a face and "What a noise!" It goes down and Mother starts up "Has all nature broke[n] loose?"

Mother was all her life a screamer. Her sudden scream at the table, when a spoon fell on a dish or any other clang occurred, often terrified the stranger guest, but to me it gilded many occasions, mightily adding to the comicalness of the situation.

In the summer of 1885 we made the plan of going with Mother to Plymouth to keep there with her her fiftieth wedding day. We found that the Town of Concord was going to celebrate the 250th Anniversary of its founding. In the fifty years, things had come round to make the anniversary on the same day of the week as in 1835, Saturday, September 12*th* and as Father then delivered the oration at the Celebration on that day and on Monday 14*th* arrived in Plymouth and was married, so would we all attend the Celebration in Concord on Saturday 12*th* and arrive in Plymouth on Monday 14*th* to repair with Mother at half past seven to the room in which she was married.

This was one of the best times of my life and Mother was as happy as she could be. All Edith's family came to Concord to the Celebration which was more stirring than we had expected, and much as we had enjoyed every part of the day, the happiest part was the evening when Edward and Annie came in, all was talked over and we found Edward too had thought everything fine, so that we were all enthusiastic together.

On Monday afternoon we reached Plymouth and all took rooms at the Samoset,[377] Mother and her three children, Will with Ralph, Violet, Cameron, Don & Edward, Edward & Annie without a single child, their three, as well as Waldo and Alexander, being left behind as too young. We went at once to the house where Mother was born, and she showed us where she and Purry had played, we asked Dr Briggs's leave to come to the Winslow house after tea, and it was most cordially given.

As usual after tea it was hard to bring Mother to be ready at the moment, but we did accomplish it, and at half past seven we all streamed into the room where she was married and were received with entire sympathy by Dr Briggs and his daughter. Presently came in Dr LeBaron Russell and Uncle George Bradford who had been present at the ceremony fifty years before. We were all delighted. This was accidental, I don't think it had been planned. Will and Edith were meditating building over their house at Naushon, and that made Will take a great interest in the architecture of the Winslow house and Dr Briggs showed us upstairs and down the family following with immense satisfaction. Mother loved every inch of the house, and her pride centred in the staircase, which Will admired. After our return to the Samoset Will said "Now let's drink your Mother's health in Polly water," so the Apollinaris[378] was brought. I think Mother had not tasted it before, certainly she liked it very much, and for many days she would recall the festive name of Polly-water, with a laugh.

In the morning some of the party went, Will & Ralph perhaps, the rest went round, before Mother was up, to see the sights of Plymouth. Mother, being ready before they returned walked over to her Father's house with me. Mrs Simmons, who then lived there, invited us in, and Mother showed me every room and told me many of the stories of her childhood hereinbefore detailed.

At dinner-time she gave us the story Aunt Harlow told of her Jackson Grandparents, and Edward highly appreciated the fun of it. In the afternoon we all visited Cousin Mary & Mr Marston Watson[379] at Hillside, and Mr Watson promised to find out for Mother where her Grandfather Cotton had lived. The rest went back to Naushon and to Concord. Mother and I stayed three days more.

It was one of the marks of age that Mother no longer remembered that she *always* felt sick in the morning. So every morning she now thought she had been taken with a serious illness. After her breakfast she felt better, and then she did not remember that she had been alarmed. In the afternoon she felt well and was full of love for her own dear town and all its inhabitants.

We had the most charming soul-contenting afternoon visiting with Mr Watson the house of her Cotton Grandparents, Mother guessed which was the room where the family sat together, the room where her Aunt Joa received the offer of marriage, & stood against the door &c[380] and he took us down to the bank of Town brook where it was interesting [See Sketch] to see the pipes in the masonry on each side of it, by which the various springs in the town poured in their plenteous contribution to its waters. Then he went with us "up to the Northward" to show us "a Spring" whose clear perfect water was led along the gutter by the road till it came to a grating down which it plunged. Other afternoons, we visited Mother's contemporaries and cousins. At Miss Kendall's we saw a portrait of Dr Kendall[,] Mother's minister, we called on a Miss Louisa Jackson, and entering her room I felt myself in the scenery of my early years. It must have been furnished about 1830 and kept by care and gentle use very nearly in *status quo* all these years. I gazed at every detail, they reminded me of Aunt Lucy's room, of our nursery and Grandma's room. Cousin Louisa was not much younger then Mother, I judged. They were glad to meet again, and

her breakfast she felt better, and then she did   345
not remember that she had been alarmed.
In the afternoon she felt well and was full of
love for her own dear town and all its inhabitants.

     We had the most charming soul-contenting
afternoon visiting with Mr Watson the house of
Mother guessed which was the room where the family sat together, the room where
she first refused the offer of marriage, & stood against the door &c
her Cotton Grandparents, and he w... us down to
the bank of Town brook where it was interesting

to see the pipes in the masonry on each side
of it, by which the various springs in the town
poured in their plenteous contribution to its water.
Then he went with us "up to the Northward" to
show us "the Pilgrim Spring" whose clear perfect
water was led along the gutter by the rose till it
came to a grating down which it plunged.
Other afternoons, we visited Mother's contemporaries
and cousins. At Miss ....'s we saw a portrait
of Dr Kendall Mother's minister. We called on a
Miss Louisa Jackson. and entering her room I felt
myself in the scenery of my early years. It must
have been furnished about 1830 and kept by care
            345

had much to say. Mother took me to Training Green and showed me Aunt Harlow's house. She said she had a Cousin Lucy Marcy,[381] but she shouldn't go to see her for Lucy Marcy had been very indignant at Joe Marcy's treatment at the hands of her Father, and she had never spoken to her and Aunt Lucy. Presently an old lady in a sunbonnet looked out of a gate and said "Is that you, Cousin Lydia? Oh! how glad I am to see you! I heard you'd come to Plymouth, and I've been hoping you'd look me up. Come in a while. I live in Aunt Harlow's house. Is this your daughter?" "Yes," said Mother, "Ellen, this is your Cousin Lucy Marcy." So we went in. The hatchet was buried in the vale of years; no one was more pleased to see Mother than she, and Mother was quite as happy that the feud was closed.

Everyone we saw was as interesting to me and to her, Mother said every tea-time, "We must stay a week longer!" and I should gladly have done so if there had been no hours in the day except from one to nine p.m. But the miseries of the rest of the time were the same each day. At nine Mother was taken ill and suffered far more with terror because Edward couldn't get to her (even if I should telegraph early in the morning) before noon tomorrow when it might be too late to save her, than she did with her sensations. So she was actively nursed till three or four o'clock, a.m. though she had occasional hours of sleep. At about four she fell asleep and waked at seven, when she called me to say she was sorry but she had waked up sick, I must pack her trunk and we must get home as soon as possible.

Then about eleven, having had her breakfast, she felt better, took a walk, and soon began to plan to remain a long time. The first days, I fought off about packing, but on the third or fourth morning I did just as I was told and we went in the noon train, Mother feeling very well and regretting that she had decided so hastily to go home.

In the summer of 1866 Edith & Will pulled down the Naushon house which was built for Don to be born in, and Will took Ralph & Cameron to Kootenay to camp out & hunt, while she brought the other children to Concord. This summer we had huckleberryings and picnics at Easterbrook, and Mother learned that she could go and could have a good time. We carried plenty of cushions, blankets & downs. I remember one picnic on the top of the lime-kiln, where Violet made us a Welsh Rarebit over an alcohol-lamp, as a very happy one. After the dinner Mother lay down on cushions, covered warm, and was read to sleep as at home.

In the December before, Miss Leavitt[382] had come to be her nurse and remained with her till her death. Mother had always exclaimed when night came "Oh I wish I had a great jallant (my sister Edith's baby-word for giant) to come and put me to bed!" Miss Leavitt was large-framed and strong and Mother had great comfort in her powerful hand. "She catches me much as you would catch a chicken," Mother once said; and Miss Legate used to say "She swoops your Mother along, and your Mother goes without a word." One day when Mother had been restless and her pillows were tossed, her hair tumbled and her cap askew, Miss Leavitt came in, shook her pillows, set Mother up against them, took off her cap and began brushing her hair. "Miss Leavitt is licking up her kitty!" said Mother with a smile of delight. Miss Leavitt, before she had been with Mother a week, said "Isn't she bright? Almost every word she says ought to be printed in the Saturday Gazette, she is so quick." She was also proud of Mother's beauty, and took great pains in dressing and decking her. Very soon she began to wash and iron all Mother's caps and collars herself, the servants did not do it well enough to please her. Her pride then extended to Mother's room and before long she washed and ironed the curtains of the bed and the bureau-covers, they were then perfect.

We began to call Mother Miss Leavitt's doll. It was very pretty to see how perfectly she finished every little detail in dressing her, and when there was an occasion for putting on her best clothes Miss Leavitt was happy. She always shook out her clean handkerchief before putting it in her pocket, she objected to its going in folded. She made the tulle caps and the bows.

In this summer of 1886 Edward & Annie were in Wayland, and when I went over to spend the day with them with Cousin Sarah, Miss Leavitt would usually prevail on Mother to follow, and at about dinner-time the carryall would come in sight Miss Leavitt driving and Mother on the back seat. One day so many of us arrived there was no room in the house large enough and Annie set the table in the tent they had out in the yard.

Haven Emerson came that autumn to go to school in Concord for a year. We had a barberrying picnic to which he came with Billy Buttrick and Philip Walcott[383] and little Ellen. All our household was there, that is Mother, Miss Leavitt, Miss Sage and I, Miss [Nelly] French, Ellen's teacher, and Mr & Mrs Emery, Anna McClure and her brother. We carried a camp-cot and camp-stools, and the gentlemen were much gratified that they could sit on them. After dinner when the rest went to gather barberries Miss Leavitt and I made up the cot with pillows and downs, Mother lay down and I read her to sleep. She enjoyed that picnic.

This year she had to give up walking, she lost her breath so easily. If breath had held out, she was otherwise strong enough. She still liked to go out into the garden, but it was hard to induce her to go to the

gate; if she did, it was with one of us on each side. But one day as she
sat at the table she saw from the dining-room window John's cat catch
a bird as she thought, and she rose and sallied forth, crossed the East
Yard and went out as far as the Dutch Codling tree, as lightly and fast
as she ever would have to rescue the victim. It proved to be a large
brown leaf that the cat was playing with and she hastened back to relieve
the anxiety on the bird's account which she supposed we must be suffering, set our minds at rest, and took her seat, neither breathless nor
fatigued.

Now became her custom to ride out every day after dinner and she
was proud that she was able to go all winter even on cold days. Edith
made her a mighty-mandarin of black silk stuffed with down, and she
carried in her lap a hot-water bottle. John usually drove her; he made
very pretty speeches to her when she sometimes thanked him. She always,
before leaving the dinner-table prepared a plate of dainties for the
horse, odds & ends of bread & pudding, and if we had fruit she added
the parings. The horse learned to connect the sight of her with a feast,
and his movements when she was in sight were always toward her. He
backed so fast when she left his head to get into the carriage, that someone had to run to hold him, so that often three were out to get her in,
John to hold the horse's head, I to hold open the door & push in her
sweeping Mandarin with her while Miss Leavitt held up her dress in
front and lifted at her elbows. In general this was a festivity. Sometimes the inconveniences & delays of the feeding made me cross.

Mother used to read to herself a great deal and a pin was her book-
mark. Many of our books still have in them the pins which she put in.
She also stuck pins in the articles in newspapers which she wished to
read again or have read to her. I find them even now sometimes when
I turn over a pile of papers.

In the first year or two after Father died I often thought she was so
feeble and wanted him so much that she would not live long. I remember saying so; but by this time I had quite ceased to have any such idea,
she seemed strong in most ways, and she and I recalled the prophecy
of her Aunt, "You'll be a stately old lady yet."

Edward's Raymond,[384] her last grandchild was born Nov. 28*th* 1880[.]
In the summer of 1887 Will & Edith's new stone house at Naushon was
finished, and they invited Mother and me to visit it and bring Miss
Leavitt. Let no one imagine it was a simple thing. The plot deep &
Machiavelli was laid beforehand[.] Many particulars had to be considered, the trunk packed in secret, the seed early sown in Mother's
mind by a pushing of the invitation, then neglected for days, then mentioned before dinner, earnestly repulsed by Mother. Then she had to

be suddenly equipped in her mantle bonnet &c by force & led by force to the carriage. This, with Mrs Sanborn's assistance (she came even to the Old Colony Depot with us) was accomplished, and was the happiest visit Mother had there; everything favoured. She liked the hall, the views of the stair-case and from it. Especially she was struck by the charm of a blazing fire in the Bay-parlour fireplace as she saw it when she came downstairs, and each room delighted her; also a drive on a glorious day to Eagle Hollow, and, most of all, of course, her Grandchildren. She did not go to Naushon again.

That autumn Anna McClure[385] came in September to stay with us eight months. She had for the first six weeks a horse and covered buggy, and invited Mother to ride with her every day. She contrived to make these rides so pleasant that Mother allowed them to last two hours instead of one which was the longest time we had before been able to keep her out. Anna had a guitar and often played and sang to her in the evenings, finally even inducing Mother to sing too. It became a regular thing, Mother & Anna's singing hymns together, Sunday evenings, to the guitar. In the spring Anna went away but often in the next two years came for Sundays, sometimes would come home from her work every night and spend the nights, through May, and she became a great boon to Mother, always able to divert her and sure to make her comfortable.

Miss Leavitt succeeded by degrees in making Mother live more like the rest of the world, less like an invalid. She often came to breakfast with us, and forgot to observe many little habits of anxious care of her health. One summer, I forget which, she and I went to visit Edward & Annie at Coffin's Beach, and she breakfasted downstairs there, and walked out to where Edward was painting the lowest drawer of the secretary by her bed. Edward's children brought almost daily by their papa to see her would climb on her bed to kiss her, then wriggle off and go to the drawer for the playthings.

They seemed to be more fond of her than I should have expected, since she could do so little personally for them. In 1889 when William was three his Aunt Alicia in the absence of his parents was amusing him and Florence and told them the story of Red-Riding-Hood, and when she came to the Wolf's pouncing on the Grandmother and eating her all up, William screamed "I can't have the Wolf eat up Grandma! Nor even Grandma Keyes!"

Raymond was a baby then. He came with his nurse and made us a visit of a week while his parents were away when he was just able to walk, and that was a happy week to Mother and me. He liked the rocking-horse, Diamond, very much. It stood in the dining-room or parlour—

wherever we were—most of the time that week, and Raymond was either on his back or offering him food; in this last Mother encouraged him.

Charley & Therchi[386] were at all times tender & charming to Mother, she always loved to have them come, and to go to see them. Whenever Bible Society met, and Therchi, Miss Legate and I were all going, Charley used to take tea with Mother and amuse her in the evening. We always found her in high spirits, on such occasions. "Sometimes it seems to me that Aunt Lidian is better with me than with other people," he once said, and he was right. There were few companions she enjoyed so much. She loved to say her German poetry to them, too.

Therchi used to bring her all sorts of good things to eat, which she had cooked herself, and flowers from her garden, and pretty presents on her birthday and New Years; and much the handsomest vases Mother ever had. It was sad that they were so often broken.

In the summer of 1888 our Don died—Judge Hoar exclaimed[387] on hearing of it, "Poor Mr Forbes has lost his junior" which was a touch of sympathy—, he died at Naushon where he was born. The funeral was at Milton, and Mother went of course, though she was so averse to going anywhere, even going to ride, at this time, that Edward & Annie didn't think she would and I think Edith had no expectation of it. But we didn't have to ask Mother to go, she had no other thought. She carried some forget-me-nots from the garden and put them in Don's dear hand. We all think her being there was sweet to Edith.

This year, I believe it was, Mother gave me on my birthday Pilgrim's Progress, and I read it to her every Sunday afternoon. It gave us both great pleasure. I hadn't read it for more than forty years though in infancy I had been at work on it most of the time, as it was very interesting to me. And Mother I think hadn't seen it for some sixty or seventy. She would always say as she went to her room after Sunday's dinner, "Now don't you want to read me some "Pilgrim's Progress"?"

In the winters she would say "I look forward with immense expectation to the coming of spring. How pleasant it will be to see the green things coming up! It seems as if I never cared so much before." But when the spring came she did not wish after 1886 or 7 to go out into the garden to see them. It seemed to her too much of an effort. "Not today, I am not well enough." We used to say when she was in the dining-room "Come into the pantry, and look out at the quarter-circle from the window." That she would consent to do, and then we would open the door onto the back piazza and get her to walk out on that and look over the railing. Then it was not very hard to get her to go down the steps to see the flowers in the round bed, and round the corner of the wing into the garden, but in the latest years, she would say "I don't want to go onto the piazza, I am afraid you will make me go down the steps." Very seldom indeed did she willingly go into the beloved garden in '91 & '92[.] "But why not, Mother? It is perfect weather, and there are plenty of flowers." "I know it, I like to see them, but it tires me and I see more things that need attention than I do flowers. So it worries me, for I am not able to attend to them[.]" In rose-time she would ask when we brought in the morning's crop of roses to have the basket put on the bed. "I want to take up every single one of them and look at it." And she did.

She had an acute illness one autumn, I should think it was in 1889 and her illusions from the fever were amusing. I remember only the one about the flies. A fly she said had come close to her and eaten a grain of sugar "I never had an opportunity before to see one so well. You have no idea of the beautiful finish of their proboscis. It is so beautifully frilled and scalloped, as if trimmed with wrought edging. It was inserting as well as an edging. Never will I allow one to be destroyed again—when the little creatures are so beautifully finished." I was away, and Edward's letter to me about her must go in here[.][388] When I came home she was still sick. I went in in the morning and she said "You don't know what I've heard. I didn't know it was possible, but I have overheard a conversation between the comforter and the blankets. Very interesting! Isn't it wonderful?" Delighted, I asked what they said. "I don't remember exactly, not all of it, they said a good deal. I think the upshot of it was that the comforter said if anyone would pull him straight they could be very comfortable."

Very entertaining it was that the comforter should have imbibed from Mother a disgust with being crooked—her bedclothes must always be straight and smooth, you remember, or the angels wouldn't come.

In the afternoon, I think it was, she said again "Oh such a conversation as the bedclothes have been holding! I believe if you had been very still you could have heard it too, I wish you had! If you could only have seen the pompous air of the comforter when he was speaking about his spots." It was a white percale comforter dotted with black dots. I am not sure that in these stories I have used Mother's very words, but I believe I wrote them down at the time, and if they are ever found, I think they will prove to agree with this version very well. Mother remembered this experience for days, believed in it, and felt a natural wonder that the bedclothes could use language among themselves.

Mrs Sanborn spent the summer of 1889 with us. What a comfort that was to us both. She used to come to the Pilgrim's Progress readings on Sunday afternoons. Then she went to ride with us and that made it easier to take Mother longer rides. There never was such an abundant crop of blackberries as that summer's, and they were a great thing for Mother. When we came to a spot where they were thick by the roadside she liked to get out and pick them, we always carried pails and often brought home one or two quarts. She forgot she was feeble and was much interested in filling her measure. She thought low-bush berries were better than the high not only in taste but in a peculiar property of restoring health to every eater.

I think she went to Boston for the last time in 1889. She was hurriedly snatched from the dinner-table, her boots put on by Miss Leavitt, her cloak by Mrs Sanborn (imported for the purpose) and her bonnet by me simultaneously while the hack drew up to the door, and Mrs Sanborn & I followed her (put in by Miss Leavitt) into it and drove off to the depot before she could catch her breath. She said she was quite unable today to go. We persevered, took her to Hovey's [Department Store] in the horse-cars, and took her to the silk counter to choose her new dress, but when we found she had no opinion and no interest in the matter we were much disappointed and even I felt really penitent when she seemed unable to get to Winter St. and thought I ought not to have brought her. We went to the milliner's and had her bonnet fitted and presently she began to revive, and paid a good deal of attention half an hour later to the purchase of white flannel. There was no longer much difficulty about walking. The last errand she did with enthusiasm, and as we drove to the depot she exclaimed "How much better this is than an afternoon in bed! I'm very glad I came. Let us do this again. I should like to tomorrow." But when tomorrow came she would not hear of it. Such was the usual course of things. She resisted going any-where, and anyone unused to her might have feared she would die on the way, so white and spent she appeared, but always (till the last time she went out, when she persistently begged to go home) she soon began to enjoy, and declared on the way home that she wouldn't have missed the visit, or the club-meeting or card-party, on any account, why she had meant to go. So I never let her off.

There was one autumn when Mother had for several days a great train of ladies. Cousin Charlotte & Cousin Sarah were both with us, Caroline Cheney[389] was making us a visit, Miss Legate, it seems to me was there, Mrs Sanborn came for a day or two, and all of them as well as Miss Leavitt and I liked to wait on her, so that when Mother moved from parlour to dining-room, or went up or down stairs, or into the garden, all seven surrounded her, and all seven were emulous to do her errands. She seemed more like a queen than ever. In the summer of 1890, perhaps it was, in the end of June[390] we were alone at tea. Miss Legate had gone home, Cousin Sarah had not yet arrived, Miss Leavitt as usual had gone to bed that she might sleep before Mother would need her at nine. The night was hot and still, the sun hadn't yet set, roses were in their glory. I ran to the kitchen and told the girl to carry out a chair into the garden then using both persuasion and some determination I induced Mother to come out with me. It was so delightful at that moment in the garden that she was in less haste than usual to go in, and consented to sit down and contemplate the scene while I cut some roses. She had as usual her black silk dress and beautiful cap, and I had thrown the light blue shawl Sally crocheted for her over her shoulders. Presently I looked round at her from a little distance and seldom have I seen a more enchanting picture than she made with the grape-arbour behind her as a background, the host of roses all round her and the last yellow rays of the setting sun a most becoming, transfiguring light on the whole scene. I gazed, and thought "Oh for Edith, or Violet, or Edward or Annie or Anna! Someone besides myself to appreciate Mother's beauty in this setting. At this very moment, by blessed chance, Mrs Sanborn came. I ran and asked her to look, and she enjoyed it as much as I. It has been a comfort to me always that that was not lost on me alone. Mother as soon as the sun set wished to go in and walked up to the house between us.

The time had come when she could no longer remember the poems she had recited to us all her life. Often, indeed every day, there were times when she wished to have Miss Leavitt, when Miss L. was having a nap, or to go to bed, when her bed was airing, and it was necessary to "take up her mind" with something for a while, and the grand resource had always been to get her to say Miss Jane Taylor's "Ann & Martha,"[391] or "Tis but the day-star's earliest, glance" or one of the Fore-fathers' Day odes, but now she attempted it in vain. On one of these occasions, I bethought me to induce her to go into the red room and stopped her at each window, saying "What happened here? What association have you with this window?" and she had one with every one. We both had a good time, she recalling particulars of each occasion that came up, and I hearing. I am sorry, I don't remember now what they were. Anna McClure died in 1890 and in dying said to her family, "I shall wait for you all, and I hope when you die I shall be allowed to come and help you through." Mother and I believe she included us, and when she spoke of dying Mother would say "I hope Anna will come." One day, as she was expressing great dread of it, I said "Anna will help you through." She brightened and said "Yes, I think she will."

A minute after she added "When I think of your Father, and Waldo—and my Father & Mother—I don't know—they seem so far off, but Anna seems near, and as if she would come[.]"

As I mentioned in speaking of her childhood[392] the fear of death was with her very great, and now it was constantly before her. When I found her alone and sat down by her, or when we were left alone she would say "Do you think we shall go to hell?" or "Do you believe in everlasting punishment?" and there was another form, when she was struck with a sense of her weakness. "It is time for me to die. I should wish to die if I thought I was good enough," and again "Oh! if I thought the Almighty would be as merciful to me as I should be to the meanest kitten, I should be willing to die."

She was always anxious that I should stay in the house after her death, and more than once wrote on a paper, "Dear Edith & Edward, it is my wish that Ellen should stay in the house, if she is willing, and that, if she isn't, she should have every piece of the furniture that she wants." Now she could no longer write; she would hold the pen, if we asked her to write her grandchildren's names in books she was to give them, and make delicate & pretty shaded lines but she had forgotten not only how to spell but how to make letters.

She would often say, "I hope the children will live in the house. I cannot bear to think of strangers' living in it[.]"

She continued to go to church till 1889, and once or twice, when I had failed to induce her to go and went without her, I met her on the steps of the church, as I came out, much pleased to surprise me. She said "After you had gone, I suddenly thought I would come and dressed in all haste. Then, when I got here, I remembered the minister's room and went into that. The door into the pulpit was open, the couch close by, and I lay down and heard the sermon as well as anybody!" When we told Mr Bulkeley he was delighted, and wished she would always do it when she did not feel able to sit up.

We sat from 188[?][393] to '89 in Miss Emeline Barrett's pew, (No.   ), for she could not longer hear in our own. One Sunday when the minister appeared in the pulpit, she turned to me and asked "Who izz it?" She never could whisper low, and this sounded to me particularly loud and breezy. I thought she wouldn't hear my answer, so wrote "Mr Abraham Jackson."[394] She put on her glasses, read it, and whispered back, "Unsanctified name!" referring to our cousin Abraham Jackson in State Prison.

In her fifty-seven years of life in Concord she had never taken root there, she was always a sojourner, her home was Plymouth, a never-dying flame of love for Plymouth burned in her heart and burst forth in praises of its people, stories of its glorious founding, reminiscences of its peaceful ways, its social life, and an enthusiastic observance of Fore-father's Day, the 22*d* of December, for it was not till 1855 I think that Plymouth people decided that it ought to be the 21*st*.

She cared for some people in Concord, and always expected to con-tribute her flowers and dishes and silver, and to go herself to every town-occasion. Yet they were not something of which she was a part. She only came. To others Soldiers' Aid Society meant Concord's work for the country, to her it meant work for the country. But of every movement of Plymouth, though only heard-of she felt herself a part. This was not willful, it was hardly conscious, purely natural.

She knew all the hymn-tunes sung in Plymouth and Brattle St. in old times, Old Hundred, Hamburg, Peterborough, Shirland, Portugal, Brattle St., Duke St., Wells, Sicilian Hymn, Greenville, Tamworth, Missionary Hymn, Watchman, Lennox, Dennis, Plegel's Hymn, Jerusa-lem, St[.] Martin's, Italiasi Hymn but, strangely enough, never learned one of the more modern ones sung constantly in Concord all of thirty years. After we had congregational singing, (in 1864 perhaps) she joined in it when we had her old tunes, but in Fayat, Illa, Gottschalk, Naomi, Mornington, Woodworth, All Saints, Boylston, Nicaea, Geer &c. never. Mr Bulkeley knew that she particularly loved Duke St. and told us he used it often for her especial benefit.

In 1891 she began to wish "to go home," usually however with "if I could only go back and find it as it was, with my Father & Mother there," and even when she did not say that, I remember no time when she did not know where she was and that that home was only a memory now. She also, in the night, called Miss Leavitt and me "Ma."

The last few years of her life we gave up going to Milton at New Years, Edward thought she was not strong enough, so all the family came together again at Bush. On these occasions, and at Thanksgiving, after Edward and his household had gone and Mother wished to go to bed, Will gave her his arm, and took her to her room, placed her in her chair by her fire and kissed her good-night. This always flattered her extremely, she would mention it afterwards with a smile of joy.

Seeing them so constantly, Mother always knew Edward's children but ceased to recognize[395] Edith's by name. Cameron would come to see her. She would light up at the sight of him, she knew he was hers, and dear, but she didn't know his name, yes, it was so with all the boys. Violet she remembered longest, but the last time Violet saw her, we asked as she beamed with delight upon her granddaughter "Who is it, Mother?" She didn't answer and we asked "Do you know who it is?"

"Yes, of course I do." "Well, what is her name?" "Experience Jenney."[396] None of us had ever heard this name. Neither has Cousin Mary Watson, for we have asked her. But Mother's great-great-grandmother was Ruth Jenney, and Experience is a regular Plymouth name. I believe that Mother must have known a person by that name. Edward Forbes a year or two before she died came and stayed with us a few days and Mother didn't call him by name, but when he was out of the room she spoke of him as "that beautiful young man." When I asked her his name she said "I don't know. I think he is one of the Boylston cousins." He was always in his later visits "that beautiful young man," indeed Mother was in love with him. One day when all of us had failed to induce her to taste her dinner Edward said "Please do, Grandma, for my sake." She smiled, pleased, and began at once, nor did she stop till she had eaten the whole. He was surprised at his success. This and all her delight in his company made us believe that something about him reminded her of Father, and Dr Holmes's immediate exclamation on seeing him a year or two after, that he resembled Father remarkably, strengthens us in this idea, and now seven years from those visits, I have come to think Edward looks more like Father than his brothers. Not only did Mother rejoice in the presence of Edward Forbes but she thought of him after he went, and more than once she said "I should like to leave my watch to that beautiful young man." In the summer a burglar entered our house and took her watch. Of course she was sorry to lose it but chiefly because the beautiful young man could not have it left to him. She often lamented it. One day [397] she said "I will have a new watch to leave him. The next time you go to Boston buy the handsomest watch you can find for me."

I took no notice of this, practically; but as weeks went on I found she never forgot it but was anxious that it should be done, and Edith and I meant to attend to it and take Edward F. with us to have his taste about it. Still, it was not done.

She left off riding out in the summer of 1892, and hardly could be led to the garden at all[.]

On the 20th of September 1892 she was ninety years old. It was impossible to make her believe it. "Mother, you are ninety years old." "Nonsense!" "But really you are, this is your ninetieth birthday." "No, you are entirely mistaken." "How old do you think you are?" "I am over eighty, I believe, I don't remember exactly, but this is the way to find out. I am two years younger than the century." "Well this is the 20th of September, 1892[.]" This statement she failed to see the force of, even to understand. We dressed her room with flowers and it pleased her. I was sorry to find she was not able to get up, for Judge Hoar had announced his intention of making a call on her, but I meant she should receive the call. He came in the afternoon and I had Mother arranged as prettily as possible. She was lying flat in her bed, but she had clean sheets and pillow-cases and counterpane and cap and nightgown. Moreover my present to her that day was a baa-lamb flannel blanket white as snow with a mitred edge of the same kind of flannel, light baby-blue, and a short sleeved jacket of the same with a little blue strip round the neck. They were both remarkably pretty. She had on the jacket and the blanket was spread over her.

I told Judge Hoar she was not up, when he came; "I am sorry," he answered, "I hoped to see her." Then I asked him if he would come up and he willingly followed. "She doesn't know much, she can't say much," I explained as we went up the front stairs. "Can she hear what I say?" "Oh! yes." "And will she understand it?" "Yes, entirely." "Oh! Very well!" he exclaimed, relieved. So he entered and walked round the bed to where Mother was. She smiled with joy and held out her hand. "Mrs Emerson, I have come to congratulate you on having had a long and beautiful and happy life. You are giving proof of wisdom, we have it on the best authority that long life is her best gift, better than some things that many people think a good deal more of, for the Bible says "Length of days is in her *right* hand, and in her *left* hand riches and honour." And he took his leave.

I remembered that Edith and Violet came, and I think more of the Grandchildren and Edward and Annie, Mrs Sanborn, Lizzy Bartlett, Gary Wheildon & Sarah Richardson;[398] many flowers and other things were brought to her. Our Farnham cousins chanced to come and Mrs Baldwin went up to see her. She had a good birthday though she was weak and in her bed.

It was in this month that one evening Miss Leavitt was frightened about her and called Cousin Sarah. They thought she was dying, and the next morning though she was better they advised me to call Edward home. He and his family had just gone to Naushon to visit Edith & Will. He came at once, but found her on the high road to health[.]

She soon got well enough to sit up part of the day, and as I remember came down to tea usually. I am no longer sure about it; but she was seldom quite herself and often talked unintelligibly, using words she made up. These words I wished to write down, but I did not, and I do not remember a single one. There was some time every day, often many times when she would be clear, but never very long.

On the 11*th* of November Miss Leavitt and I said to each other that she had seemed stronger for a few days, perhaps she would be as well as she had been in the summer. It was Friday and in the evening I went to church. When I came home I was dismayed, she must have caught cold in some way, her breath rattled. Neither Miss Leavitt or I could recall any exposure. Miss Martha Palfrey was making a visit to Miss Leavitt[.] She took a great fancy to Mother, the more that she had lately lost her own Mother and to nurse another old lady brought her dear Mother to her mind, she came into the room on Saturday several times.

In the evening Miss Leavitt called her and me. Mother had a dying look, to her, just as she had in September. It passed away, yet Miss Leavitt said she should sit by her all night. Miss Palfrey however divided the night with her. It was a peaceful one; Mother slept. It was her last night on earth.

All day Sunday her breath rattled. Edward came in the afternoon to see her. I asked him whether he thought she could live long and he said no one could tell. She might die when very cold weather came, yet she might bear it and live through the winter. He said we were not to blame for this new cold, colds sometimes came unaccountably. Dr Clarence Blake[399] was with him. They went, and I returned to Mother[.] She had much to say to me. She talked almost without intermission, but I could not divine what the words meant. After an hour I felt as if it must tire her to have no response, to talk without producing any effect, so I proposed to read to her. "What?" she asked. I considered what would sound most atractive to her and mentioned "A letter from Father to Mr Carlyle." "By all means!" she said, heartily.

I read till she fell asleep. Miss Leavitt was having her nap, Miss Legate was away making a Sunday's visit. I had my supper brought up to Mother's room. At seven it was time, by Edward's orders to give her some hot milk punch, so I waked her and asked her to drink it.

Some years before, she had exclaimed, "Ellen, in the very *articulo mortis* you will try to make me eat!" I saw that it was not improbable. It came true. She tried and said "I can't." "Isn't it good?" "Proper good." "Well, drink." She tried again and repeated, "I can't." Still I commanded & entreated. I was lifting her head. Suddenly she sat up, opened her eyes wide and looked hard at me, then relaxed. I pulled the pillows up behind her to hold her in a sitting position, noticed with joy that the rattling had stopped and she was breathing easily and again put the tumbler to her lips. After a moment, seeing she did not drink, nor refuse, I stooped and looked into her eyes. There was no life in them, and I thought she might be dying. I had never been present at a death, except when Father died and that was under ether. I had an impression that it was the rule to call others, that there might be feet to run and hands to help if anything was wanted. I wouldn't disturb Miss Leavitt's nap, so I ran down to Margaret the cook and Sadie Corning who were reading and writing in the kitchen, and asked them to bring their work upstairs.

Returning I found Mother still breathing and propped up by the pillows as I had left her. I held her wrist, but I could not tell when she ceased to breathe. When I was sure she had[,] Margaret ran to send Jim Clahane for Edward and Sadie called Miss Leavitt who was grieved that I had not sent for her before. Edward arrived wonderfully soon, and knew how to compose Mother's[400] so that she looked like herself, I could almost say like an angel, especially when Miss Leavitt brushed out her hair on the pillow on each side, her beautiful silver hair which Miss Leavitt was so proud of.

When all was attended to Edward went to telephone to Edith, and then home. Miss Leavitt and I to our rooms. Miss Legate had arrived at quarter of nine and she and S. & M. had come to look at Mother in her beauty. Both Helen & Sadie had always feared death. They said it no longer seemed to them so terrible.

Mother had said to me several times in earlier years that she had noticed that those of her friends who greatly feared to die, died in their sleep or unconscious, died without knowing it, and it seemed to her a compassion of God their timidity. "Perhaps I may be allowed to go so," she would say, and so she was.

She used to tell me of Cowper's death and that though he died in dark despair, after his death a look of joy came over his face. This thought comforted her. She would recur often to the radiance of Grandma's expression the morning after her death and say she believed the soul was not wholly disengaged from its house of clay for twelve hours after death and its experience was reflected on the face. I hoped that I might see joy on hers the next morning and indeed I expected it, but she had a look of great solemnity. Before the funeral it passed away leaving only innocence and quiet. She looked young then.

We dressed her for her coffin and put on the birthday jacket, then wrapped the birthday-blanket round her, and made her a new tulle cap such as she had always worn only without the ribbons, and we thought she was as beautiful as a picture. The coffin stood where Father's had in the study. It pleased us to have it so.

The children had prepared the service, and we went to show it to Mr Bulkeley. He said "You have not in it a word from the New Testament. For such a Christian as your Mother it seems a great mistake." We agreed and he chose some ten verses. I was grateful to him.

In Mother's life several poems had been written to her. They did not fit this occasion, we thought, as we looked them over. But Aunt Lizzy had in early years brought her one which she had found and which she told Mother seemed almost as if it had been written about her. We agreed with her as we read it that day, and asked Judge Hoar if he would read it at the funeral. He willingly did so.

We also asked Mr Bulkeley to read the hymn "Quiet from God," which she had copied into her extract-book, and had always liked to say to me.

Many, many people came to her funeral, and that gratified me very much.[401]

Notes

1. Lucy Jackson, older sister to Lidian, married Charles Brown of Boston on 18 September 1820. See note 59.

2. Charles Thomas Jackson (1805–1880), later famed for discovering the anaesthetic effects of ether. See note 256.

3. The material has a rust-red background with columns of yellow dots with black equal signs between the columns.

4. He died on 26 January 1810.

5. Charles William Lambton (1818–1831), eldest son of John George, first Earl of Durham. The engraving, by S. Cousins, shows a boy, full face, seated on a rock in contemplation. It is based on a picture by T. Lawrence belonging to Lord Durham. The engraving was published at Colnaghi, January 1827, without title. The same plate, with quotation from *Childe Harold*, was published in 1837.

6. The piece of material has a white or cream background; there are columns of black rectangles with dots in the center. Between these columns are two red dots above two red dots.

7. Probably Mrs. Martha Weston, who was known as Mrs. Patty, or more generally Ma'am Weston, wife of Coomer Weston. She held school in the house on North Street, the third below that of Miss Dr. Pierce. William T. Davis in *Plymouth Memories of an Octogenarian* (Plymouth: Memorial Press, 1906) recalls attending her school in 1826 and remembers the sanded floor and the cricket on which he sat. Mrs. Weston died on 27 July 1841.

8. Probably Mary Jackson Russell, daughter of Samuel Jackson. She married John Russell, and they lived on North Street. She would have been Mrs., not Miss.

9. On the back of the page is attached a scrap of cloth with the following note: "This, if I remember right is a calico Aunt Lucy wore when she was a little girl." The material has a dark green background with yellow dots which form squares that contain a yellow figure.

10. The *stocks* is a mold of both feet in the fourth position, that is, both feet are completely turned out. For an illustration of the stocks, see Jean Georges Noverre, *Letters on Dancing and Ballet*, trans. by Cyril W. Beaumont (London: Beaumont, 1951), p. 120.

11. Isaac Watts (1674–1748), English theologian and hymn writer.

12. Jane Taylor's *Hymns for Infant Minds* (New York: American Tract Society, 18—?). There are two copies in Emerson's library.

13. James Kendall (1769–1859), the successor of Reverend Chandler Robbins, was minister of First Church, Plymouth, from 1800 to 1859. He was born in Sterling, Massachusetts, the son of Major James Kendall.

14. No date is given but could be one of the following: James Sulliven (1807–10 December 1808), Christopher Gore (1809–1810), Elleridge Gerry (1810–1812), Caleb Strong (1812–1816).

15. The material has a medium blue background with an intricate floral design in white and in both light and dark brown.

16. One piece of material has a beige background with intricately arranged black squares mixed with brown lines which suggest a grid. The other piece has a beige background with two kinds of blocks, one a grid of brown lines and the other a brown and beige checkerboard. These are arranged in columns so as to present a diamond shape between columns.

17. Inverted on the bottom of page 21 is written in a heavy pen the following signature and date: "J Rupell Young 1868."

18. Isaac L. Hedge of Plymouth married Mary Ann Cotton, daughter of Lucy Cotton Jackson's brother, Josiah, and Rachel, daughter of the Reverend Dr. David Barnes of Scituate. This could also be Barnabas Hedge (1764–1840), a successful merchant in Plymouth. I have been unable to locate the *Samoset* or the *Columbus* in the Charles Jackson collection at the Pilgrim Society in Plymouth.

19. Ellen had originally written "North" but changed it to "Market" on 7 January 1896, adding the following note: "Mr & Mrs Marston Watson never heard of these people and thought they couldn't have been named Watson nor lived on North St. They suggested Market St. instead."

20. "Do not copy. Omit in reading aloud." is written in pencil and apparently not in Ellen's hand. "Omit in reading aloud" suggests that the manuscript might have been marked with the intention of an oral reading.

21. Mrs. Saunders and Miss Beach's Academy, Clifton Hill, Dorchester, was a fashionable boarding school for young ladies from about 1800 until as late as 1834. The house in which it was located, on the corner of Adams and East Streets, is still standing.

22. Margaret U. Gourgas (1799–1875) is buried in Linwood Cemetery, Weston; she was the daughter of John Mark Gourgas (1766–1846). She lived with her brother Francis on Monument Street.

23. Following manuscript page 109 is a poem, written on a 3" x 51/2" envelope in faded pencil. The front of the envelope is addressed to "Miss Ellen T. Emerson Concord Massachusetts." It is stamped "Jul 16 1890." and has a red, two-cent stamp cancelled in blue from Buzzards Bay, Massachusetts.

Poem recited to little Lydia Jackson by her Mother, Lucy Cotton Jackson when she saw her looking in the glass, and which 70 years later Mother recited to me, from that impression E. T. E. in Jan 1881[.]

While at the mirror, lovely maid
You trifle time away
Reflect how soon your bloom will fade
And transient charms decay
——

Turn from the glass & view your mind
On that bestow your care
Improve, correct, it till you find
No imperfection there
——

Make it the seat of every grace
Of charms that will increase
And give bright lustre to your face
When youth & beauty cease
——

Charms that will gain a worthy heart
And lasting love inspire
That will through life true bliss impart
Nor yet with life expires

Following this poem is a 51/2" x 9" brown envelope with a "Permit No. 4 Concord, N. H." for the stamp. On the return address is written "R. H. Stearns and Company / Annual Spring Sale / China, Glass and Brica-Brac / Together with / Special Offerings in Many Departments / Muslin Underwear, Household Linens, Suits, Coats and

Dresses, Millinery, Hosiery, Etc. / Beginning / Wednesday, May 19, 1915." The size and heaviness of the print varies but all is in capital letters. It is addressed to Mrs. Wm. H. Forbes, Adams St., Milton, Mass.

24. Daniel Jackson (b. 1761), her father's brother and business partner.

25. Abraham (b. 1791), Isaac Carver (b. 1799), and Jacob (b. 1794) Jackson. Other children were Daniel (b. 1787), Rebecca (b. 1789), William Morton (b. 1796), Thomas Taylor (b. 1798), and another William Morton (b. 1802). Dr. James Kendall, minister of First Parish in Plymouth, records the death of Jacob Jackson, age 62, on 22 October 1857.

26. I think that Ellen is mistaken. I cannot find an Abraham, son of Isaac Carver; however, Abraham had a son Abraham in 1821, who is probably Lidian's cousin and who handled her property. He enjoyed a long career as an embezzler but was eventually detected and punished.

27. *To scrape lint* means to scrape linen into a soft downy or fleecy substance for poultices and dressing wounds.

28. This page is dated "July 23, 1876."

29. At the beginning of this inserted letter are two statements, one indicating placement and the other, "Piece of a letter here inserted as belongs." The latter statement is in reference to the sentence, "In May 1884 . . . took a walk." which is written between the lines. There is a line drawn from the statement at the top of the letter to the sentence.

30. Daniel and Charles Jackson's counting house on Water Street was engaged in foreign navigation. After Charles's death in 1818, Daniel formed a partnership with his son Jacob but dissolved it in 1828. Daniel and Abraham then formed the firm of D. and A. Jackson and later their brother Isaac was associated with them. The last ship built by them was *Iconium* (in 1848) under Isaac C. Jackson.

31. Roland Edwin Cotton (b. 4 January 1802), son of Priscilla Jackson and Rossiter Cotton. He was Registrar of Deeds from 1837 to 1846.

32. The top of this page is cut off. On the back, in pencil, is the following: "The Winslow house, wh. mother afterwards inherited from him, came into his possession in this way." The Winslow House was built in 1754 by Edward Winslow, a great grandson of Governor Edward Winslow of the Mayflower's Company, and brother of General John Winslow. Mr. Winslow was Collector of the Port, Register of Wills and Clerk of the Courts. As a Loyalist he lost his offices at the beginning of the revolution, and became in debt to the Town of Plymouth, Thomas Davis, William Thomas, Oakes Angier and John Rowe. In 1782 the above creditors took possession under an execution against his estate, and sold the house to Thomas Jackson. In 1813 it passed under an execution from Thomas Jackson to Charles Jackson, the father of Lydia who was married in 1835 to Ralph Waldo Emerson in the Easterly front room of the first floor. In 1872 the property was sold by Mrs. Emerson to Lucia J., wife of Reverend George W. Briggs, D.D., and it was later owned by their son George Russell Briggs. This house is now the Mayflower Society House on Winslow Street, off North Street.

33. The fireset is still in the parlor of the Emerson House in Concord.

34. Ward Cotton (1770–1843) married Rebecca Jackson (b. 1800) who was sister to Priscilla, wife of Rossiter Cotton. Sophia Phillips was their daughter. Ward Cotton graduated from Harvard College in 1793 and was a minister in Boylston.

35. The chairs are still there, but there is little hint of lilac.

36. Above "Chinese tea-set" is an illegible word in pencil.

37. Bowdoin Street does not run into Bowdoin Square but into Cambridge Street, which in turn runs into Bowdoin Square a block away. Perhaps the house referred to here was that of Joseph Coolidge (1747–1820), who lived on the west corner of Bowdoin Street, or the house of Joseph Coolidge, Jr. (1773–1840), who lived at 3 Bowdoin Square.

38. The following addition appears: "tell about the appreciation of Mother's beauty E. W. E." "E. W. E." is probably Edward Waldo Emerson. The comment inserted here is not clear in its meaning. The word "Mother" is barely legible.

39. Elizabeth Davis (1803–1886), daughter of William Davis, married in 1825 Alexander Bliss, the junior partner of Daniel Webster. Bliss died in 1827 and on 16 August 1838, she married George Bancroft (1800–1891). Bancroft was secretary of the Navy under President Polk, minister to England (1846–1849), and later minister to Berlin.

40. Mary Howland Russell (1803–1862) was the daughter of Captain Nathaniel Russell and Martha LeBaron.

41. Sarah Kendall (b. 1802) was eldest daughter of Dr. James Kendall, the minister of the First Parish in Plymouth.

42. William T. Davis, *Plymouth Memories*, records that his grandfather's house adjoined the Baptist church.

43. In early 1800s Nathaniel Russell lived in a house that was on the lower corner of Middle Street and LeBaron Alley. About 1808 he moved to the house on the north side of Summer Street next to the house on the corner of Ring Lane. He lived there until 1827 when he moved into the brick house on the north corner of Court Square which he lived in until his death in 1852.

44. Captain Joseph Bartlett (1762–1835), son of Samuel and Betsey Moore Bartlett, married in 1784 Rebecca Churchill. In 1803 he built the brick house on the north corner of Court Square. According to William T. Davis, *Plymouth Memories*, it was because of severe losses during the embargoes and the War of 1812 that he moved from the house. His son, William (b. 1786), moved into the house in 1820 and kept it as a public house, named Old Colony Hotel. In a year or two, William Spooner took the house, then Ezra Cushing, followed by Nathaniel Russell in 1827.

45. This sentence is not clear. After "lived on," "North Street a little higher up than Mother did the opposite side" is cancelled. The parsonage was on Leyden Street.

46. Jane Taylor (1783–1824) was a writer of children's poetry. She and her sister Ann together produced several volumes of verses. See note 12.

47. Charles Jackson (b. 1770), son of Thomas and Sarah Taylor Jackson, died on 4 August 1818.

48. Aunt Joa was Lucy Cotton Jackson's unmarried sister, Joanna (b. 1760).

49. Lucy Cotton Jackson (b. 1768), daughter of John and Hannah Sturtevant Cotton, married Charles Jackson in 1794. She died on 15 October 1818.

50. Mrs. McKeige, of Jamaica Plain.

51. "Sidney Bartlett" is inserted in pencil. Bartlett (1799–1889) graduated from Harvard in 1818, taught school for a while, then studied law. He lived in Boston and became known as a lawyer of great learning. He refused to accept appointment as judge. He was one of the founders of the Boston Bar Association and was its first president.

52. A newspaper clipping about Sidney Bartlett follows:

"If there is any lawyer now at the bar worthy of that honor, he is Sydney Bartlett, who was a contemporary of both, has contended not unsuccessfully with them, and who, although so long a survivor of those palmy days of the bar, still remains in full possession of the faculties that originally earned him prominence. The wonderful preservation of Gladstone's powers has been during the last six months a new wonder to the world, but here is a lawyer, 10 years Gladstone's senior, who will argue a complicated case before a bench of judges with all that great ease and lucidity which he always possessed, and who according to the gossip of the bar, has a practice of $100,000 a year and fairly earns every dollar of it. Mr. Bartlett is a Harvard man, has taken little or no part in politics, and has during all his long career been most diligent in the pursuit of his profession." This is only about one-third of the article, what I judge to be the relevant part. "Mr. E. D. Sohier" and "Mr. Henry W. Paine" are also mentioned in the article.

It says that Sohier thirty-five years ago aided in the brilliant but unsuccessful defense of Professor Webster.

53. "Jacob Jackson" is cancelled.

54. "Jacob" is again cancelled and is cancelled twice more in the next sentence.

55. Margaret P. Forbes was a sister to John Murray Forbes, Edith Emerson's father-in-law.

56. Pine Bank is a recreational park on the Malden-Melrose city line.

57. Susan Bridge, who married Charles Jackson, Lidian's brother, named her first daughter Alice Bridge after her elder sister. Alice Bridge (1835–1916) married Lieut. William Arthur of the Third United States Artillery in 1867.

58. Nicholas Gouin Dufief (1776?–1834), *Nature Displayed in Her Mode of Teaching Language to Man* (Philadelphia: T. & G. Palmer, 1804). Lidian's copy (in Emerson's library) was published in 1810.

59. On 18 September 1820, Lucy married Charles Brown, who was a member of a firm of Commission Merchants at Long Wharf in Boston. He lost his money and reputation, left his family, and travelled from as far east as Constantinople to as far west as Ireland.

60. See note 39.

61. The Hedge girls are children of Barnabas Hedge and Eunice Dennie, daughter of Thaddeus Burr of Fairfield, Connecticut. Abigail (b. 1802) married Charles H. Warren; Hannah (b. 1804) married John Thomas; Eunice Dennie (b. 1806) married Chandler Robbins. Charles Henry Warren (1798–1874) graduated from Harvard in 1817. From 1839 to 1844, he was Judge of the Common Pleas Court. From 1846 to 1867, he was president of the Boston and Providence Railroad. He was president of the Massachusetts Senate in 1851 and president of the Pilgrim Society from 1845 to 1852.

62. Eliza Ann Bartlett, daughter of Captain Joseph Bartlett, married Albert Gardiner Goodwin in 1840.

63. Betsey Morton Jackson may be Elizabeth Morton (b. 1813), daughter of Daniel Jackson. She married Sebastian F. Streeter. However, she would have been much younger than the others.

64. I have been unable to locate this document.

65. In the margin is the following: "Mr Watson says it has been celebrated since 1769."

66. Daniel Webster (1782–1852), American statesman and lawyer. Lidian, as a result of their differing views on slavery, later changed her attitude about Webster.

67. Aunt Cotton was Priscilla Jackson, daughter of Thomas Jackson. She was the sister of Lidian's mother and married Rossiter (spelled also Rosseter) Cotton on 31 October 1783. The building which stood on the corner of Court and North Streets was the residence of the Cottons. In 1888, it was torn down and replaced by the Howland Building.

68. Sophia Cotton (b. 18 May 1796) married Lieut. William Lewis Gordon, United States Navy, on 23 May 1816.

69. See note 31. William T. Davis, *Plymouth Memories*, records that Rowland Edwin Cotton married Susan Augusta, daughter of Daniel Watson; their children were Rowland Edwin, Louisa, and Sudlar. The story as told by Ellen suggests that the child is a first child and that the mother died the next morning. Edwin's first wife was a Watson, but their daughter's not his wife's name was Louisa.

70. A *cricket* is a low, wooden footstool.

71. Rossiter Cotton (1758–1837) was registrar of deeds since 1789 when he succeeded his father in that position who succeeded his father in that position. He was also county treasurer. He practiced medicine for about twenty years, retiring in 1807 in Plymouth.

72. Herman Daggett, *An Abridgement of the Writings of Lewis Cornaro, A Nobleman of Venice, On Health and Long Life* (Andover: Mark Newman, 1824), p. 15: "That what we

leave, after making a hearty meal, does us more than good than what we have eaten." Lidian's copy of this work is in Emerson's library.

73. *Hydropathy* is the therapeutic use of water. This intense interest in medicine is not peculiar to Lidian as it was the medical vogue in her day for the lady of the household to be also the knowledgeable mistress of the sickroom.

74. The following is in pencil in the margin: "One pair of silk stockings still are good & sound—those she wore at her wedding."

75. In the margin on the back of the sheet is the following: "Cousin Mary Watson tells." The following is inserted in pencil and initialed by Edith Emerson Forbes on the back of manuscript page 59: "Cousin Mary Watson tells of a yellow fourpenny calico which she bought at Mr Josiah Davis's & in which she looked like a Queen as she sat in the morning sunshine nursing her baby. She also had a purple plaided silk-like Royal Stuart except it was purple where scarlet should be which she bought about 1850 & which I inherited. E.E.F."

76. Probably Benjamin Marston Watson (1820–1896), son of Benjamin Marston Watson and Lucretia Burr, daughter of Jonathan Sturges of Fairfield, Connecticut. Benjamin Marston graduated from Harvard in 1839 and married in 1846 Mary, daughter of Thomas Russell. Watson enjoyed the friendship of Emerson, Alcott, and Thoreau. His sister, Lucretia Ann, married Reverend Hersey B. Goodwin, associate to Dr. Ripley in the Concord church from 1830 to 1836.

77. Mrs. Aurelio is Lucy Lothrop Goodwin (b. 1811), daughter of Isaac Goodwin and Eliza Hammatt. She married Thomas Aurelio of Fayal.

78. Mary Fenn of Concord believes that the house mentioned is the Barrett Barn House that is across the street from Wright Tavern. The house was used for a while as a home "for deserving young women of low income."

79. The widow Esther Phillips Parsons became in 1804 the third wife of Major William Jackson (1763–1836). Jackson was one of the founders of the Plymouth Bank.

80. *Senna* is the dried leaflets of certain species of Cassia used in medicine as a purgative. *Manna* is the sweetish exudate of the European flowering ash *Fraxinus ornus* and used medicinally as a gentle laxative, demulcent, and expectorant.

81. Sarah Cotton (b. 1763) married Jesse Harlow. A house on the corner of Pleasant and Sandwich Streets was built by Jesse Harlow not long after the Revolution.

82. In the margin in pencil is the following: "Wasn't it much further along? nearer Leyden."

83. Thomas Jackson (b. 1757) married in 1788 Sally May. The Plymouth Savings Bank was erected on the site of their house in 1887.

84. The following is inserted in pencil: "I believe it was a sister-in-law."

85. See note. 39.

86. See note 61.

87. Andrew L. Russell (b. 1806) graduated from Harvard in 1827 and was at one time engaged in dry goods on Central Street in Boston. He was an iron manufacturer in Plymouth who corresponded with Emerson and was interested in publishing. LeBaron, a physician in Boston, graduated from Harvard in 1832, corresponded with Emerson, and visited Carlyle. He died in 1889. Nathaniel (1801–1875) graduated from Harvard in 1820 and became associated with his father in business. Andrew, Nathaniel, and LeBaron were all sons of Captain Nathaniel Russell and brothers to Mary Howland Russell. For Edwin Cotton, see note 31.

88. These cousins were probably the children of her Uncle Ward Cotton (1770–1843), minister in Boylston. He married Rebecca Jackson, sister of Priscilla, wife of Rossiter Cotton. The Boylston cousins would be John Thomas (b. 1801), Ward Mather (b. 1804), Lydia Jackson (b. 1806), Sally May (b. 1808), Hannah Phillips (b. 1810), and Sophia Phillips.

89. Jane Taylor, *Selected Rhymes for the Nursery* (Philadelphia: Johnson and Warner, 1810). See also notes 12 and 46.

90. General Henry Dearborn is listed in the 1816 *Boston Directory* as a resident of Milk Street.

91. In the left-hand margin in pencil is the following: "Was not Madam Dearborn afterward Madam Bowdoin of Naushon?" In the right top margin in a different ink and perhaps in a different hand is the following: "Madam Dearborn married first Gov. Bowdoin of Naushon. She was the Madam Bowdoin who went away so suddenly when her husband died."

92. John Gorham Palfrey (1796–1881), Boston-born American historian, became a Unitarian minister and was pastor of the Brattle Street Church in Boston from 1818 to 1831. He became active in politics, edited the *North American Review* (1835–1843), and is best known by his *History of New England* to the Revolutionary War.

93. The opinion she held of Uncle Brown may be colored by the pain and disgrace that he brought on the family. See note 59.

94. I have not located the first modern hymnbook.

95. Aunt Parker is Sophia Cotton (b. 14 July 1755), who married Seth Parker of Falmouth on 11 July 1776.

96. Writing from Concord on 20 January 1870 to Edward, Cousin John Parker said "our rocking horse up garret came to Wood's Hole a present to a little boy whose folks kept tavern there from his friends in Roxbury some 70 yrs. ago. That Mother saw it in 1820 or so & desired it for Sophia Brown. So Cousin John carried it aboard a vessel bound for Plymouth & some drunken sailors pushed it overboard. The Captain he scolded them & made 'em look for it, & they found it, only its head was broken off in the fall but when Mother got to Plymouth, she had it all mended. Preserve this archive of the horse, I'll have it mended again."

Inscribed on the horse is: "Made 1750 bought from Sophia Parker (Wood's Hole) 1825 by L. Jackson given to children of N (Nancy) & C (Charles) Russell by them returned to Edward Waldo Emerson in 1849."

97. Sir Walter Scott (1771–1832), "The Betrothed," *The Tales of the Crusaders* (1825). Scott's works are in Emerson's library.

98. George Partridge Bradford (1807–1890) was ten years old when his mother died, and he became the special charge of her sister, Sarah Ripley. He graduated from Harvard in 1825, and three years later at the Divinity School. He opened a school in Plymouth, after three years there, continued his educational labors in several places, and about 1842 joined Brook Farm. He made several trips to Europe, did some editing, and wrote with George Ripley "Philosophical Thought in Boston" in Justin Winsor's *Memorial History of Boston*.

99. Charles Emerson, R. W. Emerson's nephew, studied medicine in Vienna and married Therchi Keveschi of Vesprin, Hungary. They had no children.

100. Johann Wolfgang von Goethe, *Wilhelm Meister's Apprenticeship* (Boston: Wells and Lilly, 1828), 3 vols. There is an 1839 edition in Emerson's library.

101. Ellen Tucker was R. W. Emerson's first wife; Lidian named her daughter Ellen in honor of her. In the left-hand margin in pencil is the following: "I had an impression that Ellen Tucker showed her new watch there to other girls & Mother heard them talking of it."

102. "The Last Dying Speech and Confession of Poor Puss" is as follows:

> "Kind masters and misses, whoever you be,
> Do stop for a moment and pity poor me!
> While here on my death-bed I try to relate
> My many misfortunes and miseries great.
>
> My dear Mother Tabby I've often heard say,
> That I *have* been a very fine cat in my day;
> But the sorrows in which my whole life has been passed
> Have spoiled all my beauty, and killed me at last.

Poor thoughtless young thing! if I recollect right,
I was kittened in March, on a clear frosty night;
And before I could see, or was half a week old,
I nearly had perished, the barn was so cold.

But this chilly spring I got pretty well over,
And moused in the hay-loft, or played in the clover,
Or till I was weary, which seldom occurred,
Ran after my tail, which I took for a bird.

But, ah! my poor tail, and my pretty sleek ears!
The farmer's boy cut them all off with his shears:
How little I thought, when I licked them so clean,
I should be such a figure, not fit to be seen.

Some time after this, when the places were healed,
As I lay in the sun, sound asleep in the field,
Miss Fanny crept slyly, and gripping me fast,
Declared she had caught the sweet creature at last.

Ah me! how I struggled my freedom to gain,
But, alas! all my kicking and struggles were vain,
For she held me so tight in her pinafore tied,
That before she got home I had like to have died.

From this dreadful morning my sorrows arose!
Wherever I went I was followed with blows:
Some kicked me for nothing while quietly sleeping,
Or flogged me for daring the pantry to peep in.

And then the great dog! I shall never forget him;
How many a time my young master would set him,
And while I stood terrified, all of a quake,
Cry, 'Hey, cat!' and 'Seize her, boy! give her a shake!'

Sometimes, when so hungry I could not forbear
Just taking a scrap, that I thought they could spare,
Oh! what have I suffered with beating and banging,
Or starved for a fortnight, or threatened with hanging.

But kicking, and beating, and starving, and that,
I have borne with the spirit becoming a cat:
There was but one thing which I could not sustain,
So great was my sorrow, so hopeless my pain:—

One morning, laid safe in a warm little bed,
That down in the stable I'd carefully spread,
Three sweet little kittens as ever you saw,
I hid, as I thought, in some trusses of straw.

I was never so happy, I think, nor so proud,
I mewed to my kittens, and purred out aloud,
And thought with delight of the merry carousing
We'd have, when I first took them with me a-mousing.

But how shall I tell you the sorrowful ditty?
I'm sure it would melt even Growler to pity;
For the very next morning my darlings I found
Lying dead by the horse-pond, all mangled and drown

Poor darlings, I dragged them along to the stable,
And did all to warm them a mother was able;
But, alas! all my licking and mewing were vain,
And I thought I should never be happy again.

However, time gave me a little relief,
And mousing diverted the thoughts of my grief;
And at last I began to be gay and content,
Till one dreadful night I sincerely repent.

Miss Fanny was fond of a little canary,
That tempted me more than a mouse, pantry, or dairy;
So, not having eaten a morsel all day,
I flew to the bird-cage, and tore it away.

Now tell me, my friends, was the like ever heard,
That a cat should be killed for just catching a bird!
And I'm sure not the slightest suspicion I had,
But that catching a mouse was exactly as bad.

Indeed I can say, with my paw on my heart,
I would not have acted a mischievous part;
But, as dear Mother Tabby was often repeating,
I thought birds and mice were on purpose for eating.

Be this as it may, when my supper was o'er
And but a few feathers were left on the floor,
Came Fanny—and scolding, and fighting, and crying,
She gave me those bruises, of which I am dying.

But I feel that my breathing grows shorter apace,
And cold clammy sweats trickle down from my face:
I forgive little Fanny this bruise on my side—"

She stopped, gave a sigh, and a struggle, and died!

Ann and Jane Taylor

103. Compare with the following entry in Emerson's journal: "Dear husband, I wish I had never been born. I do not see how God can compensate me for the sorrow of existence." The footnote for this entry reads "The entry, presumably reporting Lidian's words, is in brown ink. Some words in blue ink are inscribed on the brown-ink entry, perhaps to alter and obscure it; no meaningful words of this inscription are recovered. Both inscriptions are heavily canceled in dark blue ink" (*The Journals and Miscellaneous Notebooks of Ralph Waldo Emerson*, ed. William H. Gilman et al. [Cambridge: Harvard University Press, 1960–], 8:365; hereafter cited as *JMN*).

104. They were the daughters of Nathan and Elizabeth (Bartlett) Bridge. Susan and Charles were married in Boston on 27 February 1834.

105. The date "1895" is inserted.

106. The Boston city directories from 1830 to 1835 list a Reverend Samuel Barrett as pastor of the Twelfth Congregational Church on Chambers Street. His residence was at 26 Hancock Street. *The Harvard University Quinquennial Catalogue of the Officers and Graduates 1636–1930* mentions a Samuel Barrett who graduated in Divinity in 1822 and who died in 1866. He served as overseer of Harvard College from 1835 to 1852. Whether this is the same Samuel Barrett I cannot be certain.

107. William Spooner came to Plymouth in 1637 as an indentured apprentice. Some of his descendants were carpenters.

108. Possibly a paraphrase of Job 29:10: "The nobles held their peace, and their tongue cleaved to the roof of their mouth."

109. Frank Browne (b. 1829), is the son of Charles and Lucy Jackson Brown. Sophia is his sister. Lidian associated the following poem by Felicia Hemans with this incident:

Casabianca

The boy stood on the burning deck,
   Whence all but he had fled;
The flame that lit the battle's wreck
   Shone round him o'er the dead.

Yet beautiful and bright he stood,
   As born to rule the storm;
A creature of heroic blood,
   A proud, though childlike, form.

The flames rolled on,—he would not go,
   Without his father's word;
That father, faint in death below,
   His voice no longer heard.

He called aloud,—"Say, father, say,
   If yet my task is done!"
He knew not that the chieftain lay
   Unconscious of his son.

"Speak, father!" once again he cried.
   "If I may yet be gone,"—
And but the booming shots replied,
   And fast the flames rolled on.

Upon his brow he felt their breath,
   And in his waving hair,
And looked from that lone post of death
   In still, yet brave despair.

And shouted but once more aloud,
   "My father! must I stay?"
While o'er him fast, through sail and shroud,
   The wreathing flames made way.

They wrapt the ship in splendour wild,
   They caught the flag on high,

And streamed above the gallant child,
Like banners in the sky.

There came a burst of thunder sound;
The boy,—Oh, where was he?
Ask of the winds, that far around
With fragments strewed the sea!

With mast, and helm, and pennon fair,
That well had borne their part;
But the noblest thing that perished there
Was that young, faithful heart.

110. Sarah Alden (Bradford) Ripley was married to Emerson's half-uncle Samuel Ripley, who received boys in his house to prepare them for college, with Sarah Ripley assuming the advanced instruction in Greek and Latin. She was one of the best Greek scholars in the country.

111. William T. Davis, *Plymouth Memories*, felt that Emerson lectured first in Plymouth in 1833 in Pilgrim Hall on Socrates. As a boy of eleven, he thought Emerson oracular and dull.

112. In the margin is written: "We called him Uncle though he was not related" and "in London still," both referring to George Bradford.

113. Ellen Sturgis (1812–1848) and her sister Caroline Sturgis (1819–1888) were Transcendentalist poets. Ellen married Dr. Robert William Hooper, of an old Marblehead Family. Caroline married William Aspinwall Tappan of New York. "Tanglewood," the Tappan estate in Lenox, Massachusetts, was given by their daughters to the Boston Symphony Orchestra.

114. At the top of the letter is written "Extract of a letter from Miss Sarah Clarke to her brother The Reverend James Freeman Clarke." The return address on printed stationery is "91 Mt. Vernon Street, Boston, Mass." The date is "February 28th. 1835." The letter is typed with some corrections made by hand.

115. Probably Elizabeth Palmer Peabody (1804–1894).

116. Mary Moody Emerson (1774–1862), Emerson's Calvinist aunt who gave him high counsels. She wore a shroud both day and night and fashioned her bed in the shape of a coffin. Her parents were Reverend William Emerson, minister of the First Parish, and Phoebe Bliss, daughter of the previous minister.

117. "Not to be read aloud or copied" follows in pencil, referring to the next four sentences.

118. The lines "The next letter...its meaning," are cancelled and also covered with a paper band, the kind that goes around stationery.

119. Charles is Emerson's brother, engaged to Elizabeth Hoar (1814–1878), daughter of Squire Samuel Hoar (1778–1856), and sister to Judge Ebenezer Rockwood Hoar (1816–1895). Charles died before they could be married; nevertheless, Elizabeth became Aunt Lizzy.

120. See note 119.

121. Emerson's grandfather, Reverend William Emerson, built the Manse for his wife Phoebe Bliss, daughter of the previous minister. The home is adjacent to the North Bridge over the Concord River. Reverend Ezra Ripley on marrying the widow Emerson lived there and served as the minister from 1778 to 1841. Hawthorne occupied the Manse from 1842 to 1846.

122. Latin for Biblical chances or lots.

123. In the margin is "Ruth III 18."

124. In the margin is "I Chron. XVII 10."

125. Emerson, *A Historical Discourse, Delivered Before the Citizens of Concord, 12th September, 1835, on the Second Centennial Anniversary of the Incorporation of the Town.* (Concord: G. F. Bemis, 1835).

126. In the margin in pencil is "and her niece & namesake L.E.J. wore them at her wedding 14 Sept. 1894."

127. The eldest son of Rossiter Cotton ("Uncle Doctor") was not Josiah but Thomas Jackson Cotton (b. 1785). He was a sea captain and married Phebe Stevens. Rossiter did not have a son named Josiah.

128. In the margin is "2 Chron. XX 12."

129. Rebecca, born 1819, and Robert (1817–1843) were children of Captain Isaac Bartlett. Both children had remarkable minds; Robert graduated from Harvard in 1836. He was tutor at Harvard in Latin from 1839–1843.

130. Zechariah 14:7. The passage is describing the day of the coming of the Lord: "But it shall be one day which shall be known to the Lord, not day, nor night: but it shall come to pass, that at evening time it shall be light."

131. The gift from Carlyle is still in the parlor over the sofa. Emerson records in his journal on 9 June 1839, "Guido's Aurora for a morning prayer, so wills & so loves us Thomas Carlyle" (*JMN*, 7:209).

132. She was George Minot's sister. The house was diagonally across from the Emerson house, but it is no longer there.

133. Above this sentence is written in pencil "omit in reading."

134. Cameron Forbes, Ellen's nephew and son of Edith and William Forbes, was appointed in 1904 Commissioner of the Philippines; later he was the Governor General. In 1930 he was appointed Ambassador to Japan. He has promoted many financial interests, among which are the Stone and Webster electric power developments, and he was chief financier of Stone and Webster. He was a partner of the J. M. Forbes Co., director of the American Telephone and Telegraph Company, the Commercial Credit Company, Copper Range Company, and United Fruit Company.

135. Possibly Benjamin or William Rodman of New Bedford.

136. Ruth Haskins Emerson (married 1796, d. 1853), Lidian's mother-in-law.

137. Harriet Martineau (1802–1876), novelist, political economist, and writer for children. In 1834 she visited the United States. There are nine volumes of her works in Emerson's library; two belong to Ellen.

138. The top of this page is cut off and the page is badly damaged around the edges. The next page begins "written at Pauline Agassiz Shaw's Jamaica Plain, June 1896."

139. The following is inserted, but since it breaks the narrative flow, it appears here: "Father always had family-prayers. Mother said it was the most beautiful of his doings. He read the Bible with her and Grandma, and then made the prayer which always touched the doings of the last 24 hours and brought them into right proportion and significance, the light of heaven through those prayers seemed to shine into every nook and corner of their life."

140. "Charles Duval," E. Verdier, 1877, is a red, medium-sized double, hybrid rose. It is bright, dwarf with cupped outer row of petals erect, rather curbed in and enclosing numerous smaller petals. "Boursault" is a climbing hybrid rose with purplish, double flowers.

141. Tristram Barnard Mackay was a Concord neighbor and a member of the Social Circle in Concord in 1849, resigning in 1851.

142. In 1823 Mary Merrick married Nathan Brooks, who became a prominent Concord lawyer, bank director, and secretary of an insurance company. He became a state senator in 1835. She was a member of the nominating committee of the Middlesex County Anti-Slavery Society's annual meeting at Concord on 3 April 1851.

143. Henry David Thoreau's mother and sister.

144. Sam Staples was the village jailer famed for arresting Thoreau in the summer of 1846 for nonpayment of taxes.

145. John S. Keyes, whose daughter Annie married Edward Emerson. David Loring was the son of George and Ann Loring. Edward and Judge Ebenezer Rockwood Hoar are Elizabeth's brothers.

146. Elizabeth Prichard is Frances's (Fanny's) sister. See note 314. Mary Ball and

Angelina were sisters. See note 310. Abby Tolman was the daughter of Deacon Elisha Tolman.

147. Reverend Hersey B. Goodwin, associate to Dr. Ezra Ripley from 1830 to 1836. See note 76.

148. Emerson lectured in Salem on 2, 4, 6, and 7 May in 1836. His subject was "English Biography and Literature."

149. Charles Emerson died of tuberculosis on 9 May 1836. He had recently taken over Samuel Hoar's law office in Concord. See note 119.

150. William Emerson (1801–1868), brother of Ralph Waldo.

151. In the margin is "2 Ki iv 10."

152. Ogden Haggerty is referred to in the *Letters of Ralph Waldo Emerson*, ed. Ralph L. Rusk (New York: Columbia University Press, 1939), as a resident of New York. The Madonna by Correggio is still in the parlor. S. G. Ward is Samuel Gray Ward, who married Anna Barker.

153. Lucy Jackson Brown did live for a brief time in the spring of 1837 with the Thoreau family.

154. Dr. Josiah Bartlett settled in Concord in 1819 when he was twenty-three. His father, Dr. Josiah Bartlett, of Charlestown, was in practice at the Battle of Lexington. His son, George Bartlett, was talented in private theatrical and parlor amusements. He was a Concord physician for more than a half century and died in 1878.

155. The poem is "I am a parcel of vain strivings tied." It was read at Thoreau's funeral by Amos Bronson Alcott.

156. *List*, a strip of cloth.

157. He wrote to Carlyle: "My wife Lidian is an incarnation of Christianity,—I call her Asia—& keeps my philosophy from Antinomianism" (10 May 1838, *The Correspondence of Emerson and Carlyle*, ed. Joseph Slater [New York: Columbia University Press, 1964], p. 184).

158. See Emerson's journal entry of 31 October 1836 for an account of Waldo's birth (*JMN*, 5:234–235) and the poem "Threnody." Emerson's last words, "O, that beautiful boy," were thought by Lidian to be about Waldo.

159. "Did not Father raize Hersey up first, then Waldo" is inserted here in pencil. Emerson records in his journal, "This day my boy was baptized in the old church by Dr Ripley. They dressed him in the selfsame robe in which twentyseven years ago my brother Charles was baptised. Lidian has a group of departed Spirits in her eye who hovered around the patriarch & the babe" (7 May 1837, *JMN*, 5:324). Hersey Goodwin is probably son of Reverend Goodwin. See note 76.

160. William Kitchiner (1775?–1827), *The Cook's Oracle: Containing receipts for plain cookery on the most economical plan for private families* (London: A Constable & Co., 1821).

161. Written after this is: "Written at Nina Lowell's Magnolia July, 1896."

162. "This House is not a Hotel" is printed and the ink is bold.

163. In May 1839, Emerson records in his journal, "Here is my wife who has come to church in hope of being soothed & strengthened after being wounded by the sharp tongue of a slut in her house" (*JMN*, 7:197).

164. See note 116. The following anecdotes about Aunt Mary were added by Edith: "About 1857 I recall an evening when Aunt Mary was at our house & Mother in high spirits was arguing with her. Mr Sanborn was present and finally Aunt Mary said "Lidian how can you speak in so frivolous a manner? This young man will never know what a noble woman you are!"

"I believe it was this evening that Mother sat down by Aunt Mary laughing & said "I'm going to give you an invitation after your own heart. I ask you to be buried in our lot in Sleepy Hollow." Aunt Mary with asperity answered "It was a matter of no interest to her where the poor carcass should be laid"—But she soon after sent a note of apology for so answering & gratefully accepted the kind invitation. E.E.F."

165. The dates in the margin are "1855" for the covered buggy, "1870" for the perambulator, and "1890" for the wicker chariot.

166. See March 1838, *JMN*, 5:456.

167. For Emerson's record of the event and of the naming, see 25 February 1839, *JMN*, 7:170.

168. See Edwin Gittleman, *Jones Very: The Effective Years, 1833–1840* (New York: Columbia University Press, 1967), pp. 339–343, for the relationship between Very and Lidian, and for Emerson's response to it. Very was a poet and essayist from Salem, Massachusetts (1813–1880). Graduated from Harvard in 1836, he taught Greek while studying at the divinity school and in 1843 was licensed as a Unitarian preacher, but did very little preaching. He believed that all his inspirations were of divine origin; he claimed that his religious sonnets were communicated to him during visions of the Holy Ghost. He was committed for a period during 1838 to the insane asylum although Emerson and others affirmed their belief that Very was sane. Emerson helped in the selection of his *Essays and Poems* (1839), Very's only book-length work published during his lifetime.

169. Margaret Fuller (1810–1850), daughter of a stern lawyer and congressman who subjected her to such strenuous education that it affected her health but made her one of the most learned women in America. She edited the Dial (1840–1842). Amos Bronson Alcott (1799–1888), teacher, reformer, and philosopher, married Abby May. Their daughter was Louisa May. He started his educational reform in 1825 at Cheshire Academy. He opened the famous Temple School in Boston but was attacked for his methods. A member of the Transcendental Club, contributor to the Dial, founder of both the Fruitlands Utopian community in Harvard, Massachusetts (which lasted less than a year), and the Concord Summer School of Philosophy, he was a leading Transcendentalist.

170. Captain Nathaniel Russell married Martha LeBaron, daughter of Isaac LeBaron, on 18 June 1800. See note 40 for Lidian's childhood friend Mary Howland Russell. See also notes 43 and 87.

171. John Brown (1818–1890) was born in Concord, where he was active in the business of the town for thirty-five years, retiring in 1880. He was the son of Captain John Brown of the War of 1812 and the grandson of Colonel Roger Brown who took part in the Revolution and in Shays' Rebellion.

172. Probably the families of John Milton and Louisa Hosmer Cheney (Elizabeth Wells Cumming Cheney, b. 1836, was the daughter of John and Louisa), George and Ann Loring, and Reverend Hersey Goodwin.

173. See note 250 for Henry Frost. Ellen Shattuck, daughter of Daniel and Sarah was born on 6 January 1838. The Lemuel Shattuck Hospital in Boston is named for Daniel's brother, Lemuel.

174. Emerson's poem lamenting the death of little Waldo.

175. Edith drew a line through Ellen's "go to church with the cook" and inserted in pencil "stay with the cook while the family were at church. E.E.F." which is adopted here. Edith recalled a story about little Waldo and wrote it on the back of this manuscript page: "Once Waldo accompanied the girl who was drawing the baby Ellen in the wagon on an errand to Miss Minot. He stayed outside with her while the girl went in. Presently the baby began to scream. Waldo went into the house & said in his quiet deliberate voice—'Miss Minot—if you want to see Ellen's teeth you had better come out now.' "

176. "Where's Kitty?" follows in pencil, written there perhaps as a reminder of another incident.

177. A *come-outer* is a radical reformer.

178. A *Grahamite* is the follower of a vegetarian dietary system advocated in the nineteenth century by Sylvester Graham (1794–1851), who conceived the notion that alcoholic intemperance could be prevented and cured by a purely vegetable diet.

Finally, he came to advocate it as a cure for all disease. Emerson records Lidian's response to reformers in *JMN*, 8:329).

179. II Samuel 18:27: "And the watchman said, me thinketh the running of the foremost is like the running of Ahimaaz the son of Zadok. And the king said, He is a good man, and cometh with good tidings." Ahimaaz told David that the Lord had avenged him of his enemies but the second runner brought news of the death of David's son, Absalom.

180. For Charles Newcomb, see *The Journals of Charles King Newcomb*, ed. Judith Kennedy Johnson (Providence: Brown University Press, 1946). Newcomb was at Brook Farm, leaving in 1845; he was from Providence.

Caroline Sturgis, daughter of merchant William Sturgis and Elizabeth Marston (Davis) Sturgis. See note 113. At age thirteen she became friends with Margaret Fuller and met Ralph Waldo Emerson when she was sixteen. In 1836, she went with Fuller for an extended visit to the Emersons. Emerson introduced her to William Tappan in 1843 and they were married in 1847.

Charles Lane (1800–1870) was associated with James Pierrepont Greaves in England, before coming to the United States with Alcott and forming Fruitlands with him.

Frederic Henry Hedge (1805–1890), son of a Harvard professor of logic. At thirteen he accompanied George Bancroft to Germany to study. He took a Harvard degree in 1825 and spent four years in the Divinity School. From 1835 to 1850, he was a minister in Bangor, Maine. After 1836, his trips to Boston became the occasion for the gathering of the Transcendental Club. While pastor in Brookline (1857–1872) he also served as professor of ecclesiastical history at Harvard Divinity School and after 1872 was professor of German in the College.

William Henry Channing (1810–1884) was a nephew of Dr. Channing, graduate of Harvard in 1829 and from the Divinity School in 1833. He found in Transcendental metaphysics a program of social regeneration. He resigned his pulpit in 1841, organized an independent church in New York, spent some months at Brook Farm, and edited magazines for three years. After 1854 most of his time was spent in England.

Caleb Stetson (1793–1870), a member of the Transcendental Club, was an orator who delivered the Phi Beta Kappa oration in 1838.

Christopher Pearse Cranch (1813–1892) was born in Alexandria, Virginia, of a Massachusetts family. His father was made a judge of the Circuit Court by John Adams. Cranch graduated from Columbian College in 1831 and then attended Harvard Divinity School. In 1835 he followed Clarke to the West, preached in St. Louis and Cincinnati, and became an editor of the *Western Messenger*. After five years he returned to Boston and became a social being. His major work was a translation of the *Aeneid*.

181. Compare Emerson's essay on "Friendship": "But as soon as the stranger begins to intrude his partialities, his definitions, his defects into the conversation, it is all over. He has heard the first, the last and best he will ever hear from us. He is no stranger now. Vulgarity, ignorance, misapprehension are old acquaintances. Now, when he comes, he may get the order, the dress and the dinner,—but the throbbing of the heart and the communications of the soul, no more."

182. Emerson wrote in his journal: "Queenie says, 'Save me from magnificent souls. I like a small common sized one'" (1842, *JMN*, 8:242).

183. Emerson wrote in his journal: "Queenie (who has a gift to curse & swear,) will every now & then in spite of all manners & christianity rip out on Saints, reformers, & Divine Providence /in/ with the most edifying zeal. In answer to the good Burrill Curtis who asks whether trade will not check the free course of love she insists 'it shall be said that there is no love to restrain the course of, & never was that poor God did all he could but selfishness fairly carried the day'" (1841, *JMN*, 8:88). Curtis was a Brook Farmer and later a Concord resident.

184. Anna Barker, friend of Margaret Fuller, was known for her beauty. She became the wife of S. G. Ward.

185. Emerson records in his journal: "Lidian grieves aloud about the wretched negro in the horrors of the middle passage; and they are bad enough. But to such as she, these crucifixions do not come. They come to the obtuse & barbarous to whom they are not horrid but only a little worse than the old sufferings. They exchange a cannibal war for a stinking hold. They have gratifications which would be none to Lidian. The grocer never damned L. because she had not paid her bill; but the good Irish woman has that to suffer once a month. She in return never feels weakness in her back because of the slave-trade. The horrors of the middle passage are the wens & ulcers that admonish us that a violation of nature has been made preceded. I should not—the nations would not know of the extremity of the wrong but for the terrors of the retribution." (1837, *JMN*, 5:382).

186. In the margin is written "Here comes in Edith's Protest." The protest is written on sheets measuring 4½" by 6¾" and follows here:

A Protest—

I think the picture of Mother's sorrow is too dark & decided. No doubt she felt so in her dark hours & when fatigue—or dyspepsia or some wound to her over-sensitive spirit oppressed her. But she was of too hopeful and healthy a mind naturally to be always sad—She was able to enjoy a great deal. I found it one of her most charming traits that her faith was so deep and secure that she was always ready with comfort—for every one—She was also a reasonable person, and I never failed to come to a good and happy understanding with her when we had a discussion. She always made good to my mind the text "As one whom his mother comforteth." [Isaiah 66:13] (I was with her a great deal in the years when Ellen was at school & I do not think I was so unobservant a person that I should have failed to feel the sad atmosphere if she had been always so deeply unhappy.) And this motherhood extended to a large number of people. All the neighbors—all whom she ever employed looked to her for help & comfort—Miss Minot's household, The Shannons, the Bulgers, the varying occupants of the pink house, and poorhouse, the children from the little school opposite, and errand boys from the block & an army of people who had sewed for her looked on her as Justice & Mercy personified—I was amazed when Mr Watts an old farmer whom we knew only by sight sent for her to comfort him on his deathbed. One of my earliest recollections is our being sent with little parcels of tea & other comforts for the old people in the poor house. Poor old Mrs Cook brought her sorrows to Mother whose sympathy & indignation about the wrongs of her daughter led her to take a journey to help her—& when the poor girl died as she was unable to be at home on the day of the funeral she sent her women & us children to do honour to her—the first funeral I ever attended; & in looking back I see Mother was so full of sympathy with Mrs Cook she never remembered it was a new and terrible experience to us.

Another case I remember was an Irish girl—an orphan child Mary Casey who was neglected & ill-treated by the family who had her in charge—how great were the pains she took about her, visiting Squire Hoar in his office to make sure the law should be on her side & writing to Father to look up her kindred in Philadelphia & sending her on. She always had a boy protegé who would do her errands and to whom she was most motherly[.] Henry Glaskin & Tommy Hazel I remember were the last of these.

She enjoyed a great deal, she did accomplish a quantity of actual work in keeping her house well—& in good repair with her many devices, and she enjoyed her triumphs in this department—especially I remember the time of making "poverty wash-stands" of shoemaker's boxes on the side or the end with overhanging boards on top using the rounded barrel tops from the ends & covering them with cheap & pretty chintz curtains.

She enjoyed her shopping in Boston & the "openings" to which Aunty always came full of interest[;] they were a great delight to us children. On these shopping excursions she used, as soon as she and Father felt a little easier about money, to refresh herself by going to the theatre which she greatly enjoyed. In the winter Ellen was in Lenox & wished for a daguerreotype of me she took us often to try for it—both Eddy & me, and began to try for a picture of herself for us. At that time Agnes Robertson was a very popular star actress at the Museum—Mother was charmed by her and took us often to see her. Besides these pleasures, she took great comfort in her children, in Ellen's letters, in preparing boxes to send to her,—in our companionship. It was at that time that she gave up coming down to breakfast. Eddy & I used to take great delight in preparing a tray every morning to tempt her with various fruits. It was a small tray which we always covered with grape leaves and on them laid in little piles all the berries we could find, one of each kind of currants black, red, white, pink and Missouri—raspberries & thimble berries & we trimmed the edges & spaces between with the green shafts of ambrosia & balsam flowers of many colours—and then went together to offer it. I think she was always cheered, & happy in this daily "surprise."

187. The verse is "To Corinne" by Felicia Hemans and is in *Parnassus* (1875), an edition of favorite poems edited by Emerson. The poem reads "She who" rather than "She that" and the first word of the last line, which is not clear in the manuscript, should be "Lovely."

188. Jane Tuckerman, pupil of Margaret Fuller, visited Concord with Elizabeth Hoar in 1839 before going to England in 1840.

189. Sarah Hoar (Mrs. Robert Storer) was the sister of Elizabeth Hoar.

190. Both the *Boston Blue Book* of 1879 and the *Brookline Street List* of 1877–1878 list Sarah Searle as living on High Street. She failed to appear in subsequent directories. Emanuel Swedenborg (1688–1772) was a Swedish scholar best known as a Biblical theologian, though he also made important contributions to science and philosophy. After study at Uppsala University he went to England and studied physics and astronomy. In 1745, he underwent a transcendent experience and entered a period of spiritual crisis. His spiritual experiences are detailed in *Heaven and Hell* (1758), but his longest theological study, the eight-volume *Arcana coelestia* (1749–1756), explicates Genesis and Exodus.

191. *Paction* is an agreement, a compact, or a bargain.

192. Lidian wrote in a letter: "Henry has been here this evening and seen Mr Emerson but no one else. He says John took leave of all the family on Monday with perfect calmness and more than resignation. It is a beautiful fate that has been granted him and I think he was worthy of it. At first it seemed not beautiful but terrible. Since I have heard particulars and recollected all the good I have heard of him I feel as if a pure spirit had been translated. Henry has just been here—(it is now Wednesday noon) I love him for the feeling he showed and the effort he made to be cheerful. He did not give way in the least but his whole demeanour was that of one struggling with sickness of heart. He came to take his clothes—and says he does not know when he shall return to us. We are wholly indebted to John for Waldo's picture. Henry and myself each carried him to a sitting but did not succeed in keeping him in the right attitude—and still enough. But John by his faculty of interesting children succeeded in keeping him looking as he should while the impression was making" (11 January 1842).

193. William Ellery Channing (1818–1901) was the son of Walter and Barbara Perkins Channing. His father, a prominent Boston physician, was the brother of the celebrated Dr. William Ellery Channing. He was educated at Round Hill School in Northampton, Latin School, and Hubbards Academy in Brookline. He withdrew from Harvard after a few months and devoted himself to writing poetry and studying medicine with his father. In 1842, he married Ellen Fuller, Margaret Fuller's sister, and settled in Concord to be near Emerson. He became the walking companion of Thoreau.

194. Edith added the following: "Mother told us that Waldo had the little cabinet

(now in my room) to keep his treasures in. It was full of designs cut out of paper for the great castle he was to build for Ellen. Not long before his death he missed some which a girl had burned and his storm of grief and indignation was terrible—it made her feel he was too sensitive a creature to bear life."

195. See Emerson's entry on the birth of Edith, November 1841, *JMN*, 8:76–77.

196. The next manuscript page, which could be in Edith's hand, follows here (the stationery has printed in red print "NAUSHON"): "Aunt Lizzy once said to Aunt Lucy or Aunt Susan in my presence 'Lidian's necessity of perfection is to blame for many of her distresses—for instance. If Mamma sees that a hole is worn in her furniture cover—she at once finds a piece of cloth & sews it on as a patch. It is not handsome & does not match but is whole & she does not worry about it. But Lidian is unable to have it mended until she can find the exact match and is distressed by it until she can find time & strength to look up the piece or devise some way of mending it to make it as handsome as it was when new.' "

197. Annie Keyes became the wife of Edward Emerson.

198. See January 1842, *JMN*, 8:163–166.

199. He looked into Ellen's coffin also: "I visited Ellen's tomb and opened the coffin" (29 March 1832, *JMN*, 4:7).

200. See Mary R. Fenn, *Old Houses of Concord* (Concord: Old Concord Chapter of the Daughters of the American Revolution, 1974), p. 18 for Edmund Hosmer and his family.

201. Lizzie Weir (5 June 1827) was the daughter of James and Elmira Weir.

202. In the winter of 1840 Margaret Fuller held conversations in Elizabeth Peabody's bookstore at 13 West Street, Boston.

203. Written in the margin is "Edith tells me she attended to it for Mother who was in Milton that year." "except on the New Years of 1873 when the house was rebuilding after the fire and Mother was spending the winter in Milton, Father & I being abroad." is cancelled. The Emerson School, the first consolidated high school in Massachusetts, opened in 1880 on Stow Street. It was the building that is now known as the Emerson Annex. The present Emerson School, a high school opened to students in 1930, is next door.

204. See note 338. Perhaps this is the same person.

205. Edith's protest follows: "Protest by E. E. F. This statement is a very singular one. I am absolutely sure that the outside doors were closed from the cold days in November till the warm days of April—uniformly—I remember the darkness of the front entry—my difficulty in reaching & turning the knob of the front door—my preference of the East which was easier—the wrath I always felt against an East wind & my speed to shut it out even in Summer when it *would* rush round the corner of the narrow passage between the two entries. I remember James Burke opening the east door to hurry us when we were to drive to school on snowy days—also my objection to the dark shades in the windows of the front door—Uncle William's remarks must have been in the autumn before the doors were shut."

206. July 1842.

207. See note 193.

208. Ann Augusta Gray Carter is described by Edith as the writer of pretty country ballads, as the Swedenborgian lady whose *Juvenile Ballads* have been out of print since 1850. Poems of Taylor, Gray, and Follen can be found in an edition by Edith Emerson Forbes, *Favourites of a Nursery of Seventy Years Ago: And Some Others of Later Date* (Boston: Houghton Mifflin, 1916). It is dedicated to "The Descendants of Lidian Emerson."

Eliza Lee (Cabot) Follen (1789–1860) was an abolitionist and miscellaneous writer, daughter of Samuel and Sarah (Barrett) Cabot. For two years she edited the *Christian Teacher's Manual,* and later the *Child's Friend.* Her books for children were well-known, *The Well-Spent Hour* (1827) being probably the most popular.

209. The rhyme is "Ride, man, ride, lion, ride, Moolly Cow,/Ride, pussy, ride, Kadar-cut, ride Bowwow."
210. The "Fragment of an Old Song":

> Away we went to wedding
> Up to Uncle Lumper's;
> There we saw the men and boys
> And women without numbers.
> In came Uncle and Aunt,
> And in came Sister Keturah,
> In came fiddler John,
> And sawed away like fury.
> Turn your middlemost man—
> Turn your partner again—
> Turn the corner and back—
> And now you're right again.

211. "Twinkle, Twinkle, Little Star" is by Jane Taylor.
212. The anonymous "Morning Hymn for a Little Child":

> Now, before I run to play,
> Let me not forget to pray
> To God who kept me through the night
> And waked me with the morning light.
>
> Help me, Lord, to love thee more
> Than I ever loved before,
> In my work and in my play,
> Be thou with me through the day.

213. Edith's completion of the poem and added fragments follow. Part of the song "When I was a pert little Miss in my teens" appears on another sheet, probably in Edith's hand, introduced by the statement, "One of Grandmother Jackson's Songs." Below the song is the line, "When Edith told Mother about Lincoln's death".

Second Verse

> Help me Lord to love Thee more
> Than I ever loved before.
> In my work & in my play
> Be Thou with me through the day.

———

Fragments of a Poem I never saw in writing about making Hasty pudding for supper. [C]alling the children, setting out bowls, filling them with milk & then

> "Drop the pudding all about"
> It ended
> Oh what a charming supper this is
> For little masters & for Misses.
> Among green pleasant meadows [See note 220]

Mother used to sing three songs which she learned of her mother.—One was a Midshipman's Song—of which I only remember the chorus

For I'm a gay young midshipman
A jolly dashing midshipman
The foremast men are at my beck
With pride I walk the quarter deck
For I'm a gay young midshipman

Another was about the gods & goddesses going a-hunting and began—

Songs of Shepherds & rustical roundelays
The Third was

When I was a pert little miss in my teens
  More ready to laugh than to cry
How little I envied the grandeur of queens
So gay & so happy was I—
  In mischief the first
At Ah working the worst
  And if by mishap
  I caught the fool's cap
I only would sob and implore
O Aunty forgive me this one little time
Oh only forgive me this one little time
  I'll never do so any more—

But once you must know 'twas my fortune to wed—
Young Harry looked spruce & looked smart
My aunt always told me to hold up my head
But forgot to take care of my heart.

To Gretna we led them a glorious chase
Young Cupid he flourished the whip
My aunt and my uncle rode after poste haste
  But Cupid he gave them the slip—

I've finished my song
And if in the throng
My aunt should appear
For perhaps she is here—
I thus would her pardon implore
O Aunty forgive me this one little time
Oh only forgive me this one little time
I'll never do so any more.

214. Anna Letitia Aikin Barbauld (1743–1825) was a writer of children's books, poet,
critic, and essayist. Her famous *Hymns in Prose for Children* was published in 1781.
She agreed with Rousseau that a child "should steadily contemplate Nature," but
added "that by so doing he will be led to contemplate the traditional God." Four
volumes of her works are in Emerson's library, including her *Hymns in Prose for
Children* (London: John Murray, 1864). which is inscribed "Edith Emerson with Uncle
William's love, Dec. 1864."
215. Martha Mary Sherwood (1775–1851), a children's writer, was born in Worcester,
England. *Little Henry and His Bearer* went through a hundred printings up to 1884
and was translated into a dozen languages. Many Victorian children were brought up
on *The History of the Fairchild Family* (1818–1847). Her *Julian Percival* (Salem:
Whipple and Lawrence, 1837) is in Emerson's library.

216. Reverend Thomas Hopkins Gallaudet, *The Child's Book on the Soul, with questions, adapted to the use of Sunday Schools and of infant schools* (Hartford: Cooke, 1831). The fifth edition, with questions (Hartford: Belknap & Hamersley, 1836), 2 vols. in 1, is in Emerson's library, with Ellen Emerson's signature.

217. I have been unable to identify Anna Ross. A nineteenth-century Mrs. Ross of New York was a prolific writer but the title pages of her works do not give a first name.

218. Taylor, *Contributions of Q. Q. to a Periodical Work [The Youth's Magazine] with some pieces not before published*, ed. Isaac Taylor, 2 vols. (London: B. J. Holdsworth, 1824).

219. From "The Shepherd's Sabbath-Song":

> This is the Sabbath day!
> In the wide field I am alone.
> Hark! now one morning bell's sweet tone,—
> Now it has died away.
>
> Kneeling I worship Thee;
> Sweet dread doth o'er my spirit steal,
> From whispering sounds of those who kneel,
> Unseen, to pray with me.
>
> Around and far away,
> So clear and solemn is the sky,
> It seems all opening to my eye;
> This is the Sabbath day!

220. The opening line of "A Ballad" (Mary Howitt's translation from Herder):

> Among green, pleasant meadows,
>   All in a grove so wild,
> Was set a marble image
>   Of the Virgin and the Child.
>
> Here oft, on summer evenings,
>   A lovely boy would rove,
> To play beside the image
>   That sanctified the grove.
>
> Oft sat his mother by him,
>   Among the shadows dim,
> And told how the Lord Jesus
>   Was once a child like him.
>
> "And now from highest heaven
>   He doth look down each day,
> And sees whate'er thou doest;
>   And hears what thou dost say!"
>
> Thus spoke his tender mother;
>   And on an evening bright,
> When the red, round sun descended
>   Mid clouds of crimson light,

Again the boy was playing,
  And earnestly said he,
"O beautiful Child Jesus
  Come down and play with me!

"I will find thee flowers the fairest,
  And weave for thee a crown;
I will get thee ripe, red strawberries,
  If thou wilt but come down!

"O holy, holy mother,
  Put him down from off thy knee;
For in these silent meadows
  There are none to play with me!"

Thus spoke the boy so lovely,
  The while his mother heard,
And on his prayer she pondered,
  But spoke to him no word.

That selfsame night she dreamed
  A lovely dream of joy:
She thought she saw young Jesus
  There playing with her boy.

"And for the fruits and flowers
  Which thou hast brought to me,
Rich blessing shall be given
  A thousandfold to thee!

"For in the fields of heaven
  Thou shalt roam with me at will,
And of bright fruits celestial
  Thou shalt have, dear child, thy fill!"

Thus tenderly and kindly
  The fair Child Jesus spoke;
And full of careful musings,
  The anxious mother woke.

And thus it was accomplished:—
  In a short month and a day,
That lovely boy so gentle,
  Upon his deathbed lay.

And thus he spoke in dying:—
  "Oh, mother, dear, I see
That beautiful Child Jesus
  A-coming down to me!

"And in his hand He beareth
  Bright flowers as white as snow,

And red and juicy strawberries,—
Dear mother, let me go!"

He died—but that fond mother
Her sorrow did restrain,
For she knew he was with Jesus,
And she asked him not again.

221. A comment by Edith follows: "She knew them by heart & recited them. E. E. F."

222. *Mary and Her Mother, a sequel to Scriptural stories for very young children* (London: Harding Mavor & Lepard, 1824).

223. See note 10.

224. "Noises" was later written in pencil, but "motions" was not cancelled.

225. Miss Foord had tutored the Alcott children, as well as the young Emersons, during parts of 1845 and 1846. In late 1846 and early 1847 she lived with the Emersons. She left permanently on 1 April. In 1847, when she was about forty-five, she proposed to Thoreau, who returned a resounding "no." Further details of this abortive romance are given in Walter Harding, "Thoreau's Feminine Foe," *PMLA*, 69 (March 1954): 110–116.

226. "She had" is inserted in pencil above "completed." Apparently Ellen intended "but Mother's task she had not quite completed."

227. Mary Porter Tileston Hemenway (1820–1894) in 1840 married Augustus Hemenway, a Boston merchant of great wealth. Her daughter Charlotte Augusta (b. 1841) appears in the manuscript. Mrs. Hemenway was a great philanthropist. Among her many contributions were her chief concern of strengthening white and Negro education in the South, improving the homemaking skills of girls in Boston, and promoting a more general knowledge of and devotion to the American past. In 1871 she gave a substantial sum to build the Tileston Normal School in Wilmington, North Carolina, to educate poor whites; she supported the school until it closed in 1891. She also gave funds to General Samuel C. Armstrong and Booker T. Washington to aid in their work at Hampton and Tuskegee institutes. In later years she sponsored summer vacation schools for the manual training of girls (1883–1884). Out of this program emerged the need for cooking classes; Mrs. Hemenway outfitted the first school kitchen in 1885 and again provided teachers and expenses; in 1887 she founded the Boston Normal School of Cookery. She also set up the Boston Normal School of Gymnastics (later taken over by Wellesley College).

228. Lizzy and Abby are Bronson Alcott's girls; Lizzy and Barry are the children of the housekeeper, Mrs. Goodwin.

229. Probably Charles Lane. See note 180.

230. *Squill* is the cut and dried fleshy inner scales of the bulb of the white variety of *urginea scilla;* it contains one or more physiologically active gluosides and is used as an expectorant, cardiac stimulant, and diuretic. *Paregoric* is camphorated tincture of opium used to mitigate pain.

231. Antoine (Anthony) Colombe, a French-Canadian laborer, worked for Emerson, Edmund Hosmer, and others in Concord. Both Colombe and Thoreau helped with the maintenance of Emerson's property before and during his absence in Europe.

232. "Fayaway" is not clear. "Layaway" may be correct.

233. In December 1838 Emerson had bought the lot of land he called the "heater-piece" because its triangular shape resembled that of a "heater" for a flatiron.

234. "He once said . . . roof." is in pencil; "judges . . . roof" is on the back of the page. "By" is over "of" and "of" is over "from."

235. Ellen wrote "and Charlie," then inserted "(Not born)" in pencil and cancelled "Charlie."

236. Edith added the following: "Eddy went—he must have been just peeling—I well—but supposed to be more infectious as just about to have the fever, was condemned

to stay at home. Aunt Lizzy's present of a doll's bed & doll was my only consolation—A mahogany French bed. E. E. F."

237. In 1850 the Bancroft address in New York was 32 West Twenty-first Street.

238. The opening lines of Ann Augusta Gray's ballad, "The Doe and the Hunter":

A Gentle Hind with her young Fawn,
    Once, on a soft spring day,
Upon a bed of dried oak leaves
    Within a thicket lay.

The little Fawn was very young,
    He was but two days old;
His eye was bright, his color light,
    Fair was he to behold.

The mother oft looked round on him,
    With her eye so bright yet meek;
He lay close by her side,—she felt
    His breath upon her cheek.

But soft! Why is that sudden start?
    What means that upright ear?
Mother, what means that anxious eye?
    What startling sound dost hear?

Quick up she springs upon her feet,
    Her head erect and high,
And anxiously she stares around,
    With wild, wide-open eye.

The tramp of horses' hoofs is heard,
    A man dismounts near by;
O'er bush and bramble, stump and stone,
    The frightened Hind doth fly.

The man is in the thicket now;
    What will the poor Fawn do?
His limbs are weak, and close the briers
    He tries to struggle through.

He gets entangled in the thorns,—
    He's in the man's firm grasp,
And his heart flutters so with fright
    That he for breath must gasp.

And with his pretty little prize,
    The man did mount again;
The frightened creature struggled hard
    But struggled hard in vain.

But where's the Hind? Poor little one!
    Where is thy mother gone?
What? Fled away to save herself,
    And left her little Fawn?

No, no; see, yonder, where she comes;
  Oh, look! Her eye how wild!
She comes with a fearless mother's heart
  To claim her stolen child.

The man restrained his steed and stopped
  Until the Hind came near;
He wished, perhaps, to see how far
  Her love would conquer fear.

Boldly she sprang, and on the horse
  Her two fore feet did place;
And silently,—imploringly,
  Looked up in the man's face.

And as she stood, the man beheld
  With pity and surprise,
Big tears well up, and trickle down
  Out of her large dark eyes.

The man he had a gentle heart;
  "Well, take thy child," he cried,
"Bold mother!" and away she bounds,
  Her baby by her side.

239. The opening line of "The Pigeon," translated from the German by Mary Howitt:

Boy. Dear Pigeon on the house-top, say,
      Why thus you coo the livelong day,—
      Thus turn your head from side to side?

Dove. Because my soul is satisfied;
      Because the dear Creator mine,
      Doth warm me with his bright sunshine!

      Above, the Pigeon cooed for joy;
      Below, all merrily played the boy,—
      For sunshine bright doth ever call
      A gladness to the heart of all;
      And the Creator from above,
      Beheld the joy of both with love.

240. The opening line of Heber's "Evening Hymn":

God that madest earth and heaven,
  Darkness and light:
Who the day for toil has given,
  For rest the night,—
May thine angel-guards defend us,
Slumber sweet thy mercy send us,
Holy dreams and hopes attend us,
  This livelong night.

241. Fredrika Bremer (1801–1865), Swedish novelist who wrote many "fireside novels," short stories, sketches, and travel books. She lived in the United States from 1849 to 1851 and was well-received in New England, where she was admired not only for her writing but for her outspoken anti-slavery sentiments. Her report on her American visit, *The Homes of the New World* (1853), was enormously popular.

242. Marcus Spring's address was at one time 51 Exchange Place, New York. Marcus and Rebecca Spring proposed that Margaret Fuller join them on a tour of Europe, to be paid for in part by her taking care of their twelve-year-old son, Eddie. Spring was at Eaglewood, Perth Amboy, New Jersey, in 1856 (see *The Correspondence of Henry David Thoreau*, ed. Walter Harding and Carl Bode [New York: New York University Press, 1958], p. 438).

243. *The Bondmaid*, trans. M. L. Putnam (Boston: James Munroe, 1844), is in Emerson's library, inscribed: from author to Mrs. Emerson, 1850. The next four pages, which are probably in Edith's hand, follow here:

"When Miss Bremer came to our house, I had just received for a birthday present a much-loved book called the Playmate [*Playmate: A Pleasant Companion for Spare Hours*, 2d Series (London, 1847)] with a gay red & gold cover. It happened that I showed it to her. Father said 'ask Miss Bremer if she will write her name in it for you[.]' She at once drew a little picture of a boat on the fly leaf at the end of the book & wrote her name below it in pencil. Father was much pleased & he & Aunt Lucy impressed on me the value she had added to the book. Unfortunately Almira borrowed the book for her brothers and one of them with clumsy heavy hand tried to deepen the lines of the boat and spoiled it to Father's infinite disgust. Miss Bremer made two visits[;] I cannot quite remember which time it was she spent a Sunday evening. Cousin Abby Adams had been asked to meet her—probably there were some of the Ripleys and Aunt Lizzy present—the room seemed pretty full. Miss Bremer asked Cousin Abby to play our national music—and she played Yankee Doodle,—rather mortified we all were by the contrast with her Swedish hymn which she played & then proposed'to show her national dance & took Cousin Abby's hand & asked her to perform it with her. I never forgot poor Cousin Abby's drawing back—it would have been a trial to her at any time to dance a new dance before a strange company—but this was Sunday! & she drew back & some one kindly said that it was not our custom to dance on Sundays.

"Miss Bremer advised Mother to eat bananas, told her they were good for the nerves & she had found them beneficial, so Mother used to buy the half-blackened green ones which were the kind for sale then & would occasionally offer us a teaspoonful to try— they never tempted me in the least—and the first banana I ever ate was on the Azalea in 1859—this to show that bananas were not common food till after the sixties were well on."

244. Samuel Hooper (1808–1875), merchant and legislator, was born in Marblehead. His parents were John and Eunice (Hooper) Hooper. In 1832 he married Anne Sturgis and became junior partner of his father-in-law's shipping firm. Anne was sister to Ellen and Caroline Sturgis. He served three years in the Massachusetts House of Representatives and one year. in the state Senate. In 1861, he went to Congress and was re-elected six times.

245. Charles Loring Brace, *Hungary in 1851: With an Experience of the Austrian Police* (New York: Charles Scribner, 1852). Frederick Law Olmsted (1822–1903), land-scape architect. I could not locate a book by him on Hungary. In 1852–1853, he was making a tour of the Southern and Southwestern states to study the effects of slavery on agriculture.

246. See note 141.

247. William W. Wheildon (1806–1892) in 1827 established the *Bunker Hill Aurora* at Charles Town, and continued as its proprietor and editor until September 1870. In 1846, he took up his summer residence in Concord and in 1856, he moved to Concord. He was chairman of a committee of the Bunker Hill Monument Association. His 1878

publication of "History of Paul Revere's Signal Lanterns, April 18, 1775, in the Steeple of the North Church," determined the location of the lanterns. A member of the Concord Social Circle from 1848 to 1851, he lived in a large house on Main Street opposite the Concord Academy buildings.

248. In Concord, on 11 May 1852, Emerson made the welcome address to Kossuth.

249. "reviews were no longer exacted." is cancelled in pencil but has been included here to complete the statement.

250. Henry Frost (b. 1838), was the son of Reverend Barzillai and Elmira Frost. "sharpened his pencil and," "looked at its," and "and pricked Edith's neck." are cancelled in pencil; I have restored them for clarity.

Compare with this *Journal* entry for October 1848:

"Edith, who until now has been quite superior to all learning, has been smitten with ambition at Miss Whiting's school and cannot be satisfied with spelling. She spells at night on my knees with fury & will not give over; asks new words like conundrums with nervous restlessness and, as Miss W(hiting) tells me, 'will not spell at school for fear she shall miss.'

"Poor Edie struggled hard to get the white card called an 'approbation' which was given out on Saturdays but one (day) week she lost it by (losing) dropping out of a book on her way home her week's card on which her marks were recorded. This she tried hard to get safe home but she had no pocket so she put it in her book as the safest place. When half way home she looked in her book & it was there; but when she arrived at home it was gone. The next week she tried again to keep a clean bill but Henry Frost pointed his jackknife at her; Edie said, 'Don't!' & lost her 'approbation' again" (*JMN*, 11:24).

251. He was in Cincinnati, St. Louis, Springfield and Jacksonville, Illinois, and Cleveland, Ohio.

252. John Pringle Nichol. In 1848, Emerson had spent the night in Glasgow at Professor Nichol's observatory (*Letters*, 4:21–22). Nichol's book, *The Planet Neptune: An Exposition and History* (Edinburgh: John Johnstone, 1848), is in Emerson's library.

253. The following page is still connected to a Cupid pad; the front of the pad has "vol. IV, pp 162–211 1841–1850."

254. Chandler Robbins was pastor of the First Parish in Plymouth from 1760 until James Kendall came in 1800.

255. "Written at Nina Lowell's 25 July 1896" heads the next page.

256. A concise statement of Jackson's case is to be found in the anonymous *Presentation of Facts Relating to the Discovery of the Anaesthetic Effects of Ether Vapor by Charles T. Jackson and Disproving the Claim of W. T. G. Morton*. This pamphlet, based mainly on evidence collected by a Congressional committee, holds that Jackson discovered in the winter of 1841–1842 how to produce anaesthesia by means of sulphuric ether, that he communicated his discovery to Morton in 1846, and that Morton first applied ether in a surgical case at the Massachusetts General Hospital in the same year. Jackson and his family were bitter over the failure of Congress to give Jackson proper recognition, and Emerson was convinced that his brother-in-law had suffered a great injustice.

When S. F. B. Morse secured a telegraph patent in 1840, Charles Jackson claimed to have explained the method of applying electricity to telegraphic use to Morse on board the ship *Sully* in 1832. William T. Davis claims that the ship's mate, Blithen, verified Jackson's claim to him in 1846.

257. Manuscript page 213 is missing. The fragment that follows is a continuation of a thought which began on page 213.

258. Ellen writes again "this to be a daughter & when Grandma had this accident."

259. See Thoreau, *Correspondence*, pp. 261–264; Emerson, William Henry Channing, and James Freeman Clarke, *Memoirs of Margaret Fuller Ossoli* (Boston: Phillips, Sampson, 1852), 2:341–352; Emerson, *Letters*, 4:218–220; Thoreau, *Journal*, ed. Bradford Torrey (Boston: Houghton Mifflin, 1906), 2:43–44; Kenneth Walter Cameron,

"Thoreau's Notes on the Shipwreck at Fire Island," *Emerson Society Quarterly*, no. 52 (3d Quarter 1968): 97–99.

260. William Cowper, "A Poetical Epistle to Lady Austen."

261. Robert Bulkeley Emerson (1807–1859), mentally handicapped brother of Ralph Waldo.

262. The last word is not clear.

263. On 15 November 1853, Emerson lectured for the Mishawum Literature Association in Charlestown, Massachusetts.

264. Elizabeth Hoar. See note 119.

265. *Celandine* is an herb that was used to treat warts and jaundice. *Pyrola* is an herb of the wintergreen family. *Sarsaprilla* is an herb used as a tonic.

266. *Quassia* is a bitter drug that was used in brewing as a substitute for hops.

267. A *Planchette* is a small triangular board with a pointer supported by two casters and a vertical pencil which is said to spell out messages from the spirit world when the operator's fingers are placed tightly upon it.

268. Orson Squire Fowler (1809–1887), a phrenologist and author of numerous works, was graduated from Amherst College in 1834. He and his brother established the *American Phrenological Journal*.

269. See note 142.

270. "Don't read" in blue pencil precedes the following page. A somewhat vertical line in blue pencil cancels "I ... her principles." Following "principles" is a closing parenthesis in blue pencil. "Finally, her principles ... and ‹ wrong" is cancelled with a line in blue pencil.

271. Ellen is unclear in text about the year and added below "1853" a "2", then a "3."

272. The page that follows appears to be in Edith's hand. The date is in blue ink, the rest in brown. Beginning "From a letter from E. T. E. to E. E. F. 13 March 1888," it continues: "I began about the snow but did not quite finish. You should have seen its beauty. I just called Mother to her bay window to admire the garden & pines and she exclaimed "Now here is trouble indeed! The cats will get under the piazza & won't be able to get out, and they will suffer!" It seemed to me most characteristic, the far-fetched difficulty relating to the dumb animal is as spontaneous in her thought as it is foreign to everybody else's."

The next fifteen pages are an addition by Edith. Pale blue ink begins a folded piece of paper with writing on all four sides; the writing continues on similarly folded paper.

Addition by Edith

"One thing always filled me with admiration and determination and persistance of her charity at immense cost of suffering to herself. Dinner at one o'clock was an hour of suffering—the sun was high, and she had no appetite—everything seemed more dreadful to her then than at other times, but her mind was never diverted from her pensioners. Almost every day she sent for a bowl to be filled with her superior mutton broth to be saved for some invalid, or an extra plate to take out a helping of roast beef or mutton or turkey, for some one who never had roasts because she lived alone; and before she went upstairs, she arranged for the sending of it with a few flowers perhaps,—she put aside some food for Dolly—she prepared something to carry to her jays—she would then before she would lie down hunt up the newspaper to send to a soldier who was slowly dying at the pink-house, or prepare a bottle of her wine or beer to be sent to Mrs Weir—and with many groans & sighs of discomfort put all these in train to be delivered before she dropped down exhausted for her nap. When her suffering made her excited & despairing & she would remember every sorrow & wrong and pace the room fast—it was surprising and comforting to me to see, if only I had the presence of mind to run for ice water or fill up her quassia cup & make her lie down, how instantaneously the sorrow was diverted—the calm look of relief would come over her face & she would lie quietly and soon enjoy the reading & go to sleep and awake with no recurrence to the grievance that had been uppermost. The power of a 'cup of cold water' seemed to me almost miraculous.

"When Father wished especially to be hospitable to the stranger girls and boys that came to Mr Sanborn's school—we had tea parties of six or eight of them quite often. I should say that Ellen was at school in Boston probably or at any rate had not begun to enjoy company & was afraid of boys & gentlemen & did not undertake to entertain them. Lizzy Storer [probably the niece of Elizabeth Hoar whose sister was Sarah Hoar Storer] used to come & plan for me the charades which we would act together for our amusement, Mother and one or two of the guests being the audience. Mother was delighted with these charades—Lizzy's fun, spirit-rappings, women's rights speeches &c were as fine as could be—we both thought, and she was always our most sympathetic auditor. She gave us every chance for such festivities—and made nothing of the trouble of our using the parlour for stage when we had tableaux & when we acted Beauty & The beast—Edward's Plays too in the barn gave her much delight Bombastes Furioso [by William Barnes Rhodes (1772–1826), a tragic burlesque opera in one act] especially.

"She used always to enjoy reading to us when we were little, a book of verses called Fresh Flowers—written by Mrs Gordon [Mrs. Katharine Parker Gordon, *Fresh Flowers for my Children* (Boston: S. G. Simpkins, 1842)] whom Mother knew in youth—and she told us that Mrs Gordon was considered to look exactly like her—& she knew it was true for once meeting her suddenly she (perhaps both) had started thinking it was a mirror she was approaching. A new edition of Fresh Flowers was printed—in it was a new thing the rhymed journal which she had written in the name of her daughter Grace three years old, from Rio—to her aunt at home. This was very interesting to Eddy & me. I knew it almost by heart. In 1856 probably we were spending the spring vacation at Aunt Susan's in Somerset St and were asked to go with Johnny to a party at the Rev Mr Stickney's in Ashburton Place for Bessy Stickney. After playing games awhile we were asked to draw little slips of paper from a basket & on each we found a number and there were two of each number, the boys & girls were to thus find their partners for the supper the duplicates being assigned to each other[.] I had been industriously asking the names of all the prettiest girls & was thrilled to hear that one younger than I with long dark curls was named Grace Gordon and still more when Eddy drew her for his partner. We told our story to Mother who was delighted. Aunt Susan told her yes Mrs Gordon lived right up the hill in Beacon St. Mother took me with her to call. Mrs Gordon was stout, with iron grey hair, brown complexion, square face & dark eyes—with no beauty at all. We saw Helen of whom we had read but not Grace but Mother asked that Grace might visit us sometime. When Mr George Haven [George Wallis Haven, a lawyer in Portsmouth, New Hampshire, a brother to Susan Haven Emerson, William Emerson's wife] married Mrs Halliburton and she let Helen invite me to visit her, I learned from Mary Halliburton that Grace Gordon was a friend of hers—and the next year I think the old plan was carried out & Helen Haven, Mary Halliburton & Grace Gordon came together to spend the spring vacation. The second day, I should think Helen had a sore throat & could not go out with us. We left her reading in the parlour. When we came home we found Mother in the red rocking chair holding Helen in her lap—she had found her sick & homesick—& had been rocking and comforting her & saw she was sickening with measles & had sent for the doctor. Father called me aside and asked me to look at her 'see what a perfect Mother she is! see how beautiful she looks with that little child in her arms!' Mr Haven came the next day & carried off Mary & Grace and rather to our jealous dissatisfaction left a maid to nurse Helen for we were delighted to keep & pet her. Later I made a visit to Grace Gordon at the South End one August or September & saw all the family, including the handsome sister Kate—Mrs Hoffendahl [spelling not clear, especially the last letter]

& her pretty & beautifully dressed daughter Marie. Mrs Gordon was very kind & I enjoyed the visit—but I do not know that Mother ever met her again.

"About Mother's visits to Plymouth, I remember my first when she took us three children & Abby to board two or three weeks with Mrs Cox on Court St. [The earliest Plymouth directory is 1890.] It was one of those plain houses with the steps out on the sidewalk & a small garden slanting up the hill behind such as are very common along that street. Many of them having the gardens "dyked" which means terraced but hers did not. I still see the pretty green effect of that garden path with the ripe plums overhanging it. I was too small to remember whom Mother saw or how she seemed but I know I went with her to Hillside and it probably was in that visit. There was a hen coop & chickens on the bare sandy hillside behind the house which one of the Misses Russell must have showed me which was always associated with Chicken Little—a new book Uncle George gave me[.] Ellen & we went in bathing on the shore—Mother visited one of her old friendly carpenters & asked him to make some blocks for us—instead of a set of bricks he made a house front with two pillars and a door, & coming to deliver it while we were all out set it up on those steps in the street & left it and the event of finding them there impressed steps & all on my memory. One other thing I remember about that visit Mother having prepared all with wardrobe with the greatest care for this occasion took pains to count how much she had accomplished & I recall her saying that each one of us had twenty one (I think it was) separate garments to be kept in order and put on every day.

"The next visit Mother took me to stay at Aunt Susan Jackson's in her own first home. We had a very happy visit—Uncle Charles came from Boston for Sunday— the children were all at home[;] Lucy was the baby. We had friendly visits to Cousin Jacob's family next door, I was asked by Mrs Hall who lived in the Winslow House to take tea with Alice and Mother called there. A family of Eatons lived just opposite & were much with Alice & Lizzy & sang much which pleased us. Alice used to make 'French biscuit' which Mother liked, copied with more sugar from memory & so evolved the French biscuit which was Father's favorite & the most frequent cake on our table for years. This was either 1851–2 or 3. She took me to see Cousin Edwin's family & I played with Sophia. The next visit in 1854—Mr Olney opened a boarding house in the old Hedge House in Leyden St—[Zaben Olney from Rhode Island ran the Old Colony House in Court Square from about 1836 to late 1840s or early 1850s. The hotel was sold to a Miss Russell in 1853. After 1854, he opened a hotel in the old Barnabas Hedge house on Leyden Street.] as soon as Mother heard of it she was delighted to know she could actually stay in the house where her early playmates lived—such a charming colonial house—& rooms were at once engaged for herself, Eddy & me, Ellen being at Lenox. We stayed two or three weeks and she was very happy there. We dined with Mrs Isaac Hedge, [Mrs Isaac L. Hedge was Maryann Cotton; William T. Davis records that she lived on Court Street.] took tea with the Misses Kendall, [Sarah Kendall was the daughter of Dr. James Kendall, Minister from 1800 to 1859 of First Parish Church in Plymouth. Sarah was a girlhood friend of Lidian.] Miss Mary Russell [Miss Mary Howland Russell, daughter of Captain Nathaniel Russell] & Mrs Warren & visited Cousin Mary Watson [Mary, the daughter of Thomas Russell who became, in 1846, the wife of Benjamin Marston Watson of Plymouth. She is author of "The Great Arm-Chair" and "The Humming-Bird." She is not to be confused with Mary Howland Russell, daughter of Captain Nathaniel Russell.] & her Mother Mrs Russell & Miss Jane Goodwin in Leyden St. We went to a party at Mrs Mercy Jacksons & another at the Samoset where Mr & Mrs Sidney Bartlett [See note 51] & their daughter & a Boston family named Bush late from China—and others were boarding. Mrs Charles Davis asked us to her house to a party. I think Mother was gay & talked & of course I listened with interest and did not chatter myself at any of these festivities. What else should I do? But it did not occur to me to be surprised or think that Mother was livelier than at home. Some weeks later I heard with surprise & some resentment that the Plymouth ladies noticed that when Mrs Emerson was so gay & full of conversation, her children sat & watched her dumb with amazement to see her in such spirits as she never had at home. That was the last visit I made to Plymouth with her until we went to the Samoset in 1885 to keep the fiftieth anniversary of her wedding.

"I went with her on her second visit to Naushon. Mrs Forbes on first making her acquaintance wrote to Father 'How pure her whole tone of thought is—I am glad to have my girls know her[.]' On this second visit we were met by the Azalea [yacht of J. M. Forbes. Naushon is the largest of the group of the Elizabeth Islands, very near Woods Hole with New Bedford to the northwest. It is seven and one-half miles long and about a mile and a half wide. This island was bought by Mr. John Murray Forbes and his uncle by marriage, Mr. William Swain, in 1843. Bowdoin College inherited it from the Bowdoin heirs and sold it to them. Amelia Forbes Emerson has written *The Early History of Naushon Island*.] with Ellen & Alice, Will & Malcolm on board & Aunt Lydia [Alice Bridge Jackson, oldest daughter of Dr. Charles Jackson, married William Arthur. Malcolm Forbes is a brother of Colonel William Forbes. Aunt Lydia is the widow of William Swain and was the aunt of John Murray Forbes.] was going also to the island[.] Mother sat with her & made friends. We were becalmed and did not reach Naushon till eleven—Will wrapped Mother & Aunt Lydia in white blankets from the cabin & could not resist saying Aunt Lydia looked like a small Polar bear—and when I glanced at the two white figures they were very funny indeed. Uncle William Swain had died the year before & Aunt Lydia was much interested in spiritualism and used to sit and hold long conversations with her about it in Mother's room which was the lower bedroom built for Uncle William—they used to hear remarkable rappings sometimes. But Malcolm was fond of knocking on the outside walls of the house & in the billiardroom below by way of entertaining Aunt Lydia. Mother delighted in the courtesy of the young people & declared she feared to come to the parlour to look for her spectacles or book as all the girls & boys jumped up to offer help. We had a very successful visit but Mother left me to stay longer & went home. I have an impression Mother visited Aunt Lydia in N. B. [could be M. B.] I do not know when but a friendship with Mrs Stephen Perkins [possibly son of Elisha Perkins and Mary Conant Perkins who were married 1805. He was killed in the Civil War.] came about either at Naushon or Milton.

"When Ellen Forbes died [eldest daughter of John Murray Forbes (d. 8 October 1860)] Mother wrote to Mrs Forbes a letter of such sympathy that not long after Aunt Margaret wrote to say she begged her to come & visit her that she might if possible give some consolation to her brother John because her letter had done him more good than any other he had received. Mother wrote she believed she could not do him any good by coming. She thought the written was often more effective than the spoken word. I cannot remember whether she went or not. I think Mother went twice to Seaconnet with Miss Russell & one of those times stayed long enough to gain much good."

273. Franklin Benjamin Sanborn (1831–1917) was an associate of John Brown (see note 277). As chairman of the Massachusetts Board of Charities, he took the famed teacher of Helen Keller, Anne Sullivan, out of an alms house at Tewksbury and sent her to the Perkins School for the Blind. He was editor of the *Springfield Republican* and organizer of the Alcott School of Philosophy, author, and one-time teacher of Ellen Emerson.

274. Louis Agassiz (1807–1873) was a Harvard botanist. Ellen attended his family-run school in 1855.

275. Wendell Phillips (1811–1884), famous orator and abolitionist. Mrs. George R. Russell, 1 Louisburg Square, probably the wife of Dr. George Russell of Boston. Mary Elizabeth Preston, niece of Lydia Maria Child, married George Luther Stearns (1809–1867) in 1843. Their acquaintance with Emerson seems to have begun when he

was their guest after a lecture at Medford late in 1854 or in the first week of 1855. Their interest in the anti-slavery movement brought them into contact a number of times.

276. John Murray Forbes became Edith Emerson's father-in-law when she married his son, William.

277. John Brown (1800–1859), famous American abolitionist, was hanged for treason after the raid on Harper's Ferry Arsenal. His daughters stayed with the Emersons in 1860.

278. An American celibate and communistic sect known as the "United Society of Believers in Christ's Second Appearing" and as the "Millennial Church." The society at Harvard, Massachusetts, lasted from 1791 to 1919. The only records preserved at the Fruitlands Museums of Harvard are from what was called the Church Family.

279. Hawthorne and Emerson visited the Shakers during a two-day walking expedition.

280. See note 190 for Swedenborg. Coventry Patmore (1823–1896), English poet and critic. In 1854 appeared the first part of his best-known poem, *The Angel in the House*, which was continued in *The Espousals* (1856). There are seven volumes by Patmore in Emerson's library, including *The Angel in the House*, 2 vols. (London: J. W. Parker, 1854–1856), with the inscription "R. W. from the author" (in Emerson's hand) and *The Espousals* (Boston: Ticknor and Fields, 1856).

281. Martha Munroe was the daughter of William and Patty Munroe. For seventeen years she was president of the Ladies Missionary Society of the Trinitarian Church. Her brother gave the public library to Concord.

282. *Tales from Grammer Grethel* by Frau Katherina Viehmannin, a German peasant woman of Hesse-Cassel, famous as the narrator of many of the German Märchen and legends recorded by Jakob & Wilhelm Grimm and immortalized in their *Kinder und Housmarchen*, published in 1812.

283. *Mechlin* is a delicate bobbin lace from Belgium that is used for dresses and millinery and has floral designs outlined by a glossy cordonnet against a net background of hexagonal mesh.

284. Ellen writes "a beach on Narragansett Bay I believe" and cancels "Narragansett Bay I believe."

285. Anna Jackson Lowell was the wife of Charles Lowell, the brother of James Russell Lowell.

286. Scott's "Child Dyring":

> CHILD DYRING has ridden him up
>   under öe,
>   (And O gin I were young!)
> There wedded he him sae fair a may.
>   (I' the greenwood it lists me to ride.)

> Thegither they lived for seven lang
>   year,
>   (And O, &c.)
> And they seven bairnes hae gotten
>   in fere.
>   (I' the greenwood, &c.)

> Sae Death's come there intill that
>   stead,
> And that winsome lily flower is dead.
> That swain he has ridden him up
>   under öe,

And syne he has married anither
    may.

He's married a may, and he's fessen
    her hame;
But she was a grim and a laidly
    dame.

When into the castell court drave she,
The seven bairnes stood wi' the
    tear in their ee.

The bairnes they stood wi' dule and
    doubt;—
She up wi' her foot, and she kicked
    them out.

Nor ale nor mead to the bairnes she
    gave:
"But hunger and hate frae me ye's
    have."

She took frae them the bowster blae,
And said, "Ye sall ligg i' the bare
    strae!"

She took frae them the groff wax-
    light:
Says, "Now ye sall ligg i' the mirk
    a'night!"

'Twas lang i' the night, and the
    bairnes grat:
Their mither she under the mools
    heard that;

That heard the wife under the eard
    that lay;
"For sooth maun I to my bairnies
    gae!"

That wife can stand up at our Lord's
    knee,
And "May I gang and my bairnies
    see?"

She prigges sae sair, and she prigged
    sae lang,
That he at the last gae her leave to
    gang.

"And thou sall come back when the
    cock does craw;

For thou nae langer sall bide
    awa."

Wi' her banes saw stark a bowt she
    gae;
She's riven baith wa' and marble
    gray.

When near to the dwalling she can
    gang,
The dogs they wow'd till the lift it
    rang.

When she came till the castell
    yett,
Her eldest dochter stood thereat.

"Why stand ye here, dear dochter
    mine?
How are sma brithers and sisters
    thine?"

"For sooth ye're a woman baith fair
    and fine;
But ye are nae dear mither of
    mine."—

"Och! how should I be fine or
    fair?
My cheek is pale, and the ground's
    my lair."—

"My mither was white, wi' cheek
    sae red.
But thou art wan, and liker ane
    dead?"

"Och, how should I be white and
    red;
Saw lang as I've been cauld and
    dead?"

When she came till the chalmer
    in.
Down the bairns' cheeks the tears
    did rin.

She buskit the tane, and she brushed
    it there;
She kem'd and plaited the tither's
    hair.

Till her eldest dochter syne said
    she,

"Ye bid Child Dyring come here to
me."

When he cam till the chalmer in,
Wi' angry mood she said to him;

"I left you rough o' ale and bread;
My bairnes quail for hunger and
need.

"I left ahind me braw bowsters
blae;
My bairnes are ligging i' the bare
strae.

"I left ye sae mony a groff wax-
light;
My bairnes ligg i' the mirk a'
night.

"Gin aft I come back to visit thee,
Wae, dowy, and weary thy luck
shall be."

Up spak little Kirstin in bed that
lay:
"To thy bairnies I'll do the best I may."

Aye when they heard the dog nirr
and bell.
Sae gae they the bairnies bread and
ale.

Aye when the dog did mow, in
haste,
They cross'd and sain'd themselves
frae the ghaist.

Aye whan the little dog yowl'd, with
fear
They shook at the thought that the
dead was near.

287. Alexander Bliss is probably the son of Mrs. George Bancroft.

288. Sarah Freeman Clarke (b. 1808), sister to Reverend James Freeman Clarke. See her letter, page 49. She had been a pupil in Emerson's school for young ladies, and was an artist by training. This visit was to Newport, the second week of July 1868.

289. Helen Maria Fiske Hunt Jackson (1830–1885) wrote *Verses*. This book, which contains (pp. 58–59) a "Tribute R.W.E." in Emerson's honor, was published on 7 December 1870, according to the *Boston Daily Advertiser* of that day. A copy of her *Verses*, (Boston: Roberts Bros., 1874), is still in Emerson's library at the Antiquarian House and contains a note in his hand showing that it was the gift of the author. Emerson thought her the best woman poet in America. Her novel *Ramona* was a protest on behalf of the Indians.

290. Edmund Hamilton Sears, *Regeneration,* 5th ed. (Boston: American Unitarian Association, 1856), is in Emerson's library with Lidian's signature.

291. Reverend Grindall Reynolds (1808–1894) succeeded Barzillai Frost as minister of the First Parish in Concord in 1858, and served there until he became secretary of the American Unitarian Association in 1881, serving there until his death. He was son-in-law of Judge Prescott Keyes. At this point Ellen inserted the following: "When I read Edith this, she said, 'Why yes it did! Mother went to Wayland on purpose and by way of leaving Mr Reynolds because he had in a sermon used Mr Webster with his dying words "I still live" as if they were a testimony to a future life. She said To hold up Mr Webster in a sermon as a pattern to the young even indirectly was so bad that she wished to emphasize her disapproval.'"

292. See note 291.

293. Edward was to meet Dr. Anderson in Omaha on 20 May 1862. Edward wrote Dr. Anderson in Minneapolis; a Dr. C. L. Anderson's name appears in a list of the physicians of Minneapolis in 1858 *(A Half Century of Minneapolis,* ed. Horace B. Hudson [Minneapolis: Hudson, 1908], p. 181).

294. Ralph L. Rusk credits Edith with this plea in a letter: "Which seems to you of most value to your country—the services of one private for a month or so or Father's life and work?" *(The Life of Ralph Waldo Emerson* [New York: Scribners, 1949], p. 425).

295. See introduction (p. xxv) for an account of the day: the time is July 1866.

296. See note 227.

297. James 1:24: "For he beholdeth himself, and goeth his way, and straightway forgetteth what manner of man he was."

298. I have been unable to identify Mrs. Dowd. J. H. Dowd, who in 1885 got a first class liquor license, in 1891 was fined and sentenced three months for "keeping a rum nuisance." In 1892 Frank Dowd's grocery store was moved from Bedford Street to be made into a house. These accounts at least verify the existence of a Dowd family in Concord at the time.

299. Information about Edith Davidson and her origin is in the introduction and the biography.

300. Horatio Woodman was the real founder of the Saturday Club. *The Boston Daily Advertiser* of 8 August 1870 told the story of his failure. His liabilities would reach upward of a quarter of a million. James Thomas Fields (1817–1881) was a publisher and author. A partner in a bookselling firm of Ticknor and Fields in 1854 and Fields, Osgood in 1868, he also edited the *Atlantic Monthly* from 1862 to 1870. He managed both lectures and publications for Emerson.

301. Cyrus Augustus Bartol (1813–1900), Unitarian clergyman, succeeded Charles Lowell in the West Church of Boston, serving from 1827 to 1889. He was a member of the Transcendental Club.

302. Parker's Hotel, known today as the Parker House, opened in 1854 on School Street. In 1860, the members of the Saturday Club met there regularly. Emerson gave many lectures in Boston during this period; without dates, it is nearly impossible to identify the ones attended by Lidian.

303. Storrow Higginson may be Samuel Storrow Higginson, graduate from Harvard in 1863. General Samuel Chapman Armstrong, army officer and educator (1839–1893), was mustered into service as captain of Company D, 125th Regiment, New York Infantry, 1862. After the Battle of Gettysburg he was promoted to major, and shortly thereafter was appointed lieutenant colonel of the Ninth United States Infantry, a regiment composed of Maryland Negroes which participated in the operations before Petersburg. In 1864 he was promoted to colonel and assigned to command the 8th United States Infantry, also made up of black troops. He led his regiment through the campaign which culminated in the surrender at Appomattox, and was then made a brigadier general. His service terminated in 1865. From Boston, Ellen wrote Edith (9 November 1870) about meeting General Armstrong at tea at Mrs. Hemenway's: "How interested and curious I was to see him again, this hero of my imagination for so long I was dis-

appointed in his face a little he didn't look so charming now that he is thinner and older as he did when he was a soldier, but it still felt good the sensation that he was a true steam-engine, an ardent and mighty worker. I am sorry that he has been put forward so fast and occupies such a position at an early age, but that he is good and powerful enthusiastic and practical is evident every moment, and also that he has not a moment to spare—To business, to business, and straight to the heart of things he must go."

304. In Emerson's *Letters* it is spelled "Clahan." In a letter to John Murray Forbes on 28 April 1860, Emerson writes: "Is it possible that you have any room in your farm at Naushon, this summer, for a good Irishman? James Burke, who has lived with me for eight years past, . . . he was, ten years ago, a mounted policeman in Ireland. James is a capable intelligent & faithful laborer, delights in horses, & perfect, I believe, in their care, takes care of the cows does all the ploughing digging, mowing, wood-chopping, &c of my farm (which includes a woodlot,) he never spares himself, & is a person of great virtues. He has no vice except a rare indulgence in drink, of which he is vastly ashamed, & thinks if I will only hide it, he shall never let it be known again." (*Letters*, 5:213).

305. In a letter dated 5 May 1865, Ellen wrote on the Civil War coming to an end: "Mother often says adversity is really the best happiness, and that I never could bear to hear, it seemed an ungrateful way of treating prosperity. But when I think now of War and Peace I begin to be afraid that I agree with Mother."

306. Increase Smith was a member of the Dorchester School Committee for many years. Before his settlement in Dorchester, he was the former preceptor of Derby Academy in Hingham, Massachusetts.

307. "C.B. & Q. R.R." is the Chicago, Burlington and Quincy Railroad. In a letter dated 21 March 1866, Ellen writes: "The baby's name is Ralph Emerson Forbes, I am not sure whether I told you before! he is a little bigger than the Sanborn baby was, not much prettier; but his head is rounder and he has hardly any hair, he is bright scarlet except his feet which are more crimson. He has three charms, he is soft as silk, and fat, that is something, and I love to kiss him; second, he is Edith's baby and belongs to me, so I am not afraid to take him, and am not scared when he cries; third, he is perfectly silly and absurd like all other babies and makes me laugh . . . ." She added that Will had the whooping-cough and was limited in seeing the baby.

308. Folder 38 contains the back of a pad and a profile picture of Lidian.

309. Sarah Alden Bradford Ripley was married to Emerson's half-uncle, Samuel Ripley. She died in Concord in the summer of 1867. See note 110.

310. Angelina Ball, daughter of Nehemiah Ball, lived at one time near the Inn where the Christian Science church is now.

311. John Milton's "Christmas Hymn" is part of his poem, "On the Morning of Christ's Nativity," composed in 1629.

312. The year is 1868.

313. They died in 1868, and William Emerson died in September of that year.

314. Fanny Prichard was the daughter of Moses and Jane, and they lived in a large house on Main Street, with their land going down to the river. They were very active in the church, always supplying flowers in season for the services.

315. Ellen Emerson was a passenger on the *Fredonia*, which left Boston for Fayal on 30 October (*Boston Daily Evening Transcript* 31 October 1868). The *Transcript* of 7 June 1869 tells of her return. The introduction enlarges on Ellen's account of this trip.

316. In the margin is "Jer X 19.20."

317. Written after this is "Written at Nina Lowells Sept. 1896."

318. The "I" could be a "T." Alcott sent his invitation to the organizational meeting (20 March 1849 at 12 West Street, Boston) for the "Town and Country Club" (established in July) to a William H. Knapp. It became the ancestor of the "Saturday Club" out of which grew the idea of the *Atlantic Monthly*.

319. On 17 September 1630, it was ordered by the court of assistants that the town

should be called Boston after Boston in Lincolnshire. John Cotton did not arrive in Boston until September 1633.

320. According to Mrs. Raymond Emerson (Amelia Forbes), Miss Leavitt was the sister of Mrs. Frank B. Sanborn and lived near the Sanborn house on Elm Street, opposite the Episcopal Church. Amelia Forbes, daughter of Malcolm Forbes, married Edward's son Raymond (1886—1977). Malcolm was brother to Edith's husband, William. Both Malcolm and William were sons of John Murray Forbes.

321. See note 144.

322. According to Cabot, F. C. Lowell left Emerson a letter which contained a check for five thousand dollars contributed by a few friends. At the suggestion of Dr. LeBaron Russell, between eleven and twelve thousand dollars was collected for a vacation and delivered to Emerson by Judge Hoar. (James Elliot Cabot, *A Memoir of Ralph Waldo Emerson* [Boston: Houghton, Mifflin, 1887], 2:703—706).

323. Probably Elizabeth and Mary are the daughters of Samuel and Sarah Bradford Ripley. Mary Ripley married a Simmons and had a daughter named Elizabeth. According to Mary Fenn of Concord, Lizzy Simmons was the daughter of one of the Ripley girls and lived in the Old Manse. Her brother was an artist. They were friends of the young set in Concord as well as relatives of the Emerson's in-laws.

324. William Ralph Emerson of Boston, a distant relative. According to Ina Mansur, town historian for Bedford, several members of a Cutler family moved to Bedford about 1830 from Ashby, Massachusetts. In 1870 in Bedford was Amos B. Cutler, 61, a house carpenter; George W. Cutler, 58, a house carpenter and brother of Amos B.; Emerson B. Cutler, 33, a house carpenter and son of Amos B.; and Thomas C. Cutler, 67, who in 1860 called himself a carpenter and in 1870, a farmer. The Cutler family is one of the names connected with the building of the middle of the Bedford town in the 1800s.

325. Henry Ward Beecher (1813—1887), the noted clergyman, son of Lyman Beecher. By the early 1850s his oratory was drawing crowds of 2,500.

326. Ellen cancelled "and brought down a box of sand, which she had up garret." It has been restored, as it is necessary to clarify the antecedent for "this" and "it" in the following sentence.

327. Lieutenant Edward (Ned) Jarvis Bartlett (1842—1914) was the son of Dr. Josiah Bartlett, who practiced medicine from 1820 to 1878. His son, Dr. William Bradford Bartlett, practised at Hartford and was examiner for Phoenix Life Insurance. Edward married Sally French, daughter of Judge Henry F. French and sister of Daniel Chester French, the sculptor, on 19 June 1873. Sally died in 1883. Edward was employed by Ammi C. Lombard in charge of Lewis' wharf in Boston.

328. Uncle Charles and Aunt Susan are Dr. Charles T. Jackson and his wife Susan Bridge Jackson; Lidian is their daughter; John Cotton Jackson, their son.

329. Jones Very spent a brief time at the McLean Asylum.

330. See note 32.

331. James Bradley Thayer was a lawyer who married Sophia Ripley, one of Samuel Ripley's daughters. He became professor of law at Harvard. He assisted Emerson in many of his business endeavors. There is evidence in Emerson's *Letters* that there was a draft of his will in 1874, but the final draft is dated 14 April 1876.

332. In a letter to Edith on 19 August 1870, Ellen describes this incident. Since this account shows the difference in Ellen's recording following an event and then remembering it more than twenty-five years later, and also since this shows Ellen's descriptive powers, it is set forth in its entirety. She called the cat a clownish black creature with gold eyes: "I hoped it would be long before Mother saw her, as she had a way of vanishing suddenly at the approach of any of the human race. But no! Mother soon begins to receive the most touching attentions and coy advances from this hideous object. From beneath some peony-bush or low branch of melodious and insinuating mew, and it follows her unseen through the garden. In a few days she is treated to a partial view of those gold eyes, or of the rusty and mottled tail. Now you know Mother isn't one to resist any effort on the part of the feline world to cultivate her acquaint-

ance. Ah no! she responded ardently to the first mew, talked sympathetically all the time to her invisible suitor, and used every blandishment to get her to lay aside all fear, so that it wasn't long before the cat rolled all round Mother in an agony of affection, and rubbed her head against her hand and purred her heart out, all the time she was working in the garden. One day this was inconvenient, and Mother said 'Scat!' This was too much for the sensitive animal, who immediately retired to the hedge and for several days wrung Mother's heart by mews of tender reproach, but never came in sight. This last week she has begun to come round again, having received ample and repeated apologies and explanations from Mother. Of course there is a reward offered in the kitchen for enticing in the grimalkin, and meat and milk daily in abundance outside. I objected and asked Mother to look at her ill-kept fur. A few days after Mother announced that Puss's fur was very nice but that her colors were amazing, black and maltese very injudiciously mixed after a sort of tortoise-shell fashion, which gave her a rusty and unkempt expression."

333. The Massachusetts Society for the Prevention of Cruelty to Animals was organized in 1868. Their monthly publication was *Our Dumb Animals*. Lidian is listed as an associate annual member (five-dollar contribution) for the years 1868–1873. The state had a president and the locals had an agent and vice-president. She was vice-president of the Concord branch in 1872; Emerson was vice-president from 1868 to 1872.

334. Mrs. Burke brought them in 1873.

335. George William Curtis (1824–1892), author, editor, and leader in civil service reform, spent two years at Brook Farm and two years in Concord to be near Emerson. Eugenia, Oscar, and Lidian were Charles T. Jackson's children. Theodore Lyman was the uncle of Frances Anne Eliot Foote, daughter of Honorable Samuel Eliot, the wife of Henry W. Foote. Lyman bought and improved the Gore estate in Waltham, noted for its dam, waterfall, park, and deer. "My daughter" is Edith Davidson.

336. According to Emerson's son, this was the last address that he ever composed.

337. See note 130 and page 56.

338. Elmira Flint Small was a widow. Flint was her maiden name.

339. *Letters and Social Aims*, which Cabot helped Emerson prepare for publication.

340. Emerson lectured for the Literary Societies of University of Virginia on 28 June 1876 on "The Natural and Permanent Functions of the Scholar." Emerson could not be heard clearly; the student body was rude and the press negative. The Centennial Exhibition in Philadelphia was at Fairmount Park.

341. The donkey arrived in July 1876. There is a picture of Ellen on Graciosa in Mary Miller Engel, *I Remember the Emersons* (Los Angeles: Times-Mirror, 1941). I have been unable to locate the original. In a letter Ellen describes "Miss" Graciosa as having a soft gray coat, white legs, and neat little black boots. Graciosa died in December 1894.

342. The material on the first three pages of Folder 45 seems to belong with the material on the birds on page 303. The letter is written on stationery, 4″ x 6″ with a water mark which suggests a crown. There is a 2¼″ x 4¾″ strip in the folder with "copied to page 306" on it and the first word is not clear. The letter follows here as well as the third page. A portion of the letter on Sanborn's lecture and a school dance is cancelled since it is not on the subject; the cancelled portion is not included here.

Concord Jan 14*th* 1859
Dear Edie,

I was prevented from writing last night as I proposed. Yesterday at dinner Mother was beginning to read a piece to us about the birds' beginning to sing at regular hours in the morning—Eddy (interrupting) "And then the robins begin Yeep-Yah yah-yah!" Mother (affectionately) "The darlings"

Eddy (spitefully) "Oh yes, the dears!" Mother (without noticing Eddy) "Sweet little souls!" Eddy—"Mother, there's a kind of bird that keeps a larder, and goes round catching all sorts of things to put in it, against winter comes. It's up in the north and

Mr Thoreau says, people sometimes find a thorn bush, with humming-birds and butterflies, and grasshoppers and all sorts of insects stuck on the thorns—this bird's collection." Mother (with interest, admiration and sympathy) "Oh!"—(again, with horror and commiseration) "Oh!" Eddy—"How well you can distinguish between Mother's Ohs, can't you Ellen? One for the bird, and one for the little creatures."

On one of our walks up there as we passed a hawkweed or other somewhat tall flower by the side-walk Mother quoted

> "These wild-flowers that so proudly rise
> Have each its birthright from on high"

and went on to talk of the pleasantness of the thought, expressing much sympathy with the flower in its growth and experience of life. I had not before considered their life from their own point of view.

343. "Written at Nina Lowell's Sept. 1896" heads manuscript page 306, folder 45.

344. Lizzy is probably the daughter of Sarah Hoar (Mrs. Robert Storer), Elizabeth's sister.

345. Emma Lazarus (1849–1887) in 1876 visited Concord and made the acquaintance of the Emerson circle, and while there read the proof sheets of her tragedy, *The Spagnoletto*. She is noted as the author of "The New Colossus," the sonnet engraved on a memorial tablet on the Statue of Liberty. She wrote "Sonnet of 1884—Miss Emma Lazarus to R. W. E." Her *Poems and Translations, written between the ages of fourteen and seventeen* (New York: Hurd and Houghton, 1867), and the unpublished manuscript of *The Spagnoletto* (1876), a play in five acts, are in Emerson's library.

346. This visit was 25 August 1876.

347. Actually 7 April.

348. Arthur Penrhyn Stanley (1815–1881), Dean of Westminster, was second son of Edward Stanley, bishop of Norwich. He was greatly influenced at Rugby by Dr. Arnold, the headmaster and the father of Matthew Arnold, and won all five school distinctions. In 1834 he entered Oxford, where he won the Ireland scholarship in 1837 and the same year the Newdegate prize for English verse. In December 1839, he was ordained deacon, and in 1843 priest and appointed a college tutor. Because of his father's death he left the University and accepted the canonry at Canterbury to provide a home for his mother and sisters. In December 1856, he was appointed professor of ecclesiastical history at Oxford and a canonry at Christ Church. He married Lady Augusta Bruce (1822–1876), fifth daughter of the seventh Earl of Elgin, on 22 December 1863 in Westminster Abbey. On 9 January 1864, he was installed as dean of the abbey. She died in 1876 and he never recovered from the shock of her death.

349. The visit was on 30 October 1878.

350. See note 348.

351. The Concord School of Philosophy held summer sessions from 15 July 1879 through 1888. It began in Alcott's library and continued later in a little hall, "The Chapel," on the hillside west of the Orchard House. Alcott was dean of the faculty; Emery, the director; Harris and Sanborn, secretary and treasurer. The average attendance of students was about forty but at Emerson's lecture 160 were present and at several of the other sessions more than seventy.

352. Mr. Samuel Hopkins Emery (d. February 1906) was a lawyer and director of the Concord School of Philosophy during its duration. He seldom lectured but frequently moderated.

353. Dr. William T. Harris (1835–1909) was superintendent of Public Schools in St. Louis for almost twenty years and the United States Commissioner of Education for almost another twenty years. In 1867 he established in St. Louis his *Journal of Specula-*

tive Philosophy. He was a follower of Hegel and gave ten lectures in the first session of the school.

354. Dr. H. K. Jones gave ten lectures in the first session, many of which were on Platonic philosophy.

355. Probably the family of Moses and Jane Prichard who lived on Main Street. Fanny Prichard was their daughter.

356. James Lyman Whitney in 1880 was forty-five, a Yale graduate of 1856. He had been a city librarian at Cincinnati but had come to Concord to live after taking a position at the Boston Public Library, where he was later Librarian and where, in 1909, he completed forty years of employment. He was elected to the Concord School Committee in 1880 and continued on it for seven years.

357. Emeline Barrett in 1878 had a boarding house on the corner of Monument and Court Streets. In 1892 her famous boarding house was moved from Monument Street to a lot beside the Mortuary Chapel and made into two tenements. In June 1889, Lidian and Ellen attended her eightieth birthday party.

358. I have been unable to identify Josephine Loughead. A Joseph Loughhead was master of Philadelphia's Latin School. In a letter Ellen describes Miss Loughhead as having golden locks and talks of entertaining her a number of times.

359. Perhaps Henry James (1843–1916), the novelist and critic.

360. See note 171.

361. William Watson Goodwin was professor of Greek at Harvard. He edited and revised a translation of *Plutarch's Morals* in 1870, for which Emerson wrote the introduction. His *De potentiae veterum gentium maritimae epochis apud Eusebium* (Gottingae: Dieterichiana, 1855) is in Emerson's library.

362. William Henry Furness (1802–1896) was a schoolmate of Emerson's at the Latin School. He was Emerson's lifelong (and probably his only really intimate) friend; at Emerson's death, he preached the funeral sermon. After Harvard College (1820) and the Divinity School (1823), he was called to the Unitarian Church in Philadelphia, where he had a long and distinguished career. He was a leader in the anti-slavery movement.

363. All of the following books are in Emerson's library except for his copy of Cumming's book, which is now in the Concord Free Public Library: Asa Cummings, *A Memoir of Edward Payson, late pastor of the Second Church in Portland*, 3d ed. (Boston: Crocker and Brewster, 1830); James Smith, *The Divine Drama of History and Civilization* (London: Chapman and Hall, 1854); Samuel Noble, *The Plenary Inspiration of the Scriptures Asserted, and the Principles of their Composition Investigated with a View to the Refutation of all Objections to their Divinity* (Cincinnati: Book Committee of the Western Convention, 1839); perhaps James Warner Ward, *Woman, a Poem* (Cincinnati: Ward & Taylor; New York: G. P. Putnam, 1852); the only book in Emerson's library by Guyon is Jeanne-Marie Guyon (Bouvieres De La Motte), *Opuscules Spirituels* (Cologne: J. de La Pierre, 1712); Thomas C. Upham, *Life and Religious Opinions and Experience of Madame de La Mothe Guyon* (New York: Harpers, 1847); Oliver Wendell Holmes, *The Autocrat of the Breakfast-table* (Boston: Phillips, Samson, 1859).

364. Sir Edwin Arnold (1832–1904), *The Light of Asia: or, The Great Renunciation (Mahabhinishkramana): Being the Life and Teaching of Gautama, Prince of India and Founder of Buddhism (as told in verse by an Indian Buddhist)* (London: Trübner, 1879). This poem was introduced to America through the Concord School. The volume was taken by Alcott to his publisher in Boston and was soon reprinted in this country. The book is in Emerson's library.

365. In 1881 Benjamin Bulkeley came to the church in Concord as a substitute morning preacher when he was still in his second year in the Divinity School. The congregation liked him so well they voted to accept him as their regular when he finished his course in 1882. He served until 1893, when he resigned because of the ill health of his wife. He retired from the ministry in 1924 and in his retirement served

as pastor emeritus in the Concord church until his death in 1930. He was related to the first minister, Peter Bulkeley, who was a forebearer of Ralph Waldo Emerson. He pronounced the benediction at Ellen's funeral.

366. See *Memoirs of the Members of the Social Circle*, 2d series (Cambridge: Social Circle, 1888), pp. 295–301, for Cyrus Stow (1787–1876).

367. Dr. Benjamin Fanueil Dunkin Adams (1839–1895) was born in Waltham. He was the son of Dr. Horatio Adams, one of the leading physicians of his time, and Ann Bethuen (Dunkin) Adams. He was graduated from Harvard College in 1860, and from Harvard Medical School, where he received the highest honors, in 1864. One of the most ardent advocates of establishing a Board of Health in Waltham, he was chairman from its beginning in 1880 until his removal from Waltham. He did much also to further the establishment of the Hospital and of the Old Ladies' Home. He was married in July 1868, to Catherine Hutchinson Brinley of Hartford, Connecticut. She and two of their four children, Edward Brinley and Catherine Fanueil survived him.

368. Charles Pickering Putnam (1884–1914), a physician specializing in the diseases of children, surgeon, and social worker from Boston.

369. Thomas Surette was the church organist in Concord. He was the son of Louis & Francis Jane Shattuck Surette. Mary Miller Engel, *I Remember the Emersons*, said that he played at Ellen's funeral, but the *Boston Globe* records that the organist was Miss Edith May Lang of Boston.

370. Daniel Chester French (1850–1931) was commissioned to sculpture the Minute Man statue after having studied for one year in Florence, Italy. See note 327.

371. Edith adds in pencil the following: "Not I. I was surprised & always wondered at it. E. E. F." Three pieces glued together form this sheet. There are pieces glued on before and after this second paragraph.

372. Helen A. Legate came from Leominster. She taught at and was later principal of the Concord Grammar School. At Ellen's invitation she came to live with her about 1890 and lived on in the Emerson House until her death in 1947.

373. The following is from Ellen's letter of 10 May 1884 describing this visit to Plymouth: "Then Luly pointed out Mrs. Isaac Hedge's house. 'Oh yes! Mr. William Hammatt built that house for Aunt Esther's daughter Esther Parsons.' She subsequently related that once when she was a child she went to tea there and she thinks it must have been uninvited, since they were making the wedding-cake for Miss Lucia Hammatt, Mrs. Austin's mother. Next we came in sight of the Thomas Hedge house quite unchanged, and very handsome. Mrs. Cox's was then described. Then Luly pointed to the house ahead and said 'There's Mrs Bartlett, Miss Lucia Bartlett's mother at the window.' Accordingly I looked to see if she would recognize Mother. She did and bowed. After we had passed the house I looked back and Mrs. Bartlett had come across to the other front room and was still looking at Mother. We had by this time met Mrs. Davis who turned round and walked with us. Aunt Squire's was the next place of interest on the other side of the street. Mother had boarded there ten months between leaving Uncle Doctor's and going to the Winslow house. Then Mr. Andrew Russell's house and Miss Mary Russell's, and Luly's Grandfather Watson's, and now Uncle Doctor's house was in full view and the Loud house where Mrs. Hedge and Mrs. Davis now live, is just opposite. The object of the expedition was to call on Mrs. Hedge, so Mother and I went in with Mrs. Davis, and Luly went on her ways. Here we were introduced first to Mrs. Hedge and Priscilla, then to the pictures of five generations. How puzzling it is! Mrs. Davis had a miniature tall clock, only 3 or 4 ft. high. 'Don't you remember it always in Grandma Cotton's parlour?' she asked! 'Oh yes indeed!' cried Mother. After a little call we departed, invited to tea tonight, and Mother said she was not well enough to go down North Street but would like to push along to the Town Square. So we did, and came to Uncle Thomas's house Uncle William and Aunt Esther had lived on the farther side, Uncle Thomas and Aunt Sally on the other. These were the identical steps down which Uncle William handed Aunt Esther by her finger-tips every Sunday morning as we have so often heard. It is

now occupied by milliner, photographer &c. Luly opened the door and we marched right in. 'This—oh! this was Aunt Esther's parlour, and that was Aunt Sally's.' As we mounted the stairs I asked if they were the old ones, 'Yes,!—oh yes!—but they have grown narrower and steeper.' I asked where the door at the head of the stairs led to, 'To the back of the house. In this house Sophia Brown died.' Which room? 'In one of those back rooms.' Whose room was this? 'It was Aunt Lucy's then. She was here when Sophia died. It was Frances Maynard's house then and Aunt Lucy was boarding with her. In old times it was Aunt Esther's room.' "

Frances Maynard was the daughter of Major William and Anna (Barnes) Jackson (b. 1789). Mrs. Frances Leonard Maynard married Samuel Maynard in 1821.

374. Cousin Mary, daughter of Thomas Russell married Benjamin Marston in 1846. Lulie may be her daughter, Lucretia (b. 1851).

375. Perhaps Charles W. Prescott (1858–1916), who was married to Ida L. Davis. He was President of the Massachusetts Asparagus Grower's Association.

376. In a letter dated 4 March 1885, Ellen writes that Miss Brown was a nurse engaged by Edith but that she and Lidian liked the old way better.

377. The directors of the Old Colony Railroad felt that a hotel would be profitable for business and built the Samoset, opening it on 4 March 1846. It was sold about 1850 to an association and operated from that date under various persons.

378. *Apollinaris* is the trade-mark for an effervescing alkaline mineral water from the Apollinaris spring at Neuenahr, Germany.

379. See notes 374 and 76.

380. "Mother guessed . . . door &c." is inserted in bolder ink.

381. Lucy Jackson (b. 1759), sister to Lidian's father, married Stephen Marcy. They lived on North Street. Perhaps Cousin Lucy is her daughter.

382. Caroline Leavitt (1835–1924), according to a newspaper obituary, was sister to Miss Josephine Leavitt. Mrs. Raymond Emerson thinks she was the sister to Frank B. Sanborn's second wife, Louisa Augusta Leavitt, and that she lived near the Sanborn House on Elm Street opposite the Episcopal church.

383. William Buttrick is the only settler to come over on the *Susan and Ellen* with Peter Bulkeley. I assume Billy is his descendant but I have been unable to identify him. Philip Walcott (1878–1914), the son of Charles H. Walcott, who married Florence Keyes, daughter of John S. Keyes. Philip became a lawyer in New York and died there from a fall.

384. See note 320. Mrs. Raymond Emerson gives her husband's birth date as 1886, not 1880. Ellen's next sentence covering 1887 and her following comment on Raymond suggests that she knew the year was later than 1880.

385. See Emerson, *Letters*, 4:315, 400, for Ann MacGuire. Or she could be Mrs. Emery's sister; see p. 184.

386. See note 99.

387. After this is "Written at Mrs Elliot Cabot's March, 1898."

388. There is no letter here from Edward.

389. Caroline Cheney (1814–1919) was daughter of John Milton and Louisa Hosmer Cheney. She was a Christian Scientist.

390. A Sunday in June 1891.

391. June Taylor's "Anne and Martha":

> It was a pleasant winter's night;
> The sky was clear, the stars were bright
> The air was fresh and cold.
> But all within was warm and tight;
> And the fire-flame cast a flashing light
> On the carpet red, and the ceiling white.
> And on the curtain-fold.

Here Anne and Martha idle sit,
Because the candles are not lit,
And both are tired of play.
And Anne is tired of Martha's chat
About the trimming of her hat
For her mother had said (she was sure of that)
She would trim their hats that day.

So, rising quickly as she could,
Anne went to the window, and there she stood;
The sash, which reached the floor, displayed
To view the pleasant garden-shade;
For the curtains were not drawn.

And she was pleased to stand and see
The moonlight on the laurel tree:—
How, when the wind the foliage heaves,
It sparkles on the glossy leaves;
And what soft light and shade were spread
On every bush and every bed
And what a sheet of light was spread
Over the level lawn.

She roved her eye from star to star,
And soon her thought had fled as far;
For thought has neither chain nor bar.
It ranges far and free.
And as she had not wings to fly
Amid the starry realms on high,
She marvelled that a mortal eye
Those distant worlds could see.

Their gentle mother enters now
And pleasure gladdens Martha's brow:
For lo! on either hand, she bears
With tender touch, these hats of theirs,
While, in her basket store, is seen
Some glossy yards of ribbon green:
And having now unrolled it—
She forms the bow, she twines the band:
Behold, with light and dextrous hand
And there does eager Martha stand
Suggesting this, opposing that—
And her whole soul is in her hat—
(Full large enough to hold it.)

Nor think that thoughtful Anne defers
To thank her mother, too, for hers.
She came, and with a grateful look
And duteous word, her hat she took
And bore it to its place.
Yet that fair ribbon, bright and new,
Scarce cared she if't was green or blue

For now her mind was braced with thought,
Some nobler happiness it sought,
Than e'er, with nicest art was wrought
With ribbon, pearl, or lace.

As years increased, still Anne inclined
To train and cultivate her mind,
At reason's nobler voice.
While Martha strove, with equal care
To deck her person light and fair:—
Now, reader, these pursuits compare,
Compare,—and make your choice.

392. See page 10.

393. The year is illegible.

394. Abraham Willard Jackson (1842–1911) was born in Portland, Maine. He left college to fight in the Civil War, serving as a captain in Colonel Higginson's Colored Regiment. He was a minister at Peterborough, New Hampshire, and in California. After retiring from the pulpit because of deafness resulting from his war experience, he lived in Concord for some years. Then he moved to Melrose to live with his son, who was a physician. He wrote the obituary of Ellen Emerson for the *Christian Register*.

395. Although "recognize" is cancelled, it is restored here for clarity.

396. Lidian's Uncle John Cotton (1753–1802) married Experience Jackson of Plymouth, daughter of Captain Samuel Jackson, in 1777. They had a daughter, Experience.

397. 19 November 1891.

398. Sarah A. E. Richardson (1835–1925) was a friend of Ellen's She was a teacher in the Primary School. After the death of Mrs. Emerson she lived for a while with Ellen.

399. Clarence John Blake (1843–1919) did much to establish otology in Massachusetts and was a teacher at the Harvard Medical School from 1870 to 1913. In 1874 Alexender Graham Bell consulted him in regard to the use of an imitation of the human ear as a phonautograph for use in the "electrical transmission of articulate speech," and Dr. Blake suggested the use of the human membrana tympani instead of an artificial ear. His suggestion was followed by Bell in a series of inventions that led to the invention of the telephone.

400. Perhaps Ellen intended Mother's "face."

401. Following this page are manuscript pages 378–384, numbered to suggest that they were written last, but since they make a disturbing chronological break, I am including them in this note:

"One of our pleasures in the new New Years transplanted to Milton was that Aunt Lizzy came. We had never asked her in old times in Concord. The first year, 1866 she said she felt unworthy because she brought no poems, but she had never in her life rhymed one line with another. The next year we had the baby—Ralph. Aunt Lizzy gave him a woolly dog with what I suppose was her maiden poem.

'Bow wow wow!
Whose dog art thou?
Ralph's, if he'll have me.
Aunt Lizzy gave me.
My name, you must know
Is Little Dog Snow.'

The next New Years, 1868, we had also Violet[.] Aunt Lizzy gave Edith Copsley 1869

Annals [Emily Steele Elliot, *Copsley Annals, Preserved in Proverbs* (New York: Dodd, n.d.)], with this poem

> This little storybook I bring
> her who goes a-mothering
> Who, happy wife and mother crowned,
> Has one early Violet found."

[There is an illegible word before "her who goes a-mothering."] I think it was the next year, 1869, that New Years found her sick at home unable to come, but she wrote a story which Mr Edward Hoar her brother had told her when he came home from Santa Barbara, California, a story that had interested her, and Father, into a poem, and sent it to Edith asking her to keep it to read to Ralph when he was old enough. It was George Nidiver[.] It was read at the New Years breakfast. Father was so pleased with it that he asked her leave to put it in at the end of his Essay on Courage [See this essay for the poem] in his book "Society and Solitude" which was then being printed, and Aunt Lizzy gave it.

"When Ralph was four or five, six or seven, just able to read he had a book at school which I think was Minsoes Fifth Hillard's third Reader, [George Stillman Hillard, *The Third Primary Reader* (Boston: Brewer and Tilesto, 1861)] which he enjoyed and often referred to. Edith thought the time had come to read to him George Nidiver, so she took him in her lap, told him Aunt Lizzy had written it to be saved for him when he was old enough to understand it, and read it to him. 'Do you like it?' she asked. 'Yes. It is in the Third Reader,' he said, as if that were in itself high commendation. Edith and all of us were a little disappointed that he knew it already, that it didn't come to him as a precious, personal possession, but we were also glad he had discovered it for himself, and that it now, of course, being in the school-reader, must be in the hands of thousands of children, and it amused us.

"Sometimes in the seventies, Father whose mail had become tiresome to him, consisting as it did in his old age principally of requests of his autograph so that he ceased to open it himself and left it to me to do, brought the morning's letters to my room, for I was sick, for me to see. One of them proved to be from Santa Barbara[,] California, and interesting—finally, oh how exciting! The writer said she had 'Society and Solitude' with her and as she read 'George Nidiver' she bethought her that she had heard the name Nidiver in the town frequently, it seemed a common name there, why, it would interest the people to see the poem, so she had it published in the local paper

> 'with the happy result of bringing to light
> the very old hero himself!!'

[These two lines of verse are in large, bold letters.] Father and I hailed this announcement with cries of amazement and delight. We made a plan. Not to mention it, to invite Edward & Annie and Will & Edith & Ralph and Aunt Lizzy to tea, and then read the letter!

"We wrote to Edith as soon as I got well, and asked her to bring Will & Ralph, and the day being set by her we invited the others.

"I forget now who was missing, somebody failed us, but Aunt Lizzy and the rest assembled and when supper was over, before we left the table I produced the letter and read it. [February 1875]

"When the poem was published in the local paper, I glanced at Aunt Lizzy. She looked embarrassed and annoyed, but when I came to the climax, she shone. 'Oh! oh! oh! oh!' she cried amid the general acclamation of the family, 'And 'it was me that done that, it was me, mesel'!' Glorious moment! How overjoyed we all were! Aunt Lizzy proceeded to give us the history of her exclamation.

"In 1843 when the Fitchburg railroad was building[,] a great gang of Irish labourers lately come over worked on it. They brought their families with them and erected a little village of shanties on a hillside close by our spring beyond Walden which Father and all his contemporaries called from that circumstance the Railroad Spring. I fear the name had gone with them and that now it has none. I shall try to have it perpetuated, a name is a convenience. These shanties sheltered a numerous tribe of children and Madam Hoar, Mrs Brooks, Mrs Munroe and other ladies of the town could not bear to have them grow up within our borders without schooling. They talked it over and their daughters undertook to teach those children each for a week in her turn. Aunt Lizzy was one and every morning for a week she wended her way to the farthest corner of Walden Pond and did her best to teach the children reading and arithmetic. She remembered it evidently as a thankless task for which she did not find herself fitted by nature; she was not a disciplinarian. One day at recess an innocent curly headed little three-year-old established himself in her lap and described to her with enthusiasm his first successful coast. On his brother's sled he had without accident coasted down to the path, across the path! and down another slope!! and lifting his blue eyes to her face with a look of triumph he wound up 'An' it was me that done that, it was me mesel'!' The words had remained in her mind ever since and now expressed her joy. How delightful to her were the visits of her grandchildren! and to Edward Forbes we owed a new and glorious charm in them. He began by the time Waldo was ten and Alexander seven to teach them to sing in parts. Sometimes Waldo took the air and Alexander the second, sometimes they did the other way. Edward accompanied them on his guitar when they were away from the piano. Here are two pictures [I have been unable to locate them] of them singing to their Grandma in her room taken at the Thanksgiving time of 1890. Edward usually placed Alexander on his left for A. had always a marked and most unfortunate peculiarity, that of allowing his thoughts to stray from the business in hand, his voice would at once betray when he forgot what he was about and a vigorous punch from Edward's left elbow was needed to recall his attention to his song. It delighted us all the night before—Thanksgiving night—when Cameron said 'I'll attend to Alexander, Edward, you can stick to your playing.' He seated himself by the boys, took a caressing hold of Alexander's back hair which he changed to a sharp tweak the moment his notes took a humdrum character. This did not irritate A., he smiled and sang better.

"Edward's enterprise of teaching the boys to sing was richly blessed to him, to them, to all the family. It bound the three together[;] it increased their interest in music for which nature already had fitted them, and from the beginning it gave great and increasing pleasure to their Father. He had rather dropped singing but Ralph's good voice had made him take it up because he enjoyed singing with him, and now that Alexander could furnish a good soprano they had among them a family choir that he loved to sing with, while Edward's accompaniments and criticisms helped them all, so that the singing came to be pretty regular every evening, and all Will's relations were thankful to have him still sing. They all loved his voice."

Index